Applied Time Series Econometrics

Time series econometrics is a rapidly evolving field. In particular, the cointegration revolution has had a substantial impact on applied analysis. As a consequence of the fast pace of development, there are no textbooks that cover the full range of methods in current use and explain how to proceed in applied domains. This gap in the literature motivates the present volume. The methods are sketched out briefly to remind the reader of the ideas underlying them and to give sufficient background for empirical work. The volume can be used as a textbook for a course on applied time series econometrics. The coverage of topics follows recent methodological developments. Unit root and cointegration analysis play a central part. Other topics include structural vector autoregressions, conditional heteroskedasticity, and nonlinear and nonparametric time series models. A crucial component in empirical work is the software that is available for analysis. New methodology is typically only gradually incorporated into the existing software packages. Therefore a flexible Java interface has been created that allows readers to replicate the applications and conduct their own analyses.

Helmut Lütkepohl is Professor of Economics at the European University Institute in Florence, Italy. He is on leave from Humboldt University, Berlin, where he has been Professor of Econometrics in the Faculty of Economics and Business Administration since 1992. He had previously been Professor of Statistics at the University of Kiel (1987–92) and the University of Hamburg (1985–87) and was Visiting Assistant Professor at the University of California, San Diego (1984–85). Professor Lütkepohl is Associate Editor of *Econometric Theory*, the *Journal of Applied Econometrics*, *Macroeconomic Dynamics*, *Empirical Economics*, and *Econometric Reviews*. He has published extensively in learned journals and books and is author, coauthor and editor of several books on econometrics and time series analysis. Professor Lütkepohl is the author of *Introduction to Multiple Time Series Analysis* (1991) and a *Handbook of Matrices* (1996). His current teaching and research interests include methodological issues related to the study of nonstationary, integrated time series, and the analysis of the transmission mechanism of monetary policy in the euro area.

Markus Krätzig is a doctoral student in the Department of Economics at Humboldt University, Berlin.

Themes in Modern Econometrics

Managing Editor
PETER C.B. PHILLIPS, *Yale University*

Series Editors
ERIC GHYSELS, *University of North Carolina, Chapel Hill*
RICHARD J. SMITH, *University of Warwick*

Themes in Modern Econometrics is designed to service the large and growing need for explicit teaching tools in econometrics. It will provide an organized sequence of textbooks in econometrics aimed squarely at the student population and will be the first series in the discipline to have this as its express aim. Written at a level accessible to students with an introductory course in econometrics behind them, each book will address topics or themes that students and researchers encounter daily. Although each book will be designed to stand alone as an authoritative survey in its own right, the distinct emphasis throughout will be on pedagogic excellence.

Titles in the Series

Statistics and Econometric Models: Volumes 1 and 2
CHRISTIAN GOURIEROUX and ALAIN MONFORT
Translated by QUANG VOUNG

Time Series and Dynamic Models
CHRISTIAN GOURIEROUX and ALAIN MONFORT
Translated and edited by GIAMPIERO GALLO

Unit Roots, Cointegration, and Structural Change
G.S. MADDALA and IN-MOO KIM

Generalized Method of Moments Estimation
Edited by LÁSZLÓ MÁTYÁS

Nonparametric Econometrics
ADRIAN PAGAN and AMAN ULLAH

Econometrics of Qualitative Dependent Variables
CHRISTIAN GOURIEROUX
Translated by PAUL B. KLASSEN

The Econometric Analysis of Seasonal Time Series
ERIC GHYSELS and DENISE R. OSBORN

Semiparametric Regression for the Applied Econometrician
ADONIS YATCHEW

APPLIED TIME SERIES ECONOMETRICS

Edited by

HELMUT LÜTKEPOHL
European University Institute, Florence

MARKUS KRÄTZIG
Humboldt University, Berlin

CAMBRIDGE
UNIVERSITY PRESS

PUBLISHED BY THE PRESS SYNDICATE OF THE UNIVERSITY OF CAMBRIDGE
The Pitt Building, Trumpington Street, Cambridge, United Kingdom

CAMBRIDGE UNIVERSITY PRESS
The Edinburgh Building, Cambridge CB2 2RU, UK
40 West 20th Street, New York, NY 10011-4211, USA
477 Williamstown Road, Port Melbourne, VIC 3207, Australia
Ruiz de Alarcón 13, 28014 Madrid, Spain
Dock House, The Waterfront, Cape Town 8001, South Africa

http://www.cambridge.org

First published 2004

Printed in the United States of America

Typefaces Times New Roman PS 10/12 pt. and Lucida Sans Typewriter
System LaTeX 2_ε [TB]

A catalog record for this book is available from the British Library.

Library of Congress Cataloging-in-Publication Data available.

ISBN 0 521 83919 x hardback
ISBN 0 521 54787 3 paperback

HL   To my delightful wife, Sabine

MK   To my parents

Contents

Preface

Time series econometrics is a rapidly evolving field. In particular, the cointegration revolution has had a substantial impact on applied work. As a consequence of the fast development there are no textbooks that cover the full range of methods in current use and at the same time explain how to proceed in applied work. This gap in the literature motivates the present volume. It is not an introductory time series textbook but assumes that the reader has some background in time series analysis. Therefore the methods are only sketched briefly to remind the reader of the underlying ideas. Thus the book is meant to be useful as a reference for a reader who has some methodological background and wants to do empirical work. It may also be used as a textbook for a course on applied time series econometrics if the students have sufficient background knowledge or if the instructor fills in the missing theory.

The coverage of topics is partly dictated by recent methodological developments. For example, unit root and cointegration analysis are a must for a time series econometrician, and consequently these topics are the central part of Chapters 2 and 3. Other topics include structural vector autoregressions (Chapter 4), conditional heteroskedasticity (Chapter 5), and nonlinear and nonparametric time series models (Chapters 6 and 7). The choice of topics reflects the interests and experiences of the authors. We are not claiming to cover only the most popular methods in current use. In fact, some of the methods have not been used very much in applied studies but have a great potential for the future. This holds, for example, for the nonparametric methods.

A crucial component in empirical work is the software that is available for an analysis. New methodology is typically only gradually incorporated into the existing software packages. Some project participants have developed new time series methods, and we wanted them to be available quickly in an easy-to-use form. This has required the creation of a flexible Java interface that allows the user to run GAUSS programs under a uniform menu-driven interface. The empirical examples presented in the text are carried out with this software called JMulTi (Java-based **Mul**tiple **Ti**me series software). It is available free of charge on the internet at www.jmulti.de.

A major advantage of the interface lies in its flexibility. This makes it easy to integrate new methods, and the interface is general enough to allow other software such as Ox to be connected as well. Therefore we expect rapid development of the JMulTi software such that it will shortly also include methods that are not covered in this book.

Although the JMulTi software is primarily a tool for empirical work, it has already proven helpful for classroom use as well. Because it is menu-driven and, hence, very easy to apply, the software has been found to be useful in presenting classroom examples even in more theory-oriented courses.

It is perhaps worth emphasizing that this book is not just meant to be a manual for JMulTi. It can be used together with other software packages as well, although some of the methods covered are not yet available in other software. Again, in accord with our own preferences and research interests, JMulTi includes some methods available in other software products in a different from. In particular, it provides some computer-intensive bootstrap methods that are very time consuming with current computer technology but will most likely not be a computational challenge anymore in a few years.

The important role of the software in empirical analysis has prompted us to present JMulTi in some detail in the book (see Chapter 8). We also provide most data sets used in the examples in this volume together with the program. Readers can thereby replicate any results they like, and they may also use the data in their own projects to get hands-on experience with the methods discussed in the following chapters.

The Project Story

The origins of this project go back to the times when one of us was working on an introductory multiple time series book [Lütkepohl (1991)]. Parallel to writing up the statistical theory contained in that book a menu-driven program based on GAUSS was already developed under the name MulTi [see Haase, Lütkepohl, Claessen, Moryson & Schneider (1992)]. At that time there was no suitable easy-to-use software available for many of the methods discussed in Lütkepohl (1991), and it seemed natural to provide the basis for empirical analysis by making the program available. Because of restrictions of the program design, the project was later terminated.

Some years later Alexander Benkwitz, then working at the Humboldt University in Berlin, relaunched the project by applying modern, object-oriented design principles. It started out as a Java user interface to some GAUSS procedures but rapidly evolved to a comprehensive modeling framework. Many people contributed their procedures to the project, which put the idea of reusing code to life. Major parts of JMulTi were provided by Ralf Brüggemann, Helmut

Herwartz, Carsten Trenkler, Rolf Tschernig, Markku Lanne, Stefan Lundbergh, Jörg Breitung, Christian Kascha, and Dmitri Boreiko. We thank all of them for their cooperation.

The current package includes many parts that were not available in the old MulTi, and many of the procedures already available in the older software are now improved considerably taking into account a decade of methodological development. On the other hand, there are still some methods that were included in MulTi and are not available in JMulTi. The procedures related to vector autoregressive moving average (VARMA) modeling are an example. These models have not become as popular in empirical work as some of the methods that are included in JMulTi. Given the rather complex programming task behind VARMA modeling, we think that investing our resources in other procedures was justified. Of course, it is possible that such models will be added at some stage.

With a quite powerful software for time series econometrics at hand, it seemed also natural to write an applied time series econometrics text covering our favorite models and procedures and extending the small text given away with the old MulTi. It was only after the two of us had moved to the European University Institute (EUI) in the lovely hills around Florence in 2002 that this project gained momentum. It became apparent that such a text might be useful to have for the students, and therefore we worked more intensively on both the JMulTi software and the applied time series econometrics text describing the relevant methods. Because some of the people who have written the software components for JMulTi clearly have more expert knowledge on their methods than we do, we asked them to also contribute their knowledge to this volume. We thank all the contributors for their good cooperation and help in finalizing the book.

Acknowledgments

There are also many further people who contributed significantly to this book and JMulTi in one way or other. Their names are too numerous to list them all. We would like to mention the following contributions specifically, however. Kirstin Hubrich, Carsten Trenkler, Dmitri Boreiko, Maria Eleftheriou, Aaron Mehrotra, and Sebastian Watzka gave us feedback and comments during a workshop organized in Florence at the end of March 2003. Dmitri Boreiko also produced many of the figures. Tommaso Proietti discussed an early version of JMulTi generously when he was visiting the EUI as a Jean Monnet Fellow in 2002. Stefan Kruchen, Franz Palm, and Jean-Pierre Urbain commented in particular on Chapter 7. Last, but not least, we would like to thank Scott Parris, the economics editor of Cambridge University Press, for his cheerful encouragement during the preparation of the manuscript.

Financial Support

The Deutsche Forschungsgemeinschaft, SFB 373, the European Commission under the Training and Mobility of Researchers Programme (contract No. ERBFMRXCT980213), and the Jan Wallander and Tom Hedelin Foundation (contract No. J99/37) provided financial support for which we are very grateful because it enabled us to complete this project and in particular to make the software available free of charge to the research community.

San Domenico di Fiesole and Berlin,   *Helmut Lütkepohl*
September 4, 2003   *Markus Krätzig*

Notation and Abbreviations

General Symbols

:=	equals by definition
$\Rightarrow$	implies
$\Leftrightarrow$	is equivalent to
$\sim$	is distributed as
$\overset{a}{\sim}$	is asymptotically distributed as
$\in$	element of
$\subset$	subset of
$\cup$	union
$\cap$	intersection
$\sum$	summation sign
$\prod$	product sign
$\rightarrow$	converges to, approaches
$\overset{p}{\rightarrow}$	converges in probability to
$\overset{a.s.}{\rightarrow}$	converges almost surely to
$\overset{q.m.}{\rightarrow}$	converges in quadratic mean to
$\overset{d}{\rightarrow}$	converges in distribution to
$o(\cdot)$	order of convergence to zero
$O(\cdot)$	order of convergence
$o_p(\cdot)$	order of convergence to zero in probability
$O_p(\cdot)$	order of convergence in probability
lim	limit
plim	probability limit
max	maximum
min	minimum
sup	supremum, least upper bound
log	natural logarithm
exp	exponential function

$I(\cdot)$	indicator function
$|z|$	absolute value or modulus of z
$\mathbb{R}$	real numbers
$\mathbb{R}^m$	m-dimensional Euclidean space
$\mathbb{C}$	complex numbers
L	lag operator
Δ	differencing operator
E	expectation
Var	variance
Cov	covariance, covariance matrix
MSE	mean-squared error (matrix)
Pr	probability
$l(\cdot)$	log-likelihood function
λ_{LM}, LM	Lagrange multiplier statistic
λ_{LR}, LR	likelihood ratio statistic
λ_W, W	Wald statistic
Q_h	portmanteau statistic
Q_h^*	modified portmanteau statistic
d.f.	degrees of freedom
H_0	null hypothesis
H_1	alternative hypothesis
$K(\cdot)$	kernel
T	sample size, time series length
$1991Q3$	third quarter of 1991

AIC, AIC	Akaike information criterion
FPE, FPE	final prediction error (criterion)
HQ, HQ	Hannan–Quinn (criterion)
SC, SC	Schwarz criterion

Distributions and Related Symbols

p-value	tail probability of a statistic
$pF(.,.)$	p-value of an $F(\cdot,\cdot)$ statistic
$N(\mu, \Sigma)$	(multivariate) normal distribution with mean (vector) μ and variance (covariance matrix) Σ
$\chi^2(m)$	χ^2-distribution with m degrees of freedom
$F(m, n)$	F-distribution with m numerator and n denominator degrees of freedom
$t(m)$	t-distribution with m degrees of freedom

Vector and Matrix Operations

M'	transpose of M
M^{-1}	inverse of M
$M^{1/2}$	square root of M
M^k	kth power of M
MN	matrix product of the matrices M and N
$\otimes$	Kronecker product
$\det(M)$, $\det M$	determinant of M
$|M|$	determinant of M
$\|M\|$	Euclidean norm of M
$\text{rk}(M)$, $\text{rk } M$	rank of M
$\text{tr}(M)$, $\text{tr } M$	trace of M
vec	column stacking operator
vech	column stacking operator for symmetric matrices (stacks the elements on and below the main diagonal only)
$\dfrac{\partial\varphi}{\partial\beta'}$	vector or matrix of first-order partial derivatives of φ with respect to β
$\dfrac{\partial^2\varphi}{\partial\beta\partial\beta'}$	Hessian matrix of φ, matrix of second order partial derivatives of φ with respect to β

General Matrices

I_m	$(m \times m)$ unit or identity matrix
0	zero or null matrix or vector
$0_{m \times n}$	$(m \times n)$ zero or null matrix

Stochastic Processes and Related Quantities

u_t	white noise process
v_t	white noise process
w_t	white noise process
ε_t	white noise process
y_t	stochastic process
$\bar{y}$	$:= T^{-1} \sum\limits_{t=1}^{T} y_t$, sample mean (vector)
$\Gamma_y(h)$	$:= \text{Cov}(y_t, y_{t-h})$ for a stationary process y_t
$R_y(h)$	correlation matrix corresponding to $\Gamma_y(h)$
σ_u^2	$:= \text{Var}(u_t)$ variance of univariate process u_t
Σ_u	$:= \text{E}(u_t u_t') = \text{Cov}(u_t)$, white noise covariance matrix
Σ_y	$:= \text{E}\left[(y_t - \mu)(y_t - \mu)'\right] = \text{Cov}(y_t)$, covariance matrix of a stationary process y_t
μ	mean (vector)

Abbreviations

AC	autocorrelation
ACF	autocorrelation function
ADF	augmented Dickey–Fuller (test)
AFPE	asymptotic final prediction error
AIC	Akaike information criterion
API	application programming interface
AR	autoregressive (process)
AR(p)	autoregressive process of order p
ARCH	autoregressive conditional heteroskedasticity
ARIMA	autoregressive integrated moving average (process)
ARIMA(p, d, q)	autoregressive integrated moving average process of order (p, d, q)
ARMA	autoregressive moving average (process)
ARMA(p, q)	autoregressive moving average process of order (p, q)
BEKK	Baba–Engle–Kraft–Kroner (model)
BHHH	Berndt–Hall–Hall–Hausman (algorithm)
CAFPE	corrected asymptotic final prediction error
CAPM	capital asset pricing model
CI	confidence interval
CUSUM	cumulated sum
DAFOX	German stock index for research purposes
DEM	Deutsche mark
DGP	data generation process
ESTAR	exponential smooth transition autoregression
ESTR	exponential smooth transition regression
FPE	final prediction error
GARCH	generalized autoregressive conditional heteroskedasticity
GBP	Great Britain pounds
GDP	gross domestic product
GED	general error distribution
GLS	generalized least squares
GNP	gross national product
GUI	graphical user interface
HEGY	Hylleberg–Engle–Granger–Yoo (test)
HP	Hodrick–Prescott (filter)
HQ	Hannan–Quinn (criterion)
I(d)	integrated of order d
iid	independently identically distributed
JVM	Java virtual machine
KPSS	Kwiatkowski–Phillips–Schmidt–Shin (test)

LJB	Lomnicki–Jarque–Bera (test)
LM	Lagrange multiplier (test)
LR	likelihood ratio (test)
LSTR	logistic smooth transition regression
LTW	Lütkepohl–Teräsvirta–Wolters (study)
MA	moving average (process)
MA(q)	moving average process of order q
MGARCH	multivariate generalized autoregressive conditional heteroskedasticity
ML	maximum likelihood
MSE	mean-squared error
NAR	nonlinear autoregression
OLS	ordinary least squares
PAC	partial autocorrelation
PACF	partial autocorrelation function
PAR	periodic autoregression
pdf	probability density function
QML	quasi-maximum likelihood
RESET	regression specification error test
RR	reduced rank
SC	Schwarz criterion
SDAR	seasonal dummy autoregression
SDNAR	seasonal dummy nonlinear autoregression
SHNAR	seasonal shift nonlinear autoregression
SNAR	seasonal nonlinear autoregression
STAR	smooth transition autoregression
STR	smooth transition regression
SVAR	structural vector autoregression
SVECM	structural vector error correction model
TGARCH	threshold generalized autoregressive conditional heteroskedasticity
TV-STAR	time-varying smooth transition autoregression
TV-STR	time-varying smooth transition regression
USD	U.S. dollar
VAR	vector autoregressive (process)
VAR(p)	vector autoregressive process of order p
VARMA	vector autoregressive moving average (process)
VARMA(p, q)	vector autoregressive moving average process of order (p, q)
VEC	vector error correction
VECM	vector error correction model
3SLS	three-stage least squares

Contributors

JÖRG BREITUNG
Universität Bonn, GERMANY
email: breitung@uni-bonn.de

RALF BRÜGGEMANN
Humboldt Universität zu Berlin, GERMANY
email: brueggem@wiwi.hu-berlin.de

HELMUT HERWARTZ
Christian Albrechts Universität Kiel, GERMANY
email: Herwartz@stat-econ.uni-kiel.de

MARKUS KRÄTZIG
Humboldt Universität zu Berlin, GERMANY
email: mk@mk-home.de

HELMUT LÜTKEPOHL
European University Institute, ITALY
email: helmut.luetkepohl@iue.it

TIMO TERÄSVIRTA
Stockholm School of Economics, SWEDEN
email: Timo.Terasvirta@hhs.se

ROLF TSCHERNIG
Maastricht University, THE NETHERLANDS
email: R.Tschernig@KE.unimaas.nl

1 Initial Tasks and Overview

Helmut Lütkepohl

1.1 Introduction

This book discusses tools for the econometric analysis of time series. Generally, a time series is a sequence of values a specific variable has taken on over some period of time. The observations have a natural ordering in time. Usually, when we refer to a series of observations as a time series, we assume some regularity of the observation frequency. For example, one value is available for each year in a period of thirty years, for instance. To be even more specific, consider the annual gross national product (GNP) of some country for a period of 1970 to 1999. Of course, the observation frequency could be more often than yearly. For instance, observations may be available for each quarter, each month, or even each day of a particular period. Nowadays, time series of stock prices or other financial market variables are even available at a much higher frequency such as every few minutes or seconds.

Many economic problems can be analyzed using time series data. For example, many macroeconometric analyses are based on time series data. Forecasting the future economic conditions is one important objective of many analyses. Another important goal is understanding the relations between a set of possibly related variables or uncovering the ongoings within an economic system or a specific market.

Before engaging in an econometric time series analysis it is a good idea to be clear about the objectives of the analysis. They can determine in part which models and statistical tools are suitable. A brief discussion of this initial stage of a project follows in Section 1.2. The next step is getting a good data set to work with. Some discussion of this step is provided in Sections 1.3 and 1.4. The discussion is presented in two separate sections because it is one thing to find data in some suitable data source and another issue to prepare the data for the project of interest. When a time series data set has been created, a good model has to be constructed for the data generation process (DGP). This is the stage at which the actual econometric analysis begins, and the tools discussed in this volume may be useful at that stage. A brief overview of the topics considered in this book is given in the final section of this chapter.

1.2 Setting Up an Econometric Project

As mentioned in the chapter introduction, the first stage of a time series econometric project is to clarify the objectives of the analysis. These objectives may be formulated by a customer who is interested in specific results or the solution of a particular problem. For example, the government may wish to know the tax revenues for the next quarter or year. In that case a forecast of a specific variable is desired. Sometimes the objectives are formulated in a less precise way, such as when the government wants to know the general implications of a change in a particular tax rule. Clearly, the econometrician has to narrow down the questions to be addressed in such a way that they become accessible with econometric analysis. A more precise question in this context would be, for instance, What are the implications for the income distribution of the households of the target economy? In short, it is important to be sufficiently precise about the desired targets of an analysis to be able to focus the analysis properly.

When the objectives of the analysis are specified, it is a good idea to check what economic theory has to say about the problem of interest or the general problem area. Often alternative theories exist that have something to say on a particular problem. Such theories are useful in different respects. First, they may be used to specify the framework for analysis and to choose the relevant variables that have to be included in a model. In economics it is clear that many variables interact more or less strongly. When the models and statistical tools for an econometric time series analysis are discussed in subsequent chapters, it will become clear, however, that typically only a very limited number of variables can be accommodated in a particular model. Otherwise a meaningful statistical analysis is not possible on the basis of the given data information. Therefore, it is important to narrow down the variables of central importance for an analysis. Here economic theory has an important part to play. The data usually have features that are not well explained or described by economic theory, however. For a proper econometric analysis they still have to be captured in the model for the DGP. Therefore, economic theory cannot be expected to deliver a complete statistical model but may be very helpful in providing some central relations between the variables of interest.

This aspect provides a second important ingredient for the analysis that comes from economic theory. When an econometric model has been constructed for the DGP, it should only be used for the analysis if it reflects the ongoings in the system of interest properly. Several statistical tools will be presented in the following chapters that can be used for checking the adequacy of a model. In addition, economic theory can also be used to check whether the central relations are reflected in the model. Of course, determining whether a given theory is compatible with the data may just be the main objective of an analysis. However, if a specific theory is used, for example, as the basis for choosing the variables for a forecasting model, investigating whether the theory is indeed reflected in the model may be a good check. Otherwise some other theory may have been a better basis for the choice of variables, and the final model may leave room for improvement. When the set of potentially most relevant variables is specified, it is necessary to get time series data for the actual analysis. That stage is discussed briefly in the next section.

1.3 Getting Data

There is now a wealth of databases with time series for a large number of variables. Therefore, at first sight the data collection step may seem easy. A problem arises, however, because economic theory considers abstract variables that are not always easy to measure. In any case, when it comes to measuring a variable such as GNP, the statistical office in charge has to establish a specific measurement procedure that may not be the same in some other statistical office. Moreover, many variables are not specified uniquely by economic theory. For example, what is the price level in some economy? Is it preferable to measure it in terms of consumer prices using, for example, the consumer price index (CPI), or should the GNP deflator be used? How is the CPI constructed? That depends, of course, on the weights given to prices of different goods and, hence, on the principle for index construction used by the statistical office in charge. Also, which goods are included has an important impact on the result. The basket of goods is typically adjusted every few years, and that may be important information to take into account in the statistical modeling procedure.

The problem of nonuniqueness and ambiguity of the definitions of the variables is not limited to macroeconomic data by the way. For instance, it may also not be fully clear how stock prices are collected. There are different possibilities to define the price associated with a specific day, for example. The quoted value may be the closing price at some specific stock exchange. Of course, many stocks are traded at different stock exchanges with different closing times; hence, quite different series may be obtained if a different specification is used. In addition, instead of the closing price, the price at some other time of the day may be considered.

It is not always easy to determine the exact definition or construction procedure of a particular time series. Nevertheless it should be clear that a good background knowledge about the data can be central for a good analysis. In turn, some surprising or strange results may just be a consequence of the specific definition of a particular variable. It is also possible that the definition of a variable will change over time. We have already mentioned the frequent adjustments of the basket of goods underlying CPI data. As another example consider German macroeconomic variables. Some of them refer to West Germany only before the German reunification and to all of Germany thereafter. Clearly, one could argue that the definitions of the relevant variables have changed over time.

Another problem with the data offered in many databases is that they have been adjusted, modified, or transformed in some way. Seasonal adjustment is, for instance, a standard procedure that is often applied to data published by statistical agencies. We will briefly touch on such procedures in Chapter 2, where it will become clear that quite different seasonal adjustment procedures exist. Consequently, even if the original series is the same, there may be striking differences when it is seasonally adjusted by different agencies. The reason is that defining and determining the seasonal component of a series are not easy tasks. In particular, there is no single best way to perform them. In any case, one should remember that adjusted or filtered data may be distorted in such a way that interesting features for a particular analysis are lost.

Aggregation is another issue of importance in setting up a suitable data set. Often the series of interest have different frequencies of observation. For example, many variables are recorded at monthly frequency, whereas others are available only quarterly or even annually. Although it is in principle possible to interpolate missing values of a time series, doing so entails problems. First, there is no unique best way to perform the interpolation. Secondly, seasonal fluctuations are difficult to model realistically. Ignoring them can lead to distortions of the relation with other series that have seasonal components. Generally, it should be understood that interpolation on the basis of a single series does not lead to an extension of the information content. Therefore, it is not uncommon in practice to set up a data set with several time series such that all series have the frequency of the series that is observed least frequently. Such an approach, however, may require that some series be aggregated over time (e.g., from monthly to quarterly frequency).

Again, there are different ways to aggregate a series, and it may be worth thinking about the implications of the aggregation method for the subsequent analysis. Suppose that a monthly interest rate series is given, whereas quarterly observations are available only for some other series. In that case, what is the best way to convert the monthly interest rate series into a quarterly one? Should one use the value of the last month of each quarter as the quarterly value or should an average of the values of the three months of each quarter be used? If it is not clear which variable best reflects the quantity one would like to include in the model, it is, of course, possible to perform an analysis with several different series based on different temporal aggregation schemes and to check which one results in the most satisfactory outcome. In any case, the analysis methods for sets of time series variables described in this book assume that all series are observed at the same frequency and for the same period. Therefore, if the original series do not satisfy this condition, they have to be modified accordingly.

In conclusion, getting suitable data for a particular analysis can be a very demanding part of an econometric project despite the many databases that are at our disposal today. Data from different sources may be collected or constructed in markedly different ways even if they refer to the same variable. A careful examination of the data definitions and specifications is therefore advisable at an early stage of an analysis.

1.4 Data Handling

The discussion in the previous section suggests that the data obtained from a specific source may not be in precisely the form to be used in the analysis. Data formats and codings can be – and often are – different when the data come from different sources. Therefore, it is usually necessary to arrange them in a uniform way in a common data file to be used in the software at the disposal of the econometrician. Fortunately, modern software can handle all kinds of different data formats. In other words, they can be imported into the econometric software tool, for instance, in ASCII or EXCEL format. Still it may be useful to make adjustments before the econometric analysis begins. For example, to avoid numerical problems it may be helpful to pay attention to a roughly similar order of magnitude in the actual time series numbers. For instance, it may not be a good idea to measure the GNP in billions of euros and another variable of similar order of magnitude in cents. The required operations for making the data more homogenous are often easy to perform with the software tool available. More details on data handling with the software JMulTi frequently referred to in this volume are discussed in Chapter 8.

1.5 Outline of Chapters

When the project objectives have been defined properly, the underlying economic or other subject matter theory has been evaluated, and a suitable set of time series has been prepared, the actual econometric modeling and statistical analysis can begin. Some tools for this stage of the analysis are presented in the following chapters.

Even when the objective is a joint analysis of a set of time series, it is usually a good idea to start with exploring the special properties and characteristics of the series individually. In other words, univariate analysis of the individual series typically precede a multivariate or systems analysis. The tools available for univariate analysis are presented in Chapter 2. In that chapter, some more discussion of important characteristics is given, in particular, in anticipation of a later multivariate analysis. For example, specific attention is paid to an exploration of the trending behavior of a series. Therefore, unit root tests that can help in detecting the existence of stochastic trends form a prominent part of the chapter. With respect to the models for describing univariate DGPs, the emphasis in Chapter 2 is on linear models for the conditional expectation or the first- and second-order moment part of a series because it is an advantage in many situations to construct simple models. Therefore, if a simple linear model is found to describe the data well, this is important information to carry on to a multivariate analysis.

At the multivariate level, linear models for the conditional mean such as vector autoregressions (VARs) and vector error correction models (VECMs) are again the first choice. Given that data sets are often quite limited and that even linear models can contain substantial numbers of parameters, it is sometimes difficult to go beyond the linear model case at the multivariate level. Chapter 3 discusses VECMs and VAR models, how to specify and estimate them, how to use them for forecasting purposes, and how to perform a specific kind of causality analysis. The recent empirical literature has found it useful to distinguish between the short- and long-run parts of a model. These parts are conveniently separated in a VECM by paying particular attention to a detailed modeling of the cointegration properties of the variables. Therefore, Chapter 3 emphasizes modeling of cointegrated series. In this analysis the results of preliminary unit root tests are of some importance. More generally, some univariate characteristics of the series form a basis for the choice of multivariate models and the analysis tools used at the systems level.

Once a model for the joint DGP of a set of time series of interest has been found, econometricians or economists often desire to use the model for analyzing the relations between the variables. The objective of such an analysis may be an investigation of the adequacy of a particular theory or theoretical argument. Alternatively, the aim may be a check of the model specification and its ability to represent the structure of a specific market or sector of an economy properly. Nowadays impulse responses and forecast error variance decompositions are used as tools for analyzing the relations between the variables in a dynamic econometric model. These tools are considered in Chapter 4. It turns out, however, that a mechanical application of the tools may not convey the information of interest, and therefore structural information often has to be added to the analysis. Doing so results in a structural VAR (SVAR) or structural VECM (SVECM) analysis that is also covered in Chapter 4, including the resulting additional estimation and specification problems.

If sufficient information is available in the data to make an analysis of nonlinearities and higher order moment properties desirable or possible, there are different ways to go beyond the linear models discussed so far. Of course, the choice depends to some extent on the data properties and also on the purpose of the analysis. An important extension that is often of interest for financial market data is to model the conditional second moments. In a univariate context, this means, of course, modeling the conditional variances. For multivariate systems, models for the conditional covariance matrices may be desired. Some models, estimation methods, and analysis tools for conditional heteroskedasticity are presented in Chapter 5.

Nonlinear modeling of the conditional mean is considered in Chapters 6 and 7. Chapter 6 contains a description of the parametric smooth transition (STR) model, and an organized way of building STR models is discussed and illuminated by empirical examples. An STR model may be regarded as a linear model with time-varying parameters such that the parametric form of the linear model varies smoothly with two extreme "regimes" according to an observable, usually stochastic – but in some applications deterministic – variable. The smoothness of the transition from one extreme regime to the other accounts for the name of this model. The modeling strategy described in Chapter 6 is only applicable to single-equation models, and the question of how to build nonlinear systems consisting of STR equations is not addressed in this book. The discussion in Chapter 6 also covers purely univariate smooth transition autoregressive (STAR) models that have been frequently fitted to economic and other time series.

A more general approach, as far as the form of nonlinearity is concerned, is adopted in Chapter 7, where both the conditional mean as well as the conditional variance of the DGP of a univariate series are modeled in general nonlinear form. Estimation of the nonlinear functions is done nonparametrically using suitable local approximations that can describe general nonlinear functions in a very flexible way. The drawback of the additional flexibility is, however, that more sample information is needed to get a clear picture of the underlying structures. Therefore, these methods can currently only be recommended for univariate time series analysis and, hence, the exposition in Chapter 7 is limited to this case.

In modern applied time series econometrics the computer is a vital tool for carrying out the analysis. In particular, the methods described in this volume rely heavily on extensive computations. Therefore, it is important to have software that does not create obstacles for the analysis by presenting only tools that are too limited. In the last chapter of this volume, software is therefore introduced that includes many of the methods and procedures considered in this book. Clearly, the methods for econometric time series analysis are evolving rapidly; hence, packaged, ready-to-use software can easily become obsolete. The software JMulTi introduced in Chapter 8 is supposed to be able to decrease the time gap between the development of new methods and their availability in user-friendly form. This software provides a flexible framework for checking new methods and algorithms quickly. Readers may therefore find it useful to familiarize themselves with the software as they go through the various chapters of the book. In other words, it may be worth having a look at the final chapter at an early stage and trying out the methods by replicating the examples using the JMulTi software.

2 Univariate Time Series Analysis

Helmut Lütkepohl

2.1 Characteristics of Time Series

The first step in building dynamic econometric models entails a detailed analysis of the characteristics of the individual time series variables involved. Such an analysis is important because the properties of the individual series have to be taken into account in modeling the data generation process (DGP) of a system of potentially related variables.

Some important characteristics of time series can be seen in the example series plotted in Figure 2.1. The first series consists of changes in seasonally adjusted U.S. fixed investment. It appears to fluctuate randomly around a constant mean, and its variability is homogeneous during the observation period. Some correlation between consecutive values seems possible. In contrast, the second series, representing a German long-term interest rate, evolves more slowly, although its variability is also fairly regular. The sluggish, longer term movements are often thought of as a stochastic trend. The third series represents German gross national product (GNP). It appears to evolve around a deterministic polynomial trend, and, moreover, it has a distinct seasonal movement. In addition there is a level shift in the third quarter of 1990. This shift is due to a redefinition of the series, which refers to West Germany only until the second quarter of 1990 and to the unified Germany afterwards. Although German reunification took place officially in October 1990, many economic time series were adjusted already on 1 July of that year, the date of the monetary unification. Finally, the last series in Figure 2.1 represents the daily DAFOX returns from 1985 to 1996. The DAFOX is a German stock index. It moves around a fixed mean value. The variability is quite dissimilar in different parts of the sample period. Furthermore, there is an unusually long spike in late 1989. Such an unusual value is sometimes referred to as an outlier.

To summarize, we see series in the figure with very different and clearly visible characteristics. They may evolve regularly around a fixed value, or they may have stochastic or deterministic trending behavior. Furthermore, they may

8

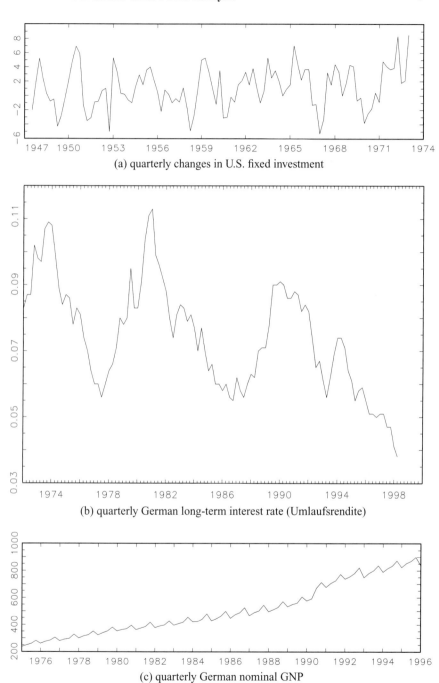

(a) quarterly changes in U.S. fixed investment

(b) quarterly German long-term interest rate (Umlaufsrendite)

(c) quarterly German nominal GNP

Figure 2.1. Example time series.

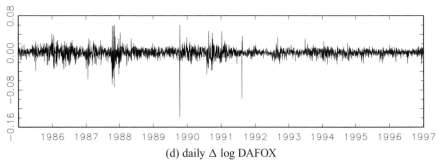

(d) daily Δ log DAFOX

Figure 2.1. (*continued*)

display seasonal movements, and they may have level shifts or outliers. All these characteristics have to be taken into account in constructing models for a set of related time series variables. Some of the characteristics may have an impact on the statistical inference procedures used in modeling and analyzing the underlying economic system. The specific characteristics of the series may be an integral part of the relationship of interest, or they may reflect features that are not of interest for the relationship under study but may still be of importance for the statistical procedures used in analyzing a given system of variables. Therefore, it is important to obtain a good understanding of the individual time series properties before a set of series is modeled jointly. Some important characteristics of the DGPs of time series will be described more formally in this chapter, and we will also present statistical quantities and procedures for analyzing these properties.

Generally, it is assumed that a given time series $y_1, \ldots, y_T$ consists of a stretch of (at least roughly) equidistant observations such as a series of quarterly values from the first quarter of 1975 (1975Q1) to the fourth quarter of 1998 (1998Q4). The fact that quarters are not of identical length will be ignored, whereas if the values of some of the quarters are missing, the observations of the time series would not be regarded as equidistant anymore. On the other hand, the DAFOX returns are often treated as a series of equidistant observations, although weekend and holiday values are missing. There are methods for dealing explicitly with missing observations. They will not be discussed here, and the reader may consult specialized literature for methods to deal with them [see, e.g., Jones (1980) and Ansley & Kohn (1983)].

In this volume, it is assumed that the time series are generated by stochastic processes. Roughly speaking, a *stochastic process* is a collection of random variables. Each time series observation is assumed to be generated by a different member of the stochastic process. The associated random variables assumed to have generated the time series observations will usually be denoted by the same symbols as the observations. Thus, a time series $y_1, \ldots, y_T$ is generated by a stochastic process $\{y_t\}_{t \in \mathsf{T}}$, where T is an index set containing the subset $\{1, \ldots, T\}$. The subscripts t are usually thought of as representing time or time periods, and the associated terminology is chosen accordingly. Note that the DGP may begin before the first time series value is observed, and it may stretch beyond the last observation period. Such an assumption is convenient for theoretical discussions, for example, of forecasting and asymptotic analysis, where the development beyond the sample period is of interest. Often T is the set of all integers or all nonnegative integers. It will be obvious from the context whether the symbol y_t refers to an observed value or the underlying random variable. To simplify the notation further we sometimes use it to denote the full stochastic process or the related time series. In that case the range of the subscript is either not important or it is understood from the context.

In this chapter many concepts, models, procedures, and theoretical results are sketched only briefly because we do not intend to provide a full introduction to univariate time series analysis but will just present some of the important background necessary for applied econometric modeling. Several time series textbooks are available with a more in-depth treatment that may be consulted for further details and discussions. Examples are Fuller (1976), Priestley (1981), Brockwell & Davis (1987), and Hamilton (1994).

2.2 Stationary and Integrated Stochastic Processes

2.2.1 Stationarity

A stochastic process y_t is called *stationary* if it has time-invariant first and second moments. In other words, y_t is stationary if

1. $E(y_t) = \mu_y$ for all $t \in T$ and
2. $E[(y_t - \mu_y)(y_{t-h} - \mu_y)] = \gamma_h$ for all $t \in T$ and all integers h such that $t - h \in T$.

The first condition means that all members of a stationary stochastic process have the same constant mean. Hence, a time series generated by a stationary stochastic process must fluctuate around a constant mean and does not have a trend, for example. The second condition ensures that the variances are also time invariant because, for $h = 0$, the variance $\sigma_y^2 = E[(y_t - \mu_y)^2] = \gamma_0$ does not depend on t. Moreover, the covariances $E[(y_t - \mu_y)(y_{t-h} - \mu_y)] = \gamma_h$ do not depend on t but just on the distance in time h of the two members of the process. Our notation is also meant to imply that the means, variances, and covariances are finite numbers. In other words, the first two moments and cross moments exist.

Clearly, some of the time series in Figure 2.1 have characteristics that make them unlikely candidates for series generated by stationary processes. For example, the German GNP series has a trend that may be better modeled by a changing mean. Moreover, the level shift in 1990 may indicate a shift in mean that is inconsistent with a constant mean for all members of the process. The changes in the variability of the DAFOX return series may violate the constant variance property of a stationary DGP. On the other hand, the U.S. investment series gives the visual impression of a time series generated by a stationary process because it fluctuates around a constant mean and the variability appears to be regular. Such a time series is sometimes referred to as a stationary time series for simplicity of terminology. From our examples it may seem that stationarity is a rare property of economic time series. Although there is some truth to this impression, it is sometimes possible to obtain stationary-looking time series by simple transformations. Some of them will be discussed shortly.

Before we go on with our discussion of stationary processes, it may be worth mentioning that there are other definitions of stationary stochastic processes that are sometimes used elsewhere in the literature. Some authors call a process with time-invariant first and second moments *covariance stationary*, and sometimes a process is defined to be stationary if all the joint distributions of $(y_t, \ldots, y_{t-h})$ are time invariant for any integer h, that is, they depend on h only and not on t. Sometimes a process satisfying this condition is described as being *strictly stationary*. This terminology will not be used here, but a process is simply called stationary if it has time-invariant first and second moments.

If the process starts in some fixed time period (e.g., if T is the set of non-negative integers), then it is possible that it needs some start-up period until the moments stabilize. In fact, it is conceivable that the moments reach a constant state only asymptotically. This happens often if the process can be made stationary by modifying the initial members of the process. In that case, the process may be called *asymptotically stationary*. We will not always distinguish between asymptotic stationarity and stationarity but will call a process stationary if stationarity can be achieved by modifying some initial variables.

Sometimes a process is called *trend-stationary* if it can be made stationary by subtracting a deterministic trend function such as a linear function of the form $\mu_0 + \mu_1 t$, where μ_0 and μ_1 are fixed parameters.

2.2.2 Sample Autocorrelations, Partial Autocorrelations, and Spectral Densities

It is not always easy to see from the plot of a time series whether it is reasonable to assume that it has a stationary DGP. For instance, the stationarity properties of the interest rate series DGP in Figure 2.1 are not obvious. Therefore, it is useful to consider some statistics related to a time series. For example, one may consider the sample autocorrelations (ACs) $\tilde{\rho}_h = \tilde{\gamma}_h/\tilde{\gamma}_0$ or $\hat{\rho}_h = \hat{\gamma}_h/\hat{\gamma}_0$ obtained from

$$\tilde{\gamma}_h = \frac{1}{T} \sum_{t=h+1}^{T} (y_t - \bar{y})(y_{t-h} - \bar{y})$$

or

$$\hat{\gamma}_h = \frac{1}{T-h} \sum_{t=h+1}^{T} (y_t - \bar{y})(y_{t-h} - \bar{y}),$$

where $\bar{y} = T^{-1} \sum_{t=1}^{T} y_t$ is the sample mean. For a series with stationary DGP, the sample autocorrelations typically die out quickly with increasing h, as in Figure 2.2, where the sample autocorrelation function (ACF) of the U.S. investment series is plotted. In contrast, the autocorrelation function of the interest rate series, which is also plotted in Figure 2.2, tapers off more slowly. Therefore, the stationarity properties of this series are less evident. We will discuss formal statistical tests for stationarity later on in Section 2.7.

In Figure 2.2, the dashed lines to both sides of the zero axis enable the reader to assess which one of the autocorrelation coefficients may be regarded as zero. Notice that the sample autocorrelations are estimates of the actual autocorrelations if the process is stationary. If it is purely random, that is, all members are mutually independent and identically distributed so that y_t and y_{t-h} are stochastically independent for $h \neq 0$, then the normalized estimated autocorrelations are asymptotically standard normally distributed, $\sqrt{T} \tilde{\rho}_h \overset{d}{\to} N(0, 1)$, and thus $\tilde{\rho}_h \approx N(0, 1/T)$. Hence, $[-2/\sqrt{T}, 2/\sqrt{T}]$ is an approximate 95% confidence interval around zero. The dashed lines in Figure 2.2 are just $\pm 2/\sqrt{T}$ lines; consequently, they give a rough indication of whether the autocorrelation coefficients may be regarded as coming from a process with true autocorrelations equal to zero. A stationary process for which all autocorrelations are zero is called *white noise* or a *white noise process*.

Clearly, on the basis of the foregoing criterion for judging the significance of the autocorrelations in Figure 2.2, the U.S. investment series is not likely to be generated by a white noise process because some autocorrelations reach outside the area between the dashed lines. On the other hand, all coefficients at higher lags are clearly between the dashed lines. Hence, the underlying autocorrelation function may be in line with a stationary DGP.

Partial autocorrelations (PACs) are also quantities that may convey useful information on the properties of the DGP of a given time series. The partial autocorrelation between y_t and y_{t-h} is the conditional autocorrelation given $y_{t-1}, \ldots, y_{t-h+1}$, that is, the autocorrelation conditional on the in-between values of the time series. Formally,

$$a_h = \mathsf{Corr}(y_t, y_{t-h} | y_{t-1}, \ldots, y_{t-h+1}).$$

The corresponding sample quantity $\hat{a}_h$ is easily obtained as the ordinary least-squares (OLS) estimator of the coefficient α_h in an autoregressive model

$$y_t = \nu + \alpha_1 y_{t-1} + \cdots + \alpha_h y_{t-h} + u_t.$$

These models are discussed in more detail in Section 2.3.1. For stationary processes, partial autocorrelations also approach zero as h goes to infinity; hence, the estimated counterparts should be small for large lags h. In Figure 2.2, the partial autocorrelation functions (PACFs) are shown for the U.S. investment series and the German long-term interest rate series. In this case they all tend to approach small values quickly for increasing h. We will see later that

autocorrelations of D investment

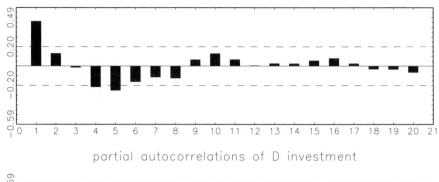

partial autocorrelations of D investment

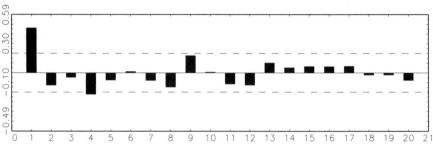

autocorrelations of long-term interest rate

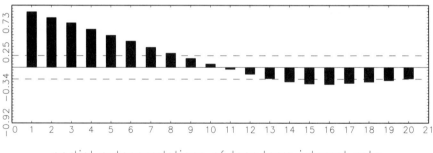

partial autocorrelations of long-term interest rate

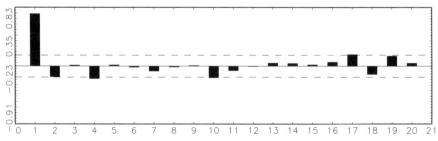

Figure 2.2. Autocorrelation functions and partial autocorrelation functions of U.S. investment and German long-term interest rate series.

autocorrelation functions and partial autocorrelation functions can give useful information on specific properties of a DGP other than stationarity.

The autocorrelations of a stationary stochastic process may be summarized compactly in the *spectral density function*. It is defined as

$$f_y(\lambda) = (2\pi)^{-1} \sum_{j=-\infty}^{\infty} \gamma_j e^{-i\lambda j} = (2\pi)^{-1} \left(\gamma_0 + 2 \sum_{j=1}^{\infty} \gamma_j \cos(\lambda j) \right),$$

(2.1)

where $i = \sqrt{-1}$ is the imaginary unit, $\lambda \in [-\pi, \pi]$ is the frequency, that is, the number of cycles in a unit of time measured in radians, and the γ_j's are the autocovariances of y_t as before. It can be shown that

$$\gamma_j = \int_{-\pi}^{\pi} e^{i\lambda j} f_y(\lambda) d\lambda.$$

Thus, the autocovariances can be recovered from the spectral density function via the integral on the right-hand side. In particular,

$$\gamma_0 = \sigma_y^2 = \int_{-\pi}^{\pi} f_y(\lambda) d\lambda.$$

In other words, for $-\pi \leq \lambda_1 < \lambda_2 \leq \pi$, the integral $\int_{\lambda_1}^{\lambda_2} f_y(\lambda) d\lambda$ represents the contribution of cycles of frequencies between λ_1 and λ_2 to the variance of y_t. Letting the distance between λ_1 and λ_2 become very small shows that $f_y(\lambda)$ may be interpreted as the contribution of cycles of frequency λ to the total variability of y_t.

A possible estimator of the spectral density is the *periodogram*, which is suggested by the definition of the spectral density in (2.1). It is obtained by replacing the autocorrelations by estimators,

$$I_y(\lambda) = (2\pi)^{-1} \left(\hat{\gamma}_0 + 2 \sum_{j=1}^{T-1} \hat{\gamma}_j \cos(\lambda j) \right).$$

Unfortunately, the periodogram is not a good estimator because it is not consistent and usually gives an imprecise impression of the spectral density. This property is a result of the increasing number of sample autocovariances included in the periodogram with growing sample size. Therefore, downweighing autocovariances for larger lags is preferable in estimating the spectral density. This results in an estimator

$$\hat{f}_y(\lambda) = (2\pi)^{-1} \left(\omega_0 \hat{\gamma}_0 + 2 \sum_{j=1}^{M_T} \omega_j \hat{\gamma}_j \cos(\lambda j) \right),$$

where the weights ω_j $(j = 1, \ldots, M_T)$ represent the so-called *spectral window* and M_T is the *truncation point*. The following examples of spectral windows

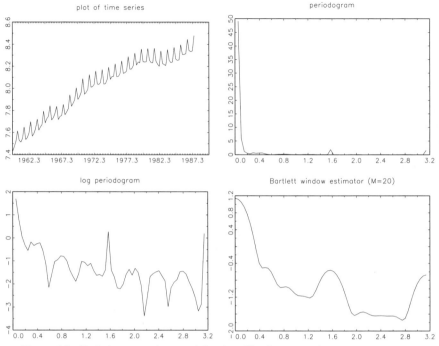

Figure 2.3. Periodogram and spectral density of log income series.

have been proposed in the literature among others:

$$\omega_j = 1 - j/M_T \quad \text{[Bartlett (1950)]}$$

$$\omega_j = \begin{cases} 1 - 6\left(\frac{j}{M_T}\right)^2 + 6\left(\frac{j}{M_T}\right)^3 & \text{for } 0 \leq j \leq \frac{M_T}{2} \\ 2\left(1 - \frac{j}{M_T}\right)^3 & \text{for } \frac{M_T}{2} \leq j \leq M_T \end{cases} \quad \text{[Parzen (1961)]}$$

[see also Priestley (1981, Sec. 6.2.3) for further proposals of spectral windows]. The weights decrease with increasing j; hence, less weight is given to $\hat{\gamma}_j$s with greater j, which are computed from fewer observations than the $\hat{\gamma}_j$s with smaller j. In other words, the autocovariance estimates based on fewer observations receive less weight. Using a spectral window such as those proposed by Bartlett or Parzen ensures consistent estimators $\hat{f}_y(\lambda)$ if the truncation point is chosen such that $M_T \to \infty$ and $M_T/T \to 0$ as $T \to \infty$.

In Figure 2.3, the logarithms of quarterly real per capita personal disposable West German income are plotted. The series has an upward trend and a distinct seasonal pattern. The trend is reflected as a spike near zero in the periodogram; that is, the very low frequencies dominate. Because the spike is so large, nothing much else can be seen in the second panel of Figure 2.3. In such a situation, it is often preferable to plot the log of the periodogram rather than the periodogram.

The logarithm is a monoton transformation and therefore ensures that larger values remain larger than smaller ones. The relative size is reduced, however. This is clearly seen in the third panel of Figure 2.3. Now it is obvious that the variability in the periodogram estimates is quite large. Therefore, we also show the log of the smoothed spectral density estimator based on a Bartlett window with window width $M_T = 20$ in the last panel of Figure 2.3. In that graph the series is seen to be dominated by very low frequency cycles (trend) and seasonal cycles. Notice the peak at frequency $2\pi/4 = 1.57$, which is the seasonal frequency of a quarterly series that completes a quarter of a cycle in each observation period. Because the frequency is measured in radians, that is, in fractions of 2π, the value 1.57 is obtained. There may be further peaks at multiples of the seasonal frequency because more than one cycle may be completed within a year, which may contribute to the appearance of a seasonal movement throughout the year. For the example series this is clearly reflected in a second peak at the right end of the graph. Note that, owing to the symmetry around frequency zero, spectral densities are typically plotted only for $\lambda \in [0, \pi]$.

Although the log income series is hardly stationary – and, hence, its spectral density may not even be properly defined – the estimate can be computed, and it may still be informative as a descriptive device. The observation that much of the spectral mass is concentrated near the zero frequency and further peaks occur around the seasonal frequencies is quite common for macroeconomic time series. Therefore, this pattern has been termed the *typical spectral shape* by Granger (1966). It describes the fact that the series is trending with long-term movements; hence, low frequencies contribute considerably to the variability of the series. In addition, the series has a strong seasonal component that contributes to the variance.

An important problem in estimating the spectral density of a time series is the choice of the window size M_T. Larger values lead to more volatile function estimates with larger variances, whereas small values of M_T result in smooth estimates that may be biased, however. For descriptive purposes, it may be worth investigating which features are of most importance for a given series by trying several different values. Alternatively, one may consult the relevant literature for a discussion on the choice of the window width and then make a more informed choice [see, e.g., Priestley (1981, Chapter 7)].

2.2.3 Data Transformations and Filters

The log transformation and rates of change. As we have seen, many economic time series have characteristics incompatible with a stationary DGP. However, in some cases simple transformations can move a series closer to stationarity. Consider, for instance, the German income series in Figure 2.4, which shows larger fluctuations for greater values of the series. In such a case, a logarithmic transformation may help to stabilize the variance. This can be seen in Figure 2.4. Of course, the trend still remains, but the variance has become more uniform

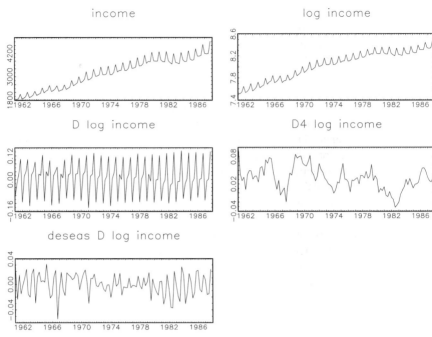

Figure 2.4. Quarterly West German real per capita personal disposable income and its transformations for the period 1961–87.

over time in the first right-hand-side panel, where the natural logarithm (log) of the series is displayed. Taking now first differences of the logs, that is, considering the quantities $\Delta \log y_t = \log y_t - \log y_{t-1}$, results in a series without a trend in the first panel of the middle row of Figure 2.4 (see D log income). Because the first differences of the logs are roughly the rates of change of the series, one way to summarize this result is that, if the original series has a trending mean and a variance proportional to the levels of the series, then the rates of change may be in line with a stationary DGP. Of course, it is possible that subject matter considerations may make it useful to study the rates of change rather than the original series. For the present example series a pronounced seasonal pattern remains in the rates of change. In such a case, considering annual rates of change may result in a more random-looking series. For the income series, the annual rates of change are obtained as $\Delta_4 \log y_t = \log y_t - \log y_{t-4}$. They are plotted in the right-hand panel in the second row of Figure 2.4 (see D4 log income). The series clearly has important characteristics of a stationary series. The last plot in Figure 2.4 will be discussed later in this section.

Generally, from a statistical point of view, taking logs may be a useful transformation to stabilize the variance of a time series if the variance of the original series increases with the level of the series. Such a transformation has implications for the distribution of the DGP, which may be important in some situations.

It is not uncommon, however, for the log transformation also to result in a series more in line with a normally distributed (Gaussian) DGP.

There are also other transformations that make economic time series look like stationary series. For example, a pronounced seasonal pattern in y_t may be due to varying means as seasons change. For instance, for a quarterly series, a different mean may be associated with every quarter. In this case, the DGP is nonstationary according to our previous definition because the mean is not time invariant. This kind of nonstationarity may, in fact, be present in the quarterly rates of change of income in Figure 2.4. However, subtracting the different quarterly means from the variables may resolve the situation and result in stationarity. For the example series the result of subtracting the seasonal means can also be seen in Figure 2.4 (see `deseas D log income`). Although the series fluctuates around a constant mean and appears to have a rather stable variance, subtracting the different quarterly means from the variables may not be the best way to transform the series in this case because some seasonal fluctuation may remain. As an alternative, the annual rates of change may be preferable. Formal statistical tests to help in deciding which transformation to use will be considered in Section 2.7.

Filtering. Time series are often filtered to extract or eliminate special features or components. Generally, a *filter* is a function of a time series that transforms it into another one. In practice many filters are linear functions. For example, if $y_1, \ldots, y_T$ is a given time series, a new series may be obtained as

$$x_t = \sum_{j=-k}^{l} \omega_j y_{t-j}, \quad t = k+1, \ldots, T-l, \tag{2.2}$$

where k and l are positive integers and $(\omega_{-k}, \ldots, \omega_0, \ldots, \omega_l)$ defines the filter with weights ω_j. Often the ω_j's are chosen so as to add up to 1, that is, $\sum_{j=-k}^{l} \omega_j = 1$, to ensure that the level of the series is maintained.

As an example, consider the filter $(\frac{1}{8}, \frac{1}{4}, \frac{1}{4}, \frac{1}{4}, \frac{1}{8})$, which gives a series

$$x_t = \frac{1}{8} y_{t-2} + \frac{1}{4} y_{t-1} + \frac{1}{4} y_t + \frac{1}{4} y_{t+1} + \frac{1}{8} y_{t+2} \tag{2.3}$$

that is a moving weighted average of consecutive values of the original series y_t. This filter may remove seasonal variation from a quarterly series y_t. To see this more clearly, suppose that y_t is a quarterly series with a different mean for each quarter, $y_t = \mu_t + z_t$, where $\mu_t = \mu_j$ if t is associated with the jth quarter and z_t is a zero mean stochastic part. In this case, if we use the filter in (2.3),

$$x_t = \frac{1}{4}(\mu_1 + \mu_2 + \mu_3 + \mu_4) + \frac{1}{8} z_{t-2} + \frac{1}{4} z_{t-1} + \frac{1}{4} z_t$$
$$+ \frac{1}{4} z_{t+1} + \frac{1}{8} z_{t+2},$$

and thus x_t has a constant mean $\frac{1}{4}(\mu_1 + \mu_2 + \mu_3 + \mu_4)$.

Often a filter is written efficiently by using the *lag operator L*, which is defined such that $Ly_t = y_{t-1}$, that is, it shifts the time index back by one period. Applying it j times gives $L^j y_t = y_{t-j}$. Also, negative powers are possible, in which case $L^{-j} y_t = y_{t+j}$, and we may define $L^0 y_t = y_t$. Using this notation, we can write the simple example filter as

$$x_t = \left(\frac{1}{8}L^{-2} + \frac{1}{4}L^{-1} + \frac{1}{4}L^0 + \frac{1}{4}L^1 + \frac{1}{8}L^2 \right) y_t.$$

More generally, a filter may simply be written as a general function of the lag operator, $\omega(L)$. For example, $\omega(L) = \sum_{j=-k}^{l} \omega_j L^j$. We will encounter several special filters in the following sections.

Filtering is often used for seasonal adjustment. In that case, if a filter such as the one in (2.2) is applied, values at the beginning and at the end of the original series y_t are lost in the filtered series x_t, which is defined for $t = k+1, \dots, T-l$ only. This feature is sometimes undesirable – especially if, for example, the series are to be used in forecasting where the latest values are of particular importance. Therefore, the filter may be modified towards the end, the beginning, or the end and the beginning of the series. Thereby complicated nonlinear filters may result. In practice, seasonal adjustment filters are usually such more complicated filters. They may also distort important features of a given series in addition to removing the seasonality. Therefore, they should not be used uncritically.

In business cycle analysis it is sometimes desirable to extract the trend from a series to get a better understanding of the business cycle fluctuations. The so-called *Hodrick–Prescott (HP) filter* is a popular tool in this context [see Hodrick & Prescott (1997)]. This filter may be defined indirectly by specifying the trend of the series $y_1, \dots, y_T$ to be the component that solves the minimization problem

$$\min_{\mu_t} \sum_{t=1}^{T} [(y_t - \mu_t)^2 + \lambda\{(\mu_{t+1} - \mu_t) - (\mu_t - \mu_{t-1})\}^2],$$

where λ is a positive constant chosen by the user of the filter. It can be shown that this minimization problem has a unique solution $\mu_1, \dots, \mu_T$ so that the filtered series μ_t has the same length as the original series y_t.

The smoothness of the filtered series is determined by the choice of λ. A large λ will magnify any changes in μ_t relative to the difference $y_t - \mu_t$ and, hence, will force μ_t to move very little. In contrast, a small value of λ will allow more movement of μ_t. The trend components (μ_t) of the German log income series for different λ values are plotted in Figure 2.5 to see the effect of λ on the solution of the minimization problem. Hodrick & Prescott (1997) have recommended a λ value of 1,600 for quarterly data, and Ravn & Uhlig (2001) have suggested using the fourth power of the change in observation

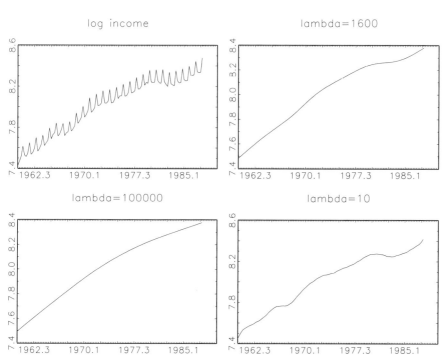

Figure 2.5. HP filtering of West German log income series with different λ values.

frequency for data observed at a different frequency. For example, yearly data are observed only one-fourth as often as quarterly data. Hence, for yearly data $\lambda = 1600/4^4 = 6.25$ is recommended.

It may be worth noting that the HP filter can be written alternatively with the help of the lag operator as

$$\omega(L) = \frac{1}{1 + \lambda(1 - L)^2(1 - L^{-1})^2},$$

although this representation does not show clearly how exactly the end effects are treated.

Typically, the difference $y_t - \mu_t$, which is called the cyclical component, is of interest for business cycle analysis.

Integrated processes. Taking first differences is a useful device for removing a series trend – either stochastic or deterministic or both. Because this transformation has been used successfully for many economic time series, a special terminology has been developed. A nonstationary stochastic process that can be made stationary by considering first differences is said to be integrated of order one (I(1)). More generally, a DGP is said to be *integrated of order d* (I(d)) if first differences have to be applied d times to make the process stationary or asymptotically stationary. Denoting the *differencing operator* by Δ (i.e., $\Delta = 1 - L$ so that for a time series or stochastic process y_t we have $\Delta y_t = y_t - y_{t-1}$), the process y_t is said to be I(d) or $y_t \sim$ I(d), if $\Delta^d y_t$ is stationary, whereas $\Delta^{d-1} y_t$ is still nonstationary. A stationary process y_t is sometimes called I(0). For reasons that will become clear later, an I(d) process with $d \geq 1$ is often called a *unit root process*, or it is said to have a *unit root*. Of course, it will not always be easy to decide on the order of integration of the DGP of a time series by looking at the plots, autocorrelations, partial autocorrelations, or spectral density estimates of the series and its differenced version. Therefore, formal statistical tests for unit roots have been developed. Some of them will be discussed in Section 2.7.

Occasionally, a distinct seasonal component can be removed by applying a *seasonal differencing operator*. If s denotes the periodicity of the season (e.g., $s = 4$ for quarterly series), then this operator is defined as $\Delta_s y_t = y_t - y_{t-s}$; hence, $\Delta_s = 1 - L^s$. If this operator removes the nonstationarity of a process, it is called a process with *seasonal unit roots*. Again the origin of this terminology will be explained in the next section. In Figure 2.4, the seasonal differences of the log income series are also depicted. In this case they represent annual rates of change and look even more stationary than quarterly rates of change.

2.3 Some Popular Time Series Models

We have already encountered a white noise process as a specific stationary stochastic process consisting of serially uncorrelated random variables. Because most economic time series exhibit serial correlation, such a model is often insufficient for describing the DGP. There are some simple parametric models, however, that have been used frequently to describe the DGPs of economic time series. In this section we will briefly discuss autoregressive (AR) processes, which were already encountered in Section 2.2.2. In addition, we will consider moving average (MA) and mixed autoregressive moving average (ARMA) models. Furthermore, we will consider autoregressive integrated moving average (ARIMA) processes and seasonal variants. To simplify the notation it is sometimes helpful to use the lag operator L, which shifts the subscript of a time series variable backwards by one period, as mentioned in the previous section.

2.3.1 Autoregressive Processes

An AR process y_t of order p (AR(p)) may be written as

$$y_t = \alpha_1 y_{t-1} + \cdots + \alpha_p y_{t-p} + u_t, \tag{2.4}$$

where u_t is an unobservable zero mean white noise process with time invariant variance $E(u_t^2) = \sigma_u^2$ and the α_i are fixed coefficients. Using the lag operator, one can write the process more compactly as

$$(1 - \alpha_1 L - \cdots - \alpha_p L^p) y_t = u_t \quad \text{or} \quad \alpha(L) y_t = u_t,$$

with $\alpha(L) = 1 - \alpha_1 L - \cdots - \alpha_p L^p$. The process is said to be *stable* if

$$\alpha(z) \neq 0 \text{ for all complex numbers } z \text{ satisfying } |z| \leq 1. \tag{2.5}$$

In that case the process can be represented as a weighted sum of past errors,

$$y_t = \alpha(L)^{-1} u_t = \phi(L) u_t = u_t + \sum_{j=1}^{\infty} \phi_j u_{t-j},$$

where $\phi(L)$ is an operator satisfying $\alpha(L)\phi(L) = 1$. Comparing coefficients shows that the ϕ_j may be obtained recursively as $\phi_j = \sum_{i=1}^{j} \phi_{j-i}\alpha_i$ for $j = 1, 2, \ldots$ with $\phi_0 = 1$ and $\alpha_i = 0$ for $i > p$. For example, if y_t is an AR(1) process, that is $y_t = \alpha_1 y_{t-1} + u_t$, the AR operator is $1 - \alpha_1 L$. It satisfies the condition (2.5) if $|\alpha_1| < 1$. In that case, $(1 - \alpha_1 L)^{-1} = \phi(L) = 1 + \alpha_1 L + \alpha_1^2 L^2 + \cdots$, and thus $\phi_j = \alpha_1^j$. Therefore, y_t has the representation

$$y_t = u_t + \sum_{j=1}^{\infty} \alpha_1^j u_{t-j}.$$

A process consisting of a weighted sum of the elements of a white noise process is called an MA process, finite order versions of which will be considered in the next section. Assuming that T is the set of all integers and, hence, the process y_t in (2.4) has been initiated in the infinite past, it is stationary (I(0)) with mean zero, variance

$$\sigma_y^2 = \gamma_0 = \sigma_u^2 \sum_{j=0}^{\infty} \phi_j^2,$$

and covariances

$$\gamma_h = \sigma_u^2 \sum_{j=0}^{\infty} \phi_{j+h}\phi_j, \quad h = \pm 1, \pm 2, \ldots .$$

For instance, for the aforementioned AR(1) process,

$$\sigma_y^2 = \gamma_0 = \sigma_u^2 \sum_{j=0}^{\infty} \alpha_1^{2j} = \sigma_u^2/(1 - \alpha_1^2)$$

and

$$\gamma_h = \sigma_u^2 \sum_{j=0}^{\infty} \alpha_1^{j+h}\alpha_1^j = \sigma_u^2 \alpha_1^h/(1 - \alpha_1^2), \quad h = \pm 1, \pm 2, \ldots .$$

For the AR(p) process (2.4), the partial autocorrelations $a_h = 0$ for $h > p$, and the spectral density is of the form

$$f_y(\lambda) = (2\pi)^{-1}\sigma_u^2|\alpha(e^{i\lambda})|^{-2},$$

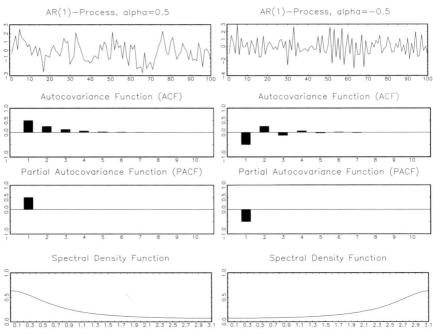

Figure 2.6. Autocorrelation functions, partial autocorrelation functions, and spectral densities of AR(1) processes.

where $| \cdot |$ denotes the modulus of a complex number. For the previously considered AR(1) example process we obtain, for instance,

$$f_y(\lambda) = \frac{1}{2\pi} \cdot \frac{\sigma_u^2}{|1 - \alpha_1 e^{i\lambda}|^2} = \frac{1}{2\pi} \cdot \frac{\sigma_u^2}{1 + \alpha_1^2 - 2\alpha_1 \cos \lambda},$$

where the relation $e^{i\lambda} = \cos \lambda + i \sin \lambda$ and the rules for working with sine and cosine functions have been used. Autocorrelation functions, partial autocorrelation functions, and spectral densities of two AR(1) processes are depicted in Figure 2.6 together with a single realization of each of the processes. Notice that the left-hand process has positive autocorrelation and is therefore less volatile than the right-hand one for which consecutive members are negatively correlated. Consequently, the spectral density of the latter process has more mass at high frequencies than that of the left-hand process.

If, for an AR(p) process, $\alpha(z) = 0$ for some complex number z with $|z| \leq 1$, the process is nonstationary. For the special case in which the AR operator has a unit root, that is, the polynomial $\alpha(z)$ has a root for $z = 1$ so that $\alpha(1) = 0$, the operator can be factored as

$$\alpha(L) = (1 - \alpha_1^* L - \cdots - \alpha_{p-1}^* L^{p-1})(1 - L).$$

Replacing $1 - L$ by Δ, we obtain an AR($p - 1$) model, $(1 - \alpha_1^* L - \cdots - \alpha_{p-1}^* L^{p-1})\Delta y_t = u_t$ for the first differences of y_t. If $\alpha^*(L) = 1 - \alpha_1^* L - \cdots - \alpha_{p-1}^* L^{p-1}$ has all its roots outside the complex unit circle, Δy_t is stationary and, hence, $y_t \sim I(1)$. If, however, $\alpha^*(z)$ has again a unit root, further differencing is necessary to obtain a stationary process, and $y_t \sim I(d)$ with $d > 1$. This relation between the unit roots of the AR operator and the integratedness of the process explains why an integrated process is sometimes called a *unit root process*.

As an example, consider the AR(2) process $y_t = 1.5y_{t-1} - 0.5y_{t-2} + u_t$. The AR operator is $\alpha(L) = 1 - 1.5L + 0.5L^2$, and thus $\alpha(1) = 1 - 1.5 + 0.5 = 0$. Hence, $\alpha(L) = (1 - 0.5L)(1 - L)$ and y_t has a unit root. It can be written alternatively as $\Delta y_t = 0.5\Delta y_{t-1} + u_t$. Clearly, $\alpha^*(z) = (1 - 0.5z)$ has a root for $z = 2$ that is outside the complex unit circle. Thus, the differenced process is stable and stationary. In other words, $y_t \sim I(1)$.

For seasonal processes, $\alpha(z)$ may have roots z on the complex unit circle with $z \neq 1$. For example, for a quarterly process there may be roots for $z = \pm i$ and -1, where $i = \sqrt{-1}$ as before. These roots are sometimes called *seasonal unit roots*, and the associated process is said to have seasonal unit roots. Notice that the quarterly seasonal differencing operator Δ_4 can be factored as $\Delta_4 = 1 - L^4 = (1 - L)(1 + iL)(1 - iL)(1 + L)$.

2.3.2 Finite-Order Moving Average Processes

If the process y_t can be represented as

$$y_t = u_t + m_1 u_{t-1} + \cdots + m_q u_{t-q}, \tag{2.6}$$

where u_t is again zero mean white noise, the process is called a moving average of order q (MA(q)). The process is stationary, and, with the help of the lag operator, it can be written more compactly as

$$y_t = (1 + m_1 L + \cdots + m_q L^q)u_t \quad \text{or} \quad y_t = m(L)u_t,$$

with $m(L) = 1 + m_1 L + \cdots + m_q L^q$. Uniqueness of the MA representation requires restrictions on the coefficients. Uniqueness is guaranteed, for example, if $m(z) \neq 0$ for complex numbers z with $|z| < 1$. If in fact $m(z) \neq 0$ for $|z| \leq 1$, the process is called *invertible*. In that case, it has an infinite order AR representation

$$m(L)^{-1} y_t = \alpha(L) y_t = y_t - \sum_{j=1}^{\infty} \alpha_j y_{t-j} = u_t,$$

where $\alpha(L)$ is such that $\alpha(L)m(L) = 1$. For example, for the MA(1) process $y_t = u_t + m_1 u_{t-1}$, invertibility is ensured if $|m_1| < 1$. In that case we get the AR representation $y_t = -\sum_{j=1}^{\infty}(-m_1)^j y_{t-j} + u_t$.

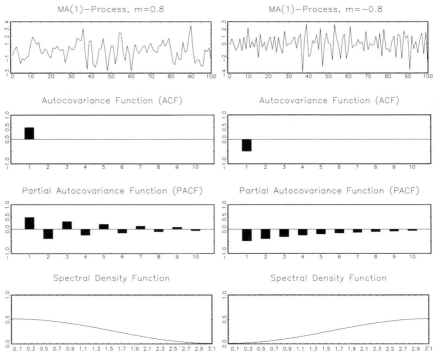

Figure 2.7. Autocorrelation functions, partial autocorrelation functions, and spectral densities of MA(1) processes.

It is easy to see that the process (2.6) has zero mean $(E(y_t) = 0)$, variance $\sigma_y^2 = \gamma_0 = \sigma_u^2 \sum_{j=0}^q m_j^2$ $(m_0 = 1)$ as well as autocovariances $\gamma_h = \sigma_u^2 \sum_{j=0}^{q-h} m_{j+h} m_j$ $(h = \pm 1, \ldots, \pm q)$, and $\gamma_h = 0$ for $h = \pm(q+1)$, $\pm(q+2)\ldots$. Moreover, the spectral density is

$$f_y(\lambda) = (2\pi)^{-1}\sigma_u^2 |m(e^{i\lambda})|^2.$$

As a special case we obtain a constant spectral density of a white noise process, $f_u(\lambda) = (2\pi)^{-1}\sigma_u^2$. For the MA(1) process $y_t = u_t + m_1 u_{t-1}$ we have

$$f_y(\lambda) = (2\pi)^{-1}\sigma_u^2 |1 + m_1 e^{i\lambda}|^2 = (2\pi)^{-1}\sigma_u^2 (1 + m_1^2 + 2m_1 \cos\lambda).$$

The autocorrelation functions, partial autocorrelation functions, and spectral densities of two first order MA processes are plotted in Figure 2.7. Obviously, the autocorrelations have a cutoff point at lag 1, whereas the partial autocorrelations taper off to zero. Thus, the behavior of these quantities, in this respect, is opposite to that of finite-order AR processes. This feature is one cornerstone in the popular Box–Jenkins specification procedure for time series models [Box & Jenkins (1976)]. In contrast, the spectral densities of AR and MA processes can be very similar. Therefore, it is difficult to distinguish between the two classes of processes on the basis of spectral density plots – especially if only estimates are available. Notice, however, that the process generating more volatile time series has a spectral density with more mass at high frequencies.

2.3.3 ARIMA Processes

A mixed ARMA process y_t with AR order p and MA order q (ARMA(p, q)) has the representation

$$y_t = \alpha_1 y_{t-1} + \cdots + \alpha_p y_{t-p} + u_t + m_1 u_{t-1} + \cdots + m_q u_{t-q}, \quad (2.7)$$

where all the symbols have the previously specified definitions. In compact lag operator notation, we have

$$\alpha(L)y_t = m(L)u_t$$

with $\alpha(L) = 1 - \alpha_1 L - \cdots - \alpha_p L^p$ and $m(L) = 1 + m_1 L + \cdots + m_q L^q$. The process is stable and stationary if $\alpha(z) \neq 0$ for $|z| \leq 1$, and it is invertible if $m(z) \neq 0$ for $|z| \leq 1$. If the process is stable, it has a pure (possibly infinite order) MA representation from which the autocorrelations can be obtained. Conversely, if the process is invertible, it has a pure (infinite order) AR representation. For mixed processes with nontrivial AR and MA parts, the autocorrelations and partial autocorrelations both do not have a cutoff point but taper off to zero gradually. The spectral density of the ARMA process (2.7) is

$$f_y(\lambda) = (2\pi)^{-1} \sigma_u^2 |m(e^{i\lambda})/\alpha(e^{i\lambda})|^2.$$

A stochastic process y_t is called an ARIMA(p, d, q) process ($y_t \sim$ ARIMA-(p, d, q)) if it is I(d) and the d times differenced process has an ARMA(p, q) representation, that is $\Delta^d y_t \sim$ ARMA(p, q). For processes with distinct seasonality, so-called seasonal models are sometimes considered. For a series with seasonal periodicity s (e.g., $s = 4$ for quarterly data), a general model form is

$$\alpha_s(L^s)\alpha(L)\Delta_s^D \Delta^d y_t = m_s(L^s)m(L)u_t,$$

where $\alpha(L) = 1 - \alpha_1 L - \cdots - \alpha_p L^p$, $\alpha_s(L^s) = 1 - \alpha_{s1} L^s - \cdots - \alpha_{sP} L^{sP}$, $m(L) = 1 + m_1 L + \cdots + m_q L^q$, and $m_s(L^s) = 1 + m_{s1} L^s + \cdots + m_{sQ} L^{sQ}$. In other words, in addition to the regular AR and MA operators, there are operators in seasonal powers of the lag operator. Such operators can sometimes result in a more parsimonious parameterization of a complex seasonal serial dependence structure than a regular nonseasonal operator. As an example consider the quarterly ARMA process $(1 - \alpha_{41} L^4)(1 - \alpha_1 L)y_t = u_t$ or $y_t = \alpha_1 y_{t-1} + \alpha_{41} y_{t-4} - \alpha_1 \alpha_{41} y_{t-5} + u_t$. Thus, although the AR part involves five lags, it can be represented with two parameters and, hence, it is parameterized more parsimoniously than a full AR(5) process. Notice that also a seasonal differencing operator may be included.

2.3.4 Autoregressive Conditional Heteroskedasticity

So far we have focused on modeling the conditional mean of the DGP of a time series given the past of the process. For example, if u_t is a white noise process of independent random variables and y_t is an AR(p) process as in (2.4), then $E(y_t|y_{t-1}, y_{t-2}, \ldots) = \alpha_1 y_{t-1} + \cdots + \alpha_p y_{t-p}$. Hence, the AR part takes care of the conditional mean of y_t. Engle (1982) observed that, for series with large outliers and volatility clustering as in the DAFOX return series in Figure 2.1, the conditional second moments may have an important structure as well. Therefore, he introduced *autoregressive conditional heteroskedasticity* (ARCH) models. By now the acronym ARCH stands for a wide range of models for changing conditional volatility. In this section the original models and generalized ARCH (GARCH) models will be introduced briefly. A more extensive introduction to modeling conditional heteroskedasticity is given in Chapter 5.

Consider the univariate AR(p) model (2.4). The residuals u_t of this model are said to follow an autoregressive conditionally heteroskedastic process of order q (ARCH(q)) if the conditional distribution of u_t, given its past $\Omega_{t-1} = \{u_{t-1}, u_{t-2}, \ldots\}$, has zero mean and the conditional variance is

$$\sigma_t^2 = \mathsf{Var}(u_t|\Omega_{t-1}) = \mathsf{E}(u_t^2|\Omega_{t-1}) = \gamma_0 + \gamma_1 u_{t-1}^2 + \cdots + \gamma_q u_{t-q}^2,$$

(2.8)

that is, $u_t|\Omega_{t-1} \sim (0, \sigma_t^2)$. Of course, alternatively the u_ts may be the residuals of a more general time series model.

Originally, Engle (1982) in his seminal paper on ARCH models assumed the conditional distribution to be normal, $u_t|\Omega_{t-1} \sim N(0, \sigma_t^2)$. Even with this special distributional assumption the model is capable of generating series with characteristics similar to those of many observed financial time series. In particular, it is capable of generating series with volatility clustering and outliers similar to the DAFOX series in Figure 2.1. Although the conditional distribution is normal, the unconditional distribution will generally be markedly nonnormal. Furthermore, the u_ts will be serially uncorrelated, that is, they are white noise.

The German long-term interest rate series is considered as an example. We have fitted an AR(4) model to the data, and the residuals together with autocorrelations and autocorrelations of the squared residuals are shown in Figure 2.8. The residual series shows some variation in its variability. Whereas the variance is low at the end, there is a substantially larger volatility in some earlier periods. Although the autocorrelation function is consistent with a white noise process, the autocorrelations of the squared residuals clearly show that there may be some dependence structure in the second moments.

It was observed by some researchers that, for many series, an ARCH process with fairly large order is necessary to capture the dynamics in the conditional variances. Therefore, Bollerslev (1986) and Taylor (1986) have proposed gaining greater parsimony by extending the model in a way similar to the approach

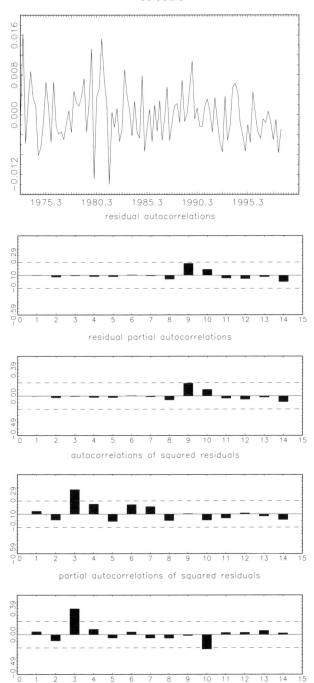

Figure 2.8. Plots of residuals from AR(4) model for German long-term interest rate, autocorrelations, and partial autocorrelations of residuals and squared residuals.

used for extending the AR model when we moved to mixed ARMA models. They suggested the *generalized* ARCH (GARCH) model with conditional variances given by

$$\sigma_t^2 = \gamma_0 + \gamma_1 u_{t-1}^2 + \cdots + \gamma_q u_{t-q}^2 + \beta_1 \sigma_{t-1}^2 + \cdots + \beta_n \sigma_{t-n}^2. \quad (2.9)$$

These models are abbreviated as GARCH(q, n). They generate processes with existing unconditional variance if and only if the coefficient sum

$$\gamma_1 + \cdots + \gamma_q + \beta_1 + \cdots + \beta_m < 1.$$

If this condition is satisfied, u_t has a constant *un*conditional variance given by

$$\sigma_u^2 = \frac{\gamma_0}{1 - \gamma_1 - \cdots - \gamma_q - \beta_1 - \cdots - \beta_n}.$$

A more extensive discussion of ARCH-type processes is provided in Chapter 5. For the remainder of this chapter, a basic knowledge of these models is sufficient.

2.3.5 Deterministic Terms

So far we have considered purely stochastic processes with zero mean. In practice, such processes are rarely sufficient for an adequate representation of real-life time series. Consider, for instance, the U.S. investment series in Figure 2.1, which may be generated by a stationary process. Its mean is not likely to be zero, however. Consequently, we have to allow at least for a nonzero mean term. For many series, more general deterministic terms may be required. For example, a polynomial trend term or seasonal dummy variables may have to be included.

We will do so by adding such deterministic terms simply to the stochastic part of the process, that is, we assume that the observable process y_t is equal to $\mu_t + x_t$, where μ_t is a purely deterministic part and x_t is a purely stochastic process. For example, x_t may be an ARIMA process, whereas $\mu_t = \mu$ or $\mu_t = \mu_0 + \mu_1 t$ or $\mu_t = \mu_0 + \mu_1 t + \delta_1 s_{1t} + \cdots + \delta_q s_{qt}$ are examples of deterministic terms. Here s_{it} represents a seasonal dummy variable that has the value 1 if t refers to the ith season but is zero otherwise. The number of seasons is assumed to be q.

Although there may be series for which our assumption of an additive relation between the deterministic and stochastic parts of the DGP does not hold, the assumption is often not very restrictive in practice and it is therefore usually supposed to hold in the following chapters.

2.4 Parameter Estimation

2.4.1 Estimation of AR Models

Estimation of AR processes is particularly easy because it can be done by ordinary least squares (OLS). Therefore, it will be considered first before we comment on the estimation of more complicated models. If the deterministic term is linear in the unknown parameters, it can be included in a straightforward way in the regression model used for estimation. To simplify the presentation, we assume that the deterministic term consists of a constant only, that is, $\mu_t = \mu$ and thus $y_t = \mu + x_t$; hence, $\alpha(L)y_t = \alpha(L)\mu + \alpha(L)x_t = \alpha(1)\mu + u_t$. The estimation equation then becomes

$$y_t = \nu + \alpha_1 y_{t-1} + \cdots + \alpha_p y_{t-p} + u_t, \tag{2.10}$$

where $\nu = \alpha(1)\mu = (1 - \alpha_1 - \cdots - \alpha_p)\mu$. If it is assumed that presample values $y_{-p+1}, \ldots, y_0$ are available in addition to the sample values $y_1, \ldots, y_T$, the OLS estimator of $\alpha = (\nu, \alpha_1, \ldots, \alpha_p)'$ is

$$\hat{\alpha} = \left(\sum_{t=1}^{T} Y_{t-1} Y'_{t-1} \right)^{-1} \sum_{t=1}^{T} Y_{t-1} y_t,$$

where $Y_{t-1} = (1, y_{t-1}, \ldots, y_{t-p})'$. If the process is stationary and does not have unit roots, then, under standard assumptions [see, e.g., Brockwell & Davis (1987)],

$$\sqrt{T}(\hat{\alpha} - \alpha) \xrightarrow{d} N\left(0, \sigma_u^2 \operatorname{plim} \left(T^{-1} \sum_{t=1}^{T} Y_{t-1} Y'_{t-1} \right)^{-1} \right)$$

or, written in a more intuitive although less precise way,

$$\hat{\alpha} \approx N\left(\alpha, \sigma_u^2 \left(\sum_{t=1}^{T} Y_{t-1} Y'_{t-1} \right)^{-1} \right).$$

The residual variance may be estimated consistently as

$$\hat{\sigma}_u^2 = \frac{1}{T - p - 1} \sum_{t=1}^{T} \hat{u}_t^2 \quad \text{or} \quad \tilde{\sigma}_u^2 = \frac{1}{T} \sum_{t=1}^{T} \hat{u}_t^2,$$

where $\hat{u}_t = y_t - Y'_{t-1}\hat{\alpha}$ ($t = 1, \ldots, T$) are the OLS residuals.

As an example we have estimated an AR(4) model for the U.S. investment series. The first four observations are set aside as presample values, and consequently we have sample values for $1948Q2 - 1972Q4$; hence, $T = 99$. The resulting estimated model is

$$y_t = \underset{(2.76)}{0.82} + \underset{(4.86)}{0.51} \, y_{t-1} - \underset{(-0.83)}{0.10} \, y_{t-2} + \underset{(0.54)}{0.06} \, y_{t-3} - \underset{(-2.02)}{0.22} \, y_{t-4} + \hat{u}_t,$$

where the t-ratios of the estimated parameters (e.g., $t_{\hat{\alpha}_i} = \hat{\alpha}_i / \hat{\sigma}_{\hat{\alpha}_i}$) are given in parentheses. Here $\hat{\sigma}_{\hat{\alpha}_i}$ denotes an estimator of the standard deviation of $\hat{\alpha}_i$. In other words, $\hat{\sigma}_{\hat{\alpha}_i}$ is the square root of the diagonal element of $\hat{\sigma}_u^2 (\sum_{t=1}^{T} Y_{t-1} Y'_{t-1})^{-1}$, which corresponds to $\hat{\alpha}_i$.

It may be worth noting that OLS estimation of the model (2.10) is equivalent to maximum likelihood (ML) estimation conditional on the initial values if the process is normally distributed (Gaussian). In that case, the estimators have asymptotic optimality properties. Moreover, the results for the AR coefficients also hold if y_t is I(1) and the AR order is greater than one ($p > 1$). In that case, the covariance matrix of the asymptotic distribution is singular, however [see, e.g., Sims, Stock & Watson (1990)]. This fact has, for instance, implications for setting up F-tests for hypotheses regarding the coefficients. Therefore, although the asymptotic theory remains largely intact for unit root processes, it may still be preferable to treat them in a different way, in particular, if inference regarding the unit root is of interest. This issue is discussed in more detail in Section 2.7. If y_t is known to be I(d), then it is preferable to set up a stable model for $\Delta^d y_t$.

2.4.2 Estimation of ARMA Models

If a model for the DGP of a time series involves MA or GARCH terms, estimation becomes more difficult because the model is then nonlinear in the parameters. It is still possible to set up the Gaussian likelihood function and use ML or, if the conditional distributions of the observations are not Gaussian (normally distributed), quasi-ML estimation. The joint density of the random variables $y_1, \ldots, y_T$ may be written as a product of conditional densities

$$f(y_1, \ldots, y_T) = f(y_1) \cdot f(y_2 | y_1) \cdots f(y_T | y_{T-1}, \ldots, y_1).$$

Hence, the log-likelihood function for an ARMA(p, q) process $\alpha(L) y_t = m(L) u_t$ has the form

$$l(\alpha_1, \ldots, \alpha_p, m_1, \ldots, m_q) = \sum_{t=1}^{T} l_t(\cdot), \tag{2.11}$$

where

$$l_t(\cdot) = -\frac{1}{2} \log 2\pi - \frac{1}{2} \log \sigma_u^2 - (m(L)^{-1} \alpha(L) y_t)^2 / 2\sigma_u^2$$

if the conditional distributions of the y_t are normally distributed. Maximizing the log-likelihood results in ML or quasi-ML estimators in the usual way. The optimization problem is highly nonlinear and should observe inequality restrictions that ensure a unique, stable ARMA representation. Notice that, for uniqueness, the model must be such that cancellation of parts of the MA term with parts of the AR operator is not possible. Under general conditions, the resulting estimators will then have an asymptotic normal distribution, which may be used for inference.

Because iterative algorithms usually have to be used in optimizing the log-likelihood, start-up values for the parameters are required. Different procedures may be used for this purpose. They depend on the model under consideration. For example, for an ARMA model, one may first fit a pure AR model with long order h by OLS. Denoting the residuals by $\hat{u}_t(h)$ ($t = 1, \ldots, T$), one may then obtain OLS estimates of the parameters from the regression equation

$$y_t = \alpha_1 y_{t-1} + \cdots + \alpha_p y_{t-p} + u_t + m_1 \hat{u}_{t-1}(h) + \cdots + m_q \hat{u}_{t-q}(h).$$

These estimates may be used for starting up an iterative maximization of the log-likelihood function.

2.5 Model Specification

Specifying the kinds of models we have discussed so far requires deciding on the orders of the various operators and possibly deterministic terms and distributional assumptions. This can be done by fitting a model, which includes all the terms that may be of interest, and then performing tests for model adequacy and model reduction in the usual way. This approach is limited by the fact, however, that the parameters in an overspecified ARMA model may not be unique; therefore, the estimators do not have the usual asymptotic properties. Thus, model selection procedures are often applied for specifying the orders. We discuss some of them in the context of pure AR models next.

2.5.1 AR Order Specification Criteria

Many of the AR order selection criteria are of the general form

$$Cr(n) = \log \tilde{\sigma}_u^2(n) + c_T \varphi(n),$$

where $\tilde{\sigma}_u^2(n) = T^{-1} \sum_{t=1}^{T} \hat{u}_t(n)^2$ is the error variance estimator based on the OLS residuals $\hat{u}_t(n)$ from an AR model of order n, c_T is a sequence indexed by the sample size, and $\varphi(n)$ is a function that penalizes large AR orders. For the criteria discussed in this section, $\varphi(n)$ is the order of the fitted process and c_T is a weighting factor that may depend on the sample size. The way this factor is chosen effectively distinguishes the different criteria. The first term on the right-hand side, $\log \tilde{\sigma}_u^2(n)$, measures the fit of a model with order n. This term decreases for increasing order because there is no correction for degrees of freedom in the variance estimator. It is important to notice, however, that the sample size is assumed to be constant for all orders n and, hence, the number of presample values set aside for estimation is determined by the maximum order p_{max}, say. The order that minimizes the criterion is chosen as estimator $\hat{p}$ of the true AR order p.

The following are examples of criteria that have been used in practice:

$$AIC(n) = \log \tilde{\sigma}_u^2(n) + \frac{2}{T} n \qquad \text{[Akaike (1973, 1974)]},$$

Table 2.1. *Order selection criteria for U.S. investment series*

	n										
	0	1	2	3	4	5	6	7	8	9	10
$AIC(n)$	2.170	1.935	1.942	1.950	1.942	1.963	1.990	2.018	1.999	1.997	2.032
$HQ(n)$	2.180	1.956	1.974	1.997	1.995	2.027	2.065	2.104	2.097	2.107	2.153
$SC(n)$	2.195	1.987	2.020	2.059	2.073	2.122	2.176	2.231	2.241	2.268	2.331

$$HQ(n) = \log \tilde{\sigma}_u^2(n) + \frac{2 \log \log T}{T} n \qquad \text{[Hannan \& Quinn (1979)]}$$

and

$$SC(n) = \log \tilde{\sigma}_u^2(n) + \frac{\log T}{T} n \qquad \text{[Schwarz (1978) and}$$
$$\text{Rissanen (1978)]}.$$

Here the term c_T equals $2/T$, $2 \log \log T/T$, and $\log T/T$ for the Akaike information criterion (AIC), the Hannan-Quinn criterion (HQ), and the Schwarz criterion (SC), respectively. The criteria have the following properties: AIC asymptotically overestimates the order with positive probability, HQ estimates the order consistently (plim $\hat{p} = p$), and SC is even strongly consistent ($\hat{p} \to p$ a.s.) under quite general conditions if the actual DGP is a finite-order AR process and the maximum order $p_{\max}$ is larger than the true order. These results hold for both stationary and integrated processes [Paulsen (1984)]. Denoting the orders selected by the three criteria by $\hat{p}(AIC)$, $\hat{p}(HQ)$, and $\hat{p}(SC)$, respectively, the following relations hold even in small samples of fixed size $T \geq 16$ [see Lütkepohl (1991, Chapters 4 and 11)]:

$$\hat{p}(SC) \leq \hat{p}(HQ) \leq \hat{p}(AIC).$$

Thus, using SC results in more parsimonious specifications with fewer parameters than HQ and AIC if there are differences in the orders chosen by the three criteria.

In Table 2.1, the values of the order selection criteria for the U.S. investment series are given. They all suggest an order of 1, although it was seen earlier that the coefficient attached to lag four has a t-value greater than 2. Using the t-ratios of the estimated coefficients and reducing the lag length by 1 if the t-ratio of the coefficient associated with the highest lag is smaller than 2 or some other threshold value is another obvious possibility for choosing the lag length. Of course, by relying on model selection criteria one may end up with a different model than with sequential testing procedures or other possible tools for choosing the AR order.

2.5.2 Specifying More General Models

In principle, model selection criteria may also be used in specifying more general models such as ARMA processes. One possible difficulty may be that estimation of many models with different orders is required, some of which have overspecified orders, and thus cancellation of parts of the AR and MA operators is possible. In that case iterative algorithms may not converge owing to the nonuniqueness of parameters. Therefore, simpler estimation methods are sometimes proposed for ARMA models at the specification stage. For example, the method for computing start-up values for ML estimation may be used (see Section 2.4.2). In other words, an AR(h) model with large order h is fitted first by OLS to obtain residuals $\hat{u}_t(h)$. Then models of the form

$$y_t = \alpha_1 y_{t-1} + \cdots + \alpha_n y_{t-n} + u_t + m_1 \hat{u}_{t-1}(h) + \cdots + m_l \hat{u}_{t-l}(h)$$
$$(2.12)$$

are fitted for all combinations (n, l) for which $n, l \le p_{\max} < h$. The combination of orders minimizing a criterion

$$Cr(n, l) = \log \tilde{\sigma}_u^2(n, l) + c_T \varphi(n, l)$$

is then chosen as an estimator for the true order (p, q). This procedure was proposed by Hannan & Rissanen (1982). It is therefore known as the *Hannan–Rissanen procedure*. Here the symbols have definitions analogous to those of the pure AR case. In other words, $\tilde{\sigma}_u^2(n, l) = T^{-1} \sum_{t=1}^{T} \hat{u}_t(n, l)^2$, where $\hat{u}_t(n, l)$ is the residual from fitting (2.12) by OLS, c_T is a sequence depending on the sample size T, and $\varphi(n, l)$ is a function that penalizes large orders. For example, the corresponding AIC is now

$$AIC(n, l) = \log \tilde{\sigma}_u^2(n, l) + \frac{2}{T}(n + l).$$

Here the choice of h and $p_{\max}$ may affect the estimated ARMA orders. Hannan & Rissanen (1982) have suggested letting h increase slightly faster than $\log T$. In any case, h needs to be greater than $p_{\max}$, which in turn may depend on the data of interest. For example, $p_{\max}$ should take into account the observation frequency.

Generally, there may be deterministic terms in the DGP. They can, of course, be accommodated in the procedure. For example, if the observations fluctuate around a nonzero mean, the sample mean should be subtracted, that is, the observations should be mean-adjusted before the Hannan–Rissanen procedure is applied. Similarly, if the series has a deterministic linear trend, $\mu_0 + \mu_1 t$, then the trend parameters may be estimated by OLS in a first step and the estimated trend function is subtracted from the original observations before the order selection procedure is applied. Alternatively, the linear trend may be estimated

Table 2.2. *Hannan–Rissanen model selection for generated AR(1)*
($y_t = 0.5y_{t-1} + u_t$) with $h = 8$ and $p_{max} = 4$

Selection criterion	AR order	MA order				
		0	1	2	3	4
	0	0.259	0.093	0.009	−0.013	−0.002
	1	−0.055*	−0.034	−0.017	−0.001	0.019
AIC	2	−0.034	−0.012	0.004	0.017	0.032
	3	−0.012	0.011	0.006	0.028	0.049
	4	0.005	0.028	0.026	0.045	0.060

from the first-stage AR(h) approximation, and the corresponding trend function may be subtracted from the y_t's before the ARMA order selection routine is applied. It is also worth noting that, in this procedure, the stochastic part is assumed to be stationary. Therefore, if the original series is integrated, it should be differenced appropriately to make it stationary.

For illustration, $T = 100$ observations were generated with the AR(1) process $y_t = 0.5y_{t-1} + u_t$, and the Hannan–Rissanen procedure was applied with $h = 8$ and $p_{max} = 4$. These settings may be realistic for a quarterly series. The results obtained with the AIC criterion are shown in Table 2.2. In this case the ARMA orders $p = 1$ and $q = 0$ are detected correctly. Although the series was generated without a deterministic term, a constant term is included in the procedure. More precisely, the sample mean is subtracted from the y_t's before the procedure is applied.

There are also other formal statistical procedures for choosing ARMA orders [e.g., Judge, Griffiths, Hill, Lütkepohl & Lee (1985, Section 7.5)]. A more subjective method is the classical *Box–Jenkins approach* to ARMA model specification. It relies on an examination of the sample autocorrelations and partial autocorrelations of a series to decide on the orders. As we have seen in Section 2.3, the true autocorrelations of a pure MA process have a cutoff point corresponding to the MA order, whereas the partial autocorrelations of such processes taper off. In contrast, for pure, finite-order AR processes the autocorrelations taper off, whereas the partial autocorrelations have a cutoff point corresponding to the AR order. These facts can help in choosing AR and MA orders.

For example, in Figure 2.9 sample autocorrelations and partial autocorrelations of AR(1) and AR(2) processes are depicted that illustrate the point. In particular, the autocorrelations and partial autocorrelations of the first AR(1) clearly reflect the theoretical properties of the corresponding population quantities (see also Figure 2.6). The dashed lines in the figures are $\pm 2/\sqrt{T}$ bounds around the zero line that can be used to assess whether the estimated quantities are different from zero, as explained in Section 2.2.2. Generally, it is important to keep in mind that the sampling variability of the autocorrelations and

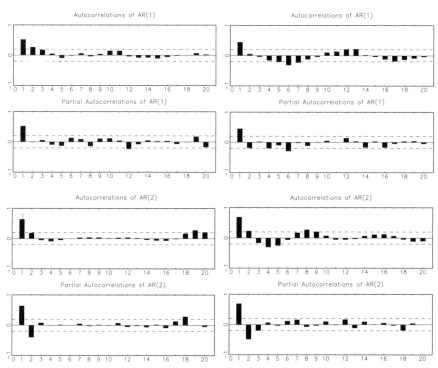

Figure 2.9. Estimated autocorrelations and partial autocorrelations of artificially generated AR(1) and AR(2) time series (AR(1): $y_t = 0.5y_{t-1} + u_t$; AR(2): $y_t = y_{t-1} -
0.5y_{t-2} + u_t$; sample size $T = 100$).

partial autocorrelations may lead to patterns that are not easily associated with
a particular process order. For example, the second set of autocorrelations and
partial autocorrelations of an AR(1) process shown in Figure 2.9 are generated
with the same DGP, $y_t = 0.5y_{t-1} + u_t$, as the first set, and still they cannot be
associated quite so easily with an AR(1) process.

Also for the AR(2) processes underlying Figure 2.9, specifying the order
correctly from the estimated autocorrelations and partial autocorrelations is
not easy. In fact, the pattern for the first AR(2) process is similar to the one of
an MA(1) process shown in Figure 2.7, and the pattern obtained for the second
AR(2) time series could easily come from a mixed ARMA process. In summary,
the estimated autocorrelations and partial autocorrelations in Figure 2.9 show
that guessing the ARMA orders from these quantities can be a challenge. This
experience should not be surprising because even the true theoretical autocorrelations and partial autocorrelations of AR, MA, and mixed ARMA processes
can be very similar. Therefore, it is not easy to discriminate between them on
the basis of limited sample information.

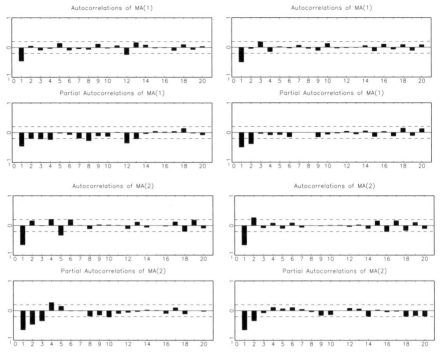

Figure 2.10. Estimated autocorrelations and partial autocorrelations of artificially generated MA(1) and MA(2) time series (MA(1): $y_t = u_t - 0.7u_{t-1}$; MA(2): $y_t = u_t - u_{t-1} + 0.5u_{t-2}$; sample size $T = 100$).

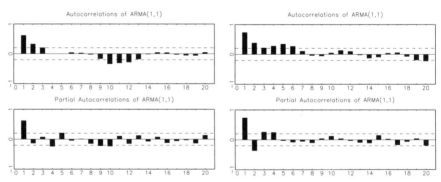

Figure 2.11. Estimated autocorrelations and partial autocorrelations of artificially generated ARMA(1,1) time series (DGP: $y_t = 0.5y_{t-1} + u_t + 0.5u_{t-1}$; sample size $T = 100$).

Table 2.3. *Hannan–Rissanen model selection for generated MA(2)*
$(y_t = u_t - u_{t-1} + 0.5u_{t-2})$ *with* $h = 8$ *and* $p_{max} = 4$

Selection criterion	AR order	MA order				
		0	1	2	3	4
	0	0.820	0.358	0.155	0.171	0.164
	1	0.192	0.118	0.131	0.115*	0.134
AIC	2	0.127	0.138	0.153	0.134	0.157
	3	0.138	0.159	0.162	0.156	0.179
	4	0.144	0.151	0.173	0.178	0.201
	0	0.820	0.386	0.212	0.255	0.277
	1	0.220	0.174*	0.216	0.227	0.275
SC	2	0.183	0.223	0.266	0.275	0.326
	3	0.223	0.272	0.303	0.325	0.376
	4	0.257	0.292	0.342	0.375	0.426

A similar situation can be observed in Figures 2.10 and 2.11, where sample autocorrelations and partial autocorrelations of MA(1), MA(2), and ARMA(1,1) processes are depicted. Although the MA(1) processes can perhaps be inferred from the estimated autocorrelations and partial autocorrelations (see also the theoretical quantities depicted in Figure 2.7), it is difficult to guess the orders of the underlying DGPs of the other time series correctly. In this context it may be of interest that using the Hannan–Rissanen procedure instead of looking at the sample autocorrelations and partial autocorrelations does not necessarily result in correct estimates of the ARMA orders. For example, we have applied the procedure to the MA(2) time series underlying the last set of autocorrelations and partial autocorrelations shown in Figure 2.10. Using an AR order of $h = 8$ in fitting a long AR in the first step of the procedure and a maximum order of $p_{max} = 4$ in the second step, we obtained the results in Table 2.3. Neither the AIC nor the SC finds the correct orders. This outcome illustrates that it may also be difficult for formal procedures to find the true ARMA orders on the basis of a time series with moderate length. Again, given the possible similarity of the theoretical autocorrelations and partial autocorrelations of ARMA processes with different orders, this observation should not be surprising. Nevertheless, less experienced time series analysts may be better off using more formal and less subjective approaches such as the Hannan–Rissanen procedure.

Also, keep in mind that finding the correct ARMA orders in the specification step of the modeling procedure may not be possible in practice anyway when real economic data are analyzed. Usually in that case no true ARMA orders exist because the actual DGP is a more complicated creature. All we can hope for is finding a good and, for the purposes of the analysis, useful approximation. Moreover, the model specification procedures should just be regarded as a preliminary way to find a satisfactory model for the DGP. These procedures need to be complemented by a thorough model checking in which modifications of, and changes to, the preliminary model are possible. Model specification procedures are described next.

2.6 Model Checking

Once a model has been specified, a range of diagnostic tools are available for checking its adequacy. Many of them are based on the model residuals. We will first present several graphical tools for checking the residuals and then turn to some tests that can be used to investigate specific properties of the residuals. Finally, the robustness and stability of the model may be checked by estimating it recursively for different subsamples. The relevant tools are described in this section.

2.6.1 Descriptive Analysis of the Residuals

Plotting the residual series of a time series model is an important way to detect possible model deficiencies. For example, outliers, inhomogeneous variances, or structural breaks may show up in the residual series. For spotting unusual residuals, a standardization of the residuals may be useful before plotting them. Denoting the residual series by $\hat{u}_t$ ($t = 1, \ldots, T$), we obtain the standardized residuals by subtracting the mean and dividing by the standard deviation; that is, the standardized residuals are $\hat{u}_t^s = (\hat{u}_t - \bar{\hat{u}})/\tilde{\sigma}_u$, where $\tilde{\sigma}_u^2 = T^{-1} \sum_{t=1}^{T} (\hat{u}_t - \bar{\hat{u}})^2$ with $\bar{\hat{u}} = T^{-1} \sum_{t=1}^{T} \hat{u}_t$. Alternatively, an adjustment for degrees of freedom may be used in the variance estimator. If the residuals are normally distributed with zero mean, roughly 95% of the standardized residuals should be in a band ± 2 around the zero line. It may also be helpful to plot the squared residuals or squared standardized residuals. Such a plot is helpful in discriminating between periods of lower and higher volatility.

Moreover, the autocorrelations and partial autocorrelations of the residuals may be worth looking at because these quantities contain information on possibly remaining serial dependence in the residuals. Similarly, the autocorrelations of the squared residuals may be informative about possible conditional heteroskedasticity. If there is no leftover autocorrelation or conditional heteroskedasticity, the autocorrelations and partial autocorrelations should be within a $\pm 2/\sqrt{T}$-band around zero with a very few exceptions. The actual asymptotic standard errors of autocorrelations computed from estimation residuals tend to be smaller than $1/\sqrt{T}$, especially for low lags [see Lütkepohl (1991, Proposition 4.6)]. Therefore, autocorrelations and partial autocorrelations associated with low lags that reach outside the $\pm 2/\sqrt{T}$-band are suspicious and give rise to concern about the adequacy of the model.

A rough impression of the main features of the residual distribution can sometimes be obtained from a plot of the estimated density. It may be determined

Table 2.4. *Some possible kernels for density estimation*

Kernel name	$K(u)$
Gaussian	$(2\pi)^{-1/2} \exp(-u^2/2)$
Biweight	$\begin{cases} \frac{15}{16}(1-u^2)^2 & \text{for } \|u\| < 1 \\ 0 & \text{otherwise} \end{cases}$
Rectangular	$\begin{cases} \frac{1}{2} & \text{for } \|u\| < 1 \\ 0 & \text{otherwise} \end{cases}$
Triangular	$\begin{cases} 1 - \|u\| & \text{for } \|u\| < 1 \\ 0 & \text{otherwise} \end{cases}$
Epanechnikov	$\begin{cases} \frac{3}{4}(1 - \frac{1}{5}u^2)/\sqrt{5} & \text{for } \|u\| < \sqrt{5} \\ 0 & \text{otherwise} \end{cases}$

using a kernel estimator of the form

$$\hat{f}_h(u) = (Th)^{-1} \sum_{t=1}^{T} K\left(\frac{u - \hat{u}_t^s}{h}\right),$$

where h is the *bandwidth* or *window width* and $K(\cdot)$ is a *kernel function*, which is typically a symmetric (about zero) probability density function (pdf). For example, the standard normal pdf, $K(u) = (2\pi)^{-1/2} \exp(-u^2/2)$, may be used. Some other possible kernels are listed in Table 2.4 (see also Chapter 7 for further discussion of kernel estimators). The choice of kernel function often does not make much difference for the estimated density. A possible value for the bandwidth is given by

$$0.9T^{-1/5} \min\{\hat{\sigma}_u, \text{interquartile range}/1.34\},$$

as recommended in Silverman (1986, p. 48). Here the interquartile range of an assumed underlying normal distribution is used. To check the implications of varying the bandwidth, h may alternatively be chosen manually [see Silverman (1986, Section 3.4) for further discussion of bandwidth choice].

In Figure 2.12, some diagnostics for the residuals of the AR(4) model for the U.S. investment series are presented. The standardized residuals are generally within the range $[-2, 2]$, as one would expect for a normally distributed series. The squared residuals show a fairly homogeneous variability of the series. Autocorrelations and partial autocorrelations also do not give rise to concern about the adequacy of the fitted model. Density estimates based on different kernels are depicted in Figure 2.13. Clearly, they differ a bit. Some have two

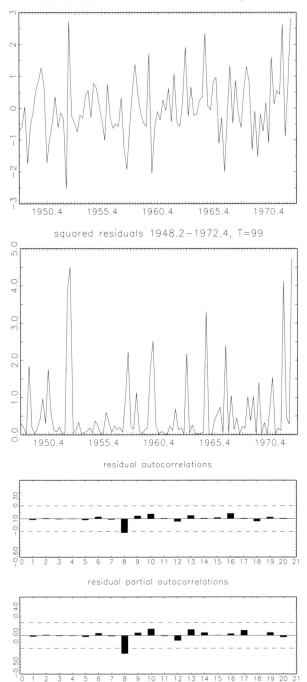

Figure 2.12. Diagnostics of AR(4) residuals of U.S. investment series.

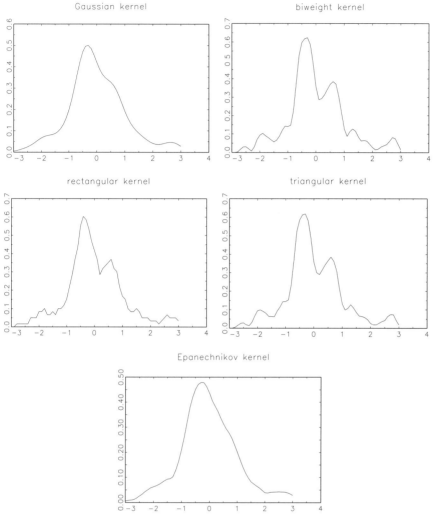

Figure 2.13. Kernel density estimates of AR(4) residuals of U.S. investment series (bandwidth $h = 0.301$).

larger peaks, whereas others point to a unimodal underlying distribution. Overall they do not provide strong evidence that the residuals are not from an underlying normal distribution.

2.6.2 Diagnostic Tests of the Residuals

Several statistical tests are available for diagnostic purposes. Tests for autocorrelation, nonnormality, ARCH, and general misspecification are often reported in the literature. We will present possible candidates in this section.

Portmanteau test for residual autocorrelation. The portmanteau test checks the null hypothesis that there is no remaining residual autocorrelation at lags 1 to h against the alternative that at least one of the autocorrelations is nonzero. In other words, the pair of hypotheses

$$H_0 : \rho_{u,1} = \cdots = \rho_{u,h} = 0$$

versus

$$H_1 : \rho_{u,i} \neq 0 \text{ for at least one } i = 1, \ldots, h$$

is tested. Here $\rho_{u,i} = \text{Corr}(u_t, u_{t-i})$ denotes an autocorrelation coefficient of the residual series. If the $\hat{u}_t$'s are residuals from an estimated ARMA(p, q) model, a possible test statistic is

$$Q_h = T \sum_{j=1}^{h} \hat{\rho}_{u,j}^2,$$

where $\hat{\rho}_{u,j} = T^{-1} \sum_{t=j+1}^{T} \hat{u}_t^s \hat{u}_{t-j}^s$. The test statistic has an approximate $\chi^2(h - p - q)$-distribution if the null hypothesis holds. This statistic is known as the *portmanteau test statistic*. The null hypothesis of no residual autocorrelation is rejected for large values of Q_h. For the limiting χ^2-distribution to hold, the number of autocorrelations included has to go to infinity ($h \to \infty$) at a suitable rate with increasing sample size. Therefore, the size of the test may be unreliable if h is too small, and it may have reduced power if h is large and, hence, many "noninformative" autocorrelations are included. Also, it has been found in Monte Carlo studies that the χ^2 approximation to the null distribution of the test statistic is a good one only for very large sample sizes T. Therefore, Ljung & Box (1978) have proposed a modified version of the portmanteau statistic for which the χ^2 approximation was found to be more suitable in some situations. In JMulTi a version is used that is in line with the corresponding multivariate statistic discussed in Chapter 3:

$$Q_h^* = T^2 \sum_{j=1}^{h} \frac{1}{T - j} \hat{\rho}_{u,j}^2 \approx \chi^2(h - p - q).$$

Clearly, remaining residual autocorrelation indicates a model defect. It may be worth trying a model with larger orders in that case.

LM test for residual autocorrelation in AR models. Another test for residual autocorrelation, sometimes known as the Breusch–Godfrey test, is based on considering an AR(h) model for the residuals

$$u_t = \beta_1 u_{t-1} + \cdots + \beta_h u_{t-h} + \text{error}_t$$

and checking the pair of hypotheses

$$H_0 : \beta_1 = \cdots = \beta_h = 0 \quad \text{versus} \quad H_1 : \beta_1 \neq 0 \text{ or } \cdots \text{ or } \beta_h \neq 0.$$

If the original model is an AR(p),

$$y_t = \nu + \alpha_1 y_{t-1} + \cdots + \alpha_p y_{t-p} + u_t, \tag{2.13}$$

the auxiliary model

$$\hat{u}_t = \nu + \alpha_1 y_{t-1} + \cdots + \alpha_p y_{t-p} + \beta_1 \hat{u}_{t-1} + \cdots + \beta_h \hat{u}_{t-h} + e_t$$

is fitted. Here $\hat{u}_t$ are the OLS residuals from the model (2.13) [see Godfrey (1988)]. It turns out that the LM statistic for the null hypothesis of interest can be obtained easily from the coefficient of determination R^2 of the auxiliary regression model as

$$LM_h = TR^2.$$

In the absence of residual autocorrelation, it has an asymptotic $\chi^2(h)$-distribution. The null hypothesis is rejected if LM_h is large and exceeds the critical value from the $\chi^2(h)$-distribution. An F version of the statistic with potentially better small sample properties may also be considered. It has the form

$$FLM_h = \frac{R^2}{1 - R^2} \cdot \frac{T - p - h - 1}{h} \approx F(h, T - p - h - 1)$$

[see Harvey (1990), Kiviet (1986), and Doornik & Hendry (1997) for details].

Lomnicki–Jarque–Bera test for nonnormality. Lomnicki (1961) and Jarque & Bera (1987) have proposed a test for nonnormality based on the third and fourth moments or, in other words, on the skewness and kurtosis of a distribution. Denoting by u_t^s the standardized true model residuals (i.e., $u_t^s = u_t / \sigma_u$), the test checks the pair of hypotheses

$$H_0 : E(u_t^s)^3 = 0 \text{ and } E(u_t^s)^4 = 3$$

versus

$$H_1 : E(u_t^s)^3 \neq 0 \text{ or } E(u_t^s)^4 \neq 3,$$

that is, it checks whether the third and fourth moments of the standardized residuals are consistent with a standard normal distribution. If the standardized estimation residuals are again denoted by $\hat{u}_t^s$, the test statistic is

$$LJB = \frac{T}{6}\left[T^{-1} \sum_{t=1}^{T} (\hat{u}_t^s)^3 \right]^2 + \frac{T}{24}\left[T^{-1} \sum_{t=1}^{T} (\hat{u}_t^s)^4 - 3 \right]^2,$$

where $T^{-1}\sum_{t=1}^{T}(\hat{u}_t^s)^3$ is a measure for the skewness of the distribution and $T^{-1}\sum_{t=1}^{T}(\hat{u}_t^s)^4$ measures the kurtosis. The test statistic has an asymptotic $\chi^2(2)$-distribution if the null hypothesis is correct, and the null hypothesis is rejected if LJB is large. If H_0 is rejected, the normal distribution is clearly also rejected. On the other hand, if the null hypothesis holds, this does not necessarily mean that the underlying distribution is actually normal but only that it has the same first four moments as the normal distribution. The test is still quite popular in practice because the first four moments are often of particular interest, and deviations from the normal distribution beyond that may not be of equal importance.

If nonnormal residuals are found, this is often interpreted as a model defect; however, much of the asymptotic theory on which inference in dynamic models is based, strictly speaking, works also for certain nonnormal residual distributions. Still, nonnormal residuals can be a consequence of neglected nonlinearities, for example. Modeling such features as well may result in a more satisfactory model with normal residuals. Sometimes, taking into account ARCH effects may help to resolve the problem. An ARCH test is therefore also performed routinely in model checking.

ARCH–LM test. A popular test for neglected conditional heteroskedasticity or, briefly, for ARCH, is based on fitting an ARCH(q) model to the estimation residuals,

$$\hat{u}_t^2 = \beta_0 + \beta_1 \hat{u}_{t-1}^2 + \cdots + \beta_q \hat{u}_{t-q}^2 + \text{error}_t, \tag{2.14}$$

and checking the null hypothesis

$$H_0 : \beta_1 = \cdots = \beta_q = 0 \quad \text{versus} \quad H_1 : \beta_1 \neq 0 \text{ or } \ldots \text{ or } \beta_q \neq 0.$$

The LM test statistic can be conveniently obtained from the coefficient of determination R^2 of the regression (2.14). More precisely, the LM statistic is

$$ARCH_{LM}(q) = TR^2.$$

It has an asymptotic $\chi^2(q)$-distribution if the null hypothesis of no conditional heteroskedasticity holds [Engle (1982)]. Large values of the test statistic indicate that H_0 is false and, hence, there may be ARCH in the residuals. In that case, it may be useful to go to Chapter 5 and consider fitting an ARCH or ARCH-type model to the residuals.

RESET. The RESET (regression specification error test) was proposed by Ramsey (1969). It is useful for testing a given model against general unspecified alternatives. It proceeds as follows. Suppose we have a model $y_t = x_t'\beta + u_t$, which may be an AR model with possibly deterministic terms and other regressors. Let us denote the OLS parameter estimator by $\hat{\beta}$ and the corresponding residuals by $\hat{u}_t$ and perform a regression

$$\hat{u}_t = x_t'\beta + \sum_{j=2}^{h} \psi_j \hat{y}_t^j + v_t,$$

where $\hat{y}_t = x_t'\hat{\beta}$. The residuals of this regression are denoted by $\hat{v}_t$. Under the null hypothesis,

$$H_0 : \psi_2 = \cdots = \psi_h = 0,$$

Table 2.5. *Diagnostics of AR(4) model for U.S. investment series*

			Tests for residual autocorrelation					
Test	Q_{16}	Q_{16}^*	Q_{24}	Q_{24}^*	LM_2	FLM_2	LM_6	FLM_6
Test statistic	6.75	7.45	10.64	12.40	0.75	0.35	5.99	0.94
Appr. distribution	$\chi^2(12)$	$\chi^2(12)$	$\chi^2(20)$	$\chi^2(20)$	$\chi^2(2)$	$F(2, 92)$	$\chi^2(6)$	$F(6, 88)$
p-value	0.87	0.83	0.96	0.90	0.69	0.71	0.42	0.47

		Other diagnostics			
Test	LJB	$ARCH_{LM}(1)$	$ARCH_{LM}(4)$	$RESET_2$	$RESET_3$
Test statistic	5.53	0.36	2.50	0.004	0.003
Appr. distribution	$\chi^2(2)$	$\chi^2(1)$	$\chi^2(4)$	$F(1, 99)$	$F(2, 99)$
p-value	0.06	0.55	0.64	0.95	1.00

there is no misspecification, and the test statistic

$$RESET_h = \frac{(\sum_{t=1}^{T} \hat{u}_t^2 - \sum_{t=1}^{T} \hat{v}_t^2)/(h-1)}{\sum_{t=1}^{T} \hat{v}_t^2/(T - K - h + 1)}$$

has an approximate $F(h - 1, T)$-distribution. Here, K is the dimension of x_t and, hence, the number of regressors in the original model. The null hypothesis of no misspecification is again rejected if the test value is large. For this test, see also Granger & Teräsvirta (1993). In practice, $h = 2$ or 3 will be sufficient to give an impression of whether the relevant model defects are present that can be detected by this test.

In Table 2.5, diagnostic tests for the AR(4) model of the U.S. investment series are given together with p-values. Recall that a p-value represents the probability of getting a test value greater than the observed one if the null hypothesis is true. Hence, the null hypothesis is actually rejected only for p-values smaller than 0.1 or 0.05. In the present case, all p-values are relatively large; consequently, none of the diagnostic tests indicate problems with the model.

2.6.3 Stability Analysis

Another important way to check a model is to investigate its stability over time. For this purpose, estimates for different subperiods are usually computed and examined. Chow tests offer a formal way to do this. They will be discussed next. Thereafter, recursive analysis, which investigates the estimator variability for successively extended samples, is discussed. Throughout this section, the underlying model is assumed to be an AR(p) process with deterministic terms.

Chow tests. Chow tests offer a classical possibility for testing for structural change. Different variants are often reported: *sample-split*, *break-point*, and *forecast tests* [see, e.g., Doornik & Hendry (1994) or Krämer & Sonnberger (1986)]. If it is assumed that a structural break may have occurred in period T_B, the sample-split and break-point tests compare the estimates from the observations associated with the period before T_B with those obtained after T_B. More precisely, the model is estimated by OLS from the full sample of T observations as well as from the first T_1 and the last T_2 observations, where $T_1 < T_B$ and $T_2 \leq T - T_B$. Denoting the resulting residuals by $\hat{u}_t$, $\hat{u}_t^{(1)}$ and $\hat{u}_t^{(2)}$, respectively, we define

$$\hat{\sigma}_u^2 = T^{-1} \sum_{t=1}^{T} \hat{u}_t^2,$$

$$\hat{\sigma}_{1,2}^2 = (T_1 + T_2)^{-1} \left(\sum_{t=1}^{T_1} \hat{u}_t^2 + \sum_{t=T-T_2+1}^{T} \hat{u}_t^2 \right),$$

$$\hat{\sigma}_{(1,2)}^2 = T_1^{-1} \sum_{t=1}^{T_1} \hat{u}_t^2 + T_2^{-1} \sum_{t=T-T_2+1}^{T} \hat{u}_t^2,$$

$$\hat{\sigma}_{(1)}^2 = T_1^{-1} \sum_{t=1}^{T_1} (\hat{u}_t^{(1)})^2,$$

and

$$\hat{\sigma}_{(2)}^2 = T_2^{-1} \sum_{t=T-T_2+1}^{T} (\hat{u}_t^{(2)})^2.$$

With this notation, the sample-split test statistic becomes

$$\lambda_{SS} = (T_1 + T_2)[\log \hat{\sigma}_{1,2}^2 - \log\{(T_1 + T_2)^{-1}(T_1\hat{\sigma}_{(1)}^2 + T_2\hat{\sigma}_{(2)}^2)\}],$$

and the break-point test statistic is

$$\lambda_{BP} = (T_1 + T_2) \log \hat{\sigma}_{(1,2)}^2 - T_1 \log \hat{\sigma}_{(1)}^2 - T_2 \log \hat{\sigma}_{(2)}^2.$$

These test statistics compare the residual variance estimate from a constant coefficient model with the residual variance estimate of a model that allows for a change in the parameters. Thereby, they check whether there are significant differences in the estimates before and after T_B. The sample-split test checks the null hypothesis that the AR coefficients and deterministic terms do not change during the sample period, whereas the break-point test checks in addition the constancy of the white noise variance.

Both test statistics are derived from likelihood ratio principles based on their respective null hypotheses. Under parameter constancy, they have limiting χ^2-distributions with k and $k + 1$ degrees of freedom, respectively. Here k is the number of restrictions imposed by assuming a constant coefficient model for the full sample period. In other words, k is the difference between the sum of the number of regression coefficients estimated in the first and last subperiods and the number of coefficients in the full sample model. Note, however, that the number of parameters may differ in the two subperiods if there are, for instance, dummy variables that are nonzero only in one of the subsamples. For the break-point test, an additional degree of freedom is obtained because the constancy of the residual variance is also tested. The parameter constancy hypothesis is rejected if the values of the test statistics λ_{SS} and/or λ_{BP} are large. It may be worth noting that the names sample-split and break-point tests are sometimes used for slightly different versions of the tests [e.g., Doornik & Hendry (1994)].

The Chow forecast test statistic has the form

$$\lambda_{CF} = \frac{T\hat{\sigma}_u^2 - T_1\hat{\sigma}_{(1)}^2}{T_1\hat{\sigma}_{(1)}^2} \cdot \frac{T_1 - K}{T - T_1},$$

where K is the number of regressors in the restricted, stable model. Thus, the test compares the full sample residual variance with the residual variance for the first subperiod. Another way of interpreting this test is that it checks whether forecasts from the model fitted to the first subsample are compatible with the observations in the second subsample [see Doornik & Hendry (1994)]. This interpretation leads us to call this test the forecast test, although this terminology is not used consistently in the literature. The test statistic has an approximate $F(T - T_1, T_1 - K)$-distribution under the null hypothesis of parameter constancy. Again, the null hypothesis is rejected for large values of λ_{CF}.

All three tests may be performed repeatedly for a range of potential break points T_B, and the results may be plotted. Thereby a visual impression of possible parameter instability is obtained. Of course, the outcomes of the repeated tests will not be independent, and rejecting the stability of the model when one of the statistics exceeds the critical value of an individual test may lead to misleading results. If a sequence of tests is performed and the test decision is based on the maximum of the test statistics, this has to be taken into account in deriving the asymptotic distribution of the test statistic. For example, if the sample-split test is applied to all periods in a set $T \subset \{1, \ldots, T\}$, then we effectively consider a test based on the test statistic

$$\sup_{T_B \in T} \lambda_{SS}.$$

The distribution of this test statistic is not χ^2 under the stability null hypothesis but was derived by Andrews (1993). Using such a test or similar tests considered by Andrews & Ploberger (1994) and Hansen (1997) is useful if the timing of a possible break point is unknown. Similar comments also apply for the forecast version of the Chow test.

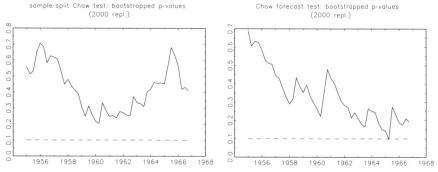

Figure 2.14. Chow tests for AR(4) model of U.S. investment series.

Unfortunately, it turns out that, in samples of common size, the χ^2 and F approximations to the actual distributions may be very poor even if a single break point is tested. The actual rejection probabilities may be much larger than the desired Type I error. Therefore, Candelon & Lütkepohl (2001) have proposed using bootstrap versions of the tests. They are obtained by estimating the model of interest, denoting the estimation residuals by $\hat{u}_t$, computing centered residuals $\hat{u}_1 - \bar{\hat{u}}, \ldots, \hat{u}_T - \bar{\hat{u}}$, and generating bootstrap residuals $u_1^*, \ldots, u_T^*$ by randomly drawing with replacement from the centered residuals. These quantities are then used to compute bootstrap time series recursively starting from given presample values $y_{-p+1}, \ldots, y_0$ for an AR(p) model. The model of interest is then reestimated with and without stability restriction and bootstrap versions of the statistics of interest – for instance, λ_{SS}^*, λ_{BP}^*, and λ_{CF}^* are computed. If these steps are repeated many times, critical values are obtained as the relevant percentage points from the empirical distributions of the bootstrap test statistics. The stability hypothesis is rejected if the original statistic (λ_{SS}, λ_{BP} or λ_{CF}) exceeds the corresponding bootstrap critical value. Alternatively, the p-values of the tests may be estimated as the fraction of times the values of the bootstrap statistics exceed the original statistics.

In Figure 2.14, bootstrapped p-values for the sample-split and forecast tests applied to the U.S. investment series are plotted. In this case the tests are applied for every quarter from $1955Q1$ to $1966Q4$. Obviously, not one of the p-values is below 5%; hence, these tests do not give rise for concern regarding the stability of the model during the period under test.

Recursive analysis. Many recursive statistics are often computed and plotted to get an impression of the stability of a model through time. For this purpose, the model is estimated using only data for $t = 1, \ldots, \tau$ and letting τ run from some small value T_1 to T. The estimates and their estimated confidence intervals are

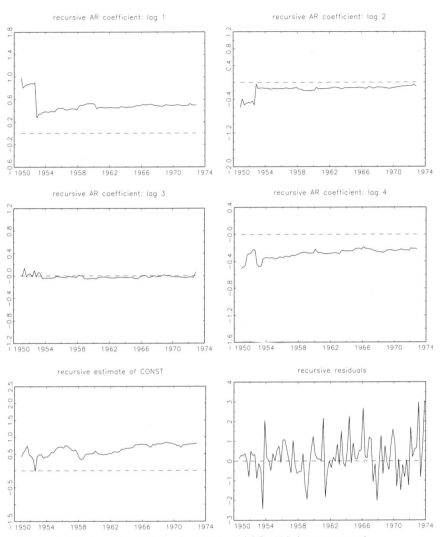

Figure 2.15. Recursive statistics for AR(4) model for U.S. investment series.

then plotted for the different τ values. Examples based on the AR(4) model for the U.S. investment series are given in Figure 2.15. Also, the series of *recursive residuals*, that is, the series of standardized one-step forecast errors from a model estimated on the basis of data up to period $\tau - 1$, is often plotted. It is also informative about possible structural changes during the sample period. More precisely, for a linear model $y_t = x_t'\beta + u_t$ $(t = 1, \ldots, T)$ with x_t $(K \times 1)$

and $\hat{\beta}_{(\tau)}$ denoting the OLS estimator based on the first τ observations only, that is,

$$\hat{\beta}_{(\tau)} = \left(\sum_{t=1}^{\tau} x_t x_t'\right)^{-1} \sum_{t=1}^{\tau} x_t y_t, \qquad \tau \geq K,$$

the recursive residuals are defined as

$$\hat{u}_\tau^{(r)} = \frac{y_\tau - x_\tau' \hat{\beta}_{(\tau-1)}}{\left(1 + x_\tau' \left(\sum_{t=1}^{\tau-1} x_t x_t'\right)^{-1} x_\tau\right)^{1/2}}, \qquad \tau = K+1, \ldots, T.$$

If x_t consists of fixed, nonstochastic regressors, the forecast error $y_\tau - x_\tau' \hat{\beta}_{(\tau-1)}$ is known to have mean zero and variance

$$\sigma_u^2 \left(1 + x_\tau' \left(\sum_{t=1}^{\tau-1} x_t x_t'\right)^{-1} x_\tau\right).$$

Hence, the recursive residuals have constant variance σ_u^2. Therefore, even if some of the regressors are stochastic, the recursive residuals are often plotted with $\pm 2\hat{\sigma}_u$ bounds, where

$$\hat{\sigma}_u^2 = (T-K)^{-1} \sum_{t=1}^{T} \hat{u}_t^2$$

is the usual residual variance estimator. Notice that here the $\hat{u}_t$'s are obtained from OLS estimation of the model based on all T observations. In other words, $\hat{u}_t = y_t - x_t' \hat{\beta}_{(T)}$. It is worth noting that the recursive residuals exist only if the inverse of $\sum_{t=1}^{\tau} x_t x_t'$ exists for all $\tau = K+1, \ldots, T$. Thus, they may not be available in the presence of dummy variables. For example, if there is an impulse dummy variable that takes a value of 1 in period T_B and is zero elsewhere, there is a zero value in x_t for $t = K+1, \ldots, T_B - 1$; hence, $\sum_{t=1}^{\tau} x_t x_t'$ will be singular for $\tau < T_B$.

The recursive coefficient estimates and recursive residuals of the U.S. investment series are plotted in Figure 2.15. The two-standard error bounds of the coefficient estimates are obtained using the square roots of the diagonal elements of the matrices

$$\hat{\sigma}_{u,\tau}^2 \left(\sum_{t=1}^{\tau} x_t x_t'\right)^{-1},$$

where

$$\hat{\sigma}_{u,\tau}^2 = \frac{1}{\tau - K} \sum_{t=1}^{\tau} (y_t - x_t' \hat{\beta}_{(\tau)})^2.$$

After a short, more volatile burn-in period, the recursive coefficients of the example model are relatively stable. Clearly, in the early period, the very small sample size on which the estimates are based induces a greater uncertainty into the estimates.

CUSUM tests. The so-called CUSUM, that is, the cumulative sum of recursive residuals,

$$CUSUM_\tau = \sum_{t=K+1}^{\tau} \hat{u}_t^{(r)}/\hat{\sigma}_u,$$

can also reveal structural changes and is therefore often plotted for $\tau = K + 1, \ldots, T$ in checking a model. The CUSUM was proposed for this purpose by Brown, Durbin & Evans (1975). If the CUSUM wanders off too far from the zero line, this is evidence against structural stability of the underlying model. A test with a significance level of about 5% is obtained by rejecting stability if $CUSUM_\tau$ crosses the lines $\pm 0.948[\sqrt{T-K} + 2(\tau - K)/\sqrt{T-K}]$ [see, e.g., Krämer & Sonnberger (1986), Krämer, Ploberger & Alt (1988), or Granger & Teräsvirta (1993, p. 85)].

This test is designed to detect a nonzero mean of the recursive residuals due to shifts in the model parameters. The test may not have much power if there is not only one parameter shift but various shifts that may compensate their impacts on the means of the recursive residuals. In that case, the CUSUM-of-squares plot based on

$$CUSUM - SQ_\tau = \sum_{t=K+1}^{\tau} (\hat{u}_t^{(r)})^2 \Bigg/ \sum_{t=K+1}^{T} (\hat{u}_t^{(r)})^2$$

may be more informative. If these quantities cross the lines given by $\pm c + (\tau - K)/(T - K)$, a structural instability is diagnosed. The constant c depends on the desired significance level, the sample size T, and the number of regressors in the model. Suitable values of c are, for instance, tabled in Johnston (1984).

In Figure 2.16, CUSUM and CUSUM-of-squares tests are shown for the AR(4) model of the U.S. investment series. Obviously, they do not give any indication of model instability because neither the *CUSUM*s nor the *CUSUM-SQ*s leave the respective areas between the dashed lines.

2.7 Unit Root Tests

Because the order of integration of a time series is of great importance for the analysis, several statistical tests have been developed for investigating it. The first set of tests checks the null hypothesis that there is a unit root against the alternative of stationarity of a DGP that may have a nonzero mean term, a deterministic linear trend, and perhaps seasonal dummy variables. The stochastic part is modeled by an AR process or, alternatively, it is accounted for by

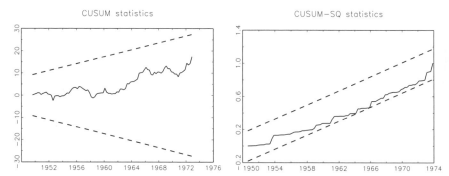

Figure 2.16. CUSUM and CUSUM-of-squares tests (5% significance level) of AR(4) model for U.S. investment series.

nonparametric techniques as in the second group of tests. The third kind of tests presented in Section 2.7.3 allow, in addition, for structural shifts as they are observed, for example, in the German GNP series in Figure 2.1. In that context, procedures are also discussed dealing with the situation in which the time of the shift is unknown. After that, so-called KPSS tests are introduced. They take a quite different view at the unit root testing problem by checking a stationarity null hypothesis against an alternative of a unit root. Finally, in the last part of this section, tests for seasonal unit roots are considered. There is a large literature on unit root testing with many more proposals and refinements that will not be covered herein. A good review of unit root testing is given, for instance, by Stock (1994).

2.7.1 Augmented Dickey–Fuller (ADF) Tests

If the DGP is an AR(p), as in (2.4), the process is integrated when $\alpha(1) = 1 - \alpha_1 - \cdots - \alpha_p = 0$, as seen in Section 2.3.1. In other words, a hypothesis of interest is $\alpha(1) = 0$. To test this null hypothesis against the alternative of stationarity of the process, it is useful to reparameterize the model. Subtracting y_{t-1} on both sides and rearranging terms results in a regression

$$\Delta y_t = \phi y_{t-1} + \sum_{j=1}^{p-1} \alpha_j^* \Delta y_{t-j} + u_t, \qquad (2.15)$$

where $\phi = -\alpha(1)$ and $\alpha_j^* = -(\alpha_{j+1} + \cdots + \alpha_p)$. In this model we wish to test the pair of hypotheses $H_0 : \phi = 0$ versus $H_1 : \phi < 0$. The so-called *augmented Dickey–Fuller* (ADF) *test* statistic is based on the t-statistic of the coefficient ϕ from an OLS estimation of (2.15) [Fuller (1976) and Dickey & Fuller (1979)]. It does not have an asymptotic standard normal distribution, but it has a non-standard limiting distribution. Critical values have been obtained by simulation, and they are available, for instance, in Fuller (1976) and Davidson & MacKinnon (1993). It turns out, however, that the limiting distribution depends on the deterministic terms that have to be included. Therefore, different critical values are used when a constant or linear trend term is added in (2.15). On the other hand, including seasonal dummies in addition to a constant or a linear trend does not result in further changes in the limiting distribution.

In these tests a decision on the AR order or, equivalently, on the number of lagged differences of y_t has to be made. This choice may be based on the model selection criteria discussed in Section 2.5, or a sequential testing procedure may be used that eliminates insignificant coefficients sequentially starting from some high-order model [see, e.g., Ng & Perron (1995)].

It may be worth noting that the limiting distribution does not depend on the α_j^* or other characteristics of the short-term dynamics. Moreover, it was shown by Said & Dickey (1984) that the tests may also be based on a finite-order AR model if the actual process is mixed ARMA. In that case the same limiting distributions are obtained as those for finite-order AR processes if the AR order approaches infinity at a suitable rate with the sample size.

In general, if the order of integration of a time series and, hence, the number of unit roots in the AR operator, are not clear, one should difference the series first as many times as deemed appropriate for making it stationary. Then a unit root test is performed for the series in this way differenced. If the unit root is rejected, a unit root test is applied to the series, which is differenced one time less than in the previous test. If again a unit root is rejected, the procedure is repeated until a unit root cannot be rejected. For example, if y_t is suspected to be I(2), then a unit root is tested for $\Delta^2 y_t$ first. If it is rejected, a unit root test is applied to Δy_t. If the unit root cannot be rejected in Δy_t, this result confirms that y_t is indeed best modeled as an I(2) series. On the other hand, if a unit root is also rejected for Δy_t, treating y_t as an I(2) series is not likely to be a good choice. The strategy for determining the number of unit roots by applying a test first to the series differenced a maximum number of times necessary for inducing stationarity was proposed by Pantula (1989) and is sometimes referred to as the *Pantula principle*. Note, however, that in this procedure, if a linear trend term is needed in the test for y_t, only a constant should be used in the test for Δy_t because, if $y_t = \mu_0 + \mu_1 t + x_t$, then $\Delta y_t = \mu_1 + \Delta x_t$. Similarly, if just a constant is deemed necessary in the test for y_t, then no deterministic term is necessary in the test for Δy_t. Analogous comments apply if higher order differences are considered.

For illustrative purposes we have applied the ADF test to the U.S. investment and the German interest rate series. Both series may have a nonzero mean but are not likely to have a linear trend component. Also there is no obvious seasonality (see Figure 2.1). For demonstration the ADF test was applied to the investment series in both forms with and without linear trend, and we have used two different lag orders. The results in Table 2.6 clearly suggest that the

Table 2.6. *ADF tests for example time series*

Variable	Deterministic term	No. of lagged differences	Test statistic	5% critical value
U.S. investment	constant and trend	0	−5.83	−3.41
		3	−5.66	
	constant	0	−5.69	−2.86
		3	−5.24	
Δinterest rate	none	0	−8.75	−1.94
		2	−4.75	
interest rate	constant	1	−1.48	−2.86
		3	−1.93	

Note: Critical values from Davidson & MacKinnon (1993, Table 20.1).

unit root null hypothesis can be rejected. For example, for lag order 3 and just a constant, the estimated model with t-values in parentheses underneath the estimates is

$$\Delta y_t = \underset{(2.76)}{0.82} - \underset{(-5.24)}{0.74} \, y_{t-1} + \underset{(1.97)}{0.25} \, \Delta y_{t-1} + \underset{(1.34)}{0.15} \, \Delta y_{t-2}$$

$$+ \underset{(2.02)}{0.22} \, \Delta y_{t-3} + \hat{u}_t.$$

The t-value of the first lag of the levels variable is just the ADF test statistic. It is clearly smaller than the 5% critical value of the relevant null distribution. Hence, the null hypothesis is rejected at this level. Notice also in Table 2.6 that the critical values are different for the case in which a linear trend is included. Of course, this is a consequence of having a different null distribution for this case than for the one in which a constant is the only deterministic term. Another issue worth mentioning perhaps is that including lagged differences in the model up to lag order 3 corresponds to a levels AR model of order 4. In other words, if the preceding model is rewritten in levels, we get an AR(4),

$$y_t = \nu_0 + \alpha_1 y_{t-1} + \alpha_2 y_{t-2} + \alpha_3 y_{t-3} + \alpha_4 y_{t-4} + u_t.$$

Therefore, the lag order used in the unit root test is in line with the AR(4) model considered earlier.

The results for the German long-term interest rate indicate that this variable may best be viewed as being I(1). From the graph and the autocorrelations and partial autocorrelations it cannot be excluded that the series is I(1). Therefore, the first differences are tested first. For both lag orders the test clearly rejects the unit root. Note that no deterministic term is included because a linear trend term is not regarded as plausible for the original series and the constant term vanishes upon differencing. Testing for a unit root in the original series, the null hypothesis is not rejected for both lag orders. Therefore we conclude that the DGP should be modeled as an I(1) process.

2.7.2 Schmidt–Phillips Tests

Schmidt & Phillips (1992) have proposed another variant of tests for the null hypothesis of a unit root when a deterministic linear trend is present. They have suggested estimating the deterministic term in a first step under the unit root hypothesis. Then the series is adjusted for the deterministic terms, and a unit root test is applied to the adjusted series. More precisely, if a deterministic trend term $\mu_t = \mu_0 + \mu_1 t$ is assumed in the DGP, the parameter μ_1 is estimated from

$$\Delta y_t = \mu_1 + \Delta x_t$$

by OLS. In other words, $\tilde{\mu}_1 = T^{-1} \sum_{t=2}^{T} \Delta y_t$. Then $\tilde{\mu}_0 = y_1 - \tilde{\mu}_1$ is used as an estimator of μ_0 and an adjusted series is obtained as $\tilde{x}_t = y_t - \tilde{\mu}_0 - \tilde{\mu}_1 t$.

Now an ADF-type test discussed previously can be applied to the adjusted series $\tilde{x}_t$ using a model without deterministic terms. To allow for more general DGPs than finite order AR processes, Schmidt & Phillips (1992), however, have proposed basing the test on a regression $\Delta \tilde{x}_t = \phi \tilde{x}_t + e_t$. The test cannot be based on the OLS estimator $\hat{\phi}$ directly or on its t-statistic $t_{\hat{\phi}}$ because the asymptotic distribution under the unit root null hypothesis depends on the dynamic structure of the error term e_t. Therefore, an adjustment factor has to be used in setting up the test statistics. Such an adjustment was previously developed by Phillips (1987) and Phillips & Perron (1988) in a related context. For the present case, Schmidt & Phillips (1992) have suggested the following two test statistics:

$$Z(\tilde{\phi}) = T\tilde{\phi}\tilde{\sigma}_\infty^2/\tilde{\sigma}_e^2 \quad \text{and} \quad Z(t_{\tilde{\phi}}) = \frac{\tilde{\sigma}_\infty}{\tilde{\sigma}_e} t_{\tilde{\alpha}}.$$

Here $\tilde{\sigma}_e^2 = T^{-1} \sum_{t=1}^{T} \tilde{e}_t^2$ is the variance estimator based on the OLS residuals of the model $y_t = v_0 + v_1 t + \rho y_{t-1} + e_t$, and

$$\tilde{\sigma}_\infty^2 = \frac{1}{T} \sum_{t=1}^{T} \tilde{e}_t^2 + 2 \sum_{j=1}^{l_q} \omega_j \left(\frac{1}{T} \sum_{t=j+1}^{T} \tilde{e}_t \tilde{e}_{t-j} \right)$$

is a nonparametric estimator of the so-called long-run variance of e_t with ω_j being a Bartlett window, $\omega_j = 1 - \frac{j}{l_q+1}$. This estimator is sometimes referred to as the *Newey–West estimator*. The asymptotic null distributions of these test statistics are different from those of the ADF statistics. Critical values for these tests are tabulated in Schmidt & Phillips (1992).

The small sample properties of the tests will depend on the choice of l_q. One possible suggestion is to use $l_q = q(T/100)^{1/4}$ with $q = 4$ or $q = 12$. Unfortunately, despite their appealing asymptotic properties, the tests may be compromised by very distorted size in small samples. Therefore, they should

Table 2.7. *Schmidt–Phillips tests for example time series*

Variable	Test	Lags l_q	Test statistic	5% critical value
U.S. investment	$Z(\tilde{\phi})$	4	−29.0	−18.1
		12	−34.1	
	$Z(t_{\tilde{\phi}})$	4	−4.23	−3.02
		12	−4.59	
interest rate	$Z(\tilde{\phi})$	4	−12.8	−18.1
		12	−14.1	
	$Z(t_{\tilde{\phi}})$	4	−2.52	−3.02
		12	−2.64	

Note: Critical values from Schmidt & Phillips (1992).

be used with caution. In fact, a test based on the OLS estimator $\hat{\phi}$ rather than its t-ratio in the model (2.15) has also been proposed by Dickey & Fuller (1979). We have not discussed this version here because of its occasional small sample distortions, which were found in simulations [see, e.g., Schwert (1989)].

To illustrate the Schmidt–Phillips tests, we have also applied them to the U.S. investment and German interest rate series. The test results are given in Table 2.7. Again, a unit root in the U.S. investment series is clearly rejected, whereas a unit root in the German interest rate is not rejected at the 5% level.

2.7.3 A Test for Processes with Level Shift

If there is a shift in the level of the DGP as, for instance, in the German GNP series in Figure 2.1, it should be taken into account in testing for a unit root because the ADF test may have very low power if the shift is simply ignored [see Perron (1989)]. One possible approach is to assume that the shift is deterministic. In that case, a shift function, which we denote by $f_t(\theta)'\gamma$, may be added to the deterministic term μ_t. Hence, we have a model

$$y_t = \mu_0 + \mu_1 t + f_t(\theta)'\gamma + x_t, \tag{2.16}$$

where θ and γ are unknown parameters or parameter vectors and the errors x_t are generated by an AR(p) process $\alpha^*(L)(1 - \rho L)x_t = u_t$ with $\alpha^*(L) = 1 - \alpha_1^* L - \cdots - \alpha_{p-1}^* L^{p-1}$.

Shift functions may, for example, be based on

$$f_t^{(1)} = d_{1t} := \begin{cases} 0, & t < T_B \\ 1, & t \geq T_B \end{cases},$$

$$f_t^{(2)}(\theta) = \begin{cases} 0, & t < T_B \\ 1 - \exp\{-\theta(t - T_B + 1)\}, & t \geq T_B \end{cases}$$

or

$$f_t^{(3)}(\theta) = \left[\frac{d_{1,t}}{1 - \theta L} : \frac{d_{1,t-1}}{1 - \theta L} \right]'.$$

The first one of these functions is a simple shift dummy variable with shift date T_B. The function does not involve any extra parameter θ. In the shift term $f_t^{(1)}\gamma$, the parameter γ is a scalar. The second shift function is based on the exponential distribution function, which allows for a nonlinear gradual shift to a new level starting at time T_B. In the shift term $f_t^{(2)}(\theta)\gamma$, both θ and γ are scalar parameters. The first one is confined to the positive real line ($\theta > 0$), whereas the second one may assume any value. Finally, the third function can be viewed as a rational function in the lag operator applied to a shift dummy d_{1t}. The actual shift term is $[\gamma_1(1 - \theta L)^{-1} + \gamma_2(1 - \theta L)^{-1}L]d_{1t}$. Here θ is a scalar parameter between 0 and 1 and $\gamma = (\gamma_1, \gamma_2)'$ is a two-dimensional parameter vector. An alternative way to write this shift function is

$$f_t^{(3)}(\theta)'\gamma = \begin{cases} 0, & t < T_B \\ \gamma_1, & t = T_B \\ \gamma_1 + \sum_{j=1}^{t-T_B} \theta^{j-1}(\theta\gamma_1 + \gamma_2), & t > T_B \end{cases}.$$

This expression offers the possibility of very general nonlinear shifts. Some possible shift functions for alternative parameter values are plotted in Figure 2.17. Notice that both $f_t^{(2)}(\theta)\gamma$ and $f_t^{(3)}(\theta)'\gamma$ can generate sharp one-time shifts at time T_B for suitable values of θ. Thus, they are more general than $f_t^{(1)}\gamma$.

Saikkonen & Lütkepohl (2002) and Lanne, Lütkepohl & Saikkonen (2002) have proposed unit root tests for the model (2.16) based on estimating the deterministic term first by a generalized least-squares (GLS) procedure and subtracting it from the original series. Then an ADF-type test is performed on the adjusted series.

If a model with linear trend and shift term is assumed, the relevant parameters $\eta = (\mu_0, \mu_1, \gamma')'$ are estimated by minimizing the generalized sum of squared errors of the model in first differences,

$$\Delta y_t = \mu_1 + \Delta f_t(\theta)'\gamma + v_t \quad (t = 2, \ldots, T),$$

where $v_t = \alpha^*(L)^{-1}u_t$. In other words, estimation is done under the unit root null hypothesis by minimizing

$$Q_p(\eta, \theta, \alpha^*) = (Y - Z(\theta)\eta)'\Sigma(\alpha^*)^{-1}(Y - Z(\theta)\eta),$$

where α^* is the vector of coefficients in $\alpha^*(L)$, $\Sigma(\alpha^*) = \text{Cov}(V)/\sigma_u^2$, $V = (v_1, \ldots, v_T)'$ the error vector of the model, $Y = [y_1, \Delta y_2, \ldots, \Delta y_T]'$ and

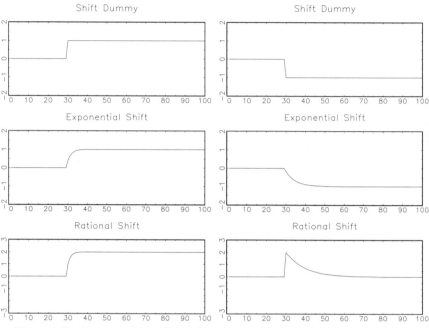

Figure 2.17. Some possible shift functions.

$Z = [Z_1 : Z_2 : Z_3]$ with $Z_1 = [1, 0, \dots, 0]'$, $Z_2 = [1, 1, \dots, 1]'$, and $Z_3 = [f_1(\theta), \Delta f_2(\theta), \dots, \Delta f_T(\theta)]'$.

Although the adjusted series $\hat{x}_t = y_t - \hat{\mu}_0 - \hat{\mu}_1 t - f_t(\hat{\theta})'\hat{\gamma}$ could be used in the ADF approach, Lanne et al. (2002) have proposed a slightly different procedure that adjusts for the estimation errors in the nuisance parameters and has worked quite well in small sample simulations. Denoting the estimator of the AR polynomial obtained by minimizing $Q_p(\eta, \theta, \alpha^*)$ by $\hat{\alpha}^*(L)$, Lanne et al. (2002) have defined $\hat{w}_t = \hat{\alpha}^*(L)\hat{x}_t$ and base the unit root test on the auxiliary regression model

$$\Delta \hat{w}_t = \nu + \phi \hat{w}_{t-1} + [\hat{\alpha}^*(L)\Delta f_t(\hat{\theta})']\pi_1 + [\hat{\alpha}^*(L)\Delta F_t(\hat{\theta})']\pi_2$$

$$+ \sum_{j=1}^{p-1} \alpha_j^\dagger \Delta \hat{x}_{t-j} + r_t$$

$$(t = p + 1, \dots, T),$$

where $F_t(\theta) = df_t/d\theta$ is the first-order derivative of $f_t(\theta)$ with respect to the θ parameter and r_t denotes an error term. The unit root test statistic is again obtained as the usual t-statistic of the estimator of ϕ based on OLS estimation of this model. As in the case of the ADF statistic, the asymptotic null distribution is nonstandard. Critical values are tabulated in Lanne et al. (2002). Again a different asymptotic distribution is obtained if the deterministic linear trend term is excluded a priori. Because the power of the test tends to improve when the linear trend is not present, it is advisable to use any prior information to this effect. If the series of interest has seasonal fluctuations, it is also possible to include seasonal dummies in addition in the model (2.16).

In executing the test it is necessary to decide on the AR order and the shift date T_B. If the latter quantity is known, the desired shift function may be included, and the AR order may be chosen in the usual way for a model in levels with the help of order selection criteria, sequential tests, and model checking tools. If the break date is unknown, Lanne, Lütkepohl & Saikkonen (2003) have recommended, on the basis of simulation results, choosing a reasonably large AR order in a first step and then picking the break date that minimizes $Q_p(\eta, \theta, \alpha^*)$. In this first step, choosing a shift dummy as shift function is recommended. Usually the choice of the break date will not be critical if it is not totally unreasonable. In other words, the unit root test is not sensitive to slight misspecification of the break date. Once a possible break date is fixed, a more detailed analysis of the AR order is called for because possible reductions of the order may improve the power of the test.

As an example, consider the German GNP series. We are considering the logs of the series because, in Figure 2.1, it can be seen that the variability increases with the level of the series. In this case the break date is known to be the third quarter of 1990, when the German monetary reunification occurred, and from then on the series refers to all of Germany whereas it refers to West Germany before that date. Therefore, we can fix T_B accordingly. Using initially the simple shift dummy variable, a constant, seasonal dummy variables, and a deterministic linear trend, both AIC and HQ favor four lagged differences, which are therefore used in the following analysis.

The series together with estimated deterministic term and the adjusted series as well as the estimated shift function for the shift dummy and the exponential shift function $f_t^{(2)}(\theta)\gamma$ are plotted in Figure 2.18. Clearly in this case the exponential shift function is almost a shift dummy because a relatively large value for θ is optimal. In Figure 2.18 the objective function, which is minimized in estimating the deterministic parameters, is also plotted as a function of θ in the lower right-hand corner. It can be seen that the objective function is a decreasing function of θ, which clearly indicates that a shift dummy describes the shift quite well because, for large values of θ, the exponential shift function is the same as a shift dummy for practical purposes. Actually, it seems reasonable to constrain θ to a range between zero and 3 only because, for $\theta = 3$, the exponential shift function almost represents an instantaneous shift to a new level. Hence, larger values are not needed to describe the range of possibilities. In this case we have also found an instantaneous shift with the rational shift function. The results are not plotted to save space. In Table 2.8 the test values for all three test statistics are given. They are all quite similar and do not provide evidence against a unit root.

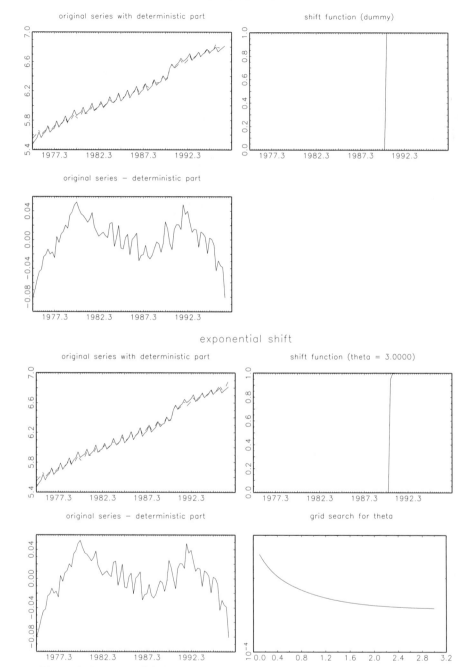

Figure 2.18. Deterministic terms and adjusted series used in unit root tests for log GNP series based on a model with four lagged differences (sample period: 1976Q2 − 1996Q4).

Table 2.8. *Unit root tests in the presence of structural shift for German log GNP using four lagged differences, a constant, seasonal dummies, and a trend*

Shift function	Test statistic	Critical values	
		10%	5%
$f_t^{(1)}\gamma$	-1.41	-2.76	-3.03
$f_t^{(2)}(\theta)\gamma$	-1.36		
$f_t^{(3)}(\theta)'\gamma$	-1.43		

Note: Critical values from Lanne et al. (2002).

Of course, there could still be other forms of structural breaks than those considered here. For example, if the series has a deterministic linear trend function, there may also be a break in the trend slope. This form of break was also considered in the literature, and appropriate unit root tests are available [see, e.g., Perron (1989)].

2.7.4 KPSS Test

Another possibility for investigating the integration properties of a series y_t is to test the null hypothesis that the DGP is stationary ($H_0 : y_t \sim I(0)$) against the alternative that it is $I(1)$ ($H_1 : y_t \sim I(1)$). Kwiatkowski, Phillips, Schmidt & Shin (1992) have derived a test for this pair of hypotheses. If it is assumed that there is no linear trend term, the point of departure is a DGP of the form

$$y_t = x_t + z_t,$$

where x_t is a random walk, $x_t = x_{t-1} + v_t$, $v_t \sim \text{iid}(0, \sigma_v^2)$, and z_t is a stationary process. In this framework the foregoing pair of hypoheses is equivalent to the pair $H_0 : \sigma_v^2 = 0$ versus $H_1 : \sigma_v^2 > 0$. If H_0 holds, y_t is composed of a constant and the stationary process z_t; hence, y_t is also stationary. Kwiatkowski et al. (1992) have proposed the following test statistic:

$$KPSS = \frac{1}{T^2} \sum_{t=1}^{T} S_t^2 / \hat{\sigma}_\infty^2,$$

where $S_t = \sum_{j=1}^{t} \hat{w}_j$ with $\hat{w}_t = y_t - \bar{y}$ and $\hat{\sigma}_\infty^2$ is an estimator of

$$\sigma_\infty^2 = \lim_{T \to \infty} T^{-1} \text{Var} \left(\sum_{t=1}^{T} z_t \right),$$

that is, $\hat{\sigma}_\infty^2$ is an estimator of the long-run variance of the process z_t. If y_t is a stationary process, S_t is $I(1)$ and the quantity in the numerator of the KPSS statistic is an estimator of its variance, which has a stochastic limit. The term in the denominator ensures that, overall, the limiting distribution is free of unknown nuisance parameters. If, however, y_t is I(1), the numerator will grow without bounds, causing the statistic to become large for large sample sizes.

To avoid strong assumptions regarding the process z_t, Kwiatkowski et al. (1992) proposed a nonparametric estimator of σ^2_∞ based on a Bartlett window having, once again, a lag truncation parameter $l_q = q(T/100)^{1/4}$:

$$\hat{\sigma}^2_\infty = \frac{1}{T}\sum_{t=1}^{T}\hat{w}_t^2 + 2\sum_{j=1}^{l_q}\omega_j\left(\frac{1}{T}\sum_{t=j+1}^{T}\hat{w}_t\hat{w}_{t-j}\right),$$

where $\omega_j = 1 - \frac{j}{l_q+1}$, as before. Using this estimator, we find that the KPSS statistic has a limiting distribution that does not depend on nuisance parameters under the null hypothesis of stationarity of y_t. Hence, critical values can be tabulated provided z_t satisfies some weak conditions. The critical values may be found, for example, in Kwiatkowski et al. (1992) or in Moryson (1998, Table 4.1). The null hypothesis of stationarity is rejected for large values of *KPSS*. One problem here is the choice of the truncation parameter l_q. Again l_4 or l_{12} may be suitable choices.

If a deterministic trend is suspected in the DGP, the point of departure is a DGP, which includes such a term,

$$y_t = \mu_1 t + x_t + z_t,$$

and the $\hat{w}_t$s are residuals from a regression

$$y_t = \mu_0 + \mu_1 t + w_t.$$

With these quantities the test statistic is computed in the same way as before. Its limiting distribution under H_0 is different from the case without a trend term, however. Critical values for the case with a trend are available from Kwiatkowski et al. (1992) or Moryson (1998, Table 5.11).

Ideally, if a series y_t is I(0), a Dickey–Fuller type test should reject the nonstationarity null hypothesis, whereas the KPSS test should not reject its null hypothesis. Such a result is pleasing because two different approaches lead to the same conclusion. In practice, such an ideal result is not always obtained for various reasons. Of course, if none of the tests reject the null hypothesis, this may be due to insufficient power of one of them. In that case it is difficult for the researcher to decide on the integration properties of y_t. It may be necessary to perform analyses under alternative assumptions for the variables involved. It is also possible that the DGP is not of the type assumed in these tests. For instance, there may be complicated and repeated structural breaks, inhomogeneous variances, long-range dependence that is not of the simple I(1) type, or heavy tailed distributions as they are sometimes observed in financial time series. Although the tests are asymptotically robust with respect to some such deviations from our ideal assumptions, there may still be an impact on the results for time series of typical length in applications.

Table 2.9. *KPSS tests for example time series*

Variable	Lags l_q	Test statistic	Critical values 10%	Critical values 5%
U.S. investment	4	0.250	0.347	0.463
	12	0.377		
interest rate	4	0.848	0.347	0.463
	12	0.465		

Note: Critical values from Kwiatkowski et al. (1992).

To illustrate the use of the KPSS test, we again use the U.S. investment and German interest rate series. The results for two different lag parameters are given in Table 2.9. In no case can the stationarity null hypothesis be rejected at the 5% level for the U.S. investment series, whereas it is rejected for the German interest rate. This result corresponds quite nicely to rejecting the unit root for the U.S. investment series and not rejecting it for the interest rate with the ADF and Schmidt–Phillips tests. Notice, however, that using $l_q = 12$ for the investment series results in a test value that is significant at the 10% level. Still, taking all the evidence together, we find that the series is better viewed as I(0) than as I(1).

KPSS tests are sometimes summarized under the heading of moving average unit root tests. The reason is that, for $\sigma_v^2 = 0$, that is, if $y_t \sim$ I(0), the first differences of y_t have a moving average term with a unit root, $\Delta y_t = z_t - \theta z_{t-1}$ with $\theta = 1$. On the other hand, if $\sigma_v^2 > 0$, then $\Delta y_t = v_t + z_t - z_{t-1} = w_t - \theta w_{t-1}$ with $\theta \neq 1$. Hence, testing stationarity of y_t against $y_t \sim$ I(1) may be accomplished by testing $H_0 : \theta = 1$ versus $H_1 : \theta \neq 1$. In other words, the hypotheses of interest can be formulated in terms of MA unit roots. Several suitable tests for this purpose have been proposed in the literature [see, e.g., Saikkonen & Luukkonen (1993b) or Tanaka (1990)]. Related work is reported by Saikkonen & Luukkonen (1993a), Leybourne & McCabe (1994), Arellano & Pantula (1995), and Tsay (1993), among others.

2.7.5 *Testing for Seasonal Unit Roots*

If it is assumed again that the DGP of a time series y_t has an AR representation, it is possible that there are roots other than 1 on the complex unit circle. For instance, if a quarterly time series has a strong seasonal component, it is possible that the seasonality and the nonstationarity can be removed partly or completely by applying a quarterly seasonal differencing operator $\Delta_4 y_t = (1 - L^4) y_t = y_t - y_{t-4}$. As noted earlier,

$$1 - L^4 = (1 - L)(1 + L)(1 + L^2)$$
$$= (1 - L)(1 + L)(1 - iL)(1 + iL). \qquad (2.17)$$

Hence, if the AR operator can be decomposed as $\alpha(L) = \alpha^*(L)(1 - L^4)$, then $\alpha(z)$ has roots for $z = 1, -1, i, -i$. All of these roots are on the complex unit circle, of course. The root $z = -1$ is called the *root at semiannual frequency*, and the complex conjugate roots $z = \pm i$ are sometimes referred to as the *annual frequency roots* because the corresponding spectral density of the DGP has peaks at the semiannual and annual frequencies if the AR operator has roots at -1 and $\pm i$, respectively. Therefore, these three roots are called *seasonal unit roots*. The root for $z = 1$ is sometimes referred to as a *zero frequency unit root* to distinguish it from the other roots.

Obviously, it is of interest to know if such unit roots exist because then it may be useful or necessary to apply the seasonal differencing operator to a series or take the seasonal unit roots into account in some other way in the subsequent analysis. Tests have been proposed by Hylleberg, Engle, Granger & Yoo (1990) to check for seasonal unit roots in quarterly time series. The idea is as follows:

If the DGP is an AR(p), as in (2.4), with AR operator $\alpha(L) = 1 - \alpha_1 L - \cdots - \alpha_p L^p$ and $p \geq 4$, this operator can be rearranged as

$$\alpha(L) = (1 - L^4) - \pi_1 L(1 + L + L^2 + L^3) + \pi_2 L(1 - L + L^2 - L^3) + (\pi_3 + \pi_4 L)(1 - L^2) - \alpha^*(L)(1 - L^4),$$

or, if (2.17) is used, as

$$\alpha(L) = (1 - L)(1 + L)(1 - iL)(1 + iL) - \pi_1 L(1 + L)(1 - iL)(1 + iL) + \pi_2 L(1 - L)(1 - iL)(1 + iL) + (\pi_3 + \pi_4 L)(1 - L)(1 + L) - \alpha^*(L)(1 - L)(1 + L)(1 - iL)(1 + iL).$$

Thus, the AR operator can be factored as follows:

$$\alpha(L) = \begin{cases} \alpha^a(L)(1 - L), & \text{if } \pi_1 = 0 \\ \alpha^b(L)(1 + L), & \text{if } \pi_2 = 0 \\ \alpha^c(L)(1 - iL)(1 + iL), & \text{if } \pi_3 = \pi_4 = 0. \end{cases}$$

Hence, $\alpha(L)$ has regular, semiannual, or annual unit roots if $\pi_1 = 0$, $\pi_2 = 0$, or $\pi_3 = \pi_4 = 0$, respectively. Therefore, Hylleberg et al. (1990) have proposed basing tests for seasonal unit roots on the model

$$\Delta_4 y_t = \pi_1 z_{1,t-1} + \pi_2 z_{2,t-1} + \pi_3 z_{3,t-1} + \pi_4 z_{3,t-2}$$

$$+ \sum_{j=1}^{p-4} \alpha_j^* \Delta_4 y_{t-j} + u_t, \tag{2.18}$$

where $z_{1t} = (1 + L)(1 - iL)(1 + iL)y_t = (1 + L + L^2 + L^3)y_t$, $z_{2t} = -(1 - L)(1 - iL)(1 + iL)y_t = -(1 - L + L^2 - L^3)y_t$ and $z_{3t} = -(1 - L)(1 + L)y_t = -(1 - L^2)y_t$. The null hypotheses $H_0 : \pi_1 = 0$, $H_0 : \pi_2 = 0$, and $H_0 : \pi_3 = \pi_4 = 0$ correspond to tests for regular, semiannual, and annual unit roots, respectively. These hypotheses can be tested by estimating the model (2.18) by OLS and considering the relevant t- and F-tests. These tests are known as HEGY *tests*. We will denote the corresponding test statistics by $t_{\hat{\pi}_1}$, $t_{\hat{\pi}_2}$, and F_{34}, respectively. Their asymptotic distributions under the respective null hypotheses are nonstandard and do not depend on the short-term dynamics manifested in the terms with lagged differences. Suitable critical values may be found in Hylleberg et al. (1990) and Franses & Hobijn (1997). "F-tests" were also considered for the joint null hypothesis that π_2, π_3, and π_4 are all zero as well as for the case that all four πs are jointly zero ($\pi_1 = \pi_2 = \pi_3 = \pi_4 = 0$). These tests will be denoted by F_{234} and F_{1234}, respectively.

Again the asymptotic distributions of the test statistics under the respective null hypotheses depend on the deterministic terms in the model. For example, if only a constant is included, another asymptotic distribution is obtained as would be the case for a model with a constant and seasonal dummy variables. Yet another distribution results if a constant, seasonal dummies, and a linear trend term are included in the model. It turns out that the t-statistic for $H_0 : \pi_1 = 0$ has the same asymptotic distribution as the corresponding ADF t-statistic if the null hypothesis holds and the t-ratio of π_2 has just the mirror distribution of the t-ratio of π_1. Notice also that individual t-tests for the significance of π_3 and π_4 have been considered as well. They are problematic, however, because the asymptotic null distribution depends on the parameters of the lagged differences [see Burridge & Taylor (2001)].

In practice, the AR order p or the number of lagged seasonal differences $\Delta_4 y_{t-j}$ has to be chosen before the HEGY tests can be performed. This may again be done by using model selection criteria. Alternatively, a fairly large order may be chosen for (2.18) first, and then the t-ratios of the estimated α_j^*s may be checked. Lagged values of $\Delta_4 y_t$ with insignificant coefficients may then be eliminated sequentially one at a time starting from the largest lag.

As an example, we consider the German log income series shown in Figure 2.4. Because both lag selection criteria AIC and HQ have suggested three lagged differences in a model with a constant, seasonal dummy variables, and a linear trend, we have estimated the corresponding model and obtained (with t-values in parentheses)

$$
\begin{aligned}
\Delta_4 y_t = \underset{(1.09)}{0.19\,sd_{1t}} + \underset{(1.83)}{0.32\,sd_{2t}} + \underset{(1.19)}{0.21\,sd_{3t}} + \underset{(2.06)}{0.36\,sd_{4t}} + \underset{(1.10)}{0.0002\,t} \\
- \underset{(-1.48)}{0.01\,z_{1,t-1}} - \underset{(-5.21)}{0.62\,z_{2,t-1}} - \underset{(-2.31)}{0.16\,z_{3,t-1}} - \underset{(-0.92)}{0.07\,z_{3,t-2}} \\
+ \underset{(2.11)}{0.25\,\Delta_4 y_{t-1}} + \underset{(2.19)}{0.27\,\Delta_4 y_{t-2}} - \underset{(-1.52)}{0.14\,\Delta_4 y_{t-3}} + \hat{u}_t.
\end{aligned}
$$

As mentioned earlier, the t-values of $z_{3,t-i}$ cannot be interpreted in the usual way. Therefore, we present the relevant test statistics for seasonal unit roots with corresponding critical values in Table 2.10. Obviously, the zero frequency and the annual unit roots cannot be rejected (see $t_{\hat{\pi}_1}$ and F_{34}). On the other hand, a

Table 2.10. *Tests for seasonal unit roots in German log income series*

Variable	Determ. terms	No. of lags	H_0	Test	Test statistic	Critical values 10%	5%
log income	constant	3	$\pi_1 = 0$	$t_{\hat{\pi}_1}$	−1.48	−3.10	−3.39
	trend		$\pi_2 = 0$	$t_{\hat{\pi}_2}$	−5.21	−2.53	−2.82
	seasonals		$\pi_3 = \pi_4 = 0$	F_{34}	3.09	5.48	6.55
			$\pi_2 = \pi_3 = \pi_4 = 0$	F_{234}	12.95	5.09	5.93
			$\pi_1 = \pi_2 = \pi_3 = \pi_4 = 0$	F_{1234}	10.81	5.55	6.31
	constant	9	$\pi_1 = 0$	$t_{\hat{\pi}_1}$	−1.53	−3.11	−3.40
	trend		$\pi_2 = 0$	$t_{\hat{\pi}_2}$	0.50	−1.61	−1.93
			$\pi_3 = \pi_4 = 0$	F_{34}	0.98	2.35	3.05
			$\pi_2 = \pi_3 = \pi_4 = 0$	F_{234}	0.74	2.18	2.74
			$\pi_1 = \pi_2 = \pi_3 = \pi_4 = 0$	F_{1234}	1.13	3.59	4.19
Δ_4 log income	constant	5	$\pi_1 = 0$	$t_{\hat{\pi}_1}$	−2.27	−2.55	−2.85
			$\pi_2 = 0$	$t_{\hat{\pi}_2}$	−6.88	−1.61	−1.93
			$\pi_3 = \pi_4 = 0$	F_{34}	32.76	2.37	3.08
			$\pi_2 = \pi_3 = \pi_4 = 0$	F_{234}	35.04	2.20	2.76
			$\pi_1 = \pi_2 = \pi_3 = \pi_4 = 0$	F_{1234}	30.49	2.83	3.36
	constant	1	$\pi_1 = 0$	$t_{\hat{\pi}_1}$	−2.62	−2.55	−2.85
			$\pi_2 = 0$	$t_{\hat{\pi}_2}$	−7.92	−1.61	−1.93
			$\pi_3 = \pi_4 = 0$	F_{34}	58.76	2.37	3.08
			$\pi_2 = \pi_3 = \pi_4 = 0$	F_{234}	56.15	2.20	2.76
			$\pi_1 = \pi_2 = \pi_3 = \pi_4 = 0$	F_{1234}	48.66	2.83	3.36

Note: Critical values from Franses & Hobijn (1997).

semiannual root is clearly rejected (see $t_{\hat{\pi}_2}$). As a consequence, F_{234} and F_{1234} also reject their respective null hypotheses.

Notice that four seasonal dummy variables (denoted by sd_{it}) are included in the model; hence, an extra constant is not included. Equivalently, a constant and three seasonal dummies could be used. Because the seasonal dummies have relatively small t-values, we have also applied seasonal unit root tests to a model without including them. The test results are also given in Table 2.10. In this case the lag order criteria favor a larger number of lagged seasonal differences. Such a result should not come as a surprise because the seasonality that was captured by the seasonal dummies in the previous model has to be taken care of by the lagged differences in the present model. Now not one of the tests can reject its respective null hypothesis at conventional significance levels. Thus, if no seasonal dummies are included, there is some evidence that seasonal differencing of the log income series is adequate. Hence, for this series, the seasonal differencing operator competes to some extent with capturing some of the seasonality by seasonal dummies.

In Table 2.10 we also give test results for the Δ_4 log income series. In this case the model selection criteria AIC and HQ suggest different lag orders, and we have included them both. Now there is some evidence that there is no additional unit root although the zero-frequency unit root cannot be rejected very clearly. It is rejected at the 10% level if just one lagged seasonal difference of the variable is added, and it cannot be rejected even at the 10% level with five lagged differences. Because unit root tests are known to have low power – in particular if many lagged differences are included – we interpret the results in Table 2.10 as weak evidence against further unit roots in Δ_4 log income.

Although in principle one should always start from a model differenced enough to obtain stationarity and if unit roots are rejected continue the unit root testing with series in which fewer differencing operators are applied, the present example shows that it is sometimes necessary to base the decision on possible unit roots on a range of tests for different levels of differencing. A mechanistic sequential procedure may not reveal all important aspects for the subsequent analysis.

For monthly series the corresponding tests for seasonal unit roots were discussed by Franses (1990) based on the observation that the seasonal differencing operator in this case can be decomposed as follows:

$$\begin{aligned}
\Delta_{12} = 1 - L^{12} = &(1 - L)(1 + L)(1 - iL)(1 + iL) \\
&\times [1 + \tfrac{1}{2}(\sqrt{3} + i)L][1 + \tfrac{1}{2}(\sqrt{3} - i)L] \\
&\times [1 - \tfrac{1}{2}(\sqrt{3} + i)L][1 - \tfrac{1}{2}(\sqrt{3} - i)L] \\
&\times [1 + \tfrac{1}{2}(\sqrt{3} + i)L][1 - \tfrac{1}{2}(\sqrt{3} - i)L] \\
&\times [1 - \tfrac{1}{2}(\sqrt{3} + i)L][1 + \tfrac{1}{2}(\sqrt{3} - i)L].
\end{aligned}$$

Moreover, an AR(p) model with $p \geq 12$ can be rearranged as

$$
\begin{aligned}
\Delta_{12} y_t = {}& \pi_1 z_{1,t-1} + \pi_2 z_{2,t-1} + \pi_3 z_{3,t-1} + \pi_4 z_{3,t-2} \\
& + \pi_5 z_{4,t-1} + \pi_6 z_{4,t-2} + \pi_7 z_{5,t-1} + \pi_8 z_{5,t-2} \\
& + \pi_9 z_{6,t-1} + \pi_{10} z_{6,t-2} + \pi_{11} z_{7,t-1} + \pi_{12} z_{7,t-2} \\
& + \sum_{j=1}^{p-12} \alpha_j^* \Delta_{12} y_{t-j} + u_t,
\end{aligned}
\tag{2.19}
$$

where

$$
\begin{aligned}
z_{1,t} &= (1 + L)(1 + L^2)(1 + L^4 + L^8) y_t \\
z_{2,t} &= -(1 - L)(1 + L^2)(1 + L^4 + L^8) y_t \\
z_{3,t} &= -(1 - L^2)(1 + L^4 + L^8) y_t \\
z_{4,t} &= -(1 - L^4)(1 - \sqrt{3}L + L^2)(1 + L^4 + L^8) y_t \\
z_{5,t} &= -(1 - L^4)(1 + \sqrt{3}L + L^2)(1 + L^4 + L^8) y_t \\
z_{6,t} &= -(1 - L^4)(1 - L^2 + L^4)(1 - L + L^2) y_t \\
z_{7,t} &= -(1 - L^4)(1 - L^2 + L^4)(1 + L + L^2) y_t.
\end{aligned}
$$

The process y_t has a regular (zero frequency) unit root if $\pi_1 = 0$, and it has seasonal unit roots if any one of the other π_is ($i = 2, \ldots, 12$) is zero. For the conjugate complex roots, $\pi_i = \pi_{i+1} = 0$ ($i = 3, 5, 7, 9, 11$) is required. The corresponding statistical hypotheses can again be checked by "t-" and "F-statistics," critical values for which are given in Franses & Hobijn (1997). If all the π_is ($i = 1, \ldots, 12$) are zero, then a stationary model for the monthly seasonal differences of the series is suitable. As in the case of quarterly series, it is also possible to include deterministic terms in the model (2.19). Again it is then necessary to use appropriately modified critical values.

Tests for seasonal unit roots have also been discussed by other authors. Examples are found in Dickey, Hasza & Fuller (1984); Canova & Hansen (1995); Beaulieu & Miron (1993); and Maddala & Kim (1998).

2.8 Forecasting Univariate Time Series

If a suitable model for the DGP of a given time series has been found, it can be used for forecasting the future development of the variable under consideration. AR processes are particularly easy to use for this purpose. Neglecting deterministic terms and assuming an AR(p) DGP, $y_t = \alpha_1 y_{t-1} + \cdots + \alpha_p y_{t-p} + u_t$, where the u_ts are generated by an independent rather than just uncorrelated white noise process, we find that the optimal (minimum MSE) 1-step forecast in period T is the conditional expectation

$$
y_{T+1|T} = \mathsf{E}(y_{T+1} | y_T, y_{T-1}, \ldots) = \alpha_1 y_T + \cdots + \alpha_p y_{T+1-p}.
\tag{2.20}
$$

Forecasts for larger horizons $h > 1$ may be obtained recursively as

$$
y_{T+h|T} = \alpha_1 y_{T+h-1|T} + \cdots + \alpha_p y_{T+h-p|T},
\tag{2.21}
$$

where $y_{T+j|T} = y_{T+j}$ for $j \leq 0$. The corresponding forecast errors are

$$
\begin{aligned}
y_{T+1} - y_{T+1|T} &= u_{T+1}, \\
y_{T+2} - y_{T+2|T} &= u_{T+2} + \phi_1 u_{T+1}, \\
&\vdots \\
y_{T+h} - y_{T+h|T} &= u_{T+h} + \phi_1 u_{T+h-1} + \cdots + \phi_{h-1} u_{T+1},
\end{aligned}
\tag{2.22}
$$

where it is easy to see by successive substitution that the ϕ_js are just the coefficients of the MA representation of the process if the process is stationary and, hence, the MA representation exists. Consequently, the ϕ_j can be computed recursively as

$$
\phi_s = \sum_{j=1}^{s} \phi_{s-j} \alpha_j, \quad s = 1, 2, \ldots
\tag{2.23}
$$

with $\phi_0 = 1$ and $\alpha_j = 0$ for $j > p$ (see Section 2.3.1). Hence, u_t is the 1-step forecast error in period $t - 1$ and the forecasts are unbiased, that is, the forecast errors have expectation 0. As mentioned earlier, these are the minimum MSE forecasts. The MSE of an h-step forecast is

$$
\sigma_y^2(h) = \mathsf{E}\{(y_{T+h} - y_{T+h|T})^2\} = \sigma_u^2 \sum_{j=0}^{h-1} \phi_j^2.
\tag{2.24}
$$

For any other h-step forecast with MSE $\bar{\sigma}_y^2(h)$, say, the difference $\bar{\sigma}_y^2(h) - \sigma_y^2(h)$ is nonnegative.

This result relies on the assumption that u_t is independent white noise, that is, u_t and u_s are independent for $s \neq t$. If u_t is uncorrelated white noise and not independent over time, the forecasts obtained recursively as

$$
y_T(h) = \alpha_1 y_T(h-1) + \cdots + \alpha_p y_T(h-p), \quad h = 1, 2, \ldots
\tag{2.25}
$$

with $y_T(j) = y_{T+j}$ for $j \leq 0$ are best *linear* forecasts [see Lütkepohl (1991, Sec. 2.2.2) for an example]. It may be worth pointing out that the forecast MSEs for I(0) variables are bounded by the unconditional variance σ_y^2 of y_t.

If the process y_t is Gaussian, that is, $u_t \sim \text{iid } N(0, \sigma_u^2)$, the forecast errors are also normal. This result may be used to set up forecast intervals of the form

$$
[y_{T+h|T} - c_{1-\gamma/2} \sigma_y(h), \ y_{T+h|T} + c_{1-\gamma/2} \sigma_y(h)],
\tag{2.26}
$$

where $c_{1-\gamma/2}$ is the $(1 - \frac{\gamma}{2})100$ percentage point of the standard normal distribution and $\sigma_y(h)$ denotes the square root of $\sigma_y^2(h)$, that is, $\sigma_y(h)$ is the standard deviation of the h-step forecast error of y_t.

Although here we have discussed the forecasts for stationary processes, the same formulas apply if y_t is I(d) with $d > 0$. Also, the ϕ_js may be computed as in (2.23). In the nonstationary case, the ϕ_js are not coefficients of an MA representation, of course, and they will not converge to zero for $j \to \infty$. As a consequence, the forecast MSEs will not converge for $h \to \infty$ but will be unbounded. Hence, the length of the forecast intervals will also be unbounded as $h \to \infty$.

For I(d) variables with $d > 0$ there is also another possibility to compute the forecasts. Suppose y_t is I(1) so that Δy_t is stationary. Then we can utilize the fact that $y_{T+h} = y_T + \Delta y_{T+1} + \cdots + \Delta y_{T+h}$. Thus, to forecast y_{T+h} in period T, we just need to get forecasts of the stationary variables Δy_{T+j} ($j = 1, \ldots, h$) and add these forecasts to y_T to get the forecast of y_{T+h}. This forecast is identical to the one obtained directly from the levels AR(p) model.

If the DGP of a variable of interest is a mixed ARMA process with infinite AR representation, this representation can in principle be used for forecasting. For practical purposes it has to be truncated at some finite lag length.

In practice we do not know the DGP exactly but have to base the forecasts on an estimated approximation of the DGP. In other words, furnishing estimated quantities with a hat, we get instead of (2.21),

$$\hat{y}_{T+h|T} = \hat{\alpha}_1 \hat{y}_{T+h-1|T} + \cdots + \hat{\alpha}_p \hat{y}_{T+h-p|T}, \tag{2.27}$$

where, of course, $\hat{y}_{T+j|T} = y_{T+j}$ for $j \leq 0$. The corresponding forecast error is

$$
\begin{aligned}
y_{T+h} - \hat{y}_{T+h|T} &= [y_{T+h} - y_{T+h|T}] + [y_{T+h|T} - \hat{y}_{T+h|T}] \\
&= \sum_{j=0}^{h-1} \phi_j u_{T+h-j} + [y_{T+h|T} - \hat{y}_{T+h|T}].
\end{aligned} \tag{2.28}
$$

At the forecast origin T, the first term on the right-hand side involves future residuals only, whereas the second term involves present and past variables only, provided only past variables have been used for estimation. Consequently, if u_t is independent white noise, the two terms are independent. Moreover, under standard assumptions, the difference $y_{T+h|T} - \hat{y}_{T+h|T}$ is small in probability as the sample size used for estimation gets large. Hence, the forecast error variance is

$$\sigma_{\hat{y}}^2(h) = \mathsf{E}\{[y_{T+h} - \hat{y}_{T+h|T}]^2\} = \sigma_y^2(h) + o(1), \tag{2.29}$$

where $o(1)$ denotes a term that approaches zero as the sample size tends to infinity. Thus, for large samples the estimation uncertainty may be ignored in evaluating the forecast precision and setting up forecast intervals. In small samples, including a correction term is preferable, however. In this case, the precision of the forecasts will depend on the precision of the estimators. Hence, if precise forecasts are desired, it is a good strategy to look for precise parameter estimators. Further details may be found in Lütkepohl (1991, Chapter 3).

Including deterministic terms in the process used for forecasting is straightforward. The appropriate value of the deterministic term is simply added to each forecast.

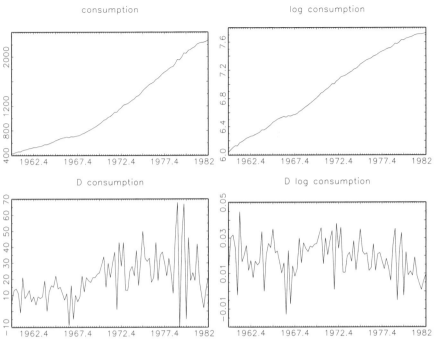

Figure 2.19. German consumption time series, $1960Q1$–$1982Q4$, and transformations of the series.

2.9 Examples

To illustrate univariate time series analysis, we consider two macroeconomic time series. The first one is a quarterly German consumption series, and the second is a Polish productivity series again with quarterly observation frequency. The analyses are discussed in detail in the next two sections.

2.9.1 German Consumption

The first series to be analyzed for illustrative purposes consists of seasonally adjusted, quarterly German consumption data for the period $1960Q1 - 1982Q4$. The series is the consumption series given in Table E.1 of Lütkepohl (1991). The time series length is $T = 92$. It is plotted together with its logs in Figure 2.19. The first differences of both series are also plotted in Figure 2.19. They reveal that constructing a model for the logs is likely to be advantageous because the changes in the log series display a more stable variance than the changes in the original series.

Otherwise, the two series have similar characteristics. In Figure 2.20 we also show the autocorrelations, partial autocorrelations, and log spectral densities

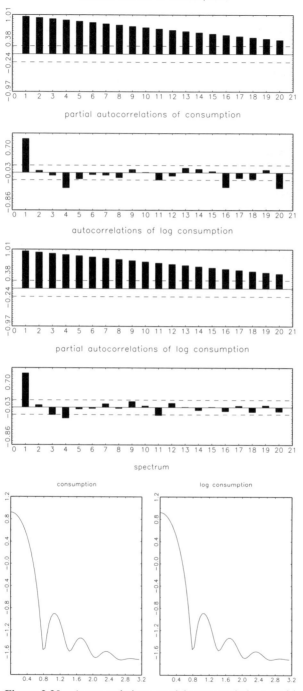

Figure 2.20. Autocorrelations, partial autocorrelations, and log spectral densities of German consumption time series.

Table 2.11. *Unit root tests for consumption time series*

Variable	Test	Deterministic terms	Lags	Test value	5% critical value
Δ log consumption	ADF	c	2	-3.13	-2.86
	KPSS	c	2	0.393	0.463
log consumption	ADF	c, t	3	-1.16	-3.41
	KPSS	c, t	3	0.232	0.146

Note: Critical values from Davidson & Mackinnon (1993, Table 20.1) and Kwiatkowski et al. (1992).

of the two series. These quantities look quite similar. The slow decay of the autocorrelations indicates that both series may have a unit root. A closer look at the partial autocorrelations reveals that there may be a problem with the seasonal adjustment of the series because, in particular, for the raw data these quantities at some seasonal lags (4, 16, 20) are larger in absolute value than the neighboring partial autocorrelations. The possible seasonal adjustment problem becomes even more apparent in the estimated spectral densities in Figure 2.20. Notice that they are plotted with a log scale. The estimates are obtained with a Bartlett window and a window size of $M_T = 10$. There are dips at the quarterly seasonal frequencies ($2\pi/4 = 1.57$ and $2 \times 2\pi/4 = \pi$). In fact, there are even dips at fractions of these frequencies at $2\pi/8$ and so forth. Hence, the seasonal adjustment procedure may have overadjusted a bit. Although this may not be a dramatic problem for the present series, it may be useful to keep this possible over adjustment in mind because it can be important for the lags to be included in the model for the DGP and for the proper interpretation of some of the model-checking statistics later in the analysis. In the following we will focus on the log consumption series and call it y_t because of the more stable variance.

Given that the log consumption series has a trending behavior and the auto-correlations indicate the possibility of a unit root, we first analyze that feature in more detail by applying unit root tests. In Table 2.11, we present the results of ADF and KPSS tests. Because we do not expect the series to have more than one unit root, the tests are first applied to Δy_t. The lag order used in the ADF test for the lagged differences is 2, as suggested by the usual model selection criteria (AIC, HQ, SC), and only a constant is included as a deterministic term. This is what is obtained from the levels model with a linear time trend when taking first differences. The test value is significant at the 5% level; hence, a unit root in the first differences is rejected at this level. The result of the KPSS test is in line with the ADF result. At the 5% level it cannot reject stationarity.

The ADF test of the levels series is based on a model with a constant and a time trend because a linear deterministic trend cannot be excluded a priori given the shape of the series plot in Figure 2.19. The number of lagged differences is 3. This value is suggested by the model for Δy_t, and it is also the choice of the model selection criteria when a maximum of $p_{max} = 14$ is allowed for. Recall that three lagged differences imply an AR(4) model when rewriting the ADF test equation in levels form. Thus, the result is consistent with the observation of a possible problem at the seasonal lags owing to the seasonal adjustment of the series.

The conclusion from the ADF test is quite clear: At the 5% level the unit root cannot be rejected. The corresponding KPSS test, again with a constant and a time trend, confirms the result. It clearly rejects stationarity at the 5% level. This outcome results with a lag truncation parameter of three, but a rejection of stationarity is also obtained with other lag orders. Overall, the test results support one unit root in the log consumption series; thus, specifying a stationary model for the first differences seems appropriate.

Therefore we have fitted an AR(3) model for Δy_t as our first guess. We have not considered mixed ARMA models because a simple low-order AR model appears to approximate the DGP well. Of course, it is still possible to bring in MA terms at a later stage if the subsequent analysis reveals that this may be advantageous. In line with the unit root test results, all model selection criteria suggest the order $p = 3$, and including a constant term is plausible on the basis of the plot in Figure 2.19. The resulting estimated model with t-values in parentheses is

$$\Delta y_t = 0.0095 - 0.11 \, \Delta y_{t-1} + 0.26 \, \Delta y_{t-2} + 0.32 \, \Delta y_{t-3} + \hat{u}_t,$$
$$\quad\quad (2.8) \quad\quad (-1.1) \quad\quad\quad (2.6) \quad\quad\quad (3.0)$$

$$\hat{\sigma}_u^2 = 1.058 \times 10^{-4}.$$

Owing to the presample values used up in differencing and estimating the foregoing model of order 3, the sample used in the OLS estimation runs from $1961Q1$ to $1982Q4$, and thus we have a sample size of $T = 88$. The reverse characteristic roots of the AR polynomial have moduli 1.30 and 1.56; therefore, the estimated AR operator clearly represents a stable, stationary model. Because the t-value of the lag-one coefficient is substantially smaller than 2 in absolute value, one could consider replacing it by zero in a final version of the model.

Before trying that modification we have confronted the present model with several specification tests. The standardized residuals of the model and the residual autocorrelations are plotted in Figure 2.21. The former quantities indicate no specific problems with outliers (unusually large or small values) or changing variability over time. The largest standardized residual is less than 3 in absolute value (see the value associated with $1966Q4$). The residual autocorrelations are plotted with estimated "exact" asymptotic 95% confidence intervals around zero, which take into account the fact that these are estimation residuals from an AR model and not observed realizations of a white noise process. Therefore, the confidence intervals are substantially smaller than the usual $\pm 2/\sqrt{T}$ at low lags. Only at higher lags do they approach the usual $\pm 2/\sqrt{T}$ bounds. In Figure 2.21, all but the first three intervals are close to these bounds. Obviously, none of the residual autocorrelations reach outside the estimated 95% confidence intervals around zero. Thus, a 5% level test of the null hypothesis that they are

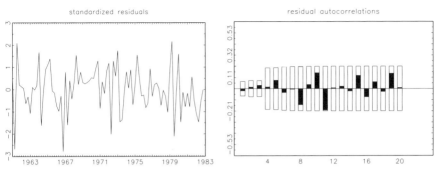

Figure 2.21. Standardized residuals and residual autocorrelations of German consumption time series; sample period: $1961Q1$–$1982Q4$, $T = 88$.

individually zero does not reject the null hypothesis of zero residual correlation. Hence, they provide no reason for concern about the adequacy of the model.

The results of a range of specification tests are shown in Table 2.12. None of the diagnostic tests indicates a specification problem. All p-values are clearly in excess of 10%. We have also done some stability analysis for the model and did not find reason for concern about its adequacy. The reader is encouraged to check recursive estimates, Chow tests, and CUSUMs to investigate the stability of the model.

Given this state of affairs, we have also estimated a restricted AR(3) model with the first lag excluded (the associated AR coefficient restricted to zero). The result is

$$\Delta y_t = \underset{(2.6)}{0.0079} + \underset{(2.7)}{0.26}\, \Delta y_{t-2} + \underset{(2.9)}{0.29}\, \Delta y_{t-3} + \hat{u}_t,$$

$$\hat{\sigma}_u^2 = 1.02 \times 10^{-4}.$$

Table 2.12. *Diagnostics for AR(3) model of Δ log consumption series*

Tests for residual autocorrelation								
Test	Q_{16}	Q_{16}^*	Q_{24}	Q_{24}^*	LM_2	FLM_2	LM_6	FLM_6
Test statistic	10.82	12.31	21.03	25.85	1.09	0.52	9.60	1.59
Appr. distribution	$\chi^2(13)$	$\chi^2(13)$	$\chi^2(21)$	$\chi^2(21)$	$\chi^2(2)$	$F(2,82)$	$\chi^2(6)$	$F(6,78)$
p-value	0.63	0.50	0.46	0.21	0.60	0.60	0.14	0.16

Other diagnostics		
Test	LJB	$ARCH_{LM}(1)$	$ARCH_{LM}(4)$
Test statistic	1.26	1.02	1.51
Appr. distribution	$\chi^2(2)$	$\chi^2(1)$	$\chi^2(4)$
p-value	0.53	0.31	0.83

Obviously, the estimated values of the other parameters have not changed much. Also the diagnostics do not give reason for concern about the model. We do not show them to save space but encourage the reader to check our assessment. It may be worth noting that the moduli of the reverse characteristic roots of the present AR polynomial are 1.26 and 1.65. Thus, they are clearly in the stable region as in the unrestricted AR(3) model.

Just to illustrate forecasting, we have also computed predictions from the estimated final model and show them with 95% forecast intervals in Figure 2.22. In the first panel, forecasts of Δy_t are depicted. As expected in a stable model, the forecasts approach the mean of the series rapidly with growing forecast horizon. Also, the width of the forecast intervals reaches a maximum quickly. The intervals reflect the overall variability in the series. Notice that these forecast intervals do not take into account the estimation uncertainty in the parameter estimates. The second panel in Figure 2.22 shows forecasts of the undifferenced series y_t, that is, these are forecasts for the trending log consumption series. Now the forecast intervals grow with increasing forecast horizon. They are in fact unbounded when the forecast horizon goes to infinity.

Forecasts can also be used to check the goodness of a model by fitting the model to a subsample and then comparing the forecasts with the actually observed values. This kind of model check is shown in the third panel of Figure 2.22. The restricted AR(3) model is fitted to data up to 1979Q4, and thus three years of data (twelve observations) at the end of the series are not used in the estimation. Forecasts are then computed for these three years, and it turns out that all actually observed values fall into the 95% forecast intervals. Thus, this check also does not raise doubts about the adequacy of the model.

2.9.2 Polish Productivity

The second example series consists of the logarithms of a seasonally unadjusted quarterly Polish productivity series for the period 1970Q1–1998Q4. Thus, we have $T = 116$ observations. The series and its first differences are plotted in Figure 2.23. The logarithms are chosen on the basis of arguments similar to those of the previous example to obtain a more stable variance. Because we have discussed this issue in the preceding example, we do not repeat it here but start from the logs.[1] Modeling the series may appear to be more challenging than the previous one because there seem to be major shifts in the series. For example, the introduction of marshal law in Poland in 1981 and the transition from a socialist to a market economy in 1989 seem to have had major impacts on the series. Although the first event is not apparent anymore in the differences, the second one leaves a clear trace in the latter series.

---

[1] For more details on the construction of the data and their sources see Lütkepohl, Saikkonen & Trenkler (2001b), where the series has been used in a larger model.

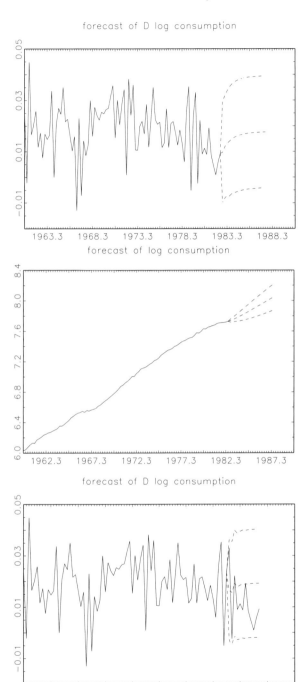

Figure 2.22. Forecasts of German consumption time series.

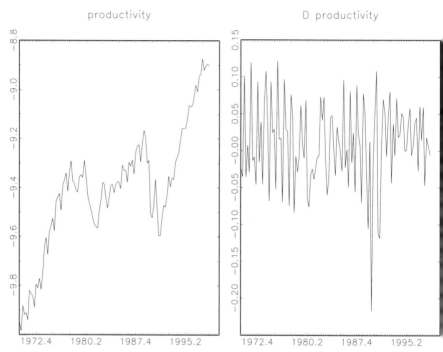

Figure 2.23. Polish productivity series, $1970Q2–1998Q4$, with first differences.

Although the series is not seasonally adjusted, it does not have a very clear seasonal pattern. Some seasonality is observable in parts of the series, however. Because this may be regarded as a sign of moving seasonality and, hence, possible seasonal unit roots, we have explored that possibility without actually expecting to find it. To avoid the strong shift in the series we have performed seasonal unit root tests on the data up to the end of 1989 only. Reducing the sample size may result in reduced power of the tests and should therefore normally be avoided. On the other hand, having a shift in the series without taking special care of it may also result in a loss of power. Therefore we use the reduced sample size in the hope that it is sufficient to reject seasonal unit roots. This rejection is indeed clearly seen in Table 2.13. All unit roots except the zero frequency one are rejected in models with time trends and with and without seasonal dummy variables. The number of lagged differences used in these tests is the one suggested by the SC and HQ criteria if a maximum lag order of 10 and no seasonal dummies are considered. With seasonal dummies, all criteria agree that no lagged differences are necessary. Even with the possibly slightly overspecified model, with seasonal dummies the seasonal unit roots are clearly rejected at the 1% level. In conclusion, although the series is not seasonally adjusted, there does not appear to be a need to worry about seasonal unit roots.

Table 2.13. *Tests for seasonal unit roots in Polish productivity, sample period 1970Q1–1989Q4*

Deterministic terms	No. of lags	H_0	Test	Test statistic	5% level critical value
constant	1	$\pi_1 = 0$	$t_{\hat{\pi}_1}$	−2.21	−3.40
trend		$\pi_2 = 0$	$t_{\hat{\pi}_2}$	−2.15	−1.93
		$\pi_3 = \pi_4 = 0$	F_{34}	4.64	3.05
		$\pi_2 = \pi_3 = \pi_4 = 0$	F_{234}	4.68	2.74
		$\pi_1 = \pi_2 = \pi_3 = \pi_4 = 0$	F_{1234}	5.31	4.19
constant	1	$\pi_1 = 0$	$t_{\hat{\pi}_1}$	−2.00	−3.39
trend		$\pi_2 = 0$	$t_{\hat{\pi}_2}$	−3.15	−2.82
seasonals		$\pi_3 = \pi_4 = 0$	F_{34}	12.79	6.55
		$\pi_2 = \pi_3 = \pi_4 = 0$	F_{234}	11.80	5.93
		$\pi_1 = \pi_2 = \pi_3 = \pi_4 = 0$	F_{1234}	11.07	6.31

Note: Critical values from Franses & Hobijn (1997).

That the zero-frequency unit root cannot be rejected may, of course, be due to reduced power of the test, which in turn may be caused by reducing the sample period and overspecifying the lag order. For a more detailed analysis of this issue we use the full sample and include a shift dummy to take care of the shift in the late 1980s or early 1990s. Because it is not fully clear where the shift actually occurred, we use the search procedure mentioned in Section 2.7.3 based on a model with a time trend and 4 lagged differences. Notice that the official shift date may not correspond to the actual shift date because economic agents may adjust their operations on the basis of knowing the official shift date in advance or possibly with some delay owing to adjustment costs. The estimated shift date is 1990Q1. Test results with this shift date and different shift functions are given in Table 2.14. The lag order is on the one hand suggested by the quarterly observation period of the series. On the other hand, the HQ and SC criteria also

Table 2.14. *Unit root tests in the presence of a structural shift in 1990Q1 for Polish productivity*

Variable	Deterministics	Shift function	Lag order	Test statistic	Critical values 10%	5%	1%
Δ productivity	constant	impulse dummy	3	−4.45	−2.58	−2.88	−3.48
productivity	constant, trend	shift dummy exponential	4	−1.77 −1.75	−2.76	−3.03	−3.55

Note: Critical values from Lanne et al. (2002).

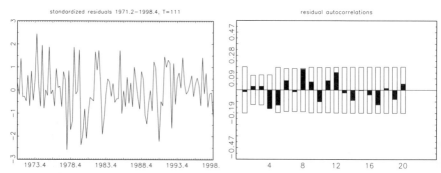

Figure 2.24. Standardized residuals and residual autocorrelations of restricted AR(4) model for Polish productivity.

favor this order when a maximum of 10 is considered. It turns out that a simple shift dummy may be sufficient for this series to capture the shift because the shift estimated with the exponential shift function is also almost an abrupt shift in period $1990Q1$. Therefore, it is not surprising that the tests with both types of shift functions reach the same conclusion. They cannot reject the unit root hypothesis.

In Table 2.14 we also give the test result for the differenced series. In this case only an impulse dummy is included for $1990Q1$ because a shift in the mean of the original series is converted to an impulse in the differenced series. Also the trend disappears as usual. In this case the unit root is clearly rejected even at the 1% level. Hence, we continue the analysis with the first differences of the series (denoted by Δy_t) and include an impulse dummy as a deterministic term in addition to a constant.

In line with the unit root analysis we consider an AR(4) model as our first choice. Estimating the model, we found that the first lag had a coefficient with a very small t-value. Therefore, we considered the following restricted AR(4) model for our series (t-values in parentheses):

$$\Delta y_t = \underset{(2.6)}{0.011} - \underset{(-6.2)}{0.27} I90Q1_t - \underset{(-2.0)}{0.15} \Delta y_{t-2} - \underset{(-3.0)}{0.22} \Delta y_{t-3}$$

$$+ \underset{(5.9)}{0.42} \Delta y_{t-4} + \hat{u}_t, \quad \hat{\sigma}_u^2 = 0.0018.$$

All roots of the AR polynomial are clearly outside the unit circle, and thus the model represents a stable, stationary process. This fairly simple model turned out to be quite satisfactory.

The standardized residuals and residual autocorrelations are depicted in Figure 2.24. With very few exceptions all standardized residuals are between ± 2. There are no outliers with absolute value substantially larger than 2, and

Table 2.15. *Diagnostics for restricted AR(4) model of* Δ *productivity*

Tests for residual autocorrelation								
Test	Q_{16}	Q^*_{16}	Q_{24}	Q^*_{24}	LM_2	FLM_2	LM_6	FLM_6
Test statistic	13.99	15.11	20.00	22.47	0.26	0.89	11.10	1.83
Appr. distr.	$\chi^2(13)$	$\chi^2(13)$	$\chi^2(21)$	$\chi^2(21)$	$\chi^2(2)$	$F(2, 103)$	$\chi^2(6)$	$F(6, 99)$
p-value	0.37	0.30	0.52	0.37	0.88	0.89	0.09	0.10

Other diagnostics			
Test		LJB	$ARCH_{LM}(1)$	$ARCH_{LM}(4)$
Test statistic		0.14	0.22	6.29
Appr. distribution		$\chi^2(2)$	$\chi^2(1)$	$\chi^2(4)$
p-value		0.93	0.64	0.18

in fact there is no indication that the residuals are not coming from a normal distribution.

The residual autocorrelations with estimated "exact" asymptotic 95% confidence intervals around zero also do not give rise to concern about remaining residual autocorrelation. The only autocorrelation coefficient reaching slightly outside the confidence interval is the one associated with lag 4. Of course, one in twenty quantities would be expected to reach outside a 95% confidence interval even if they had the assumed distribution. In this case it is suspicious that the relatively large autocorrelation coefficient is associated with the seasonal lag. The model is maintained, however, because the corresponding autocorrelation coefficient does not reach much outside the interval, and the fourth lag is included in the model.

Some more diagnostic statistics are provided in Table 2.15. They are all unsuspicious. Given the autocorrelation coefficient at lag four, the p-value of

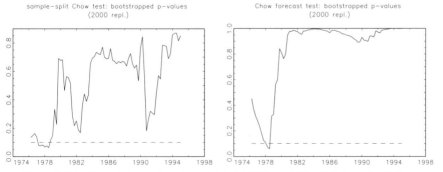

Figure 2.25. Chow test p-values for restricted AR(4) model for Polish productivity.

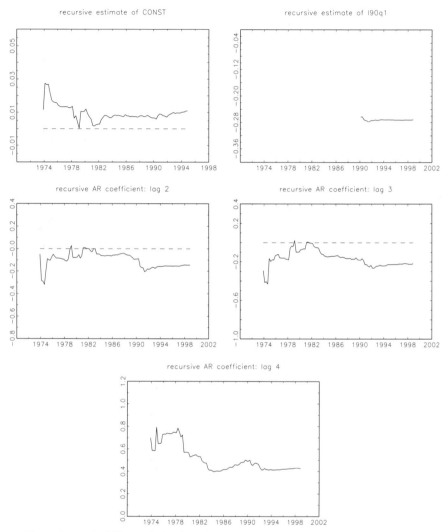

Figure 2.26. Stability analysis of restricted AR(4) model for Polish productivity.

0.09 of the LM_6 test for autocorrelation is not surprising. However, a stability analysis reveals that the model may not be stable throughout the full estimation period (see Figures 2.25 and 2.26). In particular, the Chow tests indicate instability at the beginning of the sample. The recursive parameter estimates have a different level in the earlier part of the sample than at the end. They stabilize only in the latter part of the sample period. Thus, a simple impulse dummy may not capture the full change in the DGP that has occurred during the sample

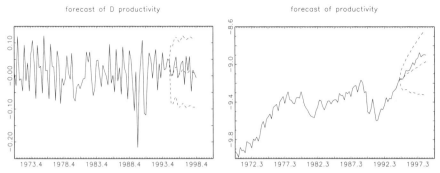

Figure 2.27. Forecasts of restricted AR(4) model for Polish productivity.

period. It may be worth investigating the situation further, with, for example, a smooth transition regression analysis (see Chapter 6).

We have also fitted the model to a truncated sample up to $1994Q4$, and we have used this model for forecasting the last four years of our original sample period. The results are presented in Figure 2.27. Even without taking into account the sampling variability in the parameter estimates, we find that all observed values are well inside the 95% forecast intervals. Of course, if all observed differences fall into their respective forecast intervals, the same has to be true for the undifferenced observations. Just for illustrative purposes, we also show them in Figure 2.27. Thus, despite the initial instability in the recursive parameter estimates, the model has some forecasting potential.

2.10 Where to Go from Here

In this chapter a range of models and techniques for analyzing single time series have been presented. Although these tools will often give useful insights into the generation mechanism of a series under consideration, they are sometimes insufficient to capture specific features of a DGP. In that case other tools have to be used. Some of them are presented in later chapters. For example, modeling second-order moments is discussed in Chapter 5, and different forms of non-linearities are considered in Chapters 6 and 7. These models may be considered if no satisfactory linear model is found using the tools of the present chapter.

If the analyst has explored the individual properties of a set of time series, it is also possible to go on and analyze them together in a system of series. Suitable multivariate models are discussed in the next two chapters.

3 Vector Autoregressive and Vector Error Correction Models

Helmut Lütkepohl

3.1 Introduction

The first step in constructing a model for a specific purpose or for a particular sector of an economy is to decide on the variables to be included in the analysis. At this stage it is usually important to take into account what economic theory has to say about the relations between the variables of interest. Suppose we want to analyze the transmission mechanism of monetary policy. An important relation in that context is the money demand function, which describes the link between the real and the monetary sector of the economy. In this relationship a money stock variable depends on the transactions volume and opportunity costs for holding money. As an example we consider German M3 as the money stock variable, GNP as a proxy for the transactions volume, a long-term interest rate R as an opportunity cost variable, and the inflation rate $Dp = \Delta p$, where p denotes the log of the GNP deflator. The latter variable may be regarded as a proxy for expected inflation, which may also be considered an opportunity cost variable. Because the quantity theory suggests a log linear relation, we focus on the variables $m = \log$ M3 and $gnp = \log$ GNP. Seasonally unadjusted quarterly series for the period 1972–98 are plotted in Figure 3.1. Of course, many more variables are related to the presently considered ones and, hence, could be included in a model for the monetary sector of the economy. However, increasing the number of variables and equations does not generally lead to a better model because doing so makes it more difficult to capture the dynamic, intertemporal relations between them. In fact, in some forecast comparisons univariate time series models were found to be superior to large-scale econometric models. One explanation for the failure of the larger models is their insufficient representation of the dynamic interactions in a system of variables.

Vector autoregressive (VAR) processes are a suitable model class for describing the data generation process (DGP) of a small or moderate set of time series variables. In these models all variables are often treated as being a priori endogenous, and allowance is made for rich dynamics. Restrictions are usually

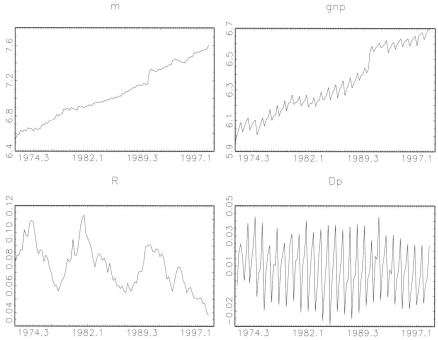

Figure 3.1. Seasonally unadjusted, quarterly German log real M3 (m), log real GNP (gnp), long-term bond rate (R), and inflation rate (Dp), 1972Q1–1998Q4.
[Data source: see Lütkepohl & Wolters (2003); see also Section 3.8 for more information on the data.]

imposed with statistical techniques instead of prior beliefs based on uncertain theoretical considerations.

From the example system shown in Figure 3.1, it is clear that special features such as trends, seasonality, and structural shifts are sometimes present in economic time series and have to be taken into account in modeling their DGP. In particular, trends have attracted considerable attention, as we have seen in Chapter 2. A situation of special interest arises if several variables are driven by a common stochastic trend, as may occur in some of the example series. In that case they have a particularly strong link that may also be of interest from an economic point of view. Following Granger (1981) and Engle & Granger (1987), variables are called *cointegrated* if they have a common stochastic trend. If cointegrating relations are present in a system of variables, the VAR form is not the most convenient model setup. In that case it is useful to consider specific parameterizations that support the analysis of the cointegration structure. The resulting models are known as *vector error correction models* (VECMs) or *vector equilibrium correction models*.

VAR models and VECMs will be discussed in this chapter. Estimation and specification issues related to these models will be considered in Sections 3.3 and 3.4, respectively. Model checking is discussed in Section 3.5, and forecasting and causality analysis are presented in Sections 3.6 and 3.7, respectively. Extensions are considered in Section 3.9. Illustrative examples are discussed throughout the chapter based on the example series in Figure 3.1. A more detailed analysis of a subset of the variables is considered in Section 3.8. Once a statistically satisfactory model for the DGP of a set of time series has been constructed, an analysis of the dynamic interactions is often of interest. Some tools available for that purpose will be introduced in the next chapter under the heading of structural modeling.

Nowadays several books are available that treat modern developments in VAR modeling and dynamic econometric analysis more generally [e.g., Lütkepohl (1991); Banerjee, Dolado, Galbraith & Hendry (1993); Hamilton (1994); Hendry (1995); Johansen (1995a); Hatanaka (1996)]. Surveys of vector autoregressive modeling include Watson (1994), Lütkepohl & Breitung (1997), and Lütkepohl (2001).

3.2 VARs and VECMs

In this section, we first introduce the basic vector autoregressive and error correction models, neglecting deterministic terms and exogenous variables. How to account for such terms will be discussed afterwards.

3.2.1 The Models

For a set of K time series variables $y_t = (y_{1t}, \ldots, y_{Kt})'$, a VAR model captures their dynamic interactions. The basic model of order p (VAR(p)) has the form

$$y_t = A_1 y_{t-1} + \cdots + A_p y_{t-p} + u_t, \tag{3.1}$$

where the A_i's are ($K \times K$) coefficient matrices and $u_t = (u_{1t}, \ldots, u_{Kt})'$ is an unobservable error term. It is usually assumed to be a zero-mean independent white noise process with time-invariant, positive definite covariance matrix $E(u_t u_t') = \Sigma_u$. In other words, the u_t's are independent stochastic vectors with $u_t \sim (0, \Sigma_u)$.

The process is *stable* if

$$\det(I_K - A_1 z - \cdots - A_p z^p) \neq 0 \text{ for } |z| \leq 1, \tag{3.2}$$

that is, the polynomial defined by the determinant of the autoregressive operator has no roots in and on the complex unit circle. On the assumption that the process has been initiated in the infinite past ($t = 0, \pm 1, \pm 2, \ldots$), it generates stationary time series that have time-invariant means, variances, and covariance structure. If the polynomial in (3.2) has a unit root (i.e., the determinant is zero for $z = 1$), then some or all of the variables are integrated. For convenience we assume for the moment that they are at most I(1). If the variables have a common stochastic trend, it is possible there are linear combinations of them that are I(0). In that case they are *cointegrated*. In other words, a set of I(1) variables is called cointegrated if a linear combination exists that is I(0). Occasionally it is convenient to consider systems with both I(1) and I(0) variables. Thereby the concept of cointegration is extended by calling any linear combination that is I(0) a cointegration relation, although this terminology is not in the spirit of the original definition because it can happen that a linear combination of I(0) variables is called a cointegration relation.

Although the model (3.1) is general enough to accommodate variables with stochastic trends, it is not the most suitable type of model if interest centers on the cointegration relations because they do not appear explicitly. The VECM form

$$\Delta y_t = \Pi y_{t-1} + \Gamma_1 \Delta y_{t-1} + \cdots + \Gamma_{p-1} \Delta y_{t-p+1} + u_t \qquad (3.3)$$

is a more convenient model setup for cointegration analysis. Here $\Pi = -(I_K - A_1 - \cdots - A_p)$ and $\Gamma_i = -(A_{i+1} + \cdots + A_p)$ for $i = 1, \ldots, p - 1$. The VECM is obtained from the levels VAR form (3.1) by subtracting y_{t-1} from both sides and rearranging terms. Because Δy_t does not contain stochastic trends by our assumption that all variables can be at most I(1), the term Πy_{t-1} is the only one that includes I(1) variables. Hence, Πy_{t-1} must also be I(0). Thus, it contains the cointegrating relations. The Γ_js ($j = 1, \ldots, p - 1$) are often referred to as the *short-run* or *short-term parameters*, and Πy_{t-1} is sometimes called the *long-run* or *long-term* part. The model in (3.3) will be abbreviated as VECM($p - 1$). To distinguish the VECM from the VAR model, we sometimes call the latter the levels version. Of course, it is also possible to determine the A_j levels parameter matrices from the coefficients of the VECM. More precisely, $A_1 = \Gamma_1 + \Pi + I_K$, $A_i = \Gamma_i - \Gamma_{i-1}$ for $i = 2, \ldots, p - 1$, and $A_p = -\Gamma_{p-1}$.

If the VAR(p) process has unit roots, that is, $\det(I_K - A_1 z - \cdots - A_p z^p) = 0$ for $z = 1$, the matrix $\Pi = -(I_K - A_1 - \cdots - A_p)$ is singular. Suppose rk(Π) $= r$. Then Π can be written as a product of ($K \times r$) matrices α and β with rk(α) $=$ rk(β) $= r$ as follows: $\Pi = \alpha\beta'$. Premultiplying an I(0) vector by some matrix results again in an I(0) process. Thus, $\beta' y_{t-1}$ is I(0) because it can be obtained by premultiplying $\Pi y_{t-1} = \alpha\beta' y_{t-1}$ with $(\alpha'\alpha)^{-1}\alpha'$. Hence, $\beta' y_{t-1}$ contains cointegrating relations. It follows that there are $r =$ rk(Π) linearly independent cointegrating relations among the components of y_t. The rank of Π is therefore referred to as the *cointegrating rank* of the system, and β is a *cointegration matrix*. For example, if there are three variables with two cointegration relations ($r = 2$), we have

$$\Pi y_{t-1} = \alpha\beta' y_{t-1} = \begin{bmatrix} \alpha_{11} & \alpha_{12} \\ \alpha_{21} & \alpha_{22} \\ \alpha_{31} & \alpha_{32} \end{bmatrix} \begin{bmatrix} \beta_{11} & \beta_{21} & \beta_{31} \\ \beta_{12} & \beta_{22} & \beta_{32} \end{bmatrix} \begin{bmatrix} y_{1,t-1} \\ y_{2,t-1} \\ y_{3,t-1} \end{bmatrix}$$

$$= \begin{bmatrix} \alpha_{11}ec_{1,t-1} + \alpha_{12}ec_{2,t-1} \\ \alpha_{21}ec_{1,t-1} + \alpha_{22}ec_{2,t-1} \\ \alpha_{31}ec_{1,t-1} + \alpha_{32}ec_{2,t-1} \end{bmatrix},$$

where

$$ec_{1,t-1} = \beta_{11}y_{1,t-1} + \beta_{21}y_{2,t-1} + \beta_{31}y_{3,t-1}$$

and

$$ec_{2,t-1} = \beta_{12}y_{1,t-1} + \beta_{22}y_{2,t-1} + \beta_{32}y_{3,t-1}.$$

The matrix α is sometimes called the *loading matrix*. It contains the weights attached to the cointegrating relations in the individual equations of the model. The matrices α and β are not unique, and thus there are many possible α and β matrices that contain the cointegrating relations or linear transformations of them. In fact, using any nonsingular ($r \times r$) matrix B, we obtain a new loading matrix αB and cointegration matrix $\beta B'^{-1}$, which satisfy $\Pi = \alpha B(\beta B'^{-1})'$. Consequently, cointegrating relations with economic content cannot be extracted purely from the observed time series. Some nonsample information is required to identify them uniquely.

The model (3.3) contains several special cases that deserve to be pointed out. If all variables are I(0), $r = K$ and the process is stationary. If $r = 0$, the term Πy_{t-1} disappears in (3.3). In that case, Δy_t has a stable VAR representation. In other words, a stable VAR representation exists for the first differences of the variables rather than the levels variables. Clearly, these boundary cases do not represent cointegrated systems in the usual sense of having a common trend. There are also other cases in which no cointegration in the original sense is present, although the model (3.3) has a cointegrating rank strictly between 0 and K. Suppose, for instance, that all variables but one are I(0); then, the cointegrating rank is $K - 1$, although the I(1) variable is not cointegrated with the other variables. Similarly, there could be $K - r$ unrelated I(1) variables and r I(0) components. Generally, for each I(0) variable in the system there can be a column in the matrix β with a unit in one position and zeros elsewhere. These cases do not represent a cointegrating relation in the original sense of the term. Still it is convenient to include these cases in the present framework because they can be accommodated easily as far as estimation and inference are concerned. Of course, the special properties of the variables may be important in the interpretation of a system and, hence, a different treatment of the special cases may be necessary in this respect. The VECM in (3.3) also indicates that, for a cointegrating rank $r > 0$, the vector of first differences of the variables, Δy_t, does not have a finite order VAR representation.

3.2.2 Deterministic Terms

Several extensions of the basic models (3.1) and (3.3) are usually necessary to represent the main characteristics of a data set of interest. From Figure 3.1, it is clear that including deterministic terms, such as an intercept, a linear trend term, or seasonal dummy variables, may be required for a proper representation of the DGP. One way to include deterministic terms is simply to add them to the stochastic part,

$$y_t = \mu_t + x_t. \tag{3.4}$$

Here μ_t is the deterministic part, and x_t is a stochastic process that may have a VAR or VECM representation, as in (3.1) or (3.3). In other words, $x_t = A_1 x_{t-1} + \cdots + A_p x_{t-p} + u_t$ or $\Delta x_t = \Pi x_{t-1} + \Gamma_1 \Delta x_{t-1} + \cdots + \Gamma_{p-1} \Delta x_{t-p+1} + u_t$. On the assumption, for instance, that μ_t is a linear trend term, that is, $\mu_t = \mu_0 + \mu_1 t$, such a model setup implies the following VAR(p) representation for y_t:

$$y_t = v_0 + v_1 t + A_1 y_{t-1} + \cdots + A_p y_{t-p} + u_t. \tag{3.5}$$

This representation is easily derived by left-multiplying (3.4) with $A(L) = I_K - A_1 L - \cdots - A_p L^p$, where L is the lag operator, as usual. Noting that $A(L) x_t = u_t$ and rearranging terms, we find that $v_0 = A(1)\mu_0 + (\sum_{j=1}^{p} j A_j)\mu_1$ and $v_1 = A(1)\mu_1$. Hence, v_0 and v_1 satisfy a set of restrictions implied by the trend parameters μ_0 and μ_1 and the VAR coefficients.

Alternatively, one may view (3.5) as the basic model without restrictions for v_i ($i = 0, 1$). In that case, the model can, in principle, generate quadratic trends if I(1) variables are included, whereas in (3.4), with a deterministic term $\mu_t = \mu_0 + \mu_1 t$, a *linear trend* term is permitted only. It is sometimes advantageous in theoretical derivations that, in (3.4), a clear partitioning of the process in a deterministic and a stochastic component be available. In some instances it is desirable to subtract the deterministic term first because the stochastic part is of primary interest in econometric analyses. Then the analysis can focus on the stochastic part containing the behavioral relations.

Of course, a VECM($p - 1$) representation equivalent to (3.5) also exists. It has the form

$$\Delta y_t = v_0 + v_1 t + \Pi y_{t-1} + \Gamma_1 \Delta y_{t-1} + \cdots + \Gamma_{p-1} \Delta y_{t-p+1} + u_t.$$

We will see in Section 3.4.2 that the restrictions on v_0 and v_1 sometimes allow absorption of the deterministic part into the cointegrating relations.

3.2.3 Exogenous Variables

Further generalizations of the model are often desirable in practice. For example, one may wish to include further stochastic variables in addition to the deterministic part. A rather general VECM form that includes all these terms is

$$\Delta y_t = \Pi y_{t-1} + \Gamma_1 \Delta y_{t-1} + \cdots + \Gamma_{p-1} \Delta y_{t-p+1} + CD_t + Bz_t + u_t, \tag{3.6}$$

where the z_ts are "unmodeled" stochastic variables, D_t contains all regressors associated with deterministic terms, and C and B are parameter matrices. The z_ts are considered unmodeled because there are no explanatory equations for them in the system (3.6). For example, if interest centers on a money demand relation, sometimes a single-equation model for Δm_t is set up and no separate equations are set up for the explanatory variables such as gnp_t and R_t.

Including unmodeled stochastic variables may be problematic for inference and analysis purposes unless the variables satisfy exogeneity requirements. Different concepts of exogeneity have been considered in the literature [see Engle, Hendry & Richard (1983)]. A set of variables z_t is said to be *weakly exogenous* for a parameter vector of interest, for instance θ, if estimating θ within a conditional model (conditional on z_t) does not entail a loss of information relative to estimating the vector in a full model that does not condition on z_t. Furthermore, z_t is said to be *strongly exogenous* if it is weakly exogenous for the parameters of the conditional model and forecasts of y_t can be made conditional on z_t without loss of forecast precision. Finally, z_t is termed *super exogenous* for θ if z_t is weakly exogenous for θ and policy actions that affect the marginal process of z_t do not affect the parameters of the conditional process. Hence, weak, strong, and super exogeneity are the relevant concepts for estimation, forecasting, and policy analysis, respectively [Ericsson, Hendry & Mizon (1998)]. In this chapter the term exogeneity refers to the relevant concept for the respective context if no specific form of exogeneity is mentioned.

All the models we have presented so far do not explicitly include instantaneous relations between the endogenous variables y_t. Therefore, they are reduced form models. In practice, it is often desirable to model the contemporaneous relations as well, and therefore it is useful to consider a *structural form*

$$A\Delta y_t = \Pi^* y_{t-1} + \Gamma_1^* \Delta y_{t-1} + \cdots + \Gamma_{p-1}^* \Delta y_{t-p+1} + C^* D_t$$
$$+ B^* z_t + v_t, \tag{3.7}$$

where the Π^*, Γ_j^* $(j = 1, \ldots, p-1)$, C^*, and B^* are structural form parameter matrices and v_t is a $(K \times 1)$ structural form error term that is typically a zero mean white noise process with time-invariant covariance matrix Σ_v. The matrix A contains the instantaneous relations between the left-hand-side variables. It has to be invertible. The reduced form corresponding to the structural model (3.7) is given in (3.6) with $\Gamma_j = A^{-1}\Gamma_j^*$ $(j = 1, \ldots, p - 1)$, $C = A^{-1}C^*$, $\Pi = A^{-1}\Pi^*$, $B = A^{-1}B^*$, and $u_t = A^{-1}v_t$. In this chapter we will primarily focus on reduced form models. Structural form models are discussed in more detail in Chapter 4. Estimation of the model parameters will be considered next.

3.3 Estimation

Because estimation of the unrestricted levels VAR representation (3.1) and the VECM (3.3) is particularly easy, these models are considered first. Afterwards, estimation under various restrictions is discussed. In this section we make the simplifying assumption that the lag order and, where used, the cointegrating rank are known. Of course, in practice these quantities also have to be specified from the data. Statistical procedures for doing so will be presented in Section 3.4. Estimation is discussed first because it is needed in the model specification procedures.

3.3.1 Estimation of an Unrestricted VAR

Given a sample $y_1, \ldots, y_T$ and presample values $y_{-p+1}, \ldots, y_0$, the K equations of the VAR model (3.1) may be estimated separately by ordinary least squares (OLS). The resulting estimator has the same efficiency as a generalized LS (GLS) estimator, as shown by Zellner (1962). Following Lütkepohl (1991), we use the notation $Y = [y_1, \ldots, y_T]$, $A = [A_1 : \cdots : A_p]$, $U = [u_1, \ldots, u_T]$ and $Z = [Z_0, \ldots, Z_{T-1}]$, where

$$Z_{t-1} = \begin{bmatrix} y_{t-1} \\ \vdots \\ y_{t-p} \end{bmatrix}.$$

Then the model (3.1) can be written as

$$Y = AZ + U \tag{3.8}$$

and the OLS estimator of A is

$$\hat{A} = [\hat{A}_1 : \cdots : \hat{A}_p] = YZ'(ZZ')^{-1}. \tag{3.9}$$

Under standard assumptions [see, e.g., Lütkepohl (1991)], the OLS estimator $\hat{A}$ is consistent and asymptotically normally distributed,

$$\sqrt{T}\text{vec}(\hat{A} - A) \overset{d}{\to} N(0, \Sigma_{\hat{A}}). \tag{3.10}$$

Here vec denotes the column stacking operator that stacks the columns of a matrix in a column vector, and $\overset{d}{\to}$ signifies convergence in distribution. A more intuitive notation for the result in (3.10) is

$$\text{vec}(\hat{A}) \overset{a}{\sim} N(\text{vec}(A), \Sigma_{\hat{A}}/T),$$

where $\overset{a}{\sim}$ indicates "asymptotically distributed as". The covariance matrix of the asymptotic distribution is $\Sigma_{\hat{A}} = \text{plim}(ZZ'/T)^{-1} \otimes \Sigma_u$ and thus an even more intuitive, albeit imprecise, way of writing the result in (3.10) is

$$\text{vec}(\hat{A}) \approx N(\text{vec}(A), (ZZ')^{-1} \otimes \Sigma_u).$$

For a normally distributed (Gaussian) I(0) process y_t, the OLS estimator in (3.9) is identical to the maximum likelihood (ML) estimator conditional on the initial values.

The OLS estimator also has the asymptotic distribution in (3.10) for non-stationary systems with integrated variables [see Park & Phillips (1988, 1989), Sims et al. (1990) and Lütkepohl (1991, Chapter 11)]. In that case it is important to note, however, that the covariance matrix $\Sigma_{\hat{A}}$ is singular, whereas it is nonsingular in the usual I(0) case. In other words, if there are integrated or cointegrated variables, some estimated coefficients or linear combinations of coefficients converge with a faster rate than $T^{1/2}$. Therefore, the usual t-, χ^2-, and F-tests for inference regarding the VAR parameters may not be valid in this case, as shown, for example, by Toda & Phillips (1993). As an example consider a univariate first-order autoregressive process $y_t = \rho y_{t-1} + u_t$. If y_t is I(1) and, hence, $\rho = 1$, the OLS estimator $\hat{\rho}$ of ρ has a nonstandard limiting distribution. The quantity $\sqrt{T}(\hat{\rho} - \rho)$ converges to zero in probability, that is, the limiting distribution has zero variance and is degenerate, whereas $T(\hat{\rho} - \rho)$ has a nondegenerate nonnormal limiting distribution (see Chapter 2). It is perhaps worth noting, however, that even in VAR models with I(1) variables, there are also many cases where no inference problems occur. As shown by Toda & Yamamoto (1995) and Dolado & Lütkepohl (1996), if all variables are I(1) or I(0) and if a null hypothesis is considered that does not restrict elements of each of the A_is ($i = 1, \ldots, p$), the usual tests have their standard asymptotic properties. For example, if the VAR order $p \geq 2$, the t-ratios have their usual asymptotic standard normal distributions because they are suitable statistics for testing that a single coefficient is zero. In other words, they test a null hypothesis constraining one coefficient only in one of the parameter matrices while leaving the other parameter matrices unrestricted.

The covariance matrix Σ_u may be estimated in the usual way. Denoting by $\hat{u}_t$ the OLS residuals, that is, $\hat{u}_t = y_t - \hat{A}Z_{t-1}$, the matrices

$$\hat{\Sigma}_u = \frac{1}{T - Kp} \sum_{t=1}^{T} \hat{u}_t \hat{u}_t' \quad \text{and} \quad \tilde{\Sigma}_u = \frac{1}{T} \sum_{t=1}^{T} \hat{u}_t \hat{u}_t' \tag{3.11}$$

are possible estimators. Both estimators are consistent and asymptotically normally distributed independently of $\hat{A}$, that is, $\sqrt{T}(\hat{\Sigma}_u - \Sigma_u)$ and $\sqrt{T}(\tilde{\Sigma}_u - \Sigma_u)$

have asymptotic normal distributions if sufficient moment conditions are imposed [see Lütkepohl (1991) and Lütkepohl & Saikkonen (1997)]. These properties are convenient for inference purposes.

As an example consider a system consisting of the German long-term interest (R_t) and inflation rate (Dp_t) plotted in Figure 3.1. Obviously, both series appear to fluctuate around a nonzero mean and, in addition, the inflation rate has a clear seasonal pattern. Therefore, in contrast to the theoretical situation just discussed, it seems useful to include deterministic components in the model. We just mention here that when they are included, the general estimation strategy remains unchanged. In other words, estimation is still done by OLS for each equation separately if the same deterministic terms are added to each equation. They can be included by extending the Z_{t-1} vectors in the foregoing formulas straightforwardly. Adding such terms does not affect the general asymptotic properties of the VAR coefficient estimators mentioned earlier. Of course, these properties are in general valid only if the model is specified properly. Hence, deleting the deterministic terms from a system for which they are needed for a proper specification may have an impact on the asymptotic properties of the estimators.

Using data from $1972\,Q2$–$1998\,Q4$ and estimating a model for $(R_t, Dp_t)'$ of order $p = 4$ with constant terms and seasonal dummies gives

$$
\begin{bmatrix} R_t \\ Dp_t \end{bmatrix} = \begin{bmatrix} 1.15 & 0.18 \\ {\scriptstyle(11.3)} & {\scriptstyle(2.1)} \\ 0.21 & 0.03 \\ {\scriptstyle(2.2)} & {\scriptstyle(0.3)} \end{bmatrix} \begin{bmatrix} R_{t-1} \\ Dp_{t-1} \end{bmatrix} + \begin{bmatrix} -0.28 & -0.03 \\ {\scriptstyle(-1.8)} & {\scriptstyle(-0.3)} \\ -0.07 & -0.06 \\ {\scriptstyle(-0.5)} & {\scriptstyle(-0.7)} \end{bmatrix} \begin{bmatrix} R_{t-2} \\ Dp_{t-2} \end{bmatrix}
$$

$$
+ \begin{bmatrix} 0.25 & 0.10 \\ {\scriptstyle(1.6)} & {\scriptstyle(1.1)} \\ 0.03 & 0.04 \\ {\scriptstyle(0.2)} & {\scriptstyle(0.4)} \end{bmatrix} \begin{bmatrix} R_{t-3} \\ Dp_{t-3} \end{bmatrix} + \begin{bmatrix} -0.26 & 0.09 \\ {\scriptstyle(-2.4)} & {\scriptstyle(1.0)} \\ -0.04 & 0.34 \\ {\scriptstyle(-0.4)} & {\scriptstyle(4.1)} \end{bmatrix} \begin{bmatrix} R_{t-4} \\ Dp_{t-4} \end{bmatrix}
$$

$$
+ \begin{bmatrix} 0.005 & 0.001 & 0.009 & -0.000 \\ {\scriptstyle(1.1)} & {\scriptstyle(0.3)} & {\scriptstyle(1.7)} & {\scriptstyle(-0.1)} \\ 0.012 & -0.034 & -0.018 & -0.016 \\ {\scriptstyle(2.9)} & {\scriptstyle(-7.1)} & {\scriptstyle(-3.6)} & {\scriptstyle(-3.4)} \end{bmatrix} \begin{bmatrix} c \\ s_{1,t} \\ s_{2,t} \\ s_{3,t} \end{bmatrix} + \begin{bmatrix} \hat{u}_{1,t} \\ \hat{u}_{2,t} \end{bmatrix}, \quad (3.12)
$$

$$
\hat{\Sigma}_u = \begin{bmatrix} 2.85 & -0.21 \\ \cdot & 2.59 \end{bmatrix} \times 10^{-5}, \qquad \widehat{\mathrm{Corr}}(u_t) = \begin{bmatrix} 1.00 & -0.08 \\ \cdot & 1.00 \end{bmatrix}.
$$

Notice that, owing to the four lagged values on the right-hand side, only data from $1973\,Q2$–$1998\,Q4$ are actually used as sample values, and thus the sample size is $T = 103$. The values for $1972\,Q2$–$1973\,Q1$ are treated as presample values. In Equation (3.12) t-values are given in parentheses underneath the coefficient estimates. If the series are generated by a stationary process, the t-ratios actually have asymptotic standard normal distributions; thus, the t-values have the usual interpretation. For example, the coefficient estimates are significant (more precisely: significantly different from zero) at the 5% level if the t-ratios have absolute values greater than 1.96. Using this rule, one finds for example, that the coefficient of Dp_{t-1} in the first equation is significant, whereas the one in the second equation is not. Generally, there are many insignificant coefficients under this rule. Therefore, model reductions may be possible. On the other hand, two of the t-ratios in the coefficient matrix attached to lag 4 are larger than 2 in absolute value. Consequently, simply reducing the VAR order and thus dropping the larger lags may not be a good strategy here. We will discuss estimation and specification of models with parameter constraints of various forms later on.

In fact, a univariate analysis of the two series reveals that both variables are well described as I(1) variables. The earlier discussion of integrated variables implies that the t-ratios maintain their usual interpretation for the VAR coefficient estimates even in this case because we have estimated a model of order greater than 1. Notice that adding deterministic terms into the model does not affect these results. The t-ratios of the parameters associated with the deterministic part may not be asymptotically standard normal, however. Therefore, the proper interpretation of the t-ratios of the coefficients in the last parameter matrix in (3.12) is not clear. It makes sense, however, that the t-ratios of the seasonal dummy variables in the inflation equation have larger absolute values than the ones in the first equation of the estimated system because Dp_t has a seasonal pattern whereas R_t is free of obvious seasonality. In general, seasonal dummies may be needed in an equation for a nonseasonal variable if some of the right-hand-side variables have a seasonal pattern, as is the case in the present model, where lags of Dp_t also appear in the R_t equation.

The estimated residual correlation matrix $\widehat{\text{Corr}}(u_t)$ is the one corresponding to the estimated covariance matrix $\hat{\Sigma}_u$, as given in JMulTi. In the present example system, the instantaneous correlation between the two variables is obviously quite small and is not significantly different from zero (at a 5% level) because it is within an interval $\pm 1.96/\sqrt{T} = \pm 0.2$ around zero.

3.3.2 Estimation of VECMs

Reduced rank ML estimation. If the cointegrating rank of the system under consideration is known, working with the VECM form (3.3) is convenient for imposing a corresponding restriction. In deriving estimators for the parameters of (3.3), the following notation is used: $\Delta Y = [\Delta y_1, \ldots, \Delta y_T]$, $Y_{-1} = [y_0, \ldots, y_{T-1}]$, $U = [u_1, \ldots, u_T]$, $\Gamma = [\Gamma_1 : \cdots : \Gamma_{p-1}]$, and $X = [X_0, \ldots, X_{T-1}]$ with

$$X_{t-1} = \begin{bmatrix} \Delta y_{t-1} \\ \vdots \\ \Delta y_{t-p+1} \end{bmatrix}.$$

For a sample with T observations and p presample values, the VECM (3.3) can now be written compactly as

$$\Delta Y = \Pi Y_{-1} + \Gamma X + U. \tag{3.13}$$

Given a specific matrix Π, the equationwise OLS estimator of Γ is easily seen to be

$$\hat{\Gamma} = (\Delta Y - \Pi Y_{-1})X'(XX')^{-1}. \tag{3.14}$$

Substituting in (3.13) and rearranging terms gives

$$\Delta YM = \Pi Y_{-1}M + \hat{U}, \tag{3.15}$$

where $M = I - X'(XX')^{-1}X$. For a given integer r, $0 < r < K$, an estimator $\hat{\Pi}$ of Π with $\text{rk}(\hat{\Pi}) = r$ can be obtained by a method known as canonical correlation analysis [see Anderson (1984)] or, equivalently, a reduced rank (RR) regression based on the model (3.15). Following Johansen (1995a), the estimator may be determined by defining

$$S_{00} = T^{-1}\Delta YM\Delta Y', \quad S_{01} = T^{-1}\Delta YMY'_{-1}, \quad S_{11} = T^{-1}Y_{-1}MY'_{-1}$$

and solving the generalized eigenvalue problem

$$\det(\lambda S_{11} - S'_{01}S_{00}^{-1}S_{01}) = 0. \tag{3.16}$$

Let the ordered eigenvalues be $\lambda_1 \geq \cdots \geq \lambda_K$ with corresponding matrix of eigenvectors $V = [b_1, \ldots, b_K]$ satisfying $\lambda_i S_{11}b_i = S'_{01}S_{00}^{-1}S_{01}b_i$ and normalized such that $V'S_{11}V = I_K$. The reduced-rank estimator of $\Pi = \alpha\beta'$ is then obtained by choosing

$$\hat{\beta} = [b_1, \ldots, b_r]$$

and

$$\hat{\alpha} = \Delta YMY'_{-1}\hat{\beta}(\hat{\beta}'Y_{-1}MY'_{-1}\hat{\beta})^{-1}, \tag{3.17}$$

that is, $\hat{\alpha}$ may be viewed as the OLS estimator from the model

$$\Delta YM = \alpha\hat{\beta}'Y_{-1}M + \tilde{U}.$$

The corresponding estimator of Π is $\hat{\Pi} = \hat{\alpha}\hat{\beta}'$. Using (3.14), we find that a feasible estimator of Γ is $\hat{\Gamma} = (\Delta Y - \hat{\Pi}Y_{-1})X'(XX')^{-1}$. Under Gaussian assumptions these estimators are ML estimators conditional on the presample values [Johansen (1988, 1991, 1995a)]. They are consistent and jointly asymptotically normal under general assumptions,

$$\sqrt{T}\text{vec}([\hat{\Gamma}_1 : \cdots : \hat{\Gamma}_{p-1}] - [\Gamma_1 : \cdots : \Gamma_{p-1}]) \xrightarrow{d} N(0, \Sigma_{\hat{\Gamma}})$$

and

$$\sqrt{T}\mathrm{vec}(\hat{\Pi} - \Pi) \xrightarrow{d} N(0, \Sigma_{\hat{\Pi}}).$$

Here the asymptotic distribution of $\hat{\Gamma}$ is nonsingular; thus, standard inference may be used for the short-term parameters Γ_j. On the other hand, the $(K^2 \times K^2)$ covariance matrix $\Sigma_{\hat{\Pi}}$ can be shown to have rank Kr and is therefore singular if $r < K$. This result is due to two factors. On the one hand, imposing the rank constraint in estimating Π restricts the parameter space and, on the other hand, Π involves the cointegration relations whose estimators have specific asymptotic properties.

In this approach the parameter estimator $\hat{\beta}$ is made unique by the normalization of the eigenvectors, and $\hat{\alpha}$ is adjusted accordingly. However, these are not econometric identification restrictions. Therefore, only the cointegration space but not the cointegration parameters are estimated consistently. To estimate the matrices α and β consistently, it is necessary to impose identifying (uniqueness) restrictions. Without such restrictions only the product $\alpha\beta' = \Pi$ can be estimated consistently. An example of identifying restrictions that has received some attention in the literature assumes that the first part of β is an identity matrix, that is, $\beta' = [I_r : \beta'_{(K-r)}]$, where $\beta_{(K-r)}$ is a $((K-r) \times r)$ matrix. For $r = 1$, this restriction amounts to normalizing the coefficient of the first variable to be 1. This normalization requires some care in choosing the order of the variables. The reason is that there may be a cointegrating relation only between a subset of variables in a given system. Therefore, normalizing an arbitrary coefficient may result in dividing by an estimate corresponding to a parameter that is actually zero because the associated variable does not belong in the cointegrating relation.

If the cointegrating rank $r > 1$, the normalization is such that

$$\beta = \begin{bmatrix} I_r \\ \beta_{(K-r)} \end{bmatrix}.$$

Given that $\mathrm{rk}(\beta) = r$, there exists a nonsingular $(r \times r)$ submatrix of β' that motivates the normalization. Notice that $\Pi = \alpha\beta' = \alpha BB^{-1}\beta'$ for any nonsingular $(r \times r)$ matrix B. Hence, choosing B such that it corresponds to the nonsingular $(r \times r)$ submatrix of β' results in a decomposition of Π, where β contains an identity submatrix. A suitable rearrangement of the variables can ensure that β' will be of the form $[I_r : \beta'_{(K-r)}]$. It should be clear, however, that such a normalization requires a suitable order of the variables. If the order of the variables is inappropriate, this can lead to major distortions. In practice, choosing the order of the variables may not be trivial. Ideally, the order should be chosen such that economically interpretable cointegrating relations result when the normalization restrictions are imposed. In choosing the order of the variables it may be helpful also to analyze cointegration between subsets of the variables before the full system is set up. A more detailed example is given in Section 3.8. Of course, different orderings may be checked. The ordering leading to the most sensible set of cointegrating relations is then maintained. An advantage of working with normalized cointegrating vectors is that they can be used directly in a two-stage procedure if a structural form model or a model with parameter restrictions is to be estimated eventually (see Section 3.3.4).

Moreover, the normalization ensures identified parameters $\beta_{(K-r)}$, and thus inference becomes possible. Generally, if uniqueness restrictions are imposed, it can be shown that $T(\hat{\beta} - \beta)$ and $\sqrt{T}(\hat{\alpha} - \alpha)$ converge in distribution [Johansen (1995a)]. Hence, the estimator of β converges with the fast rate T and is therefore sometimes called *superconsistent*. In contrast, the estimator of α converges with the usual rate $\sqrt{T}$. It has an asymptotic normal distribution under general assumptions; hence, it behaves like usual estimators in a model with stationary variables. In fact, its asymptotic distribution is the same that is obtained when $\hat{\beta}$ is replaced by the true cointegration matrix β in (3.17).

The estimators for the parameters $\beta_{(K-r)}$ have an asymptotic distribution that is multivariate normal upon appropriate normalization. More precisely, partitioning y_t as

$$
y_t = \begin{bmatrix} y_t^{(1)} \\ y_t^{(2)} \end{bmatrix},
$$

where $y_t^{(1)}$ and $y_t^{(2)}$ are $(r \times 1)$ and $((K - r) \times 1)$, respectively, and defining $Y_{-1}^{(2)} = [y_0^{(2)}, \ldots, y_{T-1}^{(2)}]$, we have

$$
\text{vec} \left\{ (\hat{\beta}_{(K-r)}' - \beta_{(K-r)}') \left(Y_{-1}^{(2)} M Y_{-1}^{(2)'} \right)^{1/2} \right\}
$$

$$
= \left[\left(Y_{-1}^{(2)} M Y_{-1}^{(2)'} \right)^{1/2} \otimes I_{K-r} \right] \text{vec}(\hat{\beta}_{(K-r)}' - \beta_{(K-r)}')
$$

$$
\xrightarrow{d} N(0, I_{K-r} \otimes (\alpha' \Sigma_u^{-1} \alpha)^{-1}),
$$

where M is the previously defined matrix from (3.15) [e.g., Reinsel (1993, Chapter 6)]. With a slight abuse of notation this result may be written as

$$
\text{vec}(\hat{\beta}_{(K-r)}') \approx N \left(\text{vec}(\beta_{(K-r)}'), (Y_{-1}^{(2)} M Y_{-1}^{(2)'})^{-1} \otimes (\alpha' \Sigma_u^{-1} \alpha)^{-1} \right).
$$

$$
\tag{3.18}
$$

Although this statement is misleading in the sense that the estimators are not really asymptotically normally distributed, it is a convenient way to think of their distributional properties when deriving inference procedures for the estimators. For example, replacing the unknown parameters in the covariance matrix by their

ML estimators, t-ratios are obtained straightforwardly by dividing the elements of $\hat{\beta}'_{(K-r)}$ by the square roots of the corresponding diagonal elements of

$$\hat{\Omega} = (Y^{(2)}_{-1} M Y^{(2)'}_{-1})^{-1} \otimes (\hat{\alpha}' \widetilde{\Sigma}_u^{-1} \hat{\alpha})^{-1}. \tag{3.19}$$

The expression in (3.18) can also be used to test composite hypotheses for $\beta_{(K-r)}$. For a given fixed $(J \times r(K-r))$ matrix R of rank J and a $(J \times 1)$ vector r, the hypothesis

$$H_0 : R\text{vec}(\beta'_{(K-r)}) = r \tag{3.20}$$

can be checked easily by a Wald test. The test statistic has an asymptotic χ^2-distribution with J degrees of freedom under H_0,

$$\lambda_W = [R\text{vec}(\hat{\beta}'_{(K-r)}) - r]'(R\hat{\Omega}R')^{-1}[R\text{vec}(\hat{\beta}'_{(K-r)}) - r] \xrightarrow{d} \chi^2(J). \tag{3.21}$$

Suppose, for instance, that the three interest rates i_1, i_2, and i_3 are driven by a common stochastic trend so that there are two cointegrating relations ($r = 2$). Then the normalized cointegration matrix has the form

$$\beta' = \begin{bmatrix} 1 & 0 & \beta_{31} \\ 0 & 1 & \beta_{32} \end{bmatrix}.$$

Suppose one now wants to test that the interest rate spreads are stationary so that the cointegrating relations are $i_1 - i_3$ and $i_2 - i_3$. In other words, one would like to test that the cointegration matrix has the form

$$\beta' = \begin{bmatrix} 1 & 0 & -1 \\ 0 & 1 & -1 \end{bmatrix}.$$

The null hypothesis of interest is then

$$H_0 : \beta_{31} = -1, \beta_{32} = -1 \quad \text{or} \quad \begin{bmatrix} 1 & 0 \\ 0 & 1 \end{bmatrix}\begin{bmatrix} \beta_{31} \\ \beta_{32} \end{bmatrix} = \begin{bmatrix} -1 \\ -1 \end{bmatrix}.$$

Hence, in this example, $R = I_2$ and $r = (-1, -1)'$. Under the null hypothesis, the resulting Wald statistic λ_W has an asymptotic $\chi^2(2)$-distribution.

As another example, consider a four-dimensional system with two cointegrating relations for which one would like to check that the cointegrating matrix satisfies

$$\beta' = \begin{bmatrix} 1 & 0 & 0 & * \\ 0 & 1 & * & 0 \end{bmatrix}.$$

Here the asterisks indicate unrestricted elements. In this case,

$$\beta'_{(K-r)} = \begin{bmatrix} 0 & * \\ * & 0 \end{bmatrix}$$

and the restrictions can be written as

$$\begin{bmatrix} 1 & 0 & 0 & 0 \\ 0 & 0 & 0 & 1 \end{bmatrix} \text{vec}(\beta'_{(K-r)}) = \begin{bmatrix} 0 \\ 0 \end{bmatrix}$$

so that

$$R = \begin{bmatrix} 1 & 0 & 0 & 0 \\ 0 & 0 & 0 & 1 \end{bmatrix} \quad \text{and} \quad r = \begin{bmatrix} 0 \\ 0 \end{bmatrix}.$$

It is perhaps interesting to note that an estimator of the levels VAR parameters A can be computed via the estimates of Π and Γ. That estimator has the advantage of imposing the cointegration restrictions on the levels version of the estimated VAR process. However, if no restrictions are imposed on α and Γ, the asymptotic distribution of the resulting estimator for A is the same as in (3.10), where no restrictions have been imposed in estimating A. Computing the covariance matrix estimator $\widetilde{\Sigma}_u$ from the residuals of the VECM estimation, we find that its asymptotic distribution is the same as if it were determined from the levels VAR form treated in the previous section. Again, it is asymptotically independent of $\hat{\Pi}$ and $\hat{\Gamma}$. Extensions of these results for the case in which the true DGP is an infinite order VAR process are considered by Saikkonen (1992) and Saikkonen & Lütkepohl (1996).

To illustrate the estimation of a VECM, we again use the German interest rate–inflation series plotted in Figure 3.1. On the basis of the levels VAR form in (3.12), three lagged differences are likely to be necessary. Because both variables are found to be I(1) in a univariate analysis, the cointegrating rank should be either 0, if no cointegration is present, or 1, if a cointegration relation is possible. The latter model is the less restricted one and, hence, has to be chosen if cointegration cannot be excluded on a priori grounds. For the presently considered variables, one cointegration relation is in fact suggested by economic theory. The so-called Fisher effect implies that the real interest rate should be stationary. In our case, where R_t is the annual nominal interest rate and Dp_t is a quarterly inflation rate, one may therefore expect that $R_t - 4Dp_t$ is a stationary variable. Consequently, this may be a cointegration relation in our system. Formal statistical tests for the number of cointegration relations are discussed in Section 3.4.2.

For our example system we have estimated a VECM with cointegrating rank $r = 1$ and three lagged differences of the two variables using data from $1973Q2$–$1998Q4$ ($T = 103$) plus four presample values. The following estimates are determined by the Johansen procedure as implemented in JMulTi

with t-statistics in parentheses:

$$\begin{bmatrix} \Delta R_t \\ \Delta Dp_t \end{bmatrix} = \begin{bmatrix} -0.10 \\ (-2.3) \\ 0.16 \\ (3.8) \end{bmatrix} \begin{bmatrix} 1.00 : -3.96 \\ (-6.3) \end{bmatrix} \begin{bmatrix} R_{t-1} \\ Dp_{t-1} \end{bmatrix} + \begin{bmatrix} 0.27 & -0.21 \\ (2.7) & (-1.4) \\ 0.07 & -0.34 \\ (0.7) & (-2.4) \end{bmatrix} \begin{bmatrix} \Delta R_{t-1} \\ \Delta Dp_{t-1} \end{bmatrix}$$

$$+ \begin{bmatrix} -0.02 & -0.22 \\ (-0.2) & (-1.8) \\ -0.00 & -0.39 \\ (-0.0) & (-3.4) \end{bmatrix} \begin{bmatrix} \Delta R_{t-2} \\ \Delta Dp_{t-2} \end{bmatrix} + \begin{bmatrix} 0.22 & -0.11 \\ (2.3) & (-1.3) \\ 0.02 & -0.35 \\ (0.2) & (-4.5) \end{bmatrix} \begin{bmatrix} \Delta R_{t-3} \\ \Delta Dp_{t-3} \end{bmatrix}$$

$$+ \begin{bmatrix} 0.002 & 0.001 & 0.009 & -0.000 \\ (0.4) & (0.3) & (1.8) & (-0.1) \\ 0.010 & -0.034 & -0.018 & -0.016 \\ (3.0) & (-7.5) & (-3.8) & (-3.6) \end{bmatrix} \begin{bmatrix} c \\ s_{1,t} \\ s_{2,t} \\ s_{3,t} \end{bmatrix} + \begin{bmatrix} \hat{u}_{1,t} \\ \hat{u}_{2,t} \end{bmatrix}, \qquad (3.22)$$

$$\widetilde{\Sigma}_u = \begin{bmatrix} 2.58 & -0.15 \\ \cdot & 2.30 \end{bmatrix} \times 10^{-5}, \qquad \widehat{\mathrm{Corr}}(u_t) = \begin{bmatrix} 1.00 & -0.06 \\ \cdot & 1.00 \end{bmatrix}.$$

Notice that the first coefficient in the cointegrating relation is normalized to 1 by JMuITi. With this normalization, the estimated cointegrating relation is quite close to what one would expect on the basis of prior considerations. In general, without normalizing the coefficient associated with R_{t-1}, such a result is unlikely because the RR estimation procedure imposes statistical uniqueness constraints on the estimated cointegration parameters, which do not take any prior economic considerations into account.

Because the first coefficient of the cointegration vector is normalized, we can use the asymptotic distribution of the second coefficient to test that it is -4, as expected, if the Fisher effect is present. For this example, $K - r = 1$, and thus $\hat{\Omega}$ is a scalar quantity that turns out to be 0.39. Hence, a t-test for $H_0 : \beta_2 = -4$ may be applied. The test statistic has the value

$$\frac{\hat{\beta}_2 + 4}{\sqrt{\hat{\Omega}}} = \frac{-3.96 + 4}{0.628} = 0.06,$$

and the null hypothesis cannot be rejected at any reasonable level of significance.

Although in general the loading coefficients are also to some extent arbitrary because they are determined by the normalization of the cointegrating vectors, their t-ratios can be interpreted in the usual way "conditional on the estimated cointegration coefficients." In other words, they can be used for assessing whether the cointegration relations resulting from our normalization enter a specific equation significantly. Because they are in fact asymptotically normal, using them with critical values from a standard normal distribution can be justified in the usual way. For our example system both estimated loading coefficients have absolute t-ratios greater than 2, which suggests that the cointegration relation is an important variable in both of the equations.

The estimators of the parameters associated with lagged differences of the variables (short-run parameters) may be interpreted in the usual way. The t-ratios are asymptotically normal under our assumptions. The same is not necessarily true for the parameters associated with deterministic terms. Their t-ratios are just given for completeness.

For VECMs, JMulTi uses the residual covariance estimate $\widetilde{\Sigma}_u$, which divides the residual sums of squares and cross products by the sample size used for estimation and does not perform a degrees-of-freedom correction. For this reason, the estimated variances for (3.22) are somewhat smaller than those of the less restricted system (3.12). Notice that imposing a cointegrating rank of $r < 2$ implies a restriction relative to a full VAR(4) model for the levels variables. The residual correlation matrix returned by JMulTi is always the one corresponding to the estimated covariance matrix. Consequently, in the present case it is based on $\widetilde{\Sigma}_u$.

As mentioned earlier, it is also possible to transform back from the VECM to the levels VAR form. The resulting estimates for the model in (3.22) are

$$
\begin{bmatrix} R_t \\ Dp_t \end{bmatrix} = \begin{bmatrix} \underset{(10.6)}{1.17} & \underset{(0.9)}{0.20} \\ \underset{(2.2)}{0.22} & \underset{(0.2)}{0.04} \end{bmatrix} \begin{bmatrix} R_{t-1} \\ Dp_{t-1} \end{bmatrix} + \begin{bmatrix} \underset{(-1.9)}{-0.29} & \underset{(-0.2)}{-0.01} \\ \underset{(-0.5)}{-0.07} & \underset{(-0.7)}{-0.05} \end{bmatrix} \begin{bmatrix} R_{t-2} \\ Dp_{t-2} \end{bmatrix}
$$

$$
+ \begin{bmatrix} \underset{(1.6)}{0.24} & \underset{(1.4)}{0.12} \\ \underset{(0.2)}{0.02} & \underset{(0.6)}{0.04} \end{bmatrix} \begin{bmatrix} R_{t-3} \\ Dp_{t-3} \end{bmatrix} + \begin{bmatrix} \underset{(-2.3)}{-0.22} & \underset{(1.3)}{0.11} \\ \underset{(-0.2)}{-0.02} & \underset{(4.5)}{0.35} \end{bmatrix} \begin{bmatrix} R_{t-4} \\ Dp_{t-4} \end{bmatrix}
$$

$$
+ \begin{bmatrix} \underset{(0.4)}{0.002} & \underset{(0.3)}{0.001} & \underset{(1.8)}{0.009} & \underset{(-0.1)}{-0.000} \\ \underset{(3.0)}{0.010} & \underset{(-7.5)}{-0.034} & \underset{(-3.8)}{-0.018} & \underset{(-3.6)}{-0.016} \end{bmatrix} \begin{bmatrix} c \\ s_{1,t} \\ s_{2,t} \\ s_{3,t} \end{bmatrix} + \begin{bmatrix} \hat{u}_{1,t} \\ \hat{u}_{2,t} \end{bmatrix}.
$$

Comparing these estimates and t-ratios with those of the unrestricted model in (3.12) shows that most of them are quite similar, and thus imposing the rank of 1 does not appear to be very restrictive. Some of the t-ratios have changed a bit, however (see, for example, the coefficients of Dp_{t-1} and Dp_{t-3} in the first equation).

A simple two-step (S2S) estimator for the cointegration matrix. Another simple method for estimating the cointegration matrix takes advantage of the fact that the VECM (3.3) can be written in the form

$$
\Delta y_t - \Pi_1 y_{t-1}^{(1)} - \Gamma X_{t-1} = \Pi_2 y_{t-1}^{(2)} + u_t, \tag{3.23}
$$

where $y_{t-1}^{(1)}$ is $(r \times 1)$, $y_{t-1}^{(2)}$ is $((K-r) \times 1)$, $\Gamma = [\Gamma_1 : \cdots : \Gamma_{p-1}]$, and $X_{t-1}' = [\Delta y_{t-1}', \ldots, \Delta y_{t-p+1}']$, as before. The matrices Π_1 and Π_2 are $(K \times r)$ and $(K \times (K-r))$, respectively, such that $[\Pi_1 : \Pi_2] = \Pi = \alpha \beta'$. Normalizing the cointegration matrix such that $\beta' = [I_r : \beta_{(K-r)}']$ gives $\Pi_1 = \alpha$ and $\Pi_2 = \alpha \beta_{(K-r)}'$. Premultiplying (3.23) by $(\alpha' \Sigma_u^{-1} \alpha)^{-1} \alpha' \Sigma_u^{-1}$ and defining

$$w_t - (\alpha' \Sigma_u^{-1} \alpha)^{-1} \alpha' \Sigma_u^{-1} (\Delta y_t - \alpha y_{t-1}^{(1)} - \Gamma X_{t-1}),$$

gives

$$w_t = \beta_{(K-r)}' y_{t-1}^{(2)} + v_t, \tag{3.24}$$

where $v_t = (\alpha' \Sigma_u^{-1} \alpha)^{-1} \alpha' \Sigma_u^{-1} u_t$ is an r-dimensional white noise process with mean zero and covariance matrix $\Sigma_v = (\alpha' \Sigma_u^{-1} \alpha)^{-1}$.

If α, Γ, and Σ_u were given, $\beta_{(K-r)}'$ could be estimated from (3.24) by OLS. Because the former parameters are unknown in practice, the following two-step procedure may be used. In the first step, we eliminate the short-term parameters by replacing them with their OLS estimators given Π as in (3.14), and we consider the concentrated model (3.15),

$$\Delta Y M = \Pi Y_{-1} M + \hat{U}.$$

Using this model we estimate Π by OLS. Denoting the estimator by $\tilde{\Pi} = [\tilde{\Pi}_1 : \tilde{\Pi}_2]$ and the corresponding residual covariance estimator by $\tilde{\Sigma}_u = T^{-1} (\Delta Y - \tilde{\Pi} Y_{t-1}) M (\Delta Y - \tilde{\Pi} Y_{t-1})'$ and using $\tilde{\alpha} = \tilde{\Pi}_1$, we define

$$\tilde{W} = (\tilde{\alpha}' \tilde{\Sigma}_u^{-1} \tilde{\alpha})^{-1} \tilde{\alpha}' \tilde{\Sigma}_u^{-1} (\Delta Y - \tilde{\alpha} Y_{-1}^{(1)}),$$

where $Y_{-1}^{(1)} = [y_0^{(1)}, \ldots, y_{T-1}^{(1)}]$. Now the second step follows in which $\beta_{(K-r)}'$ is estimated by OLS from

$$\tilde{W} M = \beta_{(K-r)}' Y_{-1}^{(2)} M + \tilde{V}, \tag{3.25}$$

that is,

$$\tilde{\beta}_{(K-r)}' = \tilde{W} M Y_{-1}^{(2)'} \left(Y_{-1}^{(2)} M Y_{-1}^{(2)'} \right)^{-1}, \tag{3.26}$$

where $Y_{-1}^{(2)} = [y_0^{(2)}, \ldots, y_{T-1}^{(2)}]$.

This simple two-step (S2S) estimator has the same asymptotic distribution as the ML estimator [see Reinsel (1993, Chapter 6) and Ahn & Reinsel (1990)]. Thus, for inference purposes we may pretend that $\text{vec}(\tilde{\beta}_{(K-r)}')$ has an approximate normal distribution, $N(\text{vec}(\beta_{(K-r)}'), \Omega)$, where from (3.25) a possible estimator of the covariance matrix is now

$$\tilde{\Omega} = (Y_{-1}^{(2)} M Y_{-1}^{(2)'})^{-1} \otimes \tilde{\Sigma}_v.$$

Here $\tilde{\Sigma}_v = T^{-1} (\tilde{W} - \tilde{\beta}_{(K-r)}' Y_{-1}^{(2)}) M (\tilde{W} - \tilde{\beta}_{(K-r)}' Y_{-1}^{(2)})'$ is the residual covariance matrix estimator from (3.25).

The S2S estimator may be used in the usual way to obtain estimators of the other parameters in the model by employing (3.17) and the formulas following that equation. The estimator can be extended straightforwardly to the case in which deterministic terms are present.

Because the ML estimator is computationally unproblematic in the present case, the usefulness of the S2S estimator may not be obvious at this stage. It will be seen later, however, that it has advantages when restrictions are to be imposed on the cointegrating vectors.

For the interest rate–inflation example we obtain

$$R_t = \underset{(0.61)}{3.63} \, Dp_t + \text{error}_t$$

using again the model with three lagged differences, seasonal dummies and a samples period $1972Q2 - 1998Q4$ including presample values. Here the estimated standard error is given in parentheses underneath the coefficient estimate. Clearly, the estimate differs somewhat from the one obtained with the Johansen ML procedure [see Equation (3.22)]. The value 4 is still well within a two-standard error interval around the estimate, however. Thus, the S2S estimator confirms that 4 may be an acceptable value of the cointegration parameter.

3.3.3 Restricting the Error Correction Term

If restrictions are available for the cointegration space from economic theory, for instance, it is useful to take them into account in estimating the VECM parameters. The error correction term can be restricted by imposing constraints on β, α, or both. These two types of restrictions are discussed in turn next.

Restrictions for the cointegration relations. If only identifying restrictions for the cointegration relations are available, estimation may proceed as described in the previous section, and then the identified estimator of β may be obtained by a suitable transformation of $\hat{\beta}$. For example, if β is just a single vector, a normalization of the first component may be obtained by dividing the vector $\hat{\beta}$ by its first component, as discussed in the previous section.

Sometimes over-identifying restrictions are available for the cointegration matrix. They can be handled easily if they can be written in the form $\beta = H\varphi$, where H is some known, fixed $(K \times s)$ matrix and φ is $(s \times r)$ with $s \geq r$. For example, in a system with three variables and one cointegration relation, if $\beta_{31} = -\beta_{21}$, we have

$$\beta = \begin{bmatrix} \beta_{11} \\ \beta_{21} \\ -\beta_{21} \end{bmatrix} = \begin{bmatrix} 1 & 0 \\ 0 & 1 \\ 0 & -1 \end{bmatrix} \begin{bmatrix} \beta_{11} \\ \beta_{21} \end{bmatrix} = H\varphi,$$

and thus $\varphi = (\beta_{11}, \beta_{21})'$. If the restrictions can be represented in this form, Y_{-1} is simply replaced by $H'Y_{-1}$ in the quantities entering the generalized eigenvalue problem (3.16), that is, we have to solve

$$\det(\lambda H' S_{11} H - H' S'_{01} S_{00}^{-1} S_{01} H) = 0 \tag{3.27}$$

for λ to get $\lambda_1^H \geq \cdots \geq \lambda_s^H$. The eigenvectors corresponding to $\lambda_1^H, \ldots, \lambda_r^H$ are the estimators of the columns of φ. Denoting the resulting estimator by $\hat{\varphi}$ gives a restricted estimator $\hat{\beta} = H\hat{\varphi}$ for β and corresponding estimators of α and Γ, as in (3.17) and the following equations.

More generally, restrictions may be available in the form $\beta = [H_1\varphi_1, H_2\varphi_2]$, where H_j is $(K \times s_j)$ and φ_j is $(s_j \times r_j)$ $(j = 1, 2)$ with $r_1 + r_2 = r$. For instance, if there are three variables $(K = 3)$ and two cointegrating relations $(r = 2)$, one zero restriction on the last element of the second cointegrating vector can be represented as

$$\beta = \begin{bmatrix} \beta_{11} & \beta_{12} \\ \beta_{21} & \beta_{22} \\ \beta_{31} & 0 \end{bmatrix} = [H_1\varphi_1, H_2\varphi_2]$$

with $H_1 = I_3$, $\varphi_1 = (\beta_{11}, \beta_{21}, \beta_{31})'$,

$$H_2 = \begin{bmatrix} 1 & 0 \\ 0 & 1 \\ 0 & 0 \end{bmatrix}$$

and $\varphi_2 = (\beta_{12}, \beta_{22})'$. In that case, restricted ML estimation is still not difficult but requires an iterative optimization, whereas the S2S estimator is available in closed form, as we will see now.

In general, if the restrictions can be represented in the form

$$\text{vec}(\beta'_{(K-r)}) = \mathcal{H}\eta + h$$

(where $\mathcal{H}$ is a fixed matrix, h a fixed vector, and η a vector of free parameters), the second step of the S2S estimator given in (3.26) may be based on the vectorized, modified model

$$\text{vec}(\widetilde{W}M) = (MY_{-1}^{(2)'} \otimes I_r)\text{vec}(\beta'_{(K-r)}) + \text{vec}(\tilde{V})$$
$$= (MY_{-1}^{(2)'} \otimes I_r)(\mathcal{H}\eta + h) + \text{vec}(\tilde{V}),$$

and thus

$$\text{vec}(\widetilde{W}M) - (MY_{-1}^{(2)'} \otimes I_r)h = (MY_{-1}^{(2)'} \otimes I_r)\mathcal{H}\eta + \text{vec}(\tilde{V}).$$

Defining $\tilde{z} = \text{vec}(\widetilde{W}M) - (MY_{-1}^{(2)'} \otimes I_r)h$, we find that the feasible GLS estimator of η is

$$\tilde{\eta} = \left[\mathcal{H}'(Y_{-1}^{(2)}MY_{-1}^{(2)'} \otimes \widetilde{\Sigma}_v^{-1})\mathcal{H} \right]^{-1} \mathcal{H}'(Y_{-1}^{(2)}M \otimes \widetilde{\Sigma}_v^{-1})\tilde{z},$$

where $\widetilde{\Sigma}_v^{-1}$ is the covariance matrix estimator from an unrestricted S2S estimation based on (3.25). Again, with some abuse of notation, we have

$$\tilde{\eta} \approx N\left(\eta, \left[\mathcal{H}'(Y_{-1}^{(2)}MY_{-1}^{(2)'} \otimes \Sigma_v^{-1})\mathcal{H} \right]^{-1} \right),$$

which can be used for inference for η. For example, the t-ratios can be obtained and interpreted in the usual manner by dividing the parameter estimators by the corresponding square roots of the diagonal elements of the covariance matrix estimator.

Using the restricted estimator $\hat{\beta}_{(K-r)}^R$ obtained from $\text{vec}(\hat{\beta}_{(K-r)}^{R'}) = \mathcal{H}\tilde{\eta} + h$, a restricted estimator of the cointegration matrix is

$$\hat{\beta}_R' = [I_r : \hat{\beta}_{(K-r)}^{R'}].$$

This restricted estimator can, for example, be used in a multistage procedure in systems estimation, where restrictions are also imposed on the short-run parameters (see Section 3.3.4).

For the German interest rate–inflation system we have the extreme case that the cointegrating vector may be regarded as being known completely from economic theory, and thus we may fix $\beta' = (1, -4)$. Doing so and estimating the system again by single-equation OLS with the new regressor variable $R_{t-1} - 4Dp_{t-1}$ in each of the equations yields

$$\begin{bmatrix} \Delta R_t \\ \Delta Dp_t \end{bmatrix} = \begin{bmatrix} -0.10 \\ \scriptstyle(-2.3) \\ 0.16 \\ \scriptstyle(3.8) \end{bmatrix} (R_{t-1} - 4Dp_{t-1}) + \begin{bmatrix} 0.27 & -0.21 \\ \scriptstyle(2.7) & \scriptstyle(-1.4) \\ 0.07 & -0.34 \\ \scriptstyle(0.7) & \scriptstyle(-2.4) \end{bmatrix} \begin{bmatrix} \Delta R_{t-1} \\ \Delta Dp_{t-1} \end{bmatrix}$$

$$+ \begin{bmatrix} -0.02 & -0.22 \\ \scriptstyle(-0.2) & \scriptstyle(-1.8) \\ -0.00 & -0.39 \\ \scriptstyle(-0.0) & \scriptstyle(-3.4) \end{bmatrix} \begin{bmatrix} \Delta R_{t-2} \\ \Delta Dp_{t-2} \end{bmatrix} + \begin{bmatrix} 0.22 & -0.11 \\ \scriptstyle(2.3) & \scriptstyle(-1.3) \\ 0.02 & -0.35 \\ \scriptstyle(0.2) & \scriptstyle(-4.5) \end{bmatrix} \begin{bmatrix} \Delta R_{t-3} \\ \Delta Dp_{t-3} \end{bmatrix}$$

$$+ \begin{bmatrix} 0.001 & 0.001 & 0.009 & -0.000 \\ \scriptstyle(0.4) & \scriptstyle(0.3) & \scriptstyle(1.8) & \scriptstyle(-0.1) \\ 0.010 & -0.034 & -0.018 & -0.016 \\ \scriptstyle(3.0) & \scriptstyle(-7.5) & \scriptstyle(-3.8) & \scriptstyle(-3.6) \end{bmatrix} \begin{bmatrix} c \\ s_{1,t} \\ s_{2,t} \\ s_{3,t} \end{bmatrix} + \begin{bmatrix} \hat{u}_{1,t} \\ \hat{u}_{2,t} \end{bmatrix}. \quad (3.28)$$

The coefficient estimates are almost the same as in (3.22). Only some of the t-values have changed slightly owing to the restriction on the cointegration vector.

Weak exogeneity restrictions. Linear restrictions on the loading matrix α of the type $\alpha = G\psi$ with G a given fixed $(K \times s)$ matrix and ψ a $(s \times r)$ parameter matrix with $s \geq r$ can also be imposed easily. For example, one may wish to consider the restriction that some or all of the cointegration relations do not enter a particular equation. Such a restriction is of special interest because it implies weak exogeneity of specific variables for the cointegrating parameters. More precisely, a variable is *weakly exogenous for the cointegrating parameters* if none of the cointegration relations enter the equation for that variable. For instance, in a three-variable system $(K = 3)$ with two cointegration relations $(r = 2)$ we may wish to consider the case that the third variable is weakly exogenous. Hence,

$$
\alpha = \begin{bmatrix} \alpha_{11} & \alpha_{12} \\ \alpha_{21} & \alpha_{22} \\ 0 & 0 \end{bmatrix} = \begin{bmatrix} 1 & 0 \\ 0 & 1 \\ 0 & 0 \end{bmatrix} \begin{bmatrix} \alpha_{11} & \alpha_{12} \\ \alpha_{21} & \alpha_{22} \end{bmatrix} = G\psi,
$$

where G and ψ are defined in the obvious way.

Suppose that we wish to impose the restriction $\alpha = G\psi$ with $\mathrm{rk}(G) = s$. This can be done by premultiplying (3.15) by $(G'G)^{-1}G'$ and performing an RR regression on a transformed model. An estimator of ψ is thereby obtained denoted as $\hat{\psi}$. The restricted estimator of α is then $\hat{\alpha} = G\hat{\psi}$. Formally the estimator of ψ may be obtained via the solution of an appropriately modified generalized eigenvalue problem, similar to (3.16) [Johansen (1995a)].

Again, more general restrictions of the form $\alpha = [G_1\psi_1, \ldots, G_r\psi_r]$ can be handled in principle. In this case, iterative algorithms are necessary for imposing them. If we combine this approach with the one considered previously for restrictions on β, it is also possible to restrict α and β simultaneously. An alternative way to impose restrictions on the loading coefficients and short-term part of the model is described in the next section.

3.3.4 Estimation of Models with More General Restrictions and Structural Forms

For a general structural form model such as (3.7) with restrictions on the loading coefficients (α), the short-term parameters (Γ), and other parameter matrices, efficient estimation is more difficult. First of all, identifying restrictions are needed. They are typically available in the form of zero restrictions on A, Γ_j^* $(j = 1, \ldots, p - 1)$, C^*, and B^*. In addition, there may be a rank restriction for Π^* given by the number of cointegrating relations. If identifying restrictions are available for the cointegrating relations, the loading matrix α^* or both, Π^* may be replaced by the product $\alpha^*\beta^{*\prime}$. Restrictions for α^* typically are zero constraints, which means that some cointegrating relations are excluded from some of the equations of the system. Usually it is possible to estimate β^* in a first stage. For example, if we use a reduced form and ignore the structural restrictions, the RR regression procedure described in Section 3.3.2 or the S2S procedure of Section 3.3.2 may be employed. If there is just one cointegrating relation, it may alternatively be estimated by a single-equation procedure. Notice, for example, that the first equation of the VECM (3.3) has the form

$$\Delta y_{1t} = \pi_{11} y_{1,t-1} + \cdots + \pi_{1K} y_{K,t-1} + \gamma_1 \Delta y_{t-1}$$

$$+ \cdots + \gamma_{p-1} \Delta y_{t-p+1} + u_{1t},$$

where the π_{1j}'s are the elements of the first row of Π and γ_j is the first row of Γ_j ($j = 1, \ldots, p - 1$). This equation may be estimated by OLS to yield estimates $\hat{\pi}_{1j}$ of the π_{1j}s. Denoting the first element of α by α_1, we have $(\pi_{11}, \ldots, \pi_{1K}) = \alpha_1 \beta'$. Hence, an estimate $\hat{\beta}$ with normalized first element may be obtained as $\hat{\beta}' = (1, \hat{\pi}_{12}/\hat{\pi}_{11}, \ldots, \hat{\pi}_{1K}/\hat{\pi}_{11})$, where it is assumed that $\alpha_1 \neq 0$ so that the cointegration relation is actually present in the first equation. A similar estimate may also be available in a structural form setting.

The first-stage estimator $\hat{\beta}^*$, for example, may be treated as fixed in a second-stage estimation of the structural form because the estimators of the cointegrating parameters converge at a better rate than the estimators of the short-term parameters. In other words, a systems estimation procedure may be applied to

$$A\Delta y_t = \alpha^* \hat{\beta}^{*'} y_{t-1} + \Gamma_1^* \Delta y_{t-1} + \cdots + \Gamma_{p-1}^* \Delta y_{t-p+1}$$

$$+ C^* D_t + B^* z_t + \hat{v}_t. \tag{3.29}$$

If only exclusion restrictions are imposed on the parameter matrices in this form, standard econometric systems estimation procedures such as three-stage LS (3SLS) [e.g., Judge et al. (1985)] or similar methods may be applied that result in estimators of the short-term parameters with the usual asymptotic properties.

Some care is necessary, however, with respect to the treatment of exogenous and deterministic variables. Generally, no problems arise if all exogenous variables are I(0). In this case parameter estimators with the usual properties are obtained. If z_t contains I(1) variables, the properties of the estimators depend on the cointegration properties of z_t. In particular, cointegration between unmodeled and endogenous variables has to be taken into account appropriately [see, e.g., Boswijk (1995)]. Numerous articles deal with estimating models containing integrated variables. Examples are Phillips (1987, 1991), Phillips & Durlauf (1986), Phillips & Hansen (1990), and Phillips & Loretan (1991). A textbook treatment is given in Davidson (2000). Some more discussion of estimating structural models is presented in Chapter 4.

Rather than including deterministic terms separately, as in (3.29), they may be included in the cointegrating relations. In this case, a suitable reparameterization of the model is called for. For intercepts and linear trend terms, the relevant reparameterizations will be presented in Section 3.4.2 in the context of testing for the cointegrating rank, where a proper treatment of deterministic terms is of particular importance. The properties of the corresponding estimators are not treated in detail here because, in a subsequent analysis of the model, the parameters of the deterministic terms are often of minor interest [see, however, Sims et al. (1990)].

3.4 Model Specification

In specifying VAR models or VECMs it is necessary to specify the lag order and, for VECMs, also the cointegrating rank. Statistical procedures that can be used to help in deciding on these quantities are available and will be discussed next. Because unrestricted VAR models and VECMs usually involve a substantial number of parameters, it is desirable to impose restrictions that reduce the dimensionality of the parameter space and thereby improve the estimation precision. Restrictions may be based on economic theory or other nonsample information and on statistical procedures. Such procedures for imposing restrictions on the deterministic term, the error correction part, and the short-term parameters will be discussed subsequently.

3.4.1 Determining the Autoregressive Order

In determining the lag order of a dynamic model, in principle the same procedures are available that were already discussed for univariate models. In other words, sequential testing procedures and model selection criteria may be applied. It is useful to focus on the VAR form (3.1) at this stage because the cointegrating rank r is usually unknown when the choice of the lag order p is made. One possible approach is to start from a model with some prespecified maximum lag length, p_{max} and apply tests sequentially to determine a suitable model order. For example, the following sequence of null hypotheses may be tested until the test rejects: $H_0 : A_{p_{max}} = 0$, $H_0 : A_{p_{max}-1} = 0$, and so forth. In this procedure, a decision on p_{max} has to be made. Occasionally this quantity is chosen by some theoretical or institutional argument. For instance, one may want to include lags of at least one year, and thus four lags have to be included for quarterly data and twelve lags may be used for a monthly model. An inappropriate choice of p_{max} may not be very severe in some respect because, if the order is chosen too small, this problem may be discovered later when the final model is subjected to a series of specification tests (see Section 3.5). For example, the portmanteau test may be unsatisfactory in this case. On the other hand, an excessively large value of p_{max} may be problematic owing to its impact on the overall error probability of a sequential procedure. If a very large order p_{max} is used, a long sequence of tests may be necessary that will have an impact on the overall Type I error of the testing sequence, that is, the choice of p_{max} will have an impact on the probability of an inadequate selection of p. Again such a problem may become apparent at some later stage when other checks and criteria are also used to evaluate the model.

Instead of sequential tests one may alternatively choose the lag length by model selection procedures. Generalized versions of the criteria discussed in Chapter 2 in the univariate case are available for that purpose. The general approach is again to fit VAR(m) models with orders $m = 0, \ldots, p_{max}$ and to choose an estimator of the order p that minimizes the preferred criterion. Many of the criteria in current use have the general form

$$Cr(m) = \log \det(\widetilde{\Sigma}_u(m)) + c_T \varphi(m), \tag{3.30}$$

where $\det(\cdot)$ denotes the determinant, $\log$ is the natural logarithm, as usual, $\widetilde{\Sigma}_u(m) = T^{-1} \sum_{t=1}^{T} \hat{u}_t \hat{u}_t'$ is the residual covariance matrix estimator for a model of order m, c_T is a sequence that depends on the sample size T, and $\varphi(m)$ is a function that penalizes large VAR orders. For instance, $\varphi(m)$ may represent the number of parameters that have to be estimated in a VAR(m) model. The term $\log \det(\widetilde{\Sigma}_u(m))$ measures the fit of a model with order m. Because there is no correction for degrees of freedom in the covariance matrix estimator, the log determinant decreases (or at least does not increase) when m increases. As in the univariate case, the sample size has to be held constant; hence, the number of presample values set aside for estimation is determined by the maximum order p_{max}.

The following criteria are direct generalizations of the corresponding criteria discussed for univariate processes in Chapter 2:

$$AIC(m) = \log \det(\widetilde{\Sigma}_u(m)) + \frac{2}{T} m K^2,$$

$$HQ(m) = \log \det(\widetilde{\Sigma}_u(m)) + \frac{2 \log \log T}{T} m K^2,$$

and

$$SC(m) = \log \det(\widetilde{\Sigma}_u(m)) + \frac{\log T}{T} m K^2.$$

Again, the AIC criterion asymptotically overestimates the order with positive probability, whereas the last two criteria estimate the order consistently under quite general conditions if the actual DGP has a finite VAR order and the maximum order p_{max} is larger than the true order. These results not only hold for I(0) processes but also for I(1) processes with cointegrated variables [Paulsen (1984)]. Denoting by $\hat{p}(AIC)$, $\hat{p}(HQ)$ and $\hat{p}(SC)$ the orders selected by the three criteria, respectively, we find that the following relations hold even in small samples of fixed size $T \geq 16$ [see Lütkepohl (1991, Chapters 4 and 11)]:

$$\hat{p}(SC) \leq \hat{p}(HQ) \leq \hat{p}(AIC).$$

Model selection criteria may also be used for identifying single coefficients that may be replaced by zero or other exclusion restrictions. Possible procedures are considered in Section 3.4.5.

3.4.2 Specifying the Cointegrating Rank

If some of the variables are I(1), a VECM is the suitable modeling framework, and the cointegrating rank r has to be chosen in addition to the lag order. Sequential testing procedures based on likelihood ratio (LR)–type tests are possible statistical tools for this choice. Because Gaussian ML estimates for the reduced-form VECM are easy to compute for a given cointegrating rank, as shown in Section 3.3.2, LR test statistics are readily available. The following sequence of hypotheses may be considered:

$$
\begin{aligned}
H_0(0) &: \mathrm{rk}(\Pi) = 0 & \text{versus } H_1(0) &: \mathrm{rk}(\Pi) > 0, \\
H_0(1) &: \mathrm{rk}(\Pi) = 1 & \text{versus } H_1(1) &: \mathrm{rk}(\Pi) > 1, \\
&\quad\vdots \\
H_0(K-1) &: \mathrm{rk}(\Pi) = K-1 & \text{versus } H_1(K-1) &: \mathrm{rk}(\Pi) = K.
\end{aligned}
\tag{3.31}
$$

The testing sequence terminates, and the corresponding cointegrating rank is selected when the null hypothesis cannot be rejected for the first time. If the first null hypothesis in this sequence, $H_0(0)$, cannot be rejected, a VAR process in first differences is considered. At the other end, if all the null hypotheses can be rejected, including $H_0(K-1)$, a levels VAR process should be considered for the subsequent analysis.

Given the discussion of unit root testing, it is not surprising that, under Gaussian assumptions, the LR statistic under $H_0(r_0)$ is nonstandard. It depends on the difference $K - r_0$ and on the deterministic terms included in the DGP. In particular, the deterministic trend terms and shift dummy variables in the DGP have an impact on the null distributions of the LR tests. Therefore, LR-type tests have been derived under different assumptions regarding the deterministic term. On the assumption that the lag order is specified properly, the limiting null distributions do not depend on the short-term dynamics.

To present the tests, the model (3.4) is a convenient point of departure. Specifically, we first consider the model

$$
y_t = \mu_0 + \mu_1 t + x_t,
\tag{3.32}
$$

where x_t is a VAR(p) process. There are three cases of particular interest from a practical point of view. First, if $\mu_1 = 0$, there is just a constant mean and no deterministic trend term. In that case, $y_t - \mu_0 = x_t$, and thus $\Delta y_t = \Delta x_t$, and from the VECM form of x_t, the mean adjusted y_t is seen to have the VECM form

$$\Delta y_t = \Pi(y_{t-1} - \mu_0) + \sum_{j=1}^{p-1} \Gamma_j \Delta y_{t-j} + u_t \qquad (3.33)$$

or, if an intercept term is used,

$$\begin{aligned}
\Delta y_t &= v_0^* + \Pi y_{t-1} + \sum_{j=1}^{p-1} \Gamma_j \Delta y_{t-j} + u_t \\
&= \Pi^* \begin{bmatrix} y_{t-1} \\ 1 \end{bmatrix} + \sum_{j=1}^{p-1} \Gamma_j \Delta y_{t-j} + u_t,
\end{aligned} \qquad (3.34)$$

where $\Pi^* = [\Pi : v_0^*]$ is $(K \times (K+1))$ with $v_0^* = -\Pi\mu_0$. Notice that it follows from the absence of a deterministic trend term that the intercept can be absorbed into the cointegration relations; thus, $\Pi^* = \alpha\beta^{*\prime}$ has rank r. Both VECM versions can be used for testing the cointegrating rank. Johansen (1995a) considers the intercept version (3.34) and provides critical values for the LR test, which is known as the *trace test*. The test statistic is of the form

$$LR(r_0) = -T \sum_{j=r_0+1}^{K} \log(1 - \lambda_j),$$

where the λ_j are the eigenvalues obtained by applying RR regression techniques to (3.34). In Saikkonen & Luukkonen (1997) and Saikkonen & Lütkepohl (2000d), two-step procedures are considered in which the mean term is estimated in a first step by a feasible GLS procedure. Substituting the estimator for μ_0 in (3.33), we may apply an LR-type test based on a RR regression of (3.33). The resulting test statistic has an asymptotic distribution that is different from the one obtained for the intercept version. In fact, asymptotically the power of the test based on (3.33) is superior to that obtained from (3.34) [see Saikkonen & Lütkepohl (1999)].

A second case results if there is actually a linear deterministic trend in the DGP and, hence, $\mu_1 \neq 0$. If the trend is confined to some individual variables but is absent from the cointegration relations, we have $\beta'\mu_1 = 0$, that is, the trend parameter is orthogonal to the cointegration matrix; thus, $\Pi(y_{t-1} - \mu_0 - \mu_1(t-1)) = \Pi(y_{t-1} - \mu_0)$. Hence, for this case, using again the VECM form of $x_t = y_t - \mu_0 - \mu_1 t$, we get

$$\Delta y_t - \mu_1 = \Pi(y_{t-1} - \mu_0) + \sum_{j=1}^{p-1} \Gamma_j(\Delta y_{t-j} - \mu_1) + u_t, \qquad (3.35)$$

where $\Delta(y_t - \mu_0 - \mu_1 t) = \Delta y_t - \mu_1$ has been used. Collecting all constant terms in an intercept gives

$$\Delta y_t = v_0 + \Pi y_{t-1} + \sum_{j=1}^{p-1} \Gamma_j \Delta y_{t-j} + u_t, \qquad (3.36)$$

where $\nu_0 = -\Pi\mu_0 + (\sum_{j=1}^{p} j A_j)\mu_1$ [see Eq. (3.5)]. A test based on the trend-adjusted version (3.35) was proposed by Saikkonen & Lütkepohl (2000b). In this case the mean and trend parameters are estimated in a first step by a feasible GLS procedure, the trend is subtracted from y_t to yield $\hat{x}_t = y_t - \hat{\mu}_0 - \hat{\mu}_1 t$, and then the test statistic is computed via RR regression based on the VECM (3.35). The null distributions are tabulated in Saikkonen & Lütkepohl (2000b). Corresponding LR tests based on the intercept version of the VECM in (3.36) are treated by Johansen (1995a).

Notice, however, that the $(K \times r)$ matrix β has to satisfy $\beta'\mu_1 = 0$ with $\mu_1 \neq 0$ under the present assumptions. This requirement implies that $r < K$. Hence, if a trend is known to be present, then it should also be allowed for under the alternative; consequently, even under the alternative the rank must be smaller than K. Thus, in the present setting only tests of null hypotheses $\text{rk}(\Pi) = r_0 < K - 1$ should be performed. This result is an implication of the fact that a linear trend is assumed in at least one of the variables ($\mu_1 \neq 0$), whereas a stable model (where $r = K$) with an intercept does not generate a linear trend.

The final case of practical importance results if a fully unrestricted linear trend term is included in (3.32). In that situation we have again two types of VECMs. Using the VECM of $x_t = y_t - \mu_0 - \mu_1 t$ gives

$$\Delta y_t - \mu_1 = \Pi(y_{t-1} - \mu_0 - \mu_1(t-1)) + \sum_{j=1}^{p-1} \Gamma_j(\Delta y_{t-j} - \mu_1) + u_t,$$
(3.37)

and, rearranging the deterministic terms, we get

$$\Delta y_t = \nu + \Pi^+ \begin{bmatrix} y_{t-1} \\ t-1 \end{bmatrix} + \sum_{j=1}^{p-1} \Gamma_j \Delta y_{t-j} + u_t,$$
(3.38)

where $\Pi^+ = \alpha[\beta' : \eta]$ is a $(K \times (K+1))$ matrix of rank r with $\eta = -\beta'\mu_1$. Furthermore, $\nu = -\Pi\mu_0 + (I_K - \Gamma_1 - \cdots - \Gamma_{p-1})\mu_1$. In this case both the variables and the cointegration relations may have a deterministic linear trend. Again, the test statistics can be obtained conveniently via RR regression applied to the VECMs by using the techniques of Section 3.3.2. The model (3.38) takes into account the fact that the linear trend term can be absorbed into the cointegration relation. Otherwise a quadratic trend would be possible in the variables that is, however, excluded by the model statement in (3.32). Alternatively, a test may once more be based on prior trend adjustment and estimation of (3.37) with estimated μ_0 and μ_1. The trend parameters are again estimated in a first step by a GLS procedure [see Saikkonen & Lütkepohl (2000d) for details and Lütkepohl & Saikkonen (2000) for critical values]. Neither of the two resulting

Table 3.1. *Models and LR-type tests for cointegration*

Assumption for deterministic term	Model setup [reference]
μ_0 arbitrary, $\mu_1 = 0$	$\Delta y_t = \Pi^* \begin{bmatrix} y_{t-1} \\ 1 \end{bmatrix} + \sum_{j=1}^{p-1} \Gamma_j \Delta y_{t-j} + u_t$ [Johansen (1995a)]
	$\Delta y_t = \Pi(y_{t-1} - \mu_0) + \sum_{j=1}^{p-1} \Gamma_j \Delta y_{t-j} + u_t$ [Saikkonen & Luukkonen (1997), Saikkonen & Lütkepohl (2000d)]
μ_0 arbitrary $\mu_1 \neq 0, \beta'\mu_1 = 0$	$\Delta y_t = \nu_0 + \Pi y_{t-1} + \sum_{j=1}^{p-1} \Gamma_j \Delta y_{t-j} + u_t$ [Johansen (1995a)]
	$\Delta y_t - \mu_1 = \Pi(y_{t-1} - \mu_0) + \sum_{j=1}^{p-1} \Gamma_j(\Delta y_{t-j} - \mu_1) + u_t$ [Saikkonen & Lütkepohl (2000b)]
μ_0, μ_1 arbitrary	$\Delta y_t = \nu + \Pi^+ \begin{bmatrix} y_{t-1} \\ t-1 \end{bmatrix} + \sum_{j=1}^{p-1} \Gamma_j \Delta y_{t-j} + u_t$ [Johansen (1992, 1994, 1995a)]
	$\Delta y_t - \mu_1 = \Pi(y_{t-1} - \mu_0 - \mu_1(t-1))$ $\qquad + \sum_{j=1}^{p-1} \Gamma_j(\Delta y_{t-j} - \mu_1) + u_t$ [Saikkonen & Lütkepohl (2000d), Lütkepohl & Saikkonen (2000)]

test versions was found to be superior in all situations; hence, both tests may be applied.

All the tests are summarized in Table 3.1. Suitable critical values based on the asymptotic null distributions may be found in the references given in that table as well. It is worth noting that seasonal dummy variables may be added to the deterministic term. This will not change the asymptotic properties of the tests. On the other hand, other dummy variables may have an impact on the asymptotic distribution of the tests. A particular case of practical relevance is discussed shortly.

We have applied cointegration tests to check the cointegrating rank of the German interest rate–inflation system. Because the series do not have an apparent linear trend, we just include a constant and seasonal dummy variables. The AIC suggests including three lagged differences, whereas HQ and SC favor a specification without lagged differences. Therefore we have applied the cointegration tests using both types of models. The results of the Johansen trace tests and the tests proposed by Saikkonen and Lütkepohl (S&L tests) are presented in Table 3.2. It turns out that the Johansen test rejects rank 0 and does not reject rank 1 for both lag orders. Thus, on the basis of this test, one would continue the analysis with a model with one cointegration relation. The

Table 3.2. *Tests for cointegration in the German interest rate–inflation system*

Test	No. of lagged differences	Null hypothesis	Test value	Critical values 90%	Critical values 95%
Johansen	0	$r = 0$	89.72	17.79	19.99
		$r = 1$	1.54	7.50	9.13
	3	$r = 0$	21.78	17.79	19.99
		$r = 1$	4.77	7.50	9.13
S&L	0	$r = 0$	28.21	10.35	12.21
		$r = 1$	0.41	2.98	4.14
	3	$r = 0$	10.13	10.35	12.21
		$r = 1$	2.42	2.98	4.14

Notes: Sample period: $1972Q2$–$1998Q4$ (including presample values). Deterministic terms: constant and seasonal dummies. Critical values from Johansen (1995a, Tables 15.1 and 15.2) for the S&L and Johansen tests, respectively.

situation is slightly different for the S&L tests. Applying on S&L test, one clearly finds rank one when no lagged differences are included. Otherwise the test cannot reject the null hypothesis $r = 0$ at the 10% level. This result reflects the possible loss in power caused by using long lag lengths. Still the test value is close to the 90% quantile of the asymptotic distribution. Hence, the overall conclusion is that working with one cointegrating relation is a reasonable choice.

Structural shifts. If there is a structural shift in the level of the DGP and if the shift can be captured by adding dummy variables to the deterministic part of the process, including such terms in the model leads to a change in the asymptotic distributions of the Johansen-type tests for the cointegrating rank. In fact, the null distributions will depend on where the shifts have occurred in the sampling period [see Johansen, Mosconi & Nielsen (2000)]. In contrast, Saikkonen & Lütkepohl (2000c) have extended their approach to DGPs with level shifts and have shown that, for their tests, the limiting null distributions are unaffected. For the case of shifts in period τ, they consider the following model:

$$y_t = \mu_0 + \mu_1 t + \delta d_{t\tau} + x_t,$$

where μ_i ($i = 0, 1$) and δ are unknown ($K \times 1$) parameter vectors. The quantity $d_{t\tau}$ is a dummy variable defined as

$$d_{t\tau} = \begin{cases} 0, & t < \tau, \\ 1, & t \geq \tau, \end{cases}$$

that is, $d_{t\tau}$ is a shift dummy variable representing a shift in period τ. The unobserved error process x_t is again assumed to have a VECM($p - 1$) form. Then the observed process y_t can be shown to have a VECM representation

$$\Delta y_t = v + \Pi^{\text{shift}} \begin{bmatrix} y_{t-1} \\ t - 1 \\ d_{t-1,\tau} \end{bmatrix} + \sum_{j=1}^{p-1} \Gamma_j \Delta y_{t-j} + \sum_{j=0}^{p-1} \gamma_j \Delta d_{t-j,\tau} + u_t,$$

where v is, as in (3.38), $\Pi^{\text{shift}} = \alpha[\beta' : \eta : \theta]$ is $(K \times (K + 2))$ of rank r, $\eta = -\beta'\mu_1$, $\theta = -\beta'\delta$, and

$$\gamma_j = \begin{cases} \delta, & j = 0, \\ -\Gamma_j \delta, & j = 1, \ldots, p - 1. \end{cases}$$

Here $\Delta d_{t-j,\tau}$ is an impulse dummy variable with value 1 in period $t = \tau + j$ and 0 elsewhere.

For a given value of the shift date τ, the deterministic part of the DGP can be estimated by RR regression if the nonlinear restrictions between the parameters in the model are ignored, that is, the γ_js are estimated unrestrictedly. Given that the restrictions occur in coefficient vectors of impulse dummies only, Saikkonen & Lütkepohl (2000c) have suggested ignoring them because doing so is not expected to do great damage to the properties of the other estimators, even in small samples. Once estimates of the parameters associated with the x_t process are available, they can again be used to estimate the parameters of the deterministic terms by a feasible GLS procedure. The observations are then adjusted for deterministic terms, and cointegration tests are based on the adjusted series as previously. The resulting test statistics for the cointegrating rank have the same limiting distributions under the null hypothesis as in the previous section, where no shift term was present. In other words, the asymptotic critical values to be used depend only on the assumptions regarding the trend terms and can be found in the references given in Table 3.1. Of course, the case where $\mu_1 = 0$ is known a priori (hence, no linear trend appears in the model) can be treated analogously.

For illustration we use the German GNP, money (M3), and interest rate (R) series plotted in Figure 3.1. As mentioned in the introduction to this chapter, the three variables may be related by a money demand function, where the demand for money depends on the transactions volume, represented by GNP, and opportunity costs for holding money, represented by R. Thus, the three series may be cointegrated. The cointegrating rank of these three variables was actually investigated by Lütkepohl & Wolters (2003). For $gnp = \log$ GNP and $m = \log$ M3 there may be a deterministic linear trend, and unit root tests provide evidence for a stochastic trend as well. Moreover, the series have a seasonal component; thus, seasonal dummy variables will be included in the model underlying the cointegration tests and there is a clear shift in the third quarter of 1990, where the German reunification occurred. This level shift can

Table 3.3. *Tests for the cointegrating rank of the German money demand system*

Test	No. of lagged differences	Null hypothesis	Test value	Critical values 90%	95%
Johansen	0	$r = 0$	33.75	39.08	42.20
		$r = 1$	10.67	22.95	25.47
		$r = 2$	4.04	10.56	12.39
	2	$r = 0$	25.50	39.08	42.20
		$r = 1$	12.51	22.95	25.47
		$r = 2$	4.10	10.56	12.39
S&L	0	$r = 0$	20.31	25.90	28.47
		$r = 1$	6.41	13.89	15.92
		$r = 2$	3.60	5.43	6.83
	2	$r = 0$	16.03	25.90	28.47
		$r = 1$	6.03	13.89	15.92
		$r = 2$	4.11	5.43	6.83
S&L with shift dummy	0	$r = 0$	35.31	25.90	28.47
		$r = 1$	12.43	13.89	15.92
		$r = 2$	0.15	5.43	6.83
	4	$r = 0$	13.60	25.90	28.47
		$r = 1$	5.62	13.89	15.92
		$r = 2$	1.04	5.43	6.83

Notes: Deterministic terms in all models: constant, linear trend, and seasonal dummies. Sample period: $1972Q1-1998Q4$ (including presample values). Critical values from Johansen (1995a, Table 15.4) for the Johansen tests and Lütkepohl & Saikkonen (2000, Table 1) for the S&L tests.

perhaps be taken care of by a shift dummy $S90Q3_t$, which is 1 from $1990Q3$ onwards and 0 before that date.

We have performed cointegrating rank tests with and without the shift dummy to show the consequences of ignoring a structural break. The results are given in Table 3.3. A linear trend, which is not assumed to be orthogonal to the cointegration relations, and seasonal dummies are included in all the tests, and the observation period is $1972Q1-1998Q4$. The first few observations are used as presample values in the usual way. The number of presample values depends on the number of lagged differences included in the model. Different lag orders are suggested by the AIC and HQ criteria and are therefore also used in the tests. It turns out that none of the tests find cointegration if no shift dummy is included in the model, whereas there is at least some evidence for one cointegration relation if $S90Q3$ is included. More precisely, a cointegration rank of zero is clearly rejected if the HQ lag order zero is considered. Hence, not being able to reject a cointegrating rank of zero when the shift is ignored may be a power problem. Thus, in this case it pays to account for the shift.

Some remarks. A comprehensive survey of the properties of LR-type tests for the cointegrating rank as well as numerous other tests that have been proposed in the literature is given by Hubrich, Lütkepohl & Saikkonen (2001). We refer the interested reader to that article for further details. Here we will only add a few specific remarks.

Instead of the pair of hypotheses in (3.31), one may alternatively test $H_0(r_0)$: $rk(\Pi) = r_0$ versus $H_1^*(r_0)$: $rk(\Pi) = r_0 + 1$. LR tests for this pair of hypotheses were also pioneered by Johansen (1988, 1991) and are known as *maximum eigenvalue tests*. They are based on a statistic

$$LR_{max}(r_0) = -T \log(1 - \lambda_{r_0+1})$$

and can be applied for all the different cases listed in Table 3.1. They also have nonstandard limiting distributions. Critical values can be found in the literature cited in the foregoing. Lütkepohl, Saikkonen & Trenkler (2001a) have compared several different maximum eigenvalue and trace tests and found that the latter have sometimes slightly more distorted sizes than the former in small samples but may also have power advantages.

The limiting distributions of the LR statistics are not only valid for normally distributed (Gaussian) processes but also under more general distributional assumptions even if the LR statistics are computed under Gaussian assumptions. In that situation these tests are just quasi-LR tests. Saikkonen & Luukkonen (1997) have demonstrated that some of the tests remain asymptotically valid even if they are based on a finite order model although the true DGP has an infinite VAR order. This result is of interest because, in practice, tests for unit roots and cointegration are usually applied to the univariate series or subsystems first to determine the order of integration for the individual variables or the cointegrating properties of a subset of variables. However, if the full system of variables is driven by a finite-order VAR process, then the generating process of the individual variables may be of the infinite-order autoregressive type [see Lütkepohl (1991, Section 6.6)]. Hence, for the sake of consistency it is reassuring to know that the tests remain valid for this case. Lütkepohl & Saikkonen (1999) have analyzed this situation in more detail. In particular, these authors consider the impact of lag length selection in this context.

There is a notable difference between the asymptotic properties of the tests and their actual performance for samples of the size typically available in economics. The properties of the tests in small samples depend quite strongly on the lag order chosen. Working with a low-order model that does not capture the serial dependence in the data well may lead to size distortions, whereas choosing an unnecessarily large lag order may spoil the power of the tests. Thus, it is a good strategy to perform tests for different lag orders and to check the

Table 3.4. *Hypotheses and tests concerning the deterministic term in a system of K variables and a given cointegrating rank r*

H_0	H_1	Asymptotic distribution of LR statistic
μ_0 arbitrary, $\mu_1 = 0$	μ_0 arbitrary, $\mu_1 \neq 0$, $\beta'\mu_1 = 0$	$\chi^2(K - r)$
μ_0 arbitrary, $\mu_1 \neq 0$, $\beta'\mu_1 = 0$	μ_0, μ_1 arbitrary	$\chi^2(r)$

robustness of the results. A large-scale simulation study comparing the small sample properties of many of the tests was performed by Hubrich et al. (2001). The tests presented herein were found to perform relatively well compared with other possible tests for the cointegrating rank.

Instead of the sequential testing procedures, model selection criteria may be used for determining the cointegrating rank. This possibility is considered, for instance, by Lütkepohl & Poskitt (1998) and Gonzalo & Pitarakis (1998).

3.4.3 Choice of Deterministic Term

The foregoing discussion of the implications of the deterministic term for tests of the cointegrating rank reveals that a proper choice of that term is important. Of course, if a linear time trend is regarded as a possibility, one could just include such a term in the process in fully general form to be on the safe side. This, however, may result in a substantial power loss if the time trend is not needed in the model. In Doornik, Hendry & Nielsen (1998), small sample and asymptotic evidence is presented that, not taking into account a deterministic trend actually present in the DGP, may result in major size distortions, and their study confirms that including an unnecessary trend term may result in a loss of power [see also Hubrich et al. (2001)].

Therefore, in applied work, investing some effort in a proper trend specification is worthwhile. This is often based on subject matter considerations or a visual inspection of the plots of the time series under study. For instance, a deterministic linear trend is often regarded as unlikely for interest rates for theoretical reasons. Consequently, if a system of interest rates is analyzed, including a mean term may be sufficient.

There are also statistical procedures that can aid in deciding on the deterministic components. Specifically, tests are proposed in Johansen (1994, 1995a) for hypotheses regarding the deterministic term within his Gaussian likelihood framework. Apart from dummy variables, the most general deterministic term in the VAR or VECM form of the processes considered thus far is $\mu_0 + \mu_1 t$. To formulate the tests for the deterministic terms we list the hypotheses of interest in Table 3.4. Because the ML estimators of the corresponding models can be obtained easily, as seen in the previous section, LR tests are obvious possibilities. The test statistics have asymptotic χ^2-distributions under the null hypothesis. For some pairs of hypotheses of interest, the corresponding asymptotic distributions are given in Table 3.4 [see Johansen (1994)]. As usual, the Gaussian framework is convenient in deriving the tests, whereas the limiting distributions of the test statistics remain valid under more general conditions.

For example, in the German interest rate–inflation system we have assumed that no linear trend is required in the model. We can now check this assumption using the first test in Table 3.4. For this purpose, we use a model with cointegrating rank 1 and without lagged differences. In other words, we use the lag order favored by the HQ and SC criteria. We estimate a model with the constant term restricted to the cointegrating relation and one with an unrestricted constant term. The likelihood ratio statistic is easily obtained from the determinants of the residual covariance matrices by taking natural logs and multiplying the difference by $T = 106$. In this case a value of 2.07 is obtained that has to be compared with a critical value of a $\chi^2(1)$-distribution because $K = 2$ and $r = 1$. Given that, for instance, the 90% quantile of the $\chi^2(1)$-distribution is 2.7, the null hypothesis cannot be rejected at any common level. On this basis our previous decision to dispense with a linear trend term is supported.

Although such tests may be helpful in deciding on the deterministic term, one should keep in mind that they introduce an additional layer of uncertainty into the overall procedure. The tests assume a specific cointegrating rank. Thus, ideally, the cointegrating rank has to be determined before the deterministic terms are tested. Therefore, checking the robustness of the testing results for the cointegrating rank to different specifications of the deterministic terms is a useful strategy. Note also that deterministic terms other than means and linear trends may be required for a proper description of the DGP. Notably, dummy variables to account for seasonality or structural shifts may be considered. Properly specified seasonal dummies do not affect the asymptotic distribution under the null hypothesis, as shown by Johansen (1995a).

3.4.4 Testing Restrictions Related to the Cointegration Vectors and the Loading Matrix

Overidentifying linear restrictions on the cointegration space can also be tested conveniently by LR or quasi-LR tests because, under Gaussian assumptions, the restricted ML estimators are readily available, as discussed in Section 3.3.3. Testing

$$H_0 : \beta = H\varphi \quad \text{versus} \quad H_1 : \beta \neq H\varphi$$

for a given, fixed $(K \times s)$ matrix H, $r \leq s < K$, and a $(s \times r)$ parameter matrix φ is particularly easy because φ can be estimated by solving the eigenvalue problem (3.27). The corresponding LR statistic is

$$LR_H = T \sum_{i=1}^{r} [\log(1 - \lambda_i^H) - \log(1 - \lambda_i)],$$

where the λ_i's are the solutions from an "unrestricted" eigenvalue problem such as (3.16). Under H_0, LR_H has an asymptotic $\chi^2(r(K - s))$-distribution [see Johansen (1995a)]. A similar procedure can also be used if the null hypothesis is more complicated (e.g., $H_0 : \beta = [H_1\varphi_1, H_2\varphi_2]$). In that case, the ML estimators can also be obtained as described in Section 3.3.3.

Alternatively, if the restrictions can be put in the general linear form (3.20) for the normalized cointegration matrix,

$$H_0 : R\text{vec}(\beta'_{(K-r)}) = r,$$

where R is a fixed $(J \times r(K - r))$ matrix of rank J and r is a $(J \times 1)$ vector, the Wald statistic (3.21)

$$\lambda_W = [R\text{vec}(\hat{\beta}'_{(K-r)}) - r]'(R\hat{\Omega}R')^{-1}[R\text{vec}(\hat{\beta}'_{(K-r)}) - r]$$

can be used to check the restrictions. It has an asymptotic χ^2-distribution with J degrees of freedom under H_0, as seen in (3.21).

Hypotheses for the loading matrix α may also be of interest. For example, one may wish to test that some or all of the cointegrating relations do not enter a particular equation and thus that the corresponding left-hand variable is weakly exogenous for the cointegration parameters. More generally, suppose that we wish to test

$$H_0 : \alpha = G\psi \quad \text{versus} \quad H_1 : \alpha \neq G\psi,$$

where G is a given $(K \times s)$ matrix and ψ is $(s \times r)$ with $r \leq s < K$. Again the restricted estimator may be obtained by an ML procedure as described in Section 3.3.3, and the corresponding LR test statistic has a $\chi^2(r(K - s))$ limiting distribution under H_0. Moreover, there may be restrictions on both α and β that can be tested jointly by an LR test.

As an alternative we may again use Wald tests for restrictions on α by applying the results discussed in Section 3.3.4. Using a two-stage procedure in which β is estimated first and then fixed in the second stage, we may treat α in the same way as the short-run parameters. Procedures for placing restrictions on them will be discussed next.

3.4.5 Testing Restrictions for the Short-Run Parameters and Fitting Subset Models

The standard t-ratios and F-tests retain their usual asymptotic properties if they are applied to the short-run parameters in a VECM, whereas problems may arise for integrated variables in the levels VAR representation, as mentioned in Section 3.3.1. It is therefore a good idea to impose restrictions on the VECM parameters, although there are also many situations in which the tests are unproblematic for checking restrictions of the VAR coefficients, as discussed in Section 3.3.1. A particular set of restrictions for which problems arise is discussed in more detail in Section 3.7.

Instead of using statistical testing procedures, restrictions for individual parameters or groups of parameters in VARs or VECMs may be based on model selection criteria. For placing individual parameter restrictions we consider the single equations of the system. Suppose the equation of interest is of the form

$$y_{jt} = x_{1t}\theta_1 + \cdots + x_{Nt}\theta_N + u_{jt}, \quad t = 1, \ldots, T. \tag{3.39}$$

Here all right-hand-side variables are denoted by x_{kt}, including deterministic variables, constants, or unlagged endogenous variables if the equation belongs to a structural form. In some situations it is also convenient to include cointegration relations among the x_{kt}s. For example, $x_{kt} = \beta' y_{t-1}$ may be a regressor if β is a known vector. For the present purposes it is convenient to write the variable selection criteria in the form

$$CR(i_1, \ldots, i_n) = \log(SSE(i_1, \ldots, i_n)/T) + c_T n/T, \tag{3.40}$$

where $SSE(i_1, \ldots, i_n)$ is the sum of squared errors obtained by including $x_{i_1 t}, \ldots, x_{i_n t}$ in the regression model (3.39) and c_T is a sequence, as in (3.30). The following variable elimination strategies have, for instance, been considered in the literature [see, e.g., Brüggemann & Lütkepohl (2001)].

Full search. Choose the regressors that minimize $CR(i_1, \ldots, i_n)$ for all subsets $\{i_1, \ldots, i_n\} \subset \{1, \ldots, N\}$, where $n = 0, \ldots, N$.   □

This procedure is computationally expensive if N is large. The set $\{1, \ldots, N\}$ has 2^N subsets. Therefore 2^N models have to be compared. The following elimination procedure proceeds sequentially and is computationally more efficient. One variable only is eliminated in each step.

Sequential elimination of regressors. Sequentially delete those regressors that lead to the largest reduction of the given selection criterion until no further reduction is possible.   □

Individual zero coefficients can also be chosen on the basis of the t-ratios of the parameter estimators. A possible strategy is to delete sequentially those regressors with the smallest absolute values of t-ratios until all t-ratios (in absolute value) are greater than some threshold value γ. Note that a single regressor is eliminated in each step only. Then new t-ratios are computed for the reduced model. Brüggemann & Lütkepohl (2001) have shown that this strategy is equivalent to the sequential elimination based on model selection criteria if the threshold value γ is chosen accordingly. More precisely, these authors show that choosing $\gamma = \{[\exp(c_T/T) - 1](T - N + j - 1)\}^{1/2}$ in the jth step of the elimination procedure results in the same final model that is obtained by sequentially minimizing the selection criterion defined by the penalty term c_T. Hence, the threshold value depends on the selection criterion via c_T, the sample size, and the number of regressors in the model. The threshold values for the t-ratios correspond to the critical values of the tests. The aforementioned AIC, HQ, and SC with $c_T(AIC) = 2$, $c_T(HQ) = 2\log\log T$, and $c_T(SC) = \log T$, respectively, may be used in these procedures. In that case, for an equation with twenty regressors and a sample size of $T = 100$, choosing a model by AIC, HQ, or SC roughly corresponds to eliminating all regressors with t-values that are not significant at the 15–20%, 10%, or 2–3% levels, respectively [see Brüggemann & Lütkepohl (2001)].

We are using the German interest rate–inflation example again to illustrate subset modeling. Restricting the error correction term as $ec_t = R_t - 4Dp_t$ and using the sequential elimination of regressors in conjunction with the AIC based on a search for restrictions on individual equations, we obtain the following model

$$
\begin{bmatrix} \Delta R_t \\ \Delta Dp_t \end{bmatrix} = \begin{bmatrix} -0.07 \\ {\scriptstyle(-3.1)} \\ 0.17 \\ {\scriptstyle(4.5)} \end{bmatrix} (R_{t-1} - 4Dp_{t-1}) + \begin{bmatrix} 0.24 & -0.08 \\ {\scriptstyle(2.5)} & {\scriptstyle(-1.9)} \\ 0 & -0.31 \\ & {\scriptstyle(-2.5)} \end{bmatrix} \begin{bmatrix} \Delta R_{t-1} \\ \Delta Dp_{t-1} \end{bmatrix}
$$

$$
+ \begin{bmatrix} 0 & -0.13 \\ & {\scriptstyle(-2.5)} \\ 0 & -0.37 \\ & {\scriptstyle(-3.6)} \end{bmatrix} \begin{bmatrix} \Delta R_{t-2} \\ \Delta Dp_{t-2} \end{bmatrix} + \begin{bmatrix} 0.20 & -0.06 \\ {\scriptstyle(2.1)} & {\scriptstyle(-1.6)} \\ 0 & -0.34 \\ & {\scriptstyle(-4.7)} \end{bmatrix} \begin{bmatrix} \Delta R_{t-3} \\ \Delta Dp_{t-3} \end{bmatrix}
$$

$$
+ \begin{bmatrix} 0 & 0 & 0.010 & 0 \\ & & {\scriptstyle(2.8)} & \\ 0.010 & -0.034 & -0.018 & -0.016 \\ {\scriptstyle(3.0)} & {\scriptstyle(-7.6)} & {\scriptstyle(-3.8)} & {\scriptstyle(-3.6)} \end{bmatrix} \begin{bmatrix} c \\ s_{1,t} \\ s_{2,t} \\ s_{3,t} \end{bmatrix} + \begin{bmatrix} \hat{u}_{1,t} \\ \hat{u}_{2,t} \end{bmatrix}. \quad (3.41)
$$

Here again the sample period $1973Q2$–$1998Q4$ plus the required presample values have been used. Obviously, quite a few coefficients are set to zero. In fact, the ΔR_t lags do not appear in the second equation anymore. The coefficients remaining in the model generally have fairly large t-ratios (in absolute value), as expected. Notice, however, that the finally chosen model was estimated by feasible GLS for the full system (3SLS). The resulting estimates are shown in Equation (3.41) with corresponding t-ratios in parentheses. Thus, in the search procedure based on individual equations, different t-ratios are the basis for variable selection. Still, generally the coefficients with large absolute *t*-ratios in the unrestricted model (3.28) are maintained in the restricted subset VECM.

It may be worth emphasizing that the same subset model selection procedure may be applied if the cointegration relation contains estimated parameters. In other words, it may be used as the second stage in a two-stage procedure in which the cointegration matrix β is estimated first and then the estimated β matrix is substituted for the true one in the second stage, where subset restrictions are determined.

3.5 Model Checking

Many statistical tools exist for checking whether a given VAR model or VECM provides an adequate representation of the DGP underlying the time series set of interest. As in the univariate case, many of them are based on the residuals of the final model. Some of them are applied to the residuals of individual equations and others are based on the full residual vectors. Graphical tools for model checking as well as recursive estimates and recursive residuals may also be considered. Some of the tools will be presented in this section.

If model defects such as residual autocorrelation or ARCH effects are detected at the checking stage, this is usually regarded as an indication that the model is a poor representation of the DGP. Efforts are then made to find a better representation by adding other variables or lags to the model, by including nonlinear terms or changing the functional form, by modifying the sampling period, or getting other data.

3.5.1 Descriptive Analysis of the Residuals

A descriptive analysis of the model residuals is at least partly based on the individual series. Therefore the graphs considered for checking univariate time series are relevant here as well. For example, plots of standardized residual series and squared residuals may be informative. Kernel density estimates may also be of interest. In addition to the autocorrelation functions of the individual series, the cross correlations are now also informative.

As an example, consider the subset VECM (3.41) of the German interest rate–inflation system. The standardized residuals, residual autocorrelations, and cross correlations are plotted in Figure 3.2. The plot of the standardized residuals indicates that some ARCH may be present in the residuals of the interest rate equation (the first equation), or there may even be a change in the structure of the relationship. Some relatively large residuals (in absolute value) in the first half of the sample period may also create problems for nonnormality tests. It may be useful to remember this point later. Although some residual autocorrelations reach outside the $\pm 2/\sqrt{T}$ bounds, they do not give rise to concern

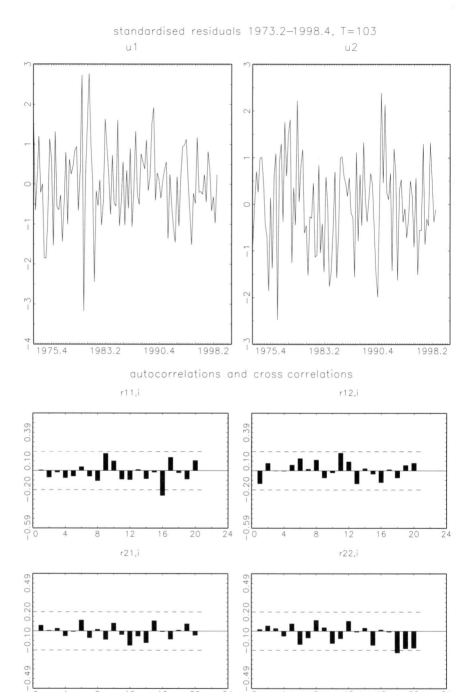

Figure 3.2. Residuals and residual autocorrelations of subset VECM (3.41) of German interest rate–inflation system (sample period: 1973*Q*2–1998*Q*4).

because the "large" autocorrelations are at high lags. Formal tests for residual autocorrelation will be discussed shortly.

3.5.2 Diagnostic Tests

A range of diagnostic tests is available for checking the model assumptions and properties formally. Tests for autocorrelation, nonnormality, and conditional heteroskedasticity are considered in this section.

Portmanteau test for autocorrelation. A formal test for residual autocorrelation may be based on the portmanteau or adjusted portmanteau statistic. The test checks the null hypothesis

$$H_0 : E(u_t u'_{t-i}) = 0, \quad i = 1, \ldots, h > p$$

against the alternative that at least one autocovariance and, hence, one autocorrelation is nonzero. The test statistic has the form

$$Q_h = T \sum_{j=1}^{h} \text{tr}(\hat{C}'_j \hat{C}_0^{-1} \hat{C}_j \hat{C}_0^{-1}),$$

where $\hat{C}_i = T^{-1} \sum_{t=i+1}^{T} \hat{u}_t \hat{u}'_{t-i}$. Suppose the $\hat{u}_t$s are residuals from a stable VAR(p) process. Then, under the null hypothesis, Q_h has an approximate $\chi^2(K^2(h - p))$-distribution. More generally, the number of degrees of freedom is determined as the difference between the autocorrelations included (K^2h) and the number of estimated VAR coefficients. The latter number can be smaller than K^2p if subset restrictions are imposed. If the test is applied to the residuals of a VECM, the parameters in the cointegration relations are not counted. As in the univariate case, the limiting χ^2-distribution is strictly valid only if $h \to \infty$ at a suitable rate with growing sample size [see Ahn (1988)]. A modified statistic with potentially superior small sample properties is the adjusted portmanteau statistic

$$Q_h^* = T^2 \sum_{j=1}^{h} \frac{1}{T - j} \text{tr}(\hat{C}'_j \hat{C}_0^{-1} \hat{C}_j \hat{C}_0^{-1}),$$

which is similar to the Ljung–Box statistic for univariate series.

In practice, the choice of h may be critical for the test result. If h is chosen too small, the χ^2-approximation to the null distribution may be very poor, whereas a large h may result in a loss of power. Therefore, in applying the test it is a good idea to try different values of h.

Another test for autocorrelation may be obtained by overfitting the VAR order; that is, a model with order $p^* > p$ is fitted and the significance of the additional lags is checked by a χ^2- or F-version of an LR or Wald test for parameter restrictions. Yet another possibility to test for residual autocorrelation is obtained by fitting a VAR model to the residuals. This variant is sometimes referred to as *Breusch–Godfrey test*. It is described next.

Breusch–Godfrey test for autocorrelation. The Breusch–Godfrey test [see, e.g., Godfrey (1988)] for hth order residual autocorrelation assumes a model

$$u_t = B_1 u_{t-1} + \cdots + B_h u_{t-h} + \text{error}_t$$

and checks

$$H_0 : B_1 = \cdots = B_h = 0 \quad \text{versus} \quad H_1 : B_1 \neq 0 \text{ or } \cdots \text{ or } B_h \neq 0.$$

For this purpose, the auxiliary model

$$\hat{u}_t = A_1 y_{t-1} + \cdots + A_p y_{t-p} + CD_t$$
$$+ B_1 \hat{u}_{t-1} + \cdots + B_h \hat{u}_{t-h} + e_t \tag{3.42}$$

or the analogous VECM form

$$\hat{u}_t = \alpha \hat{\beta}' y_{t-1} + \Gamma_1 \Delta y_{t-1} + \cdots + \Gamma_{p-1} \Delta y_{t-p+1}$$
$$+ CD_t + B_1 \hat{u}_{t-1} + \cdots + B_h \hat{u}_{t-h} + e_t \tag{3.43}$$

is considered if there are no exogenous variables and the original models are set up in reduced form without restrictions on the A_js or Γ_js. The models are estimated by OLS. Notice that the $\hat{u}_t$s with $t \leq 0$ are replaced by zero in estimating (3.42) or (3.43).

Denoting the estimated residuals by $\hat{e}_t$ ($t = 1, \ldots, T$), we obtain the following residual covariance matrix estimator from the auxiliary models:

$$\widetilde{\Sigma}_e = \frac{1}{T} \sum_{t=1}^{T} \hat{e}_t \hat{e}_t'.$$

Moreover, if we reestimate the relevant auxiliary model without the lagged residuals $\hat{u}_{t-i}$ ($i = 1, \ldots, h$), that is, impose the restrictions $B_1 = \cdots = B_h = 0$ and denote the resulting residuals by $\hat{e}_t^R$, the corresponding covariance matrix estimator is

$$\widetilde{\Sigma}_R = \frac{1}{T} \sum_{t=1}^{T} \hat{e}_t^R \hat{e}_t^{R'}.$$

The relevant LM statistic is then

$$LM_h = T \left[K - \text{tr} \left(\widetilde{\Sigma}_e \widetilde{\Sigma}_R^{-1} \right) \right].$$

It has an asymptotic $\chi^2(hK^2)$-distribution under standard assumptions. A variant of the test statistic that adjusts the "likelihood ratio" in such a way that its distribution under H_0 can be approximated well by an F-distribution was recommended by Edgerton & Shukur (1999). More precisely, they found that, in small samples, the following statistic worked well for stationary full VAR processes without subset restrictions:

$$FLM_h = \left[\left(\frac{|\widetilde{\Sigma}_R|}{|\widetilde{\Sigma}_e|} \right)^{1/s} - 1 \right] \cdot \frac{Ns - q}{Km}$$

with

$$s = \left(\frac{K^2 m^2 - 4}{K^2 + m^2 - 5} \right)^{1/2}, \quad q = \frac{1}{2}Km - 1,$$

$$N = T - n - m - \frac{1}{2}(K - m + 1),$$

where n is the number of regressors in each equation of the original system and $m = Kh$ is the number of additional regressors in the auxiliary system. The statistic is used together with critical values from an $F(hK^2, Ns - q)$-distribution.

The Brensch–Godfrey LM test is useful for testing for low order residual autocorrelation (small h), whereas a portmanteau test is preferable for larger h.

Tests for nonnormality. Multivariate tests for nonnormality can be constructed by generalizing the Lomnicki–Jarque–Bera tests described in Chapter 2. The idea is to transform the joint normal distribution in order to obtain independent components first and then apply the tests described for univariate series to the independent components. Given the residuals $\hat{u}_t$ ($t = 1, \ldots, T$) of an estimated VAR process or VECM, the residual covariance matrix is therefore estimated as

$$\widetilde{\Sigma}_u = T^{-1} \sum_{t=1}^{T} (\hat{u}_t - \bar{\hat{u}})(\hat{u}_t - \bar{\hat{u}})',$$

and the square root matrix $\widetilde{\Sigma}_u^{1/2}$ is computed. Notice that mean adjusting the estimated residuals is unnecessary if intercepts are included in the model equations. The square root $\widetilde{\Sigma}_u^{1/2}$ is obtained by computing the eigenvalues $\lambda_1, \ldots, \lambda_K$ of $\widetilde{\Sigma}_u$ and the corresponding orthonormal matrix of eigenvectors Q such that $\widetilde{\Sigma}_u = Q\Lambda Q'$ with $\Lambda = \mathrm{diag}(\lambda_1, \ldots, \lambda_K)$. Then $\widetilde{\Sigma}_u^{1/2} = Q\mathrm{diag}(\lambda_1^{1/2}, \ldots, \lambda_K^{1/2})Q'$. The tests for nonnormality can be based on the skewness and kurtosis of the standardized residuals $\hat{u}_t^s = (\hat{u}_{1t}^s, \ldots, \hat{u}_{Kt}^s)' = \widetilde{\Sigma}_u^{-1/2}(\hat{u}_t - \bar{\hat{u}})$:

$$\mathbf{b}_1 = (b_{11}, \ldots, b_{1K})' \quad \text{with} \quad b_{1k} = T^{-1} \sum_{t=1}^{T} (\hat{u}_{kt}^s)^3$$

and

$$\mathbf{b}_2 = (b_{21}, \ldots, b_{2K})' \quad \text{with} \quad b_{2k} = T^{-1} \sum_{t=1}^{T} (\hat{u}_{kt}^s)^4.$$

Possible test statistics are

$$s_3^2 = T\mathbf{b}_1'\mathbf{b}_1/6$$

and, if we define the $(K \times 1)$ vector $\mathbf{3}_K = (3, \ldots, 3)'$,

$$s_4^2 = T(\mathbf{b}_2 - \mathbf{3}_K)'(\mathbf{b}_2 - \mathbf{3}_K)/24.$$

Both statistics have asymptotic $\chi^2(K)$-distributions under the null hypothesis of normality. Moreover, under the null, $LJB_K = s_3^2 + s_4^2$ has a $\chi^2(2K)$ limiting distribution.

The standardization of the residuals used here was proposed by Doornik & Hansen (1994). Lütkepohl (1991, Chapter 4) presents an alternative way of standardizing them based on a Choleski decomposition of the residual covariance matrix. Suppose $\widetilde{P}$ is a lower triangular matrix with positive diagonal such that $\widetilde{P}\widetilde{P}' = \widetilde{\Sigma}_u$. Then the standardized residuals are defined as $\hat{u}_t^s = \widetilde{P}^{-1}(\hat{u}_t - \bar{\hat{u}})$. Computing the third and fourth moments as in the foregoing gives statistics s_{3L}^2, s_{4L}^2, and $LJB_K^L = s_{3L}^2 + s_{4L}^2$ with asymptotic $\chi^2(K)$-, $\chi^2(K)$- and $\chi^2(2K)$-distributions, respectively, under normality. The latter approach was criticized by Doornik & Hansen (1994) on the grounds that the test result may depend on the ordering of the variables because the normalization of the residuals is not invariant to the ordering of the variables. Obviously, whatever the normalization procedure, the resulting multivariate test statistic reduces to the Lomnicki–Jarque–Bera statistic for the univariate case. To get a better picture of possible deviations from normality of individual equation errors, the univariate tests may also be applied to the individual residual series separately.

ARCH–LM test. A multivariate extension of the univariate ARCH-LM test may be constructed as follows. Consider the multivariate regression model

$$\text{vech}(\hat{u}_t\hat{u}_t') = \beta_0 + B_1\text{vech}(\hat{u}_{t-1}\hat{u}_{t-1}')$$

$$+ \cdots + B_q\text{vech}(\hat{u}_{t-q}\hat{u}_{t-q}') + \text{error}_t, \tag{3.44}$$

where vech is the column-stacking operator for symmetric matrices that stacks the columns from the main diagonal downwards, β_0 is $\frac{1}{2}K(K+1)$-dimensional, and the B_js are $(\frac{1}{2}K(K+1) \times \frac{1}{2}K(K+1))$ coefficient matrices $(j = 1, \ldots, q)$. There is no ARCH in the residuals if all the B_j matrices are zero. Therefore, an ARCH test is based on the pair of hypotheses

$$H_0 : B_1 = \cdots = B_q = 0 \quad \text{versus} \quad H_1 : B_1 \neq 0 \text{ or } \cdots \text{ or } B_q \neq 0,$$

Table 3.5. *Diagnostics for subset VECM model (3.41) for German interest rate and inflation*

Test	Q_{24}	Q_{24}^*	LM_2	LM_4	LJB_2	LJB_2^l	$MARCH_{LM}(2)$
Test statistic	77.2	89.3	6.62	10.3	2.44	2.76	36.9
Appr. distribution	$\chi^2(86)$	$\chi^2(86)$	$\chi^2(8)$	$\chi^2(16)$	$\chi^2(4)$	$\chi^2(4)$	$\chi^2(18)$
p-value	0.74	0.38	0.58	0.85	0.66	0.60	0.005

which may be checked by the multivariate LM statistic

$$MARCH_{LM}(q) = \frac{1}{2}TK(K+1)R_m^2,$$

where

$$R_m^2 = 1 - \frac{2}{K(K+1)}\text{tr}(\hat{\Omega}\hat{\Omega}_0^{-1}),$$

$\hat{\Omega}$ is the residual covariance matrix of the $\frac{1}{2}K(K+1)$-dimensional regression model (3.44), and $\hat{\Omega}_0$ is the corresponding matrix with $q = 0$. The statistic is similar to the one described by Doornik & Hendry (1997, Section 10.9.2.4) and may be compared with critical values from a $\chi^2(qK^2(K+1)^2/4)$-distribution. Alternatively, an F-version based on $MARCH_{LM}(q)/[qK^2(K+1)^2/4]$ may be used.

Example. As an example we consider again the German interest rate–inflation system. Some diagnostic statistics for the subset VECM (3.41) are shown in Table 3.5. The only test that rejects its respective null hypothesis is the multivariate ARCH test. Clearly, this is not surprising given the way the residuals of the R_t equation look like (see Figure 3.2). One can also analyze the sources of the possible problem in more detail by considering the two residual series individually and performing univariate ARCH tests (see also Chapter 2). Of course, a model rejected by one of the diagnostic tests is not fully satisfactory. However, for some purposes it may still be sufficient. For example, if the linear dependencies are of major concern, the remaining ARCH in the residual series may not be a big problem. For other purposes, it may be desirable, however, to model the conditional variances properly as well. This can be done using the methods presented in Chapter 5.

3.5.3 Stability Analysis

The time invariance of a model may be checked, for example, by considering recursively estimated quantities. For this purpose, the model is estimated on the basis of the first τ observations for $\tau = T_1, \ldots, T$. Here T_1 is such that the degrees of freedom necessary for estimation are available.

Recursive estimation can be done efficiently by using updating formulas if, for example, a full VAR model is considered. However, even more complicated estimation procedures can be performed quickly a few hundred times on a modern computer. Therefore, recursive estimation does not pose serious problems as long as no iterative or simulation-based estimation procedures are necessary. For instance, using bootstrap methods for each sample size may be time-consuming.

Plotting the recursive estimates together with their standard errors or confidence intervals for $\tau = T_1, \ldots, T$ can give useful information on possible structural breaks. As an example, some recursive estimates of the subset VECM (3.41) for the German interest rate–inflation system are shown in Figure 3.3. Obviously, they are a bit erratic at the sample beginning owing to the small sample size on which they are based. Also, the larger confidence intervals around the parameter estimates at the beginning reflect the greater estimation uncertainty. Taking this uncertainty into account, one finds that the recursive estimates do not indicate parameter instability. One may take note, however, of the slight shift in the seasonal dummy variables of the inflation equation in the early 1990s. It may indicate an effect of the German reunification, which happened in 1990, and should be kept in mind in further stability checks.

Formal tests of parameter constancy are also available for vector models. For instance, CUSUM and CUSUM-of-squares tests as well as Chow tests may be used in some situations. Specifically for VECMs, tests based on the recursively computed eigenvalues used in the RR regression estimation may be considered. These tests will be presented in the next section.

CUSUM tests. CUSUM and CUSUM-of-squares tests were described in Section 2.6 of Chapter 2 for single-equation models. These tests can also be applied to the individual equations for vector models. In some cases this will lead to formally valid tests. For example, in a fully unrestricted VAR model with stationary variables, single-equation OLS estimation is efficient and the CUSUM-type tests may be applied. Also, for a VECM, where the cointegration relations are known as in the German interest rate-inflation example, single-equation estimation can be applied without problems even if there are restrictions for the parameters as in (3.41). In that case, the asymptotic efficiency of the estimators can generally be improved by using systems estimation methods. For the subset VECM (3.41), the CUSUM and CUSUM-of-squares plots are shown in Figure 3.4. They are all well inside the uncritical region and therefore do not give rise to concern about the stability of the model.

Generally, the critical bounds will not have a theoretical justification for vector models. For example, if some of the variables are integrated and appear in undifferenced form, or if estimated cointegration relations are present, the validity of the CUSUM-type tests is not clear. In that case they may still be useful

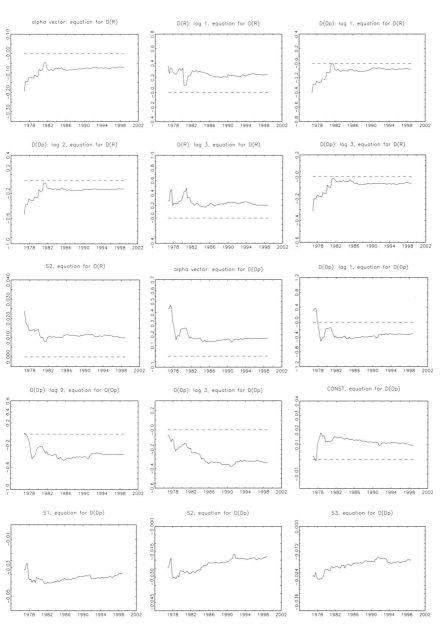

Figure 3.3. Recursive estimates of subset VECM (3.41) for German interest rate–inflation system with recursive 95% confidence intervals (sample period: $1973Q2$–$1998Q4$).

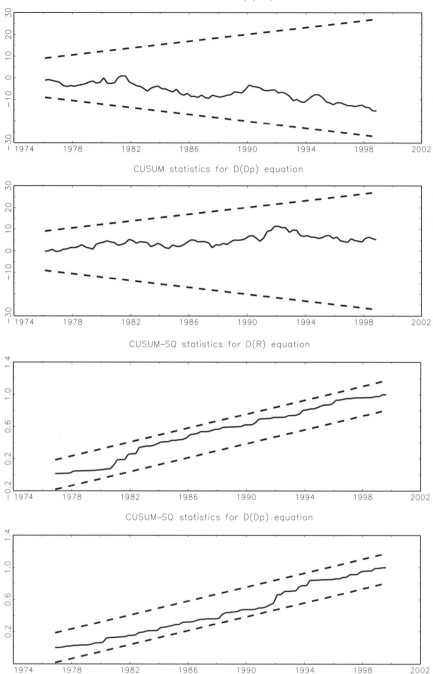

Figure 3.4. CUSUM and CUSUM-of-squares tests of subset VECM (3.41) for German interest rate–inflation system with 5% level critical bounds (sample period: 1973Q2–1998Q4).

descriptive tools for checking model stability if single-equation estimation leads to sensible estimates. The latter condition may be violated for structural form equations. [See Krämer & Sonnberger (1986), Krämer et al. (1988), and Ploberger & Krämer (1992) for further discussion of CUSUM-type tests.]

Chow tests for structural change. As is the case for univariate models, different types of Chow tests are available for vector models [see Doornik & Hendry (1997)]. We present *sample-split, break-point*, and *forecast tests*. On the assumption that a structural break may have occurred in period T_B, the model under consideration is estimated from the full sample of T observations and from the first T_1 and the last T_2 observations, where $T_1 < T_B$ and $T_2 \leq T - T_B$. The resulting residuals are denoted by $\hat{u}_t$, $\hat{u}_t^{(1)}$ and $\hat{u}_t^{(2)}$, respectively. Moreover,

$$\widetilde{\Sigma}_u = T^{-1} \sum_{t=1}^{T} \hat{u}_t \hat{u}_t',$$

$$\widetilde{\Sigma}_{1,2} = (T_1 + T_2)^{-1} \left(\sum_{t=1}^{T_1} \hat{u}_t \hat{u}_t' + \sum_{t=T-T_2+1}^{T} \hat{u}_t \hat{u}_t' \right),$$

$$\widetilde{\Sigma}_{(1,2)} = T_1^{-1} \sum_{t=1}^{T_1} \hat{u}_t \hat{u}_t' + T_2^{-1} \sum_{t=T-T_2+1}^{T} \hat{u}_t \hat{u}_t',$$

$$\widetilde{\Sigma}_{(1)} = T_1^{-1} \sum_{t=1}^{T_1} \hat{u}_t^{(1)} \hat{u}_t^{(1)'}$$

and

$$\widetilde{\Sigma}_{(2)} = T_2^{-1} \sum_{t=T-T_2+1}^{T} \hat{u}_t^{(2)} \hat{u}_t^{(2)'}.$$

With this notation, the sample-split (SS) test statistic can be written as

$$\lambda_{SS} = (T_1 + T_2)[\log \det \widetilde{\Sigma}_{1,2} - \log \det\{(T_1 + T_2)^{-1}(T_1 \widetilde{\Sigma}_{(1)} + T_2 \widetilde{\Sigma}_{(2)})\}],$$

and the break-point (BP) statistic is

$$\lambda_{BP} = (T_1 + T_2) \log \det \widetilde{\Sigma}_{(1,2)} - T_1 \log \det \widetilde{\Sigma}_{(1)} - T_2 \log \det \widetilde{\Sigma}_{(2)}.$$

If the model is time invariant, these statistics have approximate χ^2-distributions. The degrees of freedom are given by the number of restrictions imposed by assuming a constant coefficient model for the full sample period; that is, the degrees of freedom are the difference between the sum of the number of free coefficients estimated in the first and last subperiods and the number of free coefficients in the full sample model. The parameter constancy hypothesis is rejected if the value of the test statistics is large. The statistic λ_{SS} is used for a test that assumes a constant white noise covariance matrix and λ_{BP} tests against a changing Σ_u in addition [see Hansen (2003) for the asymptotic theory].

To illustrate the determination of the degrees of freedom for the tests, consider first a K-dimensional stationary VAR(p) model with constant term $y_t = \nu + A_1 y_{t-1} + \cdots + A_p y_{t-p} + u_t$. In this case the number of parameters is the same in both subperiods. Hence, counting all the VAR and deterministic parameters shows that λ_{SS} has to be used with a $\chi^2(pK^2 + K)$-distribution, whereas λ_{BP} has to be used with a $\chi^2(pK^2 + K + K(K + 1)/2)$-distribution; that is, the $K(K + 1)/2$ possibly different parameters of the white noise covariance matrix also have to be counted.

For a K-dimensional VECM, $\Delta y_t = \nu + \alpha\beta' y_{t-1} + \Gamma_1 \Delta y_{t-1} + \cdots + \Gamma_{p-1} \Delta y_{t-p+1} + u_t$, with cointegrating rank r, the situation is slightly more complicated. Now, counting all parameters in the model apart from those in Σ_u gives $2Kr + (p - 1)K^2 + K$. The degrees of freedom for the test based on λ_{SS} are, however, $2Kr - r^2 + (p - 1)K^2 + K$, where r^2 is subtracted because normalizing $\beta' = [I_r : \beta'_{(K-r)}]$ shows that r^2 of its parameters are fixed throughout the sample [see Hansen (2003)]. If in addition the cointegration matrix is held constant throughout the sample period, the degrees of freedom reduce to $Kr + (p - 1)K^2 + K$. For λ_{BP} we again have to add $K(K + 1)/2$ white noise covariance parameters to get the degrees of freedom.

Various generalizations of these tests are possible. For example, one could test for more than one break or one could check constancy of a subset of parameters keeping the remaining subsets fixed. Moreover, there may be deterministic terms in the cointegration relations, or the number of cointegration relations may change in different subperiods. These generalizations are also treated by Hansen (2003).

On the basis of approximations proposed by Rao (1973), Doornik & Hendry (1997) have suggested the following multivariate version of the Chow forecast test statistic for the situation in which a break point at time T_B is of interest:

$$\lambda_{CF} = \frac{1 - (1 - R_r^2)^{1/s}}{(1 - R_r^2)^{1/s}} \cdot \frac{Ns - q}{Kk^*} \approx F(Kk^*, Ns - q),$$

where

$$s = \left(\frac{K^2 k^{*2} - 4}{K^2 + k^{*2} - 5}\right)^{1/2}, \quad q = \frac{Kk^*}{2} - 1,$$

$$N = T - k_1 - k^* - (K - k^* + 1)/2$$

with k_1 being the number of regressors in the restricted, time-invariant model; k^* the number of forecast periods considered by the test, that is, $k^* = T - T_1$; and

$$R_r^2 = 1 - \left(\frac{T_1}{T}\right)^K |\tilde{\Sigma}_{(1)}|(|\tilde{\Sigma}_u|)^{-1}.$$

Table 3.6. *Chow tests for subset VECM model (3.41) for German interest rate and inflation*

Break point	Test	Test value	p-value	Bootstrap p-value
1982Q4	λ_{SS}	31.6	0.14	0.57
	λ_{BP}	186.7	0.00	0.08
1990Q3	λ_{SS}	35.6	0.06	0.39
	λ_{BP}	168.0	0.00	0.68

Note: Bootstrap p-values based on 2000 replications; sample period: 1973Q2–1998Q4 (plus presample values).

Again the null hypothesis of parameter constancy is rejected for large values of λ_{CF}.

As mentioned in Chapter 2 in the context of univariate analysis, Candelon & Lütkepohl (2001) have proposed using bootstrap versions of the Chow tests to improve their small sample properties. The bootstrap is set up as in the univariate case with appropriate modifications to allow for residual vectors rather than univariate residual series.

We again use the German interest rate–inflation example VECM (3.41) to illustrate the tests. In Table 3.6 results for two possible break dates are presented. The first date corresponds to a period in which the government changed in Germany, and the second one corresponds to the German unification. In each case the starting point $T - T_2 + 1$ of the second sample period is chosen such that the presample values do not overlap with data up to T_B. In other words, $T - T_2 + 1 = T_B + 4$ because there are three lagged differences and, hence, four lags of the levels variables in the model (3.41). The results illustrate several properties of the tests. First of all, the p-values based on the approximate χ^2- distributions typically differ considerably from the bootstrap p-values, the latter being often substantially larger. This illustrates the finding of Candelon & Lütkepohl (2001) that the approximate χ^2-distributions are often very poor approximations and lead to substantially higher rejection rates than the bootstrap tests. On the basis of the approximate p-values, the λ_{BP} test rejects stability for both possible break dates, whereas one would clearly not reject stability in 1990Q3 based on the bootstrap version of the test. The results in Table 3.6 also show that the tests do not always lead to the same decision. Using only the approximate distributions, one would not reject stability in 1982Q4 on the basis of the sample-split test, whereas a rejection is clear on the basis of the break-point test. Therefore, applying different tests may give additional insights in practice.

For the present example there is, however, a problem related to the interpretation of the Chow tests. In Table 3.5 we have seen that there may be some remaining ARCH and, hence, potential volatility clustering in the residuals of our model. Recall that Chow tests compare the variances for different time periods to decide on parameter constancy. Therefore, a volatility cluster in one of the subperiods may lead to the rejection of the constant parameter hypothesis not because the model parameters actually vary but because of the ARCH structure that has not been accounted for. This problem is just a special case of the more general difficulty that, if model defects are diagnosed, the actual cause of significant test results is not always obvious.

As discussed for the univariate case in Chapter 2, Section 2.6.3, the Chow tests may be performed repeatedly for a range of potential break points T_B, and the results may be plotted. If the test decision is based on the maximum of the test statistics, we are effectively considering a test based on the test statistic

$$\sup_{T_B \in \mathsf{T}} \lambda_{**},$$

where '**' stands for any of the three tests and $\mathsf{T} \subset \{1, \ldots, T\}$ is the set of periods for which the test statistic is determined. The distributions of test statistics of this kind are discussed by Andrews (1993), Andrews & Ploberger (1994), and Hansen (1997).

Recursive eigenvalues. For VECMs with cointegrated variables, Hansen & Johansen (1999) have proposed recursive statistics for stability analysis. For instance, recursive eigenvalues from (3.16) may be considered. Let $\lambda_i^{(\tau)}$ be the ith largest eigenvalue based on sample moments from the first τ observations only. If the model is time invariant, approximate 95% confidence intervals for the nonzero true eigenvalues corresponding to $\lambda_1^{(\tau)}, \ldots, \lambda_r^{(\tau)}$ are

$$\left[\frac{\lambda_i^{(\tau)}}{\lambda_i^{(\tau)} + (1 - \lambda_i^{(\tau)}) \exp(1.96\hat{\sigma}_{ii})}, \frac{\lambda_i^{(\tau)}}{\lambda_i^{(\tau)} + (1 - \lambda_i^{(\tau)}) \exp(-1.96\hat{\sigma}_{ii})} \right],$$

where $\hat{\sigma}_{ii}^2$ is $2/T$ times the $i + (i-1)[r + K(p-1)]$-th diagonal element of the matrix $\Upsilon + \Upsilon'$ obtained by defining

$$\Upsilon = (\tilde{\Sigma}^{-1} \otimes \tilde{\Sigma}^{-1})(I - \mathcal{A} \otimes \mathcal{A})^{-1}.$$

Here

$$\mathcal{A} = \begin{bmatrix} \tilde{\beta}'\tilde{\alpha} + I & \tilde{\beta}'\tilde{\Gamma}_1 & \cdots & \tilde{\beta}'\tilde{\Gamma}_{p-2} & \tilde{\beta}'\tilde{\Gamma}_{p-1} \\ \tilde{\alpha} & \tilde{\Gamma}_1 & \cdots & \tilde{\Gamma}_{p-2} & \tilde{\Gamma}_{p-1} \\ 0 & I & & 0 & 0 \\ \vdots & & \ddots & \vdots & \vdots \\ 0 & 0 & \cdots & I & 0 \end{bmatrix},$$

and $\tilde{\Sigma}$ can be determined from

$$\tilde{\Sigma} = \mathcal{A}\tilde{\Sigma}\mathcal{A}' + \tilde{\Sigma}_\varepsilon,$$

where $\tilde{\Sigma}_{\mathcal{E}}$ is the usual estimator of the covariance matrix of $(u'_t\beta, u'_t, 0, \ldots, 0)'$. Plotting the confidence intervals for consecutive sample sizes $\tau = T_1, \ldots, T$ can reveal structural breaks in the DGP. Of course, here the smallest sample size T_1 has to be large enough to permit a meaningful estimation to be made.

In Hansen & Johansen (1999), formal tests are also proposed for parameter change. For stating them we use the following notation:

$$\xi_i^{(\tau)} = \log\left(\frac{\lambda_i^{(\tau)}}{1 - \lambda_i^{(\tau)}}\right)$$

and

$$\mathcal{T}(\xi_i^{(\tau)}) = \frac{\tau}{T}|(\xi_i^{(\tau)} - \xi_i^{(T)})/\hat{\sigma}_{ii}|.$$

Thus, $\mathcal{T}(\xi_i^{(\tau)})$ compares the ith eigenvalue obtained from the full sample to the one estimated from the first τ observations only. Hansen & Johansen (1999) have shown that the maximum over all τ,

$$\sup_{T_1 \leq \tau \leq T} \mathcal{T}(\xi_i^{(\tau)}),$$

has a limiting distribution that depends on a Brownian bridge and is tabulated by Ploberger, Krämer & Kontrus (1989). Clearly, stability is rejected if the difference between the eigenvalues based on the subsamples and the full sample gets too large. Thus, if $\mathcal{T}(\xi_i^{(\tau)})$ exceeds the critical value, stability of the model is rejected.

Alternatively, a test may be based on the sum of the r largest recursive eigenvalues by considering the statistics

$$\mathcal{T}\left(\sum_{i=1}^{r} \xi_i^{(\tau)}\right) = \frac{\tau}{T}\left|\left[\sum_{i=1}^{r}(\xi_i^{(\tau)} - \xi_i^{(T)})\right]/\hat{\sigma}_{1-r}\right|.$$

Here $\hat{\sigma}_{1-r}$ is an estimator of the standard deviation of the difference

$$\sum_{i=1}^{r}(\xi_i^{(\tau)} - \xi_i^{(T)}),$$

which may be based on the relevant part of the matrix $\Upsilon + \Upsilon'$. Again, Hansen & Johansen (1999) have shown that the limiting distribution of

$$\sup_{T_1 \leq \tau \leq T} \mathcal{T}\left(\sum_{i=1}^{r} \xi_i^{(\tau)}\right)$$

is free of unknown nuisance parameters under the stability hypothesis. Thus, we may again check if the sup exceeds the critical value, in which case the stability null hypothesis is rejected.

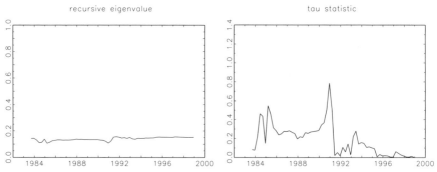

Figure 3.5. Recursive eigenvalue analysis of VECM (3.22) for the German interest rate–inflation system (with critical value for a 5% test level).

It may be worth noting that various versions of these tests make sense as stability tests. For example, if the short-term dynamics are assumed to be stable and a test of parameter change in the long-run part only is desired, one may first concentrate on the short-term parameters based on the full sample and then one may focus on recursive estimation of α and β. In that case, the Γ parameters are estimated as in (3.14) based on the full sample, and the M matrix in (3.15) is hence also based on all observations. In addition, Hansen & Johansen (1999) derived tests that may be used to test stability of the cointegration space separately.

Example. For illustration we use the unrestricted VECM (3.22) for the German interest rate–inflation data. Because the cointegrating rank $r = 1$, there is one nonzero eigenvalue. Confidence intervals for that eigenvalue are depicted in Figure 3.5. Moreover, the tau statistic $\mathcal{T}(\xi_1^{(\tau)})$ is plotted in the figure together with the critical value for a 5% level test. The recursive eigenvalue appears to be fairly stable, and the values of $\mathcal{T}(\xi_1^{(\tau)})$ are considerably smaller than the critical value. Thus, these diagnostic statistics do not indicate instability of the system.

3.6 Forecasting VAR Processes and VECMs

So far in this chapter we have focused on constructing an adequate model for the DGP of a system of variables. Once such a model has been found, it may be used for forecasting as well as economic analysis. In this section, forecasting VAR processes will be discussed first. In Section 3.7, the concept of Granger-causality will be introduced as one tool for economic analysis. The concept is based on forecast performance and has received considerable attention in the theoretical and empirical literature. Other tools for analyzing VARs and VECMs will be discussed in the next chapter.

3.6.1 Known Processes

Forecasting vector processes is completely analogous to forecasting univariate processes, as discussed in Chapter 2. The levels VAR form (3.1) is particularly convenient to use in forecasting the variables y_t. We will again initially ignore deterministic terms and exogenous variables. Moreover, it is assumed first that the process parameters are known. Suppose the u_ts are generated by an independent white noise process. In that case the minimum mean-squared error (MSE) forecast is the conditional expectation. For example, at forecast origin T, an h-step ahead forecast is obtained recursively as

$$y_{T+h|T} = A_1 y_{T+h-1|T} + \cdots + A_p y_{T+h-p|T}, \qquad (3.45)$$

where $y_{T+j|T} = y_{T+j}$ for $j \leq 0$. The corresponding forecast error is

$$y_{T+h} - y_{T+h|T} = u_{T+h} + \Phi_1 u_{T+h-1} + \cdots + \Phi_{h-1} u_{T+1}, \qquad (3.46)$$

where it can be shown by successive substitution that

$$\Phi_s = \sum_{j=1}^{s} \Phi_{s-j} A_j, \quad s = 1, 2, \ldots, \qquad (3.47)$$

with $\Phi_0 = I_K$ and $A_j = 0$ for $j > p$ [see Lütkepohl (1991, Sec. 11.3)]. As in the univariate case, u_t is the 1-step forecast error in period $t - 1$, and the forecasts are unbiased; that is, the forecast errors have expectation 0. The MSE matrix of an h-step forecast is

$$\Sigma_y(h) = \mathsf{E}\{(y_{T+h} - y_{T+h|T})(y_{T+h} - y_{T+h|T})'\} = \sum_{j=0}^{h-1} \Phi_j \Sigma_u \Phi_j'. \qquad (3.48)$$

If u_t is uncorrelated white noise and is not necessarily independent over time, the forecasts obtained via a recursion as in (3.45) are just *best linear* forecasts.

Also analogous to the univariate case, the forecast MSEs $\Sigma_y(h)$ for a stationary process converge to the unconditional covariance matrix of y_t, $\mathsf{E}[(y_t - \mathsf{E}(y_t))(y_t - \mathsf{E}(y_t))'] = \sum_{j=0}^{\infty} \Phi_j \Sigma_u \Phi_j'$. Thus, the forecast uncertainty as reflected in the MSEs is bounded even for long-term forecasts for stationary processes. In contrast, for integrated processes the MSEs are generally unbounded as the horizon h goes to infinity. Thus, the forecast uncertainty increases without bounds for forecasts of the distant future. This does not rule out, however, that forecasts of some components or linear combinations of I(1) variables have bounded MSEs. In fact, forecasts of cointegration relations have bounded MSEs even for horizons approaching infinity because they are forecasts for stationary variables.

The corresponding forecast intervals reflect these properties as well. If the process y_t is Gaussian, that is, $u_t \sim$ iid $N(0, \Sigma_u)$, the forecast errors are also multivariate normal. Using this result, the following forecast intervals can be established:

$$[y_{k,T+h|T} - c_{1-\gamma/2}\sigma_k(h), \; y_{k,T+h|T} + c_{1-\gamma/2}\sigma_k(h)]. \tag{3.49}$$

Here $c_{1-\gamma/2}$ is the $(1 - \frac{\gamma}{2})100$ percentage point of the standard normal distribution, $y_{k,T+h|T}$ denotes the kth component of $y_{T+h|T}$, and $\sigma_k(h)$ denotes the square root of the kth diagonal element of $\Sigma_y(h)$, that is, $\sigma_k(h)$ is the standard deviation of the h-step forecast error for the kth component of y_t. Obviously, if $\sigma_k(h)$ is unbounded for $h \to \infty$, the same is true for the length of the interval in (3.49).

Of course, if the DGP is modeled as a VECM, it may be rewritten in VAR form for forecasting. Alternatively, equivalent forecasting equations can be obtained directly from the VECM.

If a variable enters the system in differenced form only, it is, of course, still possible to generate forecasts of the levels. This can be done by using the relation between first differences and levels mentioned in the univariate case (see Chapter 2). More precisely, suppose that y_{kt} enters as Δy_{kt} only. Then $y_{k,T+h} = y_{k,T} + \Delta y_{k,T+1} + \cdots + \Delta y_{k,T+h}$, and thus an h-step forecast $y_{k,T+h|T} = y_{k,T} + \Delta y_{k,T+1|T} + \cdots + \Delta y_{k,T+h|T}$ may be obtained via forecasting the differences. The properties of the forecast errors including their MSEs follow from the joint distribution of the forecasts $\Delta y_{k,T+1|T}, \ldots, \Delta y_{k,T+h|T}$ [see Lütkepohl (1991)].

If deterministic or exogenous variables are present, or both, it is straightforward to extend the formula (3.45) to allow for such terms. Because the future development of deterministic variables is known by definition of the term "deterministic," they are particularly easy to handle. They may simply be added to the stochastic part. Exogenous variables may be more difficult to deal with in some respects. They are also easy to handle if their future development is known. Otherwise they have to be predicted along with the endogenous variables, in which case a model for their DGP is called for. Alternatively, if the exogenous variables are under full control of a policy maker, it may be desirable to forecast the endogenous variables conditionally on a specific future path of the exogenous variables to check the future implications of their specific values. Suppose the following reduced form model is given:

$$y_t = A_1 y_{t-1} + \cdots + A_p y_{t-p} + CD_t + Bz_t + u_t.$$

As usual, D_t summarizes the deterministic terms and z_t represents exogenous variables. In that case, one may consider conditional expectations

$$\begin{aligned}
E(y_{T+h}|y_T, y_{T-1}, \ldots, z_{T+h}, z_{T+h-1}, \ldots) \\
= A_1 E(y_{T+h-1}|\cdots) + \cdots + A_p E(y_{T+h-p}|\cdots) + CD_{T+h} + Bz_{T+h}.
\end{aligned}$$

The forecast errors and MSEs will be unaffected if there is no uncertainty in the future values of the exogenous variables.

3.6.2 Estimated Processes

So far we have worked under the assumption that the DGP is known, including its parameters. Of course, this assumption is unrealistic in practice. Therefore we will now consider the implications of using estimated VARs for the forecast precision. Denoting the optimal h-step forecast by $y_{T+h|T}$ as in (3.45) and furnishing its counterpart based on estimated coefficients by a hat give

$$\hat{y}_{T+h|T} = \hat{A}_1 \hat{y}_{T+h-1|T} + \cdots + \hat{A}_p \hat{y}_{T+h-p|T}, \tag{3.50}$$

where $\hat{y}_{T+j|T} = y_{T+j}$ for $j \leq 0$ and the $\hat{A}_i$s ($i = 1, \ldots, p$) are estimated parameters. The corresponding forecast error is

$$
\begin{aligned}
y_{T+h} - \hat{y}_{T+h|T} &= [y_{T+h} - y_{T+h|T}] + [y_{T+h|T} - \hat{y}_{T+h|T}] \\
&= \sum_{j=0}^{h-1} \Phi_j u_{T+h-j} + [y_{T+h|T} - \hat{y}_{T+h|T}].
\end{aligned} \tag{3.51}
$$

The first term on the right-hand side involves future residuals u_t with $t > T$ only, whereas the second term is determined by present and past variables if only past variables have been used for estimation. It follows that the two terms are independent if u_t is independent white noise. Moreover, under standard assumptions, the difference $y_{T+h|T} - \hat{y}_{T+h|T}$ is small in probability as the sample size used for estimation gets large and the VAR coefficients are estimated more and more precisely. Hence, the forecast error covariance matrix is

$$
\begin{aligned}
\Sigma_{\hat{y}}(h) &= \mathsf{E}\{(y_{T+h} - \hat{y}_{T+h|T})(y_{T+h} - \hat{y}_{T+h|T})'\} \\
&= \Sigma_y(h) + o(1).
\end{aligned} \tag{3.52}
$$

Here the quantity $o(1)$ denotes a term that tends to zero with increasing sample size. Thus, as far as the forecast MSE is concerned, the estimation uncertainty may be ignored in large samples. The same holds for setting up asymptotic forecast intervals. In small samples, it may still be preferable to include a correction term. Clearly, such a term will depend on the precision of the estimators. Hence, if precise forecasts are desired, it is a good strategy to look for precise parameter estimators. Further details on possible correction terms may be found in Lütkepohl (1991, Chapter 3) for the stationary case and in Reimers (1991), Engle & Yoo (1987), and Basu & Sen Roy (1987) for nonstationary processes.

Again, extensions to processes with deterministic terms and exogenous variables are straightforward. The problems associated with the use of estimated rather than known parameters are analogous to those discussed for the VAR parameters. Of course, correction factors for forecast MSEs and forecast intervals may become more complicated, depending on the terms to be included in addition to the VAR part.

Example. To give an example we have reestimated the subset VECM (3.41) using only data up to the fourth quarter of 1994, and we use that model to predict the interest rate and inflation variables for the next 16 quarters after the sample end. The resulting forecasts are presented in Figure 3.6. The 95% forecast intervals, which are also shown in the figure, do not take into account the estimation uncertainty. Notice that JMu1Ti does not provide a correction of forecast intervals for parameter estimation uncertainty if VECMs are used. In other words, the forecast intervals shown in Figure 3.6 are smaller than more precise forecast intervals based on an asymptotic approximation that takes into account estimation uncertainty. Nevertheless all of the actually observed values for the years 1995–98 are within the forecast intervals. To see this fact a little better, the forecast period is magnified in the lower part of Figure 3.6. That all observed values are within the approximate 95% forecast intervals may be viewed as an additional confirmation of the model adequacy for forecasting purposes.

In Figure 3.6 the two time series are plotted in addition to the forecasts. In these plots the time series variability can be compared with the size of the forecast intervals, and it becomes apparent that the forecast intervals reflect the overall variability of the series, as one would expect. Clearly, the intrinsic variability of a series must be taken into account in assessing the uncertainty of a forecast. Hence, it is not surprising that, especially for longer term forecasts, the overall series variability is reflected in the forecast intervals.

3.7 Granger-Causality Analysis

3.7.1 The Concept

Granger (1969) has introduced a causality concept that has become quite popular in the econometrics literature. He defines a variable y_{2t} to be causal for a time series variable y_{1t} if the former helps to improve the forecasts of the latter. Denoting by $y_{1,t+h|\Omega_t}$ the optimal h-step forecast of y_{1t} at origin t based on the set of all the *relevant* information in the universe Ω_t, we may define y_{2t} to be Granger-*non*causal for y_{1t} if and only if

$$y_{1,t+h|\Omega_t} = y_{1,t+h|\Omega_t \setminus \{y_{2,s} | s \leq t\}}, \qquad h = 1, 2, \ldots. \qquad (3.53)$$

The symbol $\mathcal{A} \setminus \mathcal{B}$ denotes the set of all elements of a set $\mathcal{A}$ not contained in the set $\mathcal{B}$. Thus, in (3.53), y_{2t} is not causal for y_{1t} if removing the past of y_{2t} from the information set does not change the optimal forecast for y_{1t} at any forecast horizon. In turn, y_{2t} is Granger-causal for y_{1t} if (3.53) does not hold for at least one h, and thus a better forecast of y_{1t} is obtained for some forecast horizon by including the past of y_{2t} in the information set. If Ω_t contains past values of y_1

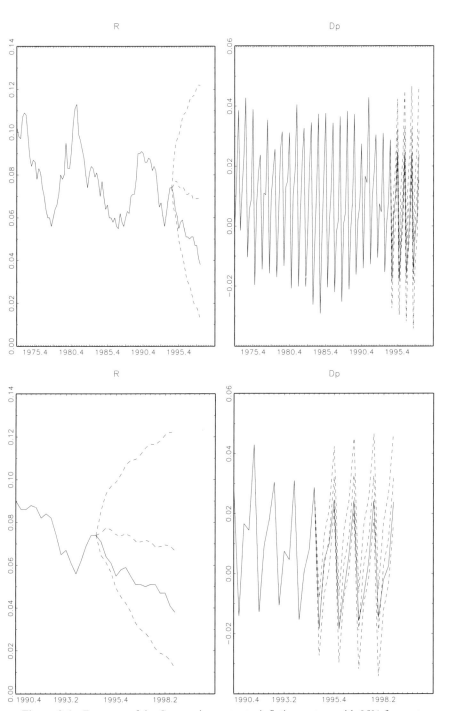

Figure 3.6. Forecasts of the German interest rate–inflation system with 95% forecast intervals based on subset VECM (3.41); estimation period: 1973*Q*2–1994*Q*4.

and y_2 only, that is, $\Omega_t = \{(y_{1,s}, y_{2,s})' | s \leq t\}$, and $(y_{1t}, y_{2t})'$ is generated by a bivariate VAR(p) process of the form

$$\begin{bmatrix} y_{1t} \\ y_{2t} \end{bmatrix} = \sum_{i=1}^{p} \begin{bmatrix} \alpha_{11,i} & \alpha_{12,i} \\ \alpha_{21,i} & \alpha_{22,i} \end{bmatrix} \begin{bmatrix} y_{1,t-i} \\ y_{2,t-i} \end{bmatrix} + u_t, \qquad (3.54)$$

then (3.53) can be shown to be equivalent to

$$\alpha_{12,i} = 0, \qquad i = 1, 2, \ldots, p. \qquad (3.55)$$

In other words, y_{2t} is not Granger-causal for y_{1t} if its lags do not appear in the y_{1t} equation. Analogously, y_{1t} is not Granger-causal for y_{2t} if the lags of the former variable do not enter the second equation.

It is perhaps worth mentioning that Granger-causality can also be investigated in the framework of the VECM. Writing that model for the presently considered bivariate case as

$$\begin{bmatrix} \Delta y_{1t} \\ \Delta y_{2t} \end{bmatrix} = \alpha\beta' \begin{bmatrix} y_{1,t-1} \\ y_{2,t-1} \end{bmatrix} + \sum_{i=1}^{p-1} \begin{bmatrix} \gamma_{11,i} & \gamma_{12,i} \\ \gamma_{21,i} & \gamma_{22,i} \end{bmatrix} \begin{bmatrix} \Delta y_{1,t-i} \\ \Delta y_{2,t-i} \end{bmatrix} + u_t,$$

one can see that (3.55) is equivalent to $\gamma_{12,i} = 0$ ($i = 1, \ldots, p - 1$) and the element in the upper right-hand corner of $\alpha\beta'$ is also zero. Of course, in a bivariate situation the cointegrating rank r can only be 0, 1, or 2, where $r = 1$ is the only instance that may involve genuine cointegration. In that case, α and β are (2×1) vectors and

$$\alpha\beta' = \begin{bmatrix} \alpha_1 \\ \alpha_2 \end{bmatrix} [\beta_1, \beta_2] = \begin{bmatrix} \alpha_1\beta_1 & \alpha_1\beta_2 \\ \alpha_2\beta_1 & \alpha_2\beta_2 \end{bmatrix}.$$

Thus, in this case, $\alpha_1\beta_2 = 0$ needs to be checked in addition to $\gamma_{12,i} = 0$ ($i = 1, \ldots, p - 1$) [see also Mosconi & Giannini (1992)]. Note that if $r = 1$, there must be Granger-causality in at least one direction (from y_{2t} to y_{1t} or from y_{1t} to y_{2t}, or both) because α and β both have rank one and, hence, cannot be zero.

Because economic systems of interest typically consist of more than two relevant variables, it is desirable to extend the concept of Granger-causality to such systems. Different possible extensions have been considered in the literature [see, e.g., Lütkepohl (1993), and Dufour & Renault (1998)]. One approach partitions the vector of all variables, y_t, into two subvectors so that $y_t = (y_{1t}', y_{2t}')'$. Then the definition in (3.53) may be used directly for the two subvectors y_{1t}, y_{2t}. If $\Omega_t = \{y_s | s \leq t\}$ and y_t is a VAR process of the form (3.54), where the $\alpha_{kh,i}$s are now submatrices of appropriate dimensions, the restrictions for noncausality are the same as in the bivariate case. For instance, y_{2t} is Granger-noncausal for y_{1t} if and only if $\alpha_{12,i} = 0$ for $i = 1, \ldots, p$ [Lütkepohl (1991, Section 2.3.1)].

If interest centers on a causal relation between two variables within a higher dimensional system, this approach is not satisfactory because a set of variables being causal for another set of variables does not necessarily imply that each member of the former set is causal for each member of the latter set. Therefore causality of y_{2t} to y_{1t} has been considered for the case in which further variables belong to the system. Different causality concepts have been proposed in this context. We will discuss them within the three-dimensional VAR process

$$y_t = \begin{bmatrix} y_{1t} \\ y_{2t} \\ y_{3t} \end{bmatrix} = \sum_{i=1}^{p} \begin{bmatrix} \alpha_{11,i} & \alpha_{12,i} & \alpha_{13,i} \\ \alpha_{21,i} & \alpha_{22,i} & \alpha_{23,i} \\ \alpha_{31,i} & \alpha_{32,i} & \alpha_{33,i} \end{bmatrix} \begin{bmatrix} y_{1,t-i} \\ y_{2,t-i} \\ y_{3,t-i} \end{bmatrix} + u_t. \tag{3.56}$$

In this system, checking causality of y_{2t} for y_{1t} by testing

$$H_0 : \alpha_{12,i} = 0, \; i = 1, \dots, p \tag{3.57}$$

is not equivalent to (3.53), however. In the present system, these restrictions are equivalent to equality of the 1-step forecasts, $y_{1,t+1|\Omega_t} = y_{1,t+1|\Omega_t \setminus \{y_{2,s}|s \leq t\}}$. The information in past y_{2t} may still be helpful in forecasting y_{1t} more than one period ahead if (3.57) holds [Lütkepohl (1993)]. The intuitive reason for this result is that there may be indirect causal links; for example, y_{2t} may have an impact on y_{3t}, which in turn may affect y_{1t}. Therefore, for higher dimensional processes the definition based on (3.53) results in more complicated nonlinear restrictions for the parameters of the VAR process. A more detailed discussion may be found in Dufour & Renault (1998).

Another concept related to Granger-causality is that of *instantaneous causality*. Roughly speaking, a variable y_{2t} is said to be instantaneously causal for another time series variable y_{1t} if knowing the value of y_2 in the forecast period helps to improve the forecasts of y_1. Formally, y_{2t} is said to be instantaneously noncausal for y_{1t} if and only if

$$y_{1,t+1|\Omega_t} = y_{1,t+1|\Omega_t \cup y_{2,t+1}}. \tag{3.58}$$

It turns out, however, that, in a bivariate VAR process, this concept reduces to a property of the model residuals. More precisely, let $u_t = (u_{1t}, u_{2t})'$ be the residual vector of the DGP of $y_t = (y_{1t}, y_{2t})'$; then, y_{2t} is not instantaneously causal for y_{1t} if and only if u_{2t} and u_{1t} are uncorrelated. In turn, y_{2t} is instantaneously causal for y_{1t} if and only if u_{1t} and u_{2t} are correlated. Consequently, the concept is fully symmetric. If y_{2t} is instantaneously causal for y_{1t}, then y_{1t} is also instantaneously causal for y_{2t}. Hence, the concept as such does not specify a causal direction. The causal direction must be known from other sources. The concept has been criticized on the grounds that correlation generally does not define a causal direction. Still, if it is known from other sources that there can only be a causal link between two variables in one direction, it may be useful to check this possibility by considering the correlation between the residuals. Generalizing the concept to higher dimensional processes creates problems similar to those encountered for Granger-causality. In other words, in the case of more than two variables there may be indirect links between them that have to be taken into account.

3.7.2 Testing for Granger-Causality

Because testing for Granger-causality requires checking whether specific coefficients are zero, standard tests for zero restrictions on VAR coefficients may be used here (χ^2- or F-tests based on the Wald principle are typically thought of in this context). Unfortunately, they may have nonstandard asymptotic properties if the VAR contains I(1) variables. In particular, Wald tests for Granger-causality are known to result in nonstandard limiting distributions depending on the cointegration properties of the system and possibly on nuisance parameters [see Toda & Phillips (1993)].

Fortunately, these problems can be overcome easily, as pointed out by Toda & Yamamoto (1995) and Dolado & Lütkepohl (1996). As mentioned in Section 3.3.1, the nonstandard asymptotic properties of the standard tests on the coefficients of cointegrated VAR processes are due to the singularity of the asymptotic distribution of the estimators. The singularity can be removed by fitting a VAR process whose order exceeds the true order, however. It can be shown that this device leads to a nonsingular asymptotic distribution of the relevant coefficients. Thus, simply overfitting the VAR order and ignoring the extra parameters in testing for Granger-causality overcomes the problems associated with standard tests – at least if asymptotic properties are of interest.

More precisely, Dolado & Lütkepohl (1996) have shown that, whenever the elements in at least one of the coefficient matrices A_i are not restricted at all under the null hypothesis, the Wald statistic has its usual limiting χ^2-distribution. Consequently, if a hypothesis is of interest involving elements from all A_i, $i = 1, \ldots, p$, as, for instance, in the noncausality restrictions in (3.55) or (3.57), standard asymptotic properties of the Wald test can be ensured simply by adding an extra (redundant) lag in estimating the parameters of the process. If the true DGP is a VAR(p) process, then, of course, a VAR($p + 1$) with $A_{p+1} = 0$ is also an appropriate model. It is important to note, however, that the test has to be performed on the A_i, $i = 1, \ldots, p$, only with the last redundant lag ignored.

This procedure can even be used if the cointegration properties of the system are unknown. If it is known that all variables are at most I(1), an extra lag may simply be added and the test may be performed on the lag-augmented model to be on the safe side. Unfortunately, the procedure is not fully efficient owing to the redundant parameters. The procedure remains valid if an intercept or other deterministic terms are included in the VAR model as a consequence of results due to Park & Phillips (1989) and Sims et al. (1990).

Testing for instantaneous causality can be done by determining the absence of instantaneous residual correlation. Because the asymptotic properties of the

Table 3.7. *Tests for causality between German interest rate and inflation based on VAR(4) model*

Causality hypothesis	Test value	Distribution	p-value
$R \xrightarrow{\text{Gr}} Dp$	2.24	$F(4, 152)$	0.07
$Dp \xrightarrow{\text{Gr}} R$	0.31	$F(4, 152)$	0.87
$R \xrightarrow{\text{inst}} Dp$	0.61	$\chi^2(1)$	0.44

Note: Sample period: $1973Q3$–$1998Q4$.

estimator of the residual covariance matrix of a VAR process are unaffected by the degree of integration and cointegration in the variables, a test statistic based on the usual Wald or likelihood ratio principles has an asymptotic χ^2-distribution under standard assumptions.

For our German interest rate–inflation example, tests for causality based on a VAR(4) model are given in Table 3.7. For the Granger-causality tests, the model is augmented by one more lag; thus, these tests are actually based on a VAR(5) model in which the relevant restrictions are, however, tested on the first four coefficient matrices. The usual Wald statistic has an asymptotic $\chi^2(4)$-distribution because four restrictions are tested. In JMulTi, an F-version of this test is used because this version often leads to a better approximation of the desired size of the test. The denominator degrees of freedom are obtained as the total number of observations used for estimation ($2T$) minus the total number of estimated parameters. In contrast, the raw χ^2 approximation is used in testing for instantaneous causality. This test is based on the residuals of a VAR(4) model. Because only one correlation coefficient is tested to be zero, the number of degrees of freedom of the approximating χ^2-distribution is one. Clearly, it is sufficient to report the test result for only one instantaneous causal direction because the test value for the other direction is identical given that it tests the very same correlation coefficient.

In Table 3.7, none of the p-values are smaller than 0.05. Hence, using a 5% significance level, none of the noncausality null hypotheses can be rejected. In other words, on the basis of these tests no causal relation between the variables can be diagnosed with any certainty. There is, however, weak evidence of a Granger-causal relation from R to Dp ($R \xrightarrow{\text{Gr}} D_p$) because the p-value of the related test is at least less than 10%. Given the previous results for the present pair of variables, the general test results are perhaps a bit surprising. First of all, on the basis of the subset VECM (3.41) one may have expected a clear causal link from Dp to R because the former variable enters the first equation of that model. A closer look confirms, however, that the t-ratios of the coefficients associated with lags of Dp are fairly small. On the other hand, no lagged differences of R appear in the ΔDp_t equation of model (3.41). In fact, R enters that equation only via the error correction term. The loading coefficient has a t-ratio of more than 4. This explains why a Granger-causal relation from R to Dp is found at least when a 10% significance level is used in the test in Table 3.7.

Generally, it is perhaps worth remembering that, if there is a cointegration relation between two variables there must also be Granger-causality in at least one direction. Despite the very clear cointegration result, the causality tests do not suggest a strong relation, and this may be a bit puzzling. It should be remembered, however, that a cointegration analysis and a Granger-causality analysis look at the data from different angles. In such a situation the view from one direction often gives a much clearer picture than from another corner. The causality tests are based on fairly large models with many parameters. The scarce sample information makes it difficult for such tests to reject the null hypothesis. In other words, the causality tests may have a power problem. This line of arguments shows that there is no conflict between the results from the cointegration analysis and the causality analysis. One of them just provides a clearer picture of the relation between the variables because of the different way it processes the sample information.

3.8 An Example

As an example we consider a system modeled around a money demand relation for Germany. This relation is of central interest for conducting a monetary policy based on targeting the money stock growth because for such a strategy the demand for money has to be predictable. In Germany the Bundesbank (German central bank) has used that strategy since the middle of the 1970s. Thus, the question of interest here is whether a stable, plausible money demand relation has existed for Germany for the period of monetary targeting by the Bundesbank.

In modeling money demand for Germany, it is worth remembering that economic theory suggests real money demand to depend on the real transactions volume and a nominal interest rate representing opportunity costs of holding money. Hence, we will consider a system with at least three variables: real money, real output and a nominal interest rate. For deciding on the specific variables to be included we note that the Bundesbank used a target value for the broad measure of the money stock M3 starting in 1988. Therefore, this variable is of particular interest here. It includes not only currency holdings but also sight deposits, time deposits for up to four years, and savings deposits. Hence, a longer term interest rate is a more suitable opportunity cost measure in the present situation than a short-term interest rate. One could even argue in favor of using the difference between a long-term rate and the interest rate on components included in M3. If different possibilities are available, one may try all of them in the course of the analysis. We decided to start with the so-called

Umlaufsrendite, which is an average bond rate. It may be thought of as a 5-year rate. We measure the transactions volume by GNP. Because the quantity theory suggests a log-linear relationship, we consider the three-dimensional system (m_t, gnp_t, R_t), where m_t is the log of real M3, gnp_t is the log of real GNP, and R_t is the nominal long-term interest rate. Of course, other variables may be important in the generation mechanism of these variables. For example, in the introduction to this chapter (see Section 3.1) we already mentioned the inflation rate as a potentially important variable. Moreover, foreign influences may play a role. Therefore, one should keep in mind that further variables may have to be added at a later stage. The decision on such variables may also depend on the purpose of the analysis. We start out with the present system and refer the reader to Lütkepohl & Wolters (2003) for an analysis of a larger system.

Because the Bundesbank started its monetary targeting policy in 1975, we use data from 1975 to 1998. The final year is chosen to be 1998 because in 1999 the euro was introduced, and the responsibility for the monetary policy shifted to the European Central Bank. Note that GNP data are only available quarterly for Germany. Therefore, we use quarterly data. For the monthly series M3 and R, we use the value published for the last month of each quarter as the corresponding quarterly value. As mentioned in Chapter 2, seasonal adjustment is an operation applied to univariate series individually; it may distort the relation between variables. Thus we use seasonally unadjusted data. In other words, we use the series m_t, gnp_t, and R_t plotted in Figure 3.1. The M3 series is deflated by the GNP deflator because that price index is also used to deflate GNP. Obviously, m_t and gnp_t have a noticeable seasonal pattern and a level shift in the third quarter of 1990 when the monetary unification of East and West Germany occurred. Since then all data refer to all of Germany, whereas, before that date, they only refer to West Germany. Clearly the level shift and the seasonality have to be taken into account in the subsequent analysis. Moreover, the trending behavior of all three series deserves consideration.

We start by investigating the unit root and univariate time series properties of the three series and just mention that all three of them are well modeled by allowing for a unit root. In fact, series similar to the present gnp_t and R_t series were already considered in Chapter 2. The appropriate tests support the conclusion that the series may be treated as I(1). We encourage the reader to confirm this result. The next step is then to investigate possible cointegration relations between the series.

We perform cointegration tests on all pairs of series before turning to the three-dimensional system. The reason is that cointegration rank tests tend to have relatively low power – especially when applied to higher dimensional systems. Therefore, applying tests to bivariate systems first is a good check of the overall plausibility and consistency of the results obtained by looking at the data from different angles. Doing this can also help in finding a proper normalization of the cointegration matrix for the estimation stage, as we will see later. Because there is a shift in the m_t and gnp_t series in the third quarter of 1990, the time when the monetary unification of East and West Germany became effective, a shift dummy variable will be included in the cointegration tests; therefore, we use the cointegration tests proposed by Saikkonen and Lütkepohl (S&L tests) (see Section 3.4.2). The results are given in Table 3.8.

In performing the tests, a few choices have to be made. In particular, the deterministic terms and the number of lagged differences in the model have to be decided. Regarding the deterministic terms, we have already mentioned that the unification shift in m_t and gnp_t makes it desirable to include a shift dummy variable in any model involving at least one of these two variables. In other words, a shift dummy should be included in all the bivariate models. In addition, m_t and gnp_t have some seasonal variation and a trending behavior that may perhaps be captured with a linear trend term. Therefore, seasonal dummy variables as well as a linear trend term are included in the test models. We leave it open whether the trend is just in the variables and, hence, orthogonal to the cointegration relations or whether a fully general linear trend is required. To avoid a decision on this issue at this point, we perform both types of tests.

Another choice that has to be made is the number of lagged differences to be included in the models on which the cointegrating rank tests are based. Notice that the lag length cannot be deduced easily from the model order used in the univariate unit root analysis because the relation between the univariate lags and those in a multivariate model is complicated and depends on the true DGP. Hence, a new choice is necessary for each of the systems considered. An easy way to make this choice is to ask the model selection criteria for suggestions. In this case, we considered a maximum lag order of 10, taking into account the data frequency and number of observations. Then VAR models for the levels series of orders 1 to 10 were fitted without any cointegration restrictions imposed, and the orders minimizing the different model selection criteria were considered. This procedure is justified here because fitting the model in the levels of the variables is equivalent to fitting a VECM without restricting the cointegrating rank. Thus, the least restricted model considered in any of the cointegration tests is used. For our systems of variables the different order selection criteria propose quite different lag orders. Therefore, we have performed cointegrating rank tests for different numbers of lags. Notice that the orders specified in Table 3.8 refer to the number of lagged differences included in the VECMs that are used for the tests. We know from Section 3.2 that this number is one less than the VAR order. The larger number of lagged differences in Table 3.8 is always the number suggested by AIC, whereas the lower number is the proposal of the HQ criterion. Recall that choosing the order too small can lead to size distortions for the tests while selecting too large an order may imply

Table 3.8. *S&L cointegration tests for German money demand system; sample period:* 1975Q1–1998Q4

Variables	Deterministic terms	No. of lagged differences	$H_0 : r = r_0$	Test statistic	Critical values 10%	5%
m, gnp	c, tr, sd, $shift$	0	$r_0 = 0$	6.86	13.89	15.92
			$r_0 = 1$	0.37	5.43	6.83
		4	$r_0 = 0$	4.91	13.89	15.92
			$r_0 = 1$	1.75	5.43	6.83
	c, $orth\ tr$, sd, $shift$	0	$r_0 = 0$	9.13	8.03	9.79
m, R	c, tr, sd, $shift$	0	$r_0 = 0$	26.71	13.89	15.92
			$r_0 = 1$	0.00	5.43	6.83
	c, $orth\ tr$, sd, $shift$	0	$r_0 = 0$	22.98	8.03	9.79
gnp, R	c, tr, sd, $shift$	0	$r_0 = 0$	8.26	13.89	15.92
			$r_0 = 1$	0.20	5.43	6.83
		6	$r_0 = 0$	8.42	13.89	15.92
			$r_0 = 1$	0.56	5.43	6.83
	c, $orth\ tr$, sd, $shift$	0	$r_0 = 0$	4.04	8.03	9.79
		6	$r_0 = 0$	9.36	8.03	9.79
m, gnp, R	c, tr, sd, $shift$	0	$r_0 = 0$	38.36	25.90	28.47
			$r_0 = 1$	9.07	13.89	15.92
			$r_0 = 2$	0.00	5.43	6.83
		4	$r_0 = 0$	19.58	25.90	28.47
			$r_0 = 1$	4.93	13.89	15.92
			$r_0 = 2$	4.53	5.43	6.83
	c, $orth\ tr$, sd, $shift$	0	$r_0 = 0$	33.62	18.19	20.66
			$r_0 = 1$	9.47	8.03	9.79
		4	$r_0 = 0$	20.14	18.19	20.66
			$r_0 = 1$	4.53	8.03	9.79

Notes: c-constant, tr-linear trend, *orth* tr-linear trend orthogonal to the cointegration relations, sd-seasonal dummies, *shift*-shift dummy variable $S90Q3$; critical values from Lütkepohl & Saikkonen (2000, Table 1) for models with unrestricted trend and from Saikkonen & Lütkepohl (2000b, Table1) for models with trend orthogonal to the cointegration relations.

reductions in power. Therefore, considering different orders may provide useful insights.

All cointegration test results are given in Table 3.8, where the sample period 1975Q1–1998Q4 refers to the full series length including the presample values needed in the estimation. In other words, the actual sample is shorter when more lagged differences are included. For the (m_t, gnp_t) and (gnp_t, R_t) systems there is very strong evidence for a cointegration rank of zero. In other words, the two variables in each of these systems do not appear to be cointegrated. Notice, however, that for both systems the rank zero hypothesis is rejected at the 10% level if the trend is restricted to be orthogonal to the cointegration relations. In total, we regard this piece of evidence as too weak to outweigh the evidence in favor of no cointegration. In contrast, for the (m_t, R_t) system the evidence is clearly in favor of one cointegration relation regardless of the assumption for the linear trend. Thus, in a three-dimensional analysis one would also expect to find at least one cointegration relation. In fact, if there is really no cointegration relation between m_t and gnp_t and also none between gnp_t and R_t, as suggested by the bivariate analysis, there cannot be a second cointegration relation between the three variables. If there were two linearly independent cointegration relations, they could always be transformed so that they would both involve just two of the variables by using the normalization of Section 3.3.2. Therefore it is reassuring that the test results for the three-dimensional system point to a cointegrating rank of 1. In line with the bivariate results, a second cointegration relation may be diagnosed at the 10% level of significance if the trend is assumed to be orthogonal to the cointegration relations and a lag order of zero, as proposed by the HQ criterion, is used. The evidence is sufficiently weak to continue the analysis with one cointegration relation. Notice that the results for the three-dimensional system in Table 3.8 are similar to those in Table 3.3, where the same variables are considered with a slightly extended sample period. Although the sampling period in this case does not change the general conclusions from the tests, it has some impact on the actual test values.

The next step in our analysis is then to search for an adequate model for the three-dimensional system of interest, $(m_t, gnp_t, R_t)'$. On the basis of our cointegration analysis results, we start out from a VECM with cointegrating rank 1 and four lagged differences. Note that the AIC suggested four lagged differences in an unrestricted model. Starting from a rather liberal specification allows us to reduce the parameter space in further steps without running the risk of neglecting important features of the DGP at an early stage. This is also the reason for including a linear time trend initially. Because a quadratic trend is not considered, the trend can be absorbed into the cointegration relation. Hence, we restrict the trend accordingly, as in (3.38). The shift dummy is included in differenced form only because it turned out to be unnecessary in the cointegration relations. Thus, we include an impulse dummy variable $I90Q3_t = \Delta S90Q3_t$ in the model. At this early stage, one could also consider a shift dummy in addition, and we ask the reader to try a model containing that term as well. Also, of course, seasonal dummies are included in all the equations. After estimating the model by the Johansen ML procedure and checking the residuals, we found the model to be a quite satisfactory

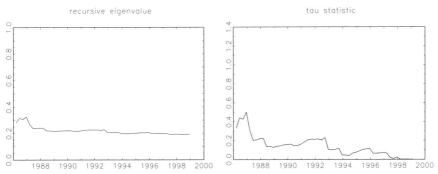

Figure 3.7. Recursive eigenvalues and stability test statistic for unrestricted VECM with cointegrating rank one, four lagged differences, constants, seasonal dummies, and a time trend restricted to the cointegration relation for German money demand system; sample period: $1975Q1$–$1998Q4$ (including presample values).

representation of the DGP. A stability analysis based an the recursive eigenvalues and the $\mathcal{T}(\xi_1^{(\tau)})$ statistic for $1986Q1$–$1998Q4$ does not give rise to concern (see Figure 3.7). In particular, the value of the test statistic does not exceed the critical value for a 5% level test, which is shown as a line near the top of the right panel of Figure 3.7. Thus, the model may be used as a starting point for model reduction.

Choosing m_t as the first variable in our model means that the coefficient of this variable in the cointegration relation will be normalized to 1 in the ML estimation procedure described in Section 3.3.2. This normalization is problematic if m_t is not actually present in the cointegration relation and, hence, has a coefficient of zero attached to it. For our present system we found, however, that m_t is possibly cointegrated with R_t in a bivariate system. This result strongly suggests that m_t is part of the cointegration relation with nonzero coefficient, which may thus be normalized to 1. The cointegration relation obtained from the ML estimation with this normalization is

$$ec_t^{tr} = m_t - \underset{(0.228)}{0.863\, gnp_t} + \underset{(0.801)}{3.781\, R_t} - \underset{(0.002)}{0.002\, t},$$

where estimated standard errors are given in parentheses. Notice that the coefficient of the trend term in the cointegration relation has an asymptotic normal distribution under standard assumptions, and thus its t-ratio can be interpreted in the usual way. Clearly, the coefficient of the trend term is not significantly different from zero at conventional levels. Therefore, we reestimated the model without the trend term and obtained the following cointegration relation:

$$ec_t^{ML} = m_t - \underset{(0.090)}{1.093\, gnp_t} + \underset{(1.267)}{6.514\, R_t}$$

or

$$m_t = \underset{(0.090)}{1.093} \, gnp_t - \underset{(1.267)}{6.514} \, R_t + ec_t^{ML},$$

where again estimated standard errors are given in parentheses. The latter equation looks like a quite plausible money demand relation, in which increases in the transactions volume increase money demand and increases in the opportunity costs for money holdings (R_t) reduce the demand for money. Because both m_t and gnp_t are in logs, the coefficient 1.093 is the estimated output elasticity. If the (log) velocity of money ($gnp_t - m_t$) is constant, one would expect a 1% increase in the transactions volume (output) to induce a 1% increase in money demand. Hence, in a simple theoretical model the output elasticity is expected to be 1. The gnp_t coefficient is in fact not far from this value and, given its standard deviation of 0.090, it is not significantly different from 1 if common significance levels are used. The reader may confirm this result using the Wald test (3.21).

Therefore it makes sense to estimate a model with a restricted cointegration vector for which the output elasticity is set to 1. Using the S2S estimator for this purpose, we obtain the long-run relation

$$m_t = gnp_t - \underset{(0.742)}{3.876} \, R_t + ec_t^{S2S}. \tag{3.59}$$

The coefficient of R_t is a semielasticity because this variable is not in logs. Thus, the elasticity is obtained as $\partial m / \partial \log R = (\partial m / \partial R)R$; therefore, for an interest rate of 5% the elasticity would be $-3.876 \times 0.05 = -0.194$, which is not an implausible value. Consequently, our estimated cointegration relation qualifies as a long-run money demand relation.

In the light of our previous results there is, however, one problem with this interpretation. In the bivariate cointegration analysis we found a cointegration relation between m_t and R_t that does not involve gnp_t. Thus, the single cointegration relation found in the three-dimensional analysis may be one between m_t and R_t only. Hence, how can we find a cointegration relation involving all three variables in the present three-dimensional analysis? Given the foregoing estimation results, gnp_t enters significantly in the cointegration relation. Both the ML and the S2S estimators confirm this result. There is indeed a slight inconsistency between the bivariate and the three-dimensional analysis. We therefore maintain all three variables in the cointegration relation. After all, eliminating gnp_t from the cointegration relation imposes a restriction on the model that is rejected by the data if the full three-dimensional information set is taken into account.

We now use the cointegration relation from (3.59) and perform a model reduction. Using a single-equation sequential elimination procedure based on the AIC results in the following estimated model, where the final estimation was done by feasible GLS (EGLS), which is equivalent to 3SLS because the model is in reduced form:

$$
\begin{bmatrix} \Delta m_t \\ \Delta gnp_t \\ \Delta R_t \end{bmatrix} = \begin{bmatrix} -0.04 \\ (-3.1) \\ 0 \\ -0.01 \\ (-1.6) \end{bmatrix} (m_{t-1} - gnp_{t-1} + 3.876 R_{t-1})
$$

$$
+ \begin{bmatrix} 0.15 & -0.18 & -0.58 \\ (2.5) & (-2.9) & (-3.4) \\ 0.22 & -0.36 & 0 \\ (2.8) & (-4.2) & \\ 0 & 0 & 0.18 \\ & & (1.8) \end{bmatrix} \begin{bmatrix} \Delta m_{t-1} \\ \Delta gnp_{t-1} \\ \Delta R_{t-1} \end{bmatrix} + \begin{bmatrix} 0 & 0 & -0.30 \\ & & (-1.6) \\ 0.25 & -0.22 & 0.37 \\ (3.1) & (-2.4) & (1.5) \\ 0 & 0 & 0 \end{bmatrix} \begin{bmatrix} \Delta m_{t-2} \\ \Delta gnp_{t-2} \\ \Delta R_{t-2} \end{bmatrix}
$$

$$
+ \begin{bmatrix} 0 & -0.09 & 0 \\ & (-1.8) & \\ 0 & 0 & 0 \\ 0 & 0 & 0.18 \\ & & (1.8) \end{bmatrix} \begin{bmatrix} \Delta m_{t-3} \\ \Delta gnp_{t-3} \\ \Delta R_{t-3} \end{bmatrix} + \begin{bmatrix} 0 & 0 & 0 \\ 0 & 0.28 & 0 \\ & (4.0) & \\ 0 & 0 & 0 \end{bmatrix} \begin{bmatrix} \Delta m_{t-4} \\ \Delta gnp_{t-4} \\ \Delta R_{t-4} \end{bmatrix}
$$

$$
+ \begin{bmatrix} 0.15 & 0.07 & -0.03 & -0.02 & -0.02 \\ (17.5) & (4.9) & (-5.4) & (-3.5) & (-4.4) \\ 0.11 & 0.04 & -0.07 & -0.03 & -0.03 \\ (8.9) & (7.7) & (-9.1) & (-4.2) & (-3.5) \\ 0 & 0.01 & 0 & 0 & 0 \\ & (1.5) & & & \end{bmatrix} \begin{bmatrix} 190Q3_t \\ c \\ s_{1,t} \\ s_{2,t} \\ s_{3,t} \end{bmatrix} + \begin{bmatrix} \hat{u}_{1,t} \\ \hat{u}_{2,t} \\ \hat{u}_{3,t} \end{bmatrix}. \tag{3.60}
$$

Here the t-values are given in parentheses. The corresponding residual covariance and correlation matrices are

$$
\widetilde{\Sigma}_u = \begin{bmatrix} 6.85 & -0.01 & 0.40 \\ \cdot & 13.3 & 1.12 \\ \cdot & \cdot & 2.59 \end{bmatrix} \times 10^{-5} \quad \text{and} \quad \widetilde{Corr} = \begin{bmatrix} 1 & -0.00 & 0.10 \\ \cdot & 1 & 0.19 \\ \cdot & \cdot & 1 \end{bmatrix}.
$$

Obviously, all off-diagonal elements of $\widetilde{Corr}$ are quite small. Given our effective sample size of $T = 91$ observations, they are all smaller than $2/\sqrt{T} = 0.21$ and thus not significantly different from zero. This can be useful information in a further analysis of the model such as when an impulse response analysis is performed (see Chapter 4).

The reader may want to check the adequacy of the model by conducting the usual diagnostic tests. They do not give rise to concern about the adequacy of the model. The only potential model defect is a significant ARCH test for the residuals of the interest rate equation. ARCH effects in the residuals of financial data series are not surprising and are not necessarily a signal of inadequate modeling of the conditional expectation of the DGP. Because we are mainly interested in the latter part in the present analysis, we decided to ignore the significant diagnostic test value. There is, however, a problem that may be caused by ARCH in the residuals. As mentioned earlier, volatility clusters can lead to significant values of Chow tests because these tests compare the residual variability in different subperiods to decide on parameter instability. If the variability differs due to ARCH effects, this may then be diagnosed as parameter instability. Therefore, checking the stability of our model with these tests may not be a fruitful exercise in this case. Given the results of the stability test based on the recursive eigenvalues, we decide to maintain the present model as a basis for economic analysis. Possible tools for such an analysis are considered in the next chapter. We encourage the reader to consider model reduction using the cointegration vectors from ML estimations with and without a linear trend term in the model and to try other model variants such as a model with a shift dummy variable.

3.9 Extensions

In this chapter we have focused on VAR and VEC models possibly enriched by deterministic and exogenous variables. Pure VAR models have become standard tools for macroeconometric analysis following the critique of static large-scale econometric models launched by Sims (1980) in an influential article. VECMs have become popular after the introduction of cointegration. A possible limitation of our discussion of these models is the assumption regarding the order of integration. We have considered I(0) and I(1) variables only. Higher order integration may be present in some variables in practice. Although some results of the present chapter remain valid in that case, it is generally a good idea to take higher order integration into account explicitly. An extensive literature on the related issues is currently unfolding [see, e.g., Johansen (1995b) and Haldrup (1998)].

The theoretical literature on multiple time series modeling has also considered more general vector models that allow for MA terms and thereby may achieve more parsimonious parameterizations. Some relevant references are Hannan & Deistler (1988), Lütkepohl (1991), and Lütkepohl & Poskitt (1996a). Extensions of these models to cointegrated systems are discussed by Lütkepohl & Claessen (1997) and Bartel & Lütkepohl (1998). Unfortunately, these models are more difficult to handle in practice and therefore have not become very popular for empirical work.

Some other model extensions of practical importance will be considered in other parts of this book. For instance, for financial time series modeling the conditional second moments are sometimes of primary interest. Multivariate ARCH-type models that can be used for this purpose will be discussed in Chapter 5. Generally, nonlinearities of unknown functional form may be treated nonparametrically, semiparametrically, or seminonparametrically. A large body of literature is currently developing on these issues. Some methods of this type for univariate series will be considered in Chapter 7. Moreover, specific forms of nonlinearities that have proved quite useful in applications will be presented in Chapter 6.

4 Structural Vector Autoregressive Modeling and Impulse Responses

Jörg Breitung, Ralf Brüggemann, and Helmut Lütkepohl

4.1 Introduction

In the previous chapter we have seen how a model for the DGP of a set of economic time series variables can be constructed. When such a model is available, it can be used for analyzing the dynamic interactions between the variables. This kind of analysis is usually done by tracing the effect of an impulse in one of the variables through the system. In other words, an impulse response analysis is performed. Although this is technically straightforward, some problems related to impulse response analysis exist that have been the subject of considerable discussion in the literature.

As argued forcefully by Cooley & LeRoy (1985), vector autoregressions have the status of "reduced form" models and therefore are merely vehicles to summarize the dynamic properties of the data. Without reference to a specific economic structure, such reduced-form VAR models are difficult to understand. For example, it is often difficult to draw any conclusion from the large number of coefficient estimates in a VAR system. As long as such parameters are not related to "deep" structural parameters characterizing preferences, technologies, and optimization behavior, the parameters do not have an economic meaning and are subject to the so-called Lucas critique.

Sims (1981, 1986), Bernanke (1986), and Shapiro & Watson (1988) put forward a new class of econometric models that is now known as *structural vector autoregression* (SVAR) or *identified VAR*. Instead of identifying the (autoregressive) coefficients, identification focuses on the errors of the system, which are interpreted as (linear combinations of) exogenous shocks. In the early applications of Sargent (1978) and Sims (1980), the innovations of the VAR were orthogonalized using a Choleski decomposition of the covariance matrix. A recursive structure was thereby imposed on the instantaneous relations between the variables. Unless there is a justification from subject matter theory for a specific recursive structure, there is some degree of arbitrariness when constructing shocks in this manner. In general, choosing a different ordering of the variables produces different shocks and, thus, the effects of the shocks on the system depend on the way the variables are arranged in the time series vector y_t. To account for this difficulty, Sims (1981) recommended trying various triangular orthogonalizations and checking the robustness of the results to the ordering of the variables.

An alternative approach to the identification of the shocks is to formulate structural equations for the errors of the system. In this case it is convenient to think of the equations as an IS curve or a money demand relation, for example, where the equations apply to the unexpected part of the variables (the *innovations*) instead of the variables themselves. If the equations are valid for the system variables, then they also apply to the unexpected part of the variables. Therefore, the identification using a set of simultaneous equations is appealing with respect to the traditional approach advocated by the Cowles Commission, and it is not surprising that this kind of identification is used widely in empirical work with SVAR models.

In recent work, the identification of shocks using restrictions on their long-run effects has become popular. In many cases, economic theory suggests that the effects of some shocks are zero in the long-run, that is, the shocks have transitory effects with respect to particular variables. For example, classical economic theory implies that the effect of nominal shocks on real variables like output or unemployment vanishes as time goes by. Such assumptions give rise to nonlinear restrictions on the parameters and may be used to identify the structure of the system.

An important difference of SVAR models with respect to traditional simultaneous equation models is that the latter usually employ many more restrictions than necessary to identify the system, that is, these models are often highly over-identified. In his famous critique, Sims (1980) described these overly restricted models as "incredible." SVAR proponents therefore try to avoid oversimplifying the structure and impose just enough restrictions to identify the parameters. Accordingly, most SVAR models are just-identified.

The impulse responses obtained from an SVAR or structural VECM (SVECM) typically are highly nonlinear functions of the model parameters. This property has implications for drawing inferences related to the impulse responses. It is known that, for the functions of interest here, standard asymptotic inference may be a poor guide in small samples. We will discuss the problem and possible solutions in Section 4.5.

The structure of this chapter is as follows. In the next section, the model framework for impulse response analysis will be reviewed briefly. The principles of impulse response analysis for a given SVAR model with identified shocks are considered in Section 4.3, the estimation of the structural parameters is addressed in Section 4.4, and statistical inference for impulse responses is treated in Section 4.5. Finally, forecast error variance decomposition as a special way of summarizing impulse responses is discussed in Section 4.6. Empirical examples are presented in some detail in Section 4.7, and conclusions follow in Section 4.8.

4.2 The Models

The most general model we have considered in the previous chapter is a structural VECM form

$$A\Delta y_t = \Pi^* y_{t-1} + \Gamma_1^* \Delta y_{t-1} + \cdots + \Gamma_{p-1}^* \Delta y_{t-p+1}$$

$$+ C^* D_t + B^* z_t + v_t, \qquad (4.1)$$

where $y_t = (y_{1t}, \ldots, y_{Kt})'$ is a $(K \times 1)$ vector of endogenous variables; z_t is a vector of exogenous or unmodeled stochastic variables; D_t contains all deterministic terms; the Π^*, Γ_j^* ($j = 1, \ldots, p - 1$), C^*, and B^* are structural form parameter matrices; and v_t is a $(K \times 1)$ structural form error that is a zero mean white noise process with time-invariant covariance matrix Σ_v. The invertible $(K \times K)$ matrix A allows modeling instantaneous relations among the variables in y_t.

As already noted, structural shocks are the central quantities in an SVAR model. These shocks are unpredictable with respect to the past of the process and are the input of a linear dynamic system generating the K-dimensional time series vector y_t. They are hence related to the residuals in (4.1). The shocks are associated with an economic meaning such as an oil price shock, exchange rate shock, or a monetary shock. Because the shocks are not directly observed, assumptions are needed to identify them. There seems to be a consensus that structural shocks should be mutually uncorrelated (and thus *orthogonal*). This assumption is required to consider the dynamic impact of an isolated shock. If the shocks were correlated, we would have to take into account the relationship between the shocks. Moreover, the decomposition into orthogonal components has a long tradition in statistical analysis and is also used in factor analysis, for example. The shocks or structural innovations, denoted by ε_t, are assumed to be related to the model residuals by linear relations $v_t = B\varepsilon_t$, where B is a $(K \times K)$ matrix.

For our present purposes, the deterministic terms are of no importance because they are not affected by impulses hitting the system. Moreover, they do not affect such impulses themselves. Therefore, for notational convenience the deterministic term is often dropped from the model. In practice this may be done by adjusting the variables or the model for deterministic terms before an analysis of the dynamic interactions between the variables is carried out. Similarly, exogenous variables, if they are under the control of some policy maker, may not react to stochastic shocks of the system and may therefore be ignored for the present purposes. Also, in macroeconometric analysis, exogeneity of a variable is often regarded as too strong a condition; therefore, all observable stochastic variables are modeled as endogenous. Instead, the error variables are viewed as the actual exogenous variables, although they are not under the control of any economic agents. Hence, instead of (4.1) we consider

$$A\Delta y_t = \Pi^* y_{t-1} + \Gamma_1^* \Delta y_{t-1} + \cdots + \Gamma_{p-1}^* \Delta y_{t-p+1} + B\varepsilon_t \qquad (4.2)$$

with $\varepsilon_t \sim (0, I_K)$. Such a model has an equivalent VAR representation for the levels variables of the form

$$A y_t = A_1^* y_{t-1} + \cdots + A_p^* y_{t-p} + B\varepsilon_t. \qquad (4.3)$$

This model is also often useful for our purposes, especially if the y_ts are stationary I(0) variables. Here the A_i^*'s ($i = 1, \ldots, p$) are ($K \times K$) coefficient matrices, as usual.

The reduced forms corresponding to the structural forms (4.2) and (4.3), respectively, are obtained by premultiplying with A^{-1},

$$\Delta y_t = \Pi y_{t-1} + \Gamma_1 \Delta y_{t-1} + \cdots + \Gamma_{p-1} \Delta y_{t-p+1} + u_t \qquad (4.4)$$

and

$$y_t = A_1 y_{t-1} + \cdots + A_p y_{t-p} + u_t, \qquad (4.5)$$

where $\Pi = A^{-1}\Pi^*, \Gamma_j = A^{-1}\Gamma_j^*$ ($j = 1, \ldots, p - 1$) and $A_j = A^{-1}A_j^*$ ($j = 1, \ldots, p$). Moreover,

$$u_t = A^{-1} B\varepsilon_t, \qquad (4.6)$$

which relates the reduced-form disturbances u_t to the underlying structural shocks ε_t.

To identify the structural form parameters, we must place restrictions on the parameter matrices. Even if the matrix A, which specifies the instantaneous relations between the variables, is set to an identity matrix ($A = I_K$), the assumption of orthogonal shocks ε_t is not sufficient to achieve identification. For a K-dimensional system, $K(K - 1)/2$ restrictions are necessary for orthogonalizing the shocks because there are $K(K - 1)/2$ potentially different instantaneous covariances. These restrictions can be obtained from a "timing scheme" for the shocks. For such an identification scheme it is assumed that the shocks may affect a subset of variables directly within the current time period, whereas another subset of variables is affected with a time lag only. An example of such an identification scheme is the triangular (or recursive) identification suggested by Sims (1980). In this model the shocks enter the equations successively so that the additional shock of the second equation does not affect the variable explained by the first equation in the same period. Similarly, the third shock does not affect the variables explained by the first and second equation in the current time period. Such a scheme is also called a *Wold causal chain system* [Wold (1960)] and is often associated with a causal chain from the first to the last variable in the system. Because the impulse responses computed from these models depend on the ordering of the variables, nonrecursive identification schemes that also allow for instantaneous effects of the variables ($A \neq I_K$) have been suggested in the literature [see, e.g., Sims (1986) and Bernanke (1986)]. Moreover, restrictions on the long-run effects of some shocks are also sometimes used to identify SVAR models [see, e.g., Blanchard & Quah (1989), Galí (1999), and King, Plosser, Stock & Watson (1991)]. In empirical applications such restrictions are suggested by economic theory or are imposed just for convenience.

In the following we discuss different types of SVAR models that have been used in applied work. The most popular kinds of restrictions can be classified as follows:

(i) $B = I_K$. The vector of innovations ε_t is modeled as an interdependent system of linear equations such that $Au_t = \varepsilon_t$. Linear restrictions on A can be written in explicit form as $\text{vec}(A) = R_A \gamma_A + r_A$, where γ_A contains all unrestricted elements of A, R_A is a suitable matrix with 0-1 elements, and r_A is a vector of normalizing constants.

(ii) $A = I_K$. In this case the model for the innovations is $u_t = B\varepsilon_t$, and to exclude some (linear combinations of the) structural shocks in particular equations, restrictions of the form $\text{vec}(B) = R_B \gamma_B + r_B$ are imposed, where γ_B contains the unrestricted elements of B and R_B is the corresponding selection matrix with 0-1 elements.

(iii) The so-called AB-model of Amisano & Giannini (1997) combines the restrictions for A and B from (i) and (ii) such that the model for the innovations is $Au_t = B\varepsilon_t$. Accordingly, the two sets of restrictions $\text{vec}(A) = R_A \gamma_A + r_A$ and $\text{vec}(B) = R_B \gamma_B + r_B$ are used to identify the system.

(iv) There may be prior information on the long-run effects of some shocks. They are measured by considering the responses of the system variables to the shocks. Therefore, it is useful to discuss impulse responses and then also to consider the long-run effects in more detail. Impulse response analysis is presented in the next section.

It is possible to check the identification of an SVAR model by using an order condition similar to the one used to check for identification of a system of simultaneous equations. The number of parameters of the reduced form VAR (leaving out the parameters attached to the lagged variables) is given by the number of nonredundant elements of the covariance matrix Σ_u, that is, $K(K+1)/2$. Accordingly, it is not possible to identify more than $K(K+1)/2$

parameters of the structural form. However, the overall number of elements of the structural form matrices A and B is $2K^2$. It follows that

$$2K^2 - \frac{K(K+1)}{2} = K^2 + \frac{K(K-1)}{2} \tag{4.7}$$

restrictions are required to identify the full model. If we set one of the matrices A or B equal to the identity matrix, then $K(K-1)/2$ restrictions remain to be imposed.

As an example, consider a recursive identification scheme. In this case, $A = I_K$ and $u_t = B\varepsilon_t$. Restricting B to be lower triangular ensures that the first component of ε_t, ε_{1t}, can have an instantaneous impact in all equations, whereas ε_{2t} cannot affect the first equation instantaneously but only all the others, and so on. Hence, the recursive structure implies just the required $K(K-1)/2$ zero restrictions.

The simple IS–LM model discussed by Pagan (1995) is another example of an AB-model. Let q_t, i_t, and m_t denote output, an interest rate, and real money, respectively. The errors of the corresponding reduced form VAR are denoted by $u_t = (u_t^q, u_t^i, u_t^m)'$. A structural model reflecting a traditional Keynesian view is

$$\begin{aligned} u_t^q &= -a_{12}u_t^i + b_{11}\varepsilon_t^{IS} & \text{(IS curve)}, \\ u_t^i &= -a_{21}u_t^q - a_{23}u_t^m + b_{22}\varepsilon_t^{LM} & \text{(inverse LM curve)}, \\ u_t^m &= b_{33}\varepsilon_t^m & \text{(money supply rule)}, \end{aligned}$$

where the structural shocks are assumed to be mutually uncorrelated. The first equation represents a traditional IS curve with a negative parameter for the interest rate innovation u_t^i. The second equation results from solving a Keynesian money demand relationship with respect to interest rate innovations. In other words, the point of departure is a relation $u_t^m = \beta_1 u_t^q + \beta_2 u_t^i + \varepsilon_t^{LM}$, where β_1 is positive because more money is used to finance a larger transactions volume. Moreover, β_2 is negative because higher interest rates lead to lower money holdings and, hence, less demand for money. Accordingly, it is expected that a_{21} is negative whereas a_{23} is positive. Finally, the third equation postulates that the innovations of the money base are driven by exogenous money supply shocks. Obviously, this model reflects a very stylized view of the economy. A more realistic representation of the economic system would involve further equations and parameter restrictions [see, e.g., Galí (1992)]. The present three equations correspond to an AB-model, which can be written as $Au_t = B\varepsilon_t$:

$$\begin{bmatrix} 1 & a_{12} & 0 \\ a_{21} & 1 & a_{23} \\ 0 & 0 & 1 \end{bmatrix} u_t = \begin{bmatrix} b_{11} & 0 & 0 \\ 0 & b_{22} & 0 \\ 0 & 0 & b_{33} \end{bmatrix} \varepsilon_t. \tag{4.8}$$

To illustrate how the restrictions implied by this model can be written using the notation defined above, we give the linear restrictions in matrix form:

$$
\mathrm{vec}(\mathsf{A}) = \begin{bmatrix} 1 \\ a_{21} \\ 0 \\ a_{12} \\ 1 \\ 0 \\ 0 \\ a_{23} \\ 1 \end{bmatrix} = \begin{bmatrix} 0\ 0\ 0 \\ 1\ 0\ 0 \\ 0\ 0\ 0 \\ 0\ 1\ 0 \\ 0\ 0\ 0 \\ 0\ 0\ 0 \\ 0\ 0\ 0 \\ 0\ 0\ 1 \\ 0\ 0\ 0 \end{bmatrix} \begin{bmatrix} a_{21} \\ a_{12} \\ a_{23} \end{bmatrix} + \begin{bmatrix} 1 \\ 0 \\ 0 \\ 0 \\ 1 \\ 0 \\ 0 \\ 0 \\ 1 \end{bmatrix}
$$

and

$$
\mathrm{vec}(\mathsf{B}) = \begin{bmatrix} b_{11} \\ 0 \\ 0 \\ 0 \\ b_{22} \\ 0 \\ 0 \\ 0 \\ b_{33} \end{bmatrix} = \begin{bmatrix} 1\ 0\ 0 \\ 0\ 0\ 0 \\ 0\ 0\ 0 \\ 0\ 0\ 0 \\ 0\ 1\ 0 \\ 0\ 0\ 0 \\ 0\ 0\ 0 \\ 0\ 0\ 0 \\ 0\ 0\ 1 \end{bmatrix} \begin{bmatrix} b_{11} \\ b_{22} \\ b_{33} \end{bmatrix}.
$$

As mentioned earlier in this section, $2K^2 - K(K+1)/2$ restrictions need to be imposed for just-identification. In our example, $K = 3$, and consequently we need $2K^2 - K(K+1)/2 = 12$ restrictions on A and B. Counting the restrictions given by (4.8), we find the model to be just-identified. There are 6 restrictions for A (3 zeros and 3 ones) and additional 6 zero restrictions for B. Given that there are enough identifying assumptions, the parameters of the SVAR model can be estimated by methods discussed in Section 4.4. Within an SVAR model the dynamic effects of structural shocks are typically investigated by an impulse response analysis, which is discussed in the following section.

4.3 Impulse Response Analysis

4.3.1 Stationary VAR Processes

If the process y_t is I(0), the effects of shocks in the variables of a given system are most easily seen in its Wold moving average (MA) representation

$$
y_t = \Phi_0 u_t + \Phi_1 u_{t-1} + \Phi_2 u_{t-2} + \cdots , \tag{4.9}
$$

where $\Phi_0 = I_K$ and the

$$\Phi_s = \sum_{j=1}^{s} \Phi_{s-j} A_j, \quad s = 1, 2, \ldots, \tag{4.10}$$

can be computed recursively, as in (3.47), from the reduced-form coefficients of the VAR in levels specified in (4.5). The coefficients of this representation may be interpreted as reflecting the responses to impulses hitting the system. The (i, j)th elements of the matrices Φ_s, regarded as a function of s, trace out the expected response of $y_{i,t+s}$ to a unit change in y_{jt}, holding constant all past values of y_t. Since the change in y_{it}, given $\{y_{t-1}, y_{t-2}, \ldots\}$, is measured by the innovation u_{it}, the elements of Φ_s represent the impulse responses of the components of y_t with respect to the u_t innovations. In the presently considered I(0) case, $\Phi_s \to 0$ as $s \to \infty$. Hence, the effect of an impulse is transitory as it vanishes over time. These impulse responses are sometimes called *forecast error impulse responses* because the u_t's are the 1-step ahead forecast errors.

Occasionally, interest centers on the accumulated effects of the impulses. They are easily obtained by adding up the Φ_s matrices. For example, the accumulated effects over all periods, the total long-run effects, are given by

$$\Phi = \sum_{s=0}^{\infty} \Phi_s = (I_K - A_1 - \cdots - A_p)^{-1}. \tag{4.11}$$

This matrix exists if the VAR process is stable (see the stability condition in (3.2)).

A critique that has been raised against forecast error impulse responses is that the underlying shocks are not likely to occur in isolation if the components of u_t are instantaneously correlated, that is, if Σ_u is not diagonal. Therefore, orthogonal innovations are preferred in an impulse response analysis, as mentioned in Section 4.2. One way to get them is to use a Choleski decomposition of the covariance matrix Σ_u. If B is a lower triangular matrix such that $\Sigma_u = \mathsf{B}\mathsf{B}'$, the orthogonalized shocks are given by $\varepsilon_t = \mathsf{B}^{-1} u_t$. Hence, we obtain the following from (4.9):

$$y_t = \Psi_0 \varepsilon_t + \Psi_1 \varepsilon_{t-1} + \cdots, \tag{4.12}$$

where $\Psi_i = \Phi_i \mathsf{B}$ $(i = 0, 1, 2, \ldots)$. Here $\Psi_0 = \mathsf{B}$ is lower triangular, and thus an ε shock in the first variable may have an instantaneous effect on all the variables, whereas a shock in the second variable cannot have an instantaneous impact on y_{1t} but only on the other variables, and so on. Thus, we have a Wold causal chain. Given that the ε shocks are instantaneously uncorrelated (orthogonal), the corresponding impulse responses are often referred to as *orthogonalized impulse responses*.

Because many matrices B exist that satisfy $\mathsf{B}\mathsf{B}' = \Sigma_u$, using a Choleski decomposition approach is to some extent arbitrary unless there are good reasons for a particular recursive structure specified by a given B. As mentioned in Section 4.1, if B is found by a lower triangular Choleski decomposition, choosing a different ordering of the variables in the vector y_t may produce different shocks. Hence, the effects of a shock may depend on the way the variables are arranged in the vector y_t. In view of this difficulty, Sims (1981) has recommended trying various triangular orthogonalizations and checking the robustness of the results with respect to the ordering of the variables if no particular ordering is suggested by subject matter theory. Using information based on the latter leads to SVAR models, of course.

As discussed earlier, in an SVAR such as (4.3), the residuals are represented as $B\varepsilon_t$ and ε_t is a ($K \times 1$) vector of structural shocks with (diagonal) covariance matrix $E(\varepsilon_t \varepsilon_t') = \Sigma_\varepsilon$, which is often specified to be an identity matrix. In any case, the structural shocks are instantaneously uncorrelated. In the AB-model the relation to the reduced form residuals is given by $Au_t = B\varepsilon_t$. Therefore, the impulse responses in a general SVAR model may be obtained from (4.12) with $\Psi_j = \Phi_j A^{-1}B$. If restrictions on the long-run effects are available, they may be placed on $\Psi = \Phi A^{-1}B$, where Φ is the matrix specified in (4.11). For example, one may want to impose the restriction that some shocks do not have any long-run effects. This is achieved by setting the respective elements of the long-run impact matrix $\Psi = \Psi_0 + \Psi_1 + \cdots$ equal to zero.

As an example we consider the model suggested by Blanchard & Quah (1989). On the basis of a simple economic model, Blanchard and Quah have identified supply shocks as having persistent effects on output whereas demand shocks are transitory. Suppose in a VAR model for $y_t = (\Delta Q_t, U_t)'$, where Q_t denotes the log of output and U_t is the unemployment rate, we wish to identify innovations that can be interpreted as supply shocks and demand shocks, $\varepsilon_t = (\varepsilon_t^s, \varepsilon_t^d)'$. Because we have $K = 2$ variables and can specify $A = I_2$, we need $K(K-1)/2 = 1$ restriction to identify the structural shocks from the VAR residuals. The effects of these shocks on the output growth rates ΔQ_t and the unemployment U_t are obtained from the Ψ_i matrices. Accumulating them gives the effects on Q_t and the accumulated unemployment rate. Thus, the restriction that demand shocks have no long-run impact on output can be imposed by constraining the (1,2)-element of the matrix $\Psi = \sum_{i=0}^{\infty} \Psi_i$ to be equal to zero. Estimation of models with long-run restrictions is discussed in Section 4.4.

4.3.2 Impulse Response Analysis of Nonstationary VARs and VECMs

Although the Wold representation does not exist for nonstationary cointegrated processes, it is easy to see from Section 3.6 that the Φ_s impulse response matrices can be computed in the same way as in (4.10) based on VARs with integrated variables or the levels version of a VECM [Lütkepohl (1991, Chapter 11) and Lütkepohl & Reimers (1992)]. In this case, the Φ_s may not converge to zero as $s \to \infty$; consequently, some shocks may have permanent effects. Of course, one may also consider orthogonalized or accumulated impulse responses. Because the Φ_s and Ψ_s may not approach zero as $s \to \infty$, the total accumulated impulse responses will generally not exist, however. Recall that for cointegrated systems the matrix $(I_K - A_1 - \cdots - A_p)$ is singular. From Johansen's version of Granger's Representation Theorem [see Johansen (1995a)] it is known, however, that if y_t is generated by a reduced-form VECM $\Delta y_t = \alpha\beta' y_{t-1} + \Gamma_1 \Delta y_{t-1} + \cdots + \Gamma_{p-1}\Delta y_{t-p+1} + u_t$, it has the following MA representation:

$$y_t = \Xi \sum_{i=1}^{t} u_i + \Xi^*(L)u_t + y_0^*,$$

where $\Xi = \beta_\perp \left(\alpha'_\perp (I_K - \sum_{i=1}^{p-1} \Gamma_i)\beta_\perp \right)^{-1} \alpha'_\perp$, $\Xi^*(L) = \sum_{j=0}^{\infty} \Xi_j^* L^j$ is an infinite-order polynomial in the lag operator with coefficient matrices Ξ_j^* that go to zero as $j \to \infty$. The term y_0^* contains all initial values. Notice that Ξ has rank $K - r$ if the cointegrating rank of the system is r. It represents the long-run effects of forecast error impulse responses, whereas the Ξ_j^*'s contain transitory effects.

Because the forecast error impulse responses based on Ξ and the Ξ_j^*'s are subject to the same criticism as for stable VAR processes, appropriate shocks have to be identified for a meaningful impulse response analysis. If u_t is replaced by $A^{-1}B\varepsilon_t$, the orthogonalized "short-run" impulse responses may be obtained as $\Xi_j^* A^{-1}B$ in a way analogous to the stationary VAR case. Moreover, the long-run effects of ε shocks are given by

$$\Xi A^{-1}B. \tag{4.13}$$

This matrix has rank $K - r$ because $\mathrm{rk}(\Xi) = K - r$ and A and B are nonsingular. Thus, the matrix (4.13) can have at most r columns of zeros. Hence, there can be at most r shocks with transitory effects (zero long-run impact), and at least $k^* = K - r$ shocks have permanent effects. Given the reduced rank of the matrix, each column of zeros stands for only k^* independent restrictions. Thus, if there are r transitory shocks, the corresponding zeros represent k^*r independent restrictions only. To identify the permanent shocks exactly we need $k^*(k^* - 1)/2$ additional restrictions. Similarly, $r(r - 1)/2$ additional contemporaneous restrictions identify the transitory shocks [see, e.g., King et al. (1991)]. Together these are a total of $k^*r + k^*(k^* - 1)/2 + r(r - 1)/2 = K(K - 1)/2$ restrictions. Hence, assuming $A = I_K$, we have just enough restrictions to identify B.

For example, in King et al. (1991) a model is considered for the log of private output (q_t), consumption (c_t), and investment (i_t). Using economic theory, King et al. inferred that all three variables should be I(1) with $r = 2$ cointegration relations and only one permanent shock. Because $k^* = 1$, the permanent shock is identified without further assumptions ($k^*(k^* - 1)/2 = 0$). For identification of the transitory shocks, $r(r - 1)/2 = 1$ further restriction is needed. Suppose a recursive structure of the transitory shocks is assumed such that the second transitory shock does not have an instantaneous impact on the first one. Placing the permanent shock first in the ε_t vector, these restrictions can be represented as follows in the foregoing framework:

$$\Xi B = \begin{bmatrix} * & 0 & 0 \\ * & 0 & 0 \\ * & 0 & 0 \end{bmatrix} \quad \text{and} \quad B = \begin{bmatrix} * & * & * \\ * & * & 0 \\ * & * & * \end{bmatrix},$$

where asterisks denote unrestricted elements. Because ΞB has rank 1, the two zero columns represent two independent restrictions only. A third restriction is placed on B, and thus we have a total of $K(K - 1)/2$ independent restrictions as required for just-identification.

In some situations A may also be specified differently from the identity matrix. In any case, long-run restrictions imply in general nonlinear restrictions on A, B, or both. To illustrate the process of deriving structural restrictions from economic theory, we will discuss a more complex example next.

An example. Long-run identifying assumptions for the ε_t shocks are typically derived from economic theory. To illustrate this point, we briefly describe a simple macroeconomic model of the labor market used by Jacobson, Vredin & Warne (1997) to investigate the effects of shocks to Scandinavian unemployment. This model consists of a production function, a labor demand relation, a labor supply, and a wage-setting relation. All variables are expressed in natural logarithms. The production function relates output gdp_t to employment e_t as follows:

$$gdp_t = \rho e_t + \theta_{1,t}, \tag{4.14}$$

where ρ measures the returns to scale. The quantity $\theta_{1,t}$ is a stochastic technology trend that follows a random walk,

$$\theta_{1,t} = \theta_{1,t-1} + \varepsilon_t^{gdp},$$

and ε_t^{gdp} is the pure technology shock. Labor demand relates employment to output and real wages $(w - p)_t$:

$$e_t = \lambda gdp_t - \eta(w - p)_t + \theta_{2,t}, \tag{4.15}$$

with an error process

$$\theta_{2,t} = \phi_d \theta_{2,t-1} + \varepsilon_t^d.$$

If $|\phi_d| < 1$, the labor demand is stationary. In that case the pure labor demand innovation ε_t^d has only temporary effects on employment. Jacobson et al. (1997)

assumed $\phi_d = 0$ a priori, which implies that the labor demand shock has no long-run effects. Within a cointegration analysis, stationarity of labor demand can be tested; hence, the a priori assumption is not needed here. In the third equation of the model, the labor force l_t is related to real wages according to

$$l_t = \pi(w - p)_t + \theta_{3,t}. \tag{4.16}$$

The exogenous labor supply trend $\theta_{3,t}$ follows a random walk

$$\theta_{3,t} = \theta_{3,t-1} + \varepsilon_t^s,$$

where ε_t^s is the underlying labor supply shock. Finally, we have the wage-setting relation

$$(w - p)_t = \delta(gdp_t - e_t) - \gamma(l_t - e_t) + \theta_{4,t} \tag{4.17}$$

stating that real wages are a function of productivity $(gdp_t - e_t)$ and unemployment $(l_t - e_t)$. The wage setting trend $\theta_{4,t}$ can be stationary or nonstationary, as determined by ϕ_w in

$$\theta_{4,t} = \phi_w\theta_{4,t-1} + \varepsilon_t^w.$$

If $|\phi_w| < 1$, the wage setting trend is stationary. Again, results from empirical analysis can be used to determine whether wage setting is stationary.

Under standard assumptions for the shocks ε^{gdp}, ε^d, ε^s, and ε^w the solution of the model (4.14)–(4.17) in terms of the variables used in the empirical analysis is given by

$$
\begin{bmatrix} gdp_t - e_t \\ e_t \\ l_t - e_t \\ (w - p)_t \end{bmatrix} = \psi \begin{bmatrix} (1 - \lambda)(1 + \gamma\pi) + \eta\gamma \\ \lambda(1 + \gamma\pi) - \eta\delta \\ \eta\delta - \lambda + (1 - \lambda)\pi\delta \\ \lambda\gamma + \delta(1 - \lambda) \end{bmatrix} \theta_{1,t} + \psi \begin{bmatrix} (\rho - 1)(1 + \gamma\pi) \\ 1 + \gamma\pi \\ (\rho - 1)\delta\pi - 1 \\ \gamma - \delta(1 - \rho) \end{bmatrix} \theta_{2,t}
$$

$$
+ \psi \begin{bmatrix} (\rho - 1)\eta\gamma \\ \eta\gamma \\ 1 - \rho\lambda + (\rho - 1)\delta\eta \\ (\rho\lambda - 1)\gamma \end{bmatrix} \theta_{3,t} + \psi \begin{bmatrix} \eta(1 - \rho) \\ -\eta \\ \eta + (1 - \rho\lambda)\pi \\ 1 - \rho\lambda \end{bmatrix} \theta_{4,t} \tag{4.18}
$$

with

$$\psi = \frac{1}{(1 - \rho\lambda)(1 + \gamma\pi) + \eta\gamma + (\rho - 1)\eta\delta}.$$

From this solution it is obvious that productivity, employment, unemployment, and real wages are driven by two random walks in productivity and labor supply. As explained earlier, the labor demand and the wage setting component can be stationary or nonstationary. In terms of the common trends literature, there are at least two and at most four common trends in this model. This implies at most two cointegration relations: a labor demand relation and a wage-setting relation. The model together with results from a cointegration analysis implies a set of identifying assumptions for the structural VECM. Suppose, for example, that two cointegration relations ($r = 2$) have been found in a four-dimensional VAR ($K = 4$) for productivity, employment, unemployment, and real wages. Consequently, only $k^* = K - r = 2$ shocks may have permanent effects. We associate the technology, the labor demand, the labor supply, and the wage-setting shocks with the equations for productivity, employment, unemployment, and real wages, respectively, such that $\varepsilon_t = (\varepsilon_t^{gdp}, \varepsilon_t^d, \varepsilon_t^s, \varepsilon_t^w)'$.

For stationarity of labor demand and wage-setting our model implies that labor demand and wage-setting shocks have no long-run impact on the system variables and, hence, the second and fourth columns of the long-run impact matrix $\Xi A^{-1}B$ are zero. To identify the two permanent shocks we have to impose $k^*(k^* - 1)/2 = 1$ additional restriction. Assuming constant returns to scale ($\rho = 1$) implies that productivity is only driven by productivity shocks ε^{gdp} in the long-run [see (4.18)]. Thus, if $A = I_K$ is assumed, these sets of restrictions can be expressed as follows in terms of the long-run impact matrix:

$$\Xi B = \begin{bmatrix} * & 0 & 0 & 0 \\ * & 0 & * & 0 \\ * & 0 & * & 0 \\ * & 0 & * & 0 \end{bmatrix}. \tag{4.19}$$

Here unrestricted elements are again indicated by asterisks. Note that, owing to the reduced rank of Ξ, we cannot simply count the zeros in (4.19) to determine the number of restrictions imposed on the model. As explained at the beginning of this section, the two zero columns represent $k^*r = 4$ linearly independent restrictions only. Hence, the zeros in (4.19) stand for only five linearly independent restrictions. In addition, we need $r(r - 1)/2 = 1$ contemporaneous restriction to disentangle the effects of the two transitory shocks. For instance, we may choose the restriction that labor demand shocks do not affect real wages on impact, that is, we set $B_{42} = 0$. In our example, a typical problem within the SVAR modeling class arises: The theoretical model does not suggest contemporaneous restrictions, and thus, defending this type of restriction may be difficult. In practice, a sensitivity analysis with respect to different contemporaneous identifying assumptions can be useful. We will employ the presented theoretical model to derive identifying assumptions in a structural VECM for Canadian labor market data in Section 4.7.3.

To compute the impulse responses we need not only the reduced form parameters but also the structural parameters. How to estimate them will be discussed in the next section before we consider inference for impulse responses in Section 4.5.

4.4 Estimation of Structural Parameters

4.4.1 SVAR Models

The estimation of the SVAR model is equivalent to the problem of estimating a simultaneous equation model with covariance restrictions. First, consider a model without restrictions on the long-run effects of the shocks. It is assumed that ε_t is white noise with $\varepsilon_t \sim N(0, I_K)$ and the basic model is a VAR(p); thus the structural form is

$$\mathsf{A}y_t = \mathsf{A}[A_1, \ldots, A_p]Y_{t-1} + \mathsf{B}\varepsilon_t, \tag{4.20}$$

where $Y'_{t-1} = (y'_{t-1}, \ldots, y'_{t-p})$. If we define $A = [A_1, \ldots, A_p]$, the corresponding reduced form is $y_t = AY_{t-1} + \mathsf{A}^{-1}\mathsf{B}\varepsilon_t$. Notice that the error term $u_t = \mathsf{A}^{-1}\mathsf{B}\varepsilon_t$. Hence, for a sample $y_1, \ldots, y_T$, if we use the notation $Y = [y_1, \ldots, y_T]$ and $Z = [Y_0, \ldots, Y_{T-1}]$, the log-likelihood function is

$$
\begin{aligned}
l(A, \mathsf{A}, \mathsf{B}) &= -\tfrac{KT}{2}\log 2\pi - \tfrac{T}{2}\log|\mathsf{A}^{-1}\mathsf{B}\mathsf{B}'\mathsf{A}'^{-1}| \\
&\quad - \tfrac{T}{2}\mathrm{tr}\{(Y - AZ)'[\mathsf{A}^{-1}\mathsf{B}\mathsf{B}'\mathsf{A}'^{-1}]^{-1}(Y - AZ)\} \\
&= \text{constant} + \tfrac{T}{2}\log|\mathsf{A}|^2 - \tfrac{T}{2}\log|\mathsf{B}|^2 \\
&\quad - \tfrac{T}{2}\mathrm{tr}\{\mathsf{A}'\mathsf{B}'^{-1}\mathsf{B}^{-1}\mathsf{A}(Y - AZ)(Y - AZ)'\}.
\end{aligned}
\tag{4.21}
$$

Here we have used the matrix rules $|\mathsf{A}^{-1}\mathsf{B}\mathsf{B}'(\mathsf{A}^{-1})'| = |\mathsf{A}^{-1}|^2|\mathsf{B}|^2 = |\mathsf{A}|^{-2}|\mathsf{B}|^2$ and $\mathrm{tr}(VW) = \mathrm{tr}(WV)$ for matrices V and W with suitable dimensions. If there are no restrictions on A, we know from Chapter 3, Section 3.3.1, that for any given A and B the function $l(A, \mathsf{A}, \mathsf{B})$ is maximized with respect to A by $\hat{A} = YZ'(ZZ')^{-1}$. Substituting this expression in (4.21) gives the concentrated log-likelihood

$$
\begin{aligned}
l_C(\mathsf{A}, \mathsf{B}) &= \text{constant} + \frac{T}{2}\log|\mathsf{A}|^2 - \frac{T}{2}\log|\mathsf{B}|^2 \\
&\quad - \frac{T}{2}\mathrm{tr}(\mathsf{A}'\mathsf{B}'^{-1}\mathsf{B}^{-1}\mathsf{A}\widetilde{\Sigma}_u),
\end{aligned}
\tag{4.22}
$$

where $\widetilde{\Sigma}_u = T^{-1}(Y - \hat{A}Z)(Y - \hat{A}Z)'$ is just the estimated covariance matrix of the VAR residuals [cf. Breitung (2001)].

It is easy to extend this approach to the case in which deterministic terms are present in the original model. Moreover, the same concentrated likelihood function is obtained if there are restrictions for A, for example, if a subset model is fitted. In this case, theoretically we just have to replace $\widetilde{\Sigma}_u$ by the residual covariance matrix of the restricted ML estimator of the reduced form. For practical purposes, the exact ML estimator is usually not used, however, because its computation requires the use of nonlinear optimization methods in general. Instead, the feasible GLS estimator, which has the same asymptotic properties as the ML estimator may be used. In that case, (4.22) is not strictly the concentrated log-likelihood, however. For simplicity we still refer to this function as the concentrated log-likelihood.

The function (4.22) is maximized with respect to A and B subject to the restrictions resulting from the structural form of the system, which for the AB-model can be written compactly as

$$
\begin{bmatrix} \text{vec } A \\ \text{vec } B \end{bmatrix} = \begin{bmatrix} R_A & 0 \\ 0 & R_B \end{bmatrix} \begin{bmatrix} \gamma_A \\ \gamma_B \end{bmatrix} + \begin{bmatrix} r_A \\ r_B \end{bmatrix}. \tag{4.23}
$$

Because no closed form solution is available, this has to be done by employing numerical optimization methods. For this purpose, Amisano & Giannini (1997) have suggested using a scoring algorithm. More precisely, estimates for γ_A and γ_B are found by iterating on

$$
\begin{bmatrix} \tilde{\gamma}_A \\ \tilde{\gamma}_B \end{bmatrix}_{i+1} = \begin{bmatrix} \tilde{\gamma}_A \\ \tilde{\gamma}_B \end{bmatrix}_i + \ell\, \mathcal{I}\left(\begin{bmatrix} \tilde{\gamma}_A \\ \tilde{\gamma}_B \end{bmatrix}_i\right)^{-1} \mathcal{S}\left(\begin{bmatrix} \tilde{\gamma}_A \\ \tilde{\gamma}_B \end{bmatrix}_i\right),
$$

where ℓ is the step length, $\mathcal{I}(\cdot)$ denotes the information matrix of the free parameters γ_A and γ_B, $\mathcal{S}(\cdot)$ is the score vector, and the subscript refers to the iteration number from which the signified estimator is obtained. If we use

$$
\mathcal{I}\left(\begin{bmatrix} \text{vec } A \\ \text{vec } B \end{bmatrix}\right)
$$

$$
= T \begin{bmatrix} [B^{-1}A]^{-1} \otimes B'^{-1} \\ -(I_K \otimes B'^{-1}) \end{bmatrix} (I_{K^2} + \mathbf{K}_{KK})
$$

$$
\times \left[([B^{-1}A]'^{-1} \otimes B^{-1}) \vdots -(I_K \otimes B^{-1}) \right]
$$

with $\mathbf{K}_{KK}$ being a $(K^2 \times K^2)$ commutation matrix defined such that for any $(K \times K)$ matrix M, $\text{vec}(M') = \mathbf{K}_{KK}\text{vec}(M)$, the information matrix for the free parameters can be shown to be

$$
\mathcal{I}\left(\begin{bmatrix} \gamma_A \\ \gamma_B \end{bmatrix}\right) = \begin{bmatrix} R'_A & 0 \\ 0 & R'_B \end{bmatrix} \mathcal{I}\left(\begin{bmatrix} \text{vec } A \\ \text{vec } B \end{bmatrix}\right) \begin{bmatrix} R_A & 0 \\ 0 & R_B \end{bmatrix}.
$$

The score vector for the free parameters is given by

$$
\mathcal{S}\left(\begin{bmatrix} \gamma_A \\ \gamma_B \end{bmatrix}\right) = \begin{bmatrix} R'_A & 0 \\ 0 & R'_B \end{bmatrix} \mathcal{S}\left(\begin{bmatrix} \text{vec } A \\ \text{vec } B \end{bmatrix}\right),
$$

where we have used

$$
\mathcal{S}\left(\begin{bmatrix} \text{vec } A \\ \text{vec } B \end{bmatrix}\right) = \begin{bmatrix} (I_K \otimes B'^{-1}) \\ -(B^{-1}A \otimes B'^{-1}) \end{bmatrix} \mathcal{S}(\text{vec}[B^{-1}A])
$$

and

$$\mathcal{S}(\text{vec}[\mathsf{B}^{-1}\mathsf{A}]) = T\text{vec}([\mathsf{B}^{-1}\mathsf{A}]'^{-1}) - T(\widetilde{\Sigma}_u \otimes I_K)\text{vec}(\mathsf{B}^{-1}\mathsf{A}).$$

Although straightforward in theory, sometimes the optimization turns out to be difficult in practice, and the choice of appropriate starting values is crucial.

Identification of the SVAR models is often checked numerically using the starting values for γ_A and γ_B. As noted by Christiano, Eichenbaum & Evans (1999), in some cases the signs of the elements in A and B are not identified even if the usual order criterion for identification is met. They have suggested normalizing the sign so that the contemporaneous impact matrix $\mathsf{A}^{-1}\mathsf{B}$ will have positive diagonal elements.

Iteration of the algorithm stops when some prespecified criterion, such as the relative change in the log-likelihood and the relative change in the parameters, is met. The resulting ML estimator is asymptotically efficient and normally distributed, where the asymptotic covariance matrix is estimated by the inverse of the information matrix. Moreover, an ML estimator for Σ_u is given by

$$\widetilde{\Sigma}_u^* = \tilde{\mathsf{A}}^{-1}\tilde{\mathsf{B}}\tilde{\mathsf{B}}'\tilde{\mathsf{A}}'^{-1}, \tag{4.24}$$

where $\tilde{\mathsf{A}}$ and $\tilde{\mathsf{B}}$ are estimators of A and B, respectively. Note that $\widetilde{\Sigma}_u^*$ only corresponds to the reduced-form estimate $\widetilde{\Sigma}_u$ if the SVAR is exactly identified. In the presence of over-identifying restrictions, an LR test statistic for these restrictions can be constructed in the usual way as

$$LR = T(\log|\widetilde{\Sigma}_u^*| - \log|\widetilde{\Sigma}_u|). \tag{4.25}$$

This statistic has an asymptotic χ^2-distribution with degrees of freedom equal to the number of over-identifying restrictions. In the AB-model this is the number of constraints imposed on A and B minus $2K^2 - K(K+1)/2 = K^2 + K(K-1)/2$.

At times a priori information on the effects of structural shocks is available that specifies the structural long-run impact matrix Ψ to be lower triangular. Examples in the literature include Blanchard & Quah (1989) and Galí (1999). As discussed in Section 4.3, in a stationary VAR model these restrictions can be imposed by restricting the elements above the main diagonal of Ψ to zero. Estimation is particularly easy in this case. For the computation of the structurally identified impulse responses it is sufficient to estimate the contemporaneous impact matrix $\mathsf{C} = \mathsf{A}^{-1}\mathsf{B}$. We note that the long-run impact matrix of structural shocks Ψ can be related to Φ by the contemporaneous impact matrix C,

$$\Psi = \Phi\mathsf{C},$$

such that

$$\Psi\Psi' = \Phi\Sigma_u\Phi'$$
$$= (I_K - A_1 - \cdots - A_p)^{-1}\Sigma_u(I_K - A_1' - \cdots - A_p')^{-1}.$$

Because Ψ is assumed to be lower triangular, it can be obtained from a Choleski decomposition of the matrix

$$(I_K - A_1 - \cdots - A_p)^{-1}\Sigma_u(I_K - A_1' - \cdots - A_p')^{-1}.$$

Replacing the unknown quantities with estimates, we find that C can be estimated by

$$\hat{C} = \hat{\Phi}^{-1}\hat{\Psi} = \hat{\Phi}^{-1}\mathrm{chol}[\hat{\Phi}\hat{\Sigma}_u\hat{\Phi}'].$$

It must be emphasized that this estimation procedure works only in stationary VAR models because $(I_K - A_1 - \cdots - A_p)^{-1}$ does not exist otherwise. Moreover, this procedure can only be used to estimate models that are exactly identified. Although this case can be seen as a fairly special model, it is sometimes useful to have a closed-form solution for estimating the structural parameters. Section 4.7 illustrates the use of different estimation techniques.

Generally, if not otherwise mentioned, the procedures described in this section are also applicable if some or all of the variables have unit roots and a levels VAR model is fitted without taking possible cointegration restrictions into account.

4.4.2 Structural VECMs

For VECMs the concentrated likelihood function (4.22) can also be used for estimating the structural parameters A and B. If no restrictions are imposed on the short-run parameters, the $\tilde{\Sigma}_u$ matrix represents the residual covariance matrix obtained from a reduced rank regression as described in Chapter 3, Section 3.3.2. If the short-run parameters are restricted or restrictions are placed on the cointegration vectors, some other estimator may be used instead of the ML estimator, and Σ_u may be estimated from the corresponding residuals.

Generally, if long-run identifying restrictions have to be considered, maximization of (4.22) is a numerically difficult task because these restrictions are typically highly nonlinear for A, B, or both. In some cases, however, it is possible to express these long-run restrictions as linear restrictions, and maximization can be done using the scoring algorithm defined above. In particular, consider a cointegrated VECM where $A = I_K$. Then restrictions that some shocks have no long-run impact on the system variables can be written in implicit form as

$$R_\Xi\mathrm{vec}(\Xi B) = 0,$$

where R_Ξ is an appropriate restriction matrix. Following Vlaar (1998) in using the rules of the vec operator, we can reformulate these restrictions as

$$R_\Xi(I_K \otimes \Xi)\mathrm{vec}(B) = R_{B,l}\mathrm{vec}(B) = 0.$$

Replacing Ξ by an estimator obtained from the reduced form, we obtain $\hat{R}_{B,l} = R_\Xi(I_K \otimes \hat{\Xi})$, which is a stochastic restriction matrix. These implicit restrictions can be translated into the explicit form used in the maximization procedure of the SVECM and, moreover, can be combined with contemporaneous restrictions on the elements of B in the form $\text{vec}(B) = R_B \gamma_B$. It is worth noting that this method also works if there are more restrictions on the structural parameters than necessary for exact identification. In other words, the method may be applied for over-identified models, and the validity of these restrictions may be tested using the LR test statistic given in (4.25).

4.5 Statistical Inference for Impulse Responses

4.5.1 Asymptotic Estimation Theory

If an estimator $\hat\theta$ of the SVAR or SVECM coefficients summarized in the vector θ is available, estimators of the impulse responses may be obtained as functions of $\hat\theta$. Formally, we write for some arbitrary impulse response coefficient $\phi = \phi(\theta)$, and thus

$$\hat\phi = \phi(\hat\theta). \tag{4.26}$$

If $\hat\theta$ has an asymptotic normal distribution,

$$\sqrt{T}(\hat\theta - \theta) \xrightarrow{d} N(0, \Sigma_{\hat\theta}), \tag{4.27}$$

the ϕ are also asymptotically normally distributed,

$$\sqrt{T}(\hat\phi - \phi) \xrightarrow{d} N(0, \sigma_{\hat\phi}^2), \tag{4.28}$$

where

$$\sigma_{\hat\phi}^2 = \frac{\partial \phi}{\partial \theta'} \Sigma_{\hat\theta} \frac{\partial \phi}{\partial \theta} \tag{4.29}$$

and $\partial\phi/\partial\theta$ denotes the vector of first-order partial derivatives of ϕ with respect to the elements of θ. The limiting result in (4.28) holds if $\sigma_{\hat\phi}^2$ is nonzero, which in turn is guaranteed if $\Sigma_{\hat\theta}$ is nonsingular and $\partial\phi/\partial\theta \neq 0$. Note that the covariance matrix $\Sigma_{\hat\theta}$ may be singular if there are constraints on the coefficients or, as mentioned in Chapter 3, if there are I(1) variables. The partial derivatives will also usually be zero in some points of the parameter space because the ϕs generally consist of sums of products of the VAR coefficients; hence, the partial derivatives will also be sums of products of such coefficients, which may be zero. Nonzero partial derivatives are guaranteed if all elements of θ are nonzero. In other words, fitting subset VAR models where all the coefficients are restricted to zero that are actually zero helps to make the asymptotics work. Of course, in practice which coefficients are zero is usually unknown. Therefore, fitting subset models as described in Chapter 3, Section 3.4.5, may be a good idea.

4.5.2 Bootstrapping Impulse Responses

In applied work, statistical inference regarding impulse responses is often based on bootstrap methods. In particular, they are frequently used to construct confidence intervals (CIs) for impulse responses because, in this way, more reliable small sample inference is occasionally possible than by using asymptotic theory [e.g., Kilian (1998)]. Moreover, the analytical expressions of the asymptotic variances of the impulse response coefficients are rather complicated [e.g., Lütkepohl (1991, Chapter 3)]. If the bootstrap is used for setting up CIs, the precise expressions of the variances are not needed; hence, deriving the analytical expressions explicitly can be avoided.

Alternative bootstrap approaches have been proposed for setting up CIs for impulse responses. They use residual-based bootstraps that proceed as follows: First the model of interest is estimated. If the estimation residuals are denoted by $\hat{u}_t$, centered residuals, $\hat{u}_1 - \bar{\hat{u}}, \ldots, \hat{u}_T - \bar{\hat{u}}$, are computed and bootstrap residuals, $u_1^*, \ldots, u_T^*$, are generated by randomly drawing them with replacement from the centered residuals. The u_t^*'s are used to compute bootstrap time series recursively starting from given presample values $y_{-p+1}, \ldots, y_0$ for a model with p lags. The model is reestimated and the quantities of interest are determined on the basis of the parameter estimates obtained in this way. Repeating these steps many times gives the empirical bootstrap distribution of the quantities of interest. From that distribution, quantiles, and hence CIs, may be obtained for the impulse responses.

In the following, the symbols ϕ, $\hat{\phi}$, and $\hat{\phi}^*$ denote some general impulse response coefficient, its estimator implied by the estimators of the model coefficients, and the corresponding bootstrap estimator, respectively. The following bootstrap CIs have, for instance, been considered in the literature [see, e.g., Benkwitz, Lütkepohl & Wolters (2001)]:

- *Standard percentile interval*
  The most common method in setting up CIs for impulse responses in practice is to use the interval

  $$CI_S = \left[s_{\gamma/2}^*, s_{(1-\gamma/2)}^* \right],$$

  where $s_{\gamma/2}^*$ and $s_{(1-\gamma/2)}^*$ are the $\gamma/2$- and $(1-\gamma/2)$-quantiles, respectively, of the empirical distribution of the $\hat{\phi}^*$. The interval CI_S is the percentile confidence interval described, for example, by Efron & Tibshirani (1993).

- *Hall's percentile interval*
  Hall (1992) presents the usual bootstrap analogy stating that the distribution of $(\hat{\phi} - \phi)$ is approximately equal to that of $(\hat{\phi}^* - \hat{\phi})$ in large samples. From this result, the interval

  $$CI_H = \left[\hat{\phi} - t_{(1-\gamma/2)}^*, \hat{\phi} - t_{\gamma/2}^* \right]$$

can be derived. Here $t^*_{\gamma/2}$ and $t^*_{(1-\gamma/2)}$ are the $\gamma/2$- and $(1-\gamma/2)$-quantiles, respectively, of the empirical distribution of $(\hat{\phi}^* - \hat{\phi})$.

• *Hall's studentized interval*
In some situations, using a studentized statistic $(\hat{\phi} - \phi)/(\widehat{\text{var}}(\hat{\phi}))^{1/2}$ for constructing confidence intervals may be advantageous. In that case, bootstrap quantiles $t^{**}_{\gamma/2}$ and $t^{**}_{1-\gamma/2}$ from the distribution of $(\hat{\phi}^* - \hat{\phi})/(\widehat{\text{var}}(\hat{\phi}^*))^{1/2}$ are used to construct an interval

$$CI_{SH} = \left[\hat{\phi} - t^{**}_{(1-\gamma/2)}(\widehat{\text{var}}(\hat{\phi}))^{1/2}, \ \hat{\phi} - t^{**}_{\gamma/2}(\widehat{\text{var}}(\hat{\phi}))^{1/2} \right].$$

In this approach the variances are estimated by a bootstrap within each bootstrap replication.

Several refinements and modifications of these intervals exist. Unfortunately, the bootstrap does not necessarily overcome the problems due to a singularity in the asymptotic distribution that results from a zero variance in (4.28). In other words, in these cases bootstrap CIs may not have the desired coverage even asymptotically. For a critical discussion, see Benkwitz, Lütkepohl & Neumann (2000).

At least three possible strategies are available to overcome the problems resulting from the different rates of convergence in the parameter space. First, one may consider bootstrap procedures that adjust to the kind of singularity in the asymptotic distribution. Some different proposals of this kind are discussed in Benkwitz et al. (2000). For instance, subsampling may be used to estimate the convergence rate of the parameter estimators in addition to the model parameters. These and other methods were shown to have drawbacks, however, in empirical applications. Either they are not very practical for processes of realistic dimension and autoregressive order or they do not perform well in samples of typical size.

A second possibility for tackling the singularity problem is to single out and eliminate the points at which problems occur before an impulse response analysis is carried out. In the present case this proposal amounts to determining all zero coefficients in a first stage of the analysis and enforcing the resulting zero restrictions in the next stage, where the resulting subset model is estimated and used for computing impulse responses. This solution is, for instance, considered by Benkwitz et al. (2001). A possible problem in this approach is the uncertainty with respect to the actual zero restrictions.

A third way out of the singularity problem is to consider a different type of modeling approach based on the assumption of a potentially infinite VAR order. In this approach it is assumed that the model order is increased when more sample information becomes available. In other words, the model order is assumed to approach infinity with the sample size at a suitable rate. An asymptotic theory has been developed by Lütkepohl (1988, 1996),

Lütkepohl & Poskitt (1991, 1996b), Lütkepohl & Saikkonen (1997), and Saikkonen & Lütkepohl (1996, 2000a) based on work by Lewis & Reinsel (1985) and Saikkonen (1992). It turns out that this asymptotic theory avoids the kind of singularity in the asymptotic distribution that causes the failure of the bootstrap procedures. On the other hand, the greater generality of the model results in an inefficiency relative to the model with finite fixed order. In practice, using subset models may be the preferred solution.

4.5.3 An Illustration

To illustrate the use of an impulse response analysis for studying the relations between the variables of a model, we consider again the German interest rate–inflation system of Chapter 3. We use the subset VECM (3.41) to account for the problems related to the construction of bootstrap confidence intervals for the impulse responses. Because no instantaneous residual correlation was found in testing for instantaneous causality, it may be reasonable for this system to consider the forecast error impulse responses. In other words, our shocks are identified by assuming that the reduced-form residuals are instantaneously un-correlated. We plot the impulse responses in Figure 4.1 together with bootstrap confidence intervals obtained using the three methods just mentioned. The standard and Hall confidence intervals are based on 2,000 bootstrap replications, and the studentized Hall intervals are based in addition on 50 replications for estimating the variances $\widehat{\text{var}}(\hat{\phi}^*)$ in each of the outer replication rounds. As a consequence, the latter CIs are rather demanding computationally. The bootstrap literature suggests that the number of bootstrap replications has to be quite large in order to obtain reliable results. In the present case it is therefore questionable if 2,000 replications are adequate. One way to check this would be to simulate CIs with increasing numbers of replications and to determine whether an increase of the number of replications leads to changes in the CIs. For the present example, similar results are also obtained with smaller numbers of replications such as 1,000. Therefore, using 2,000 replications may be sufficient.

In this particular case all three methods for computing CIs produce qualitatively similar results. Both variables react permanently to a one-time impulse in their own residuals. Also they both have an impact on each other. Notice that the cointegrating rank $r = 1$. Hence, there can be at most one transitory shock. Because we do not need such a restriction for identification and therefore do not impose it, it should not come as a surprise that both shocks have permanent effects. The feedback relation reflected in the impulse responses of our final model was not seen as clearly in a Granger-causality analysis in Chapter 3. It produced much weaker evidence for a feedback relation. One of the problems in this kind of analysis is that a lack of sample information may make it difficult to produce clear results in relatively unrestricted models.

To illustrate this point we also provide the impulse responses of an unrestricted VAR(4) model for the two variables of interest in the lower part of Figure 4.1. Given the size of the CIs, the reactions of the variables are much less clear in this experiment than in the restricted subset VECM. In particular, because no cointegration restrictions have been imposed, the long-run reactions of the variables to impulses to the system are not very clear and may not even be diagnosed to be permanent. Of course, it is important to keep in mind that our modeling effort, including the specification of the cointegration relation, is based on a statistical analysis that cannot produce definite results with certainty. Therefore, some uncertainty remains about the adequacy of the restrictions we have imposed on the final model (3.41). Consequently, the conclusions drawn from the model also have some degree of uncertainty.

4.6 Forecast Error Variance Decomposition

Forecast error variance decompositions are also popular tools for interpreting VAR models and VECMs. Recall that the h-step forecast error from a VAR model is

$$y_{T+h} - y_{T+h|T} = u_{T+h} + \Phi_1 u_{T+h-1} + \cdots + \Phi_{h-1} u_{T+1}$$

[see (3.46) in Chapter 3]. Expressing this error in terms of the structural innovations $\varepsilon_t = (\varepsilon_{1t}, \ldots, \varepsilon_{Kt})' = B^{-1} A u_t$ gives

$$y_{T+h} - y_{T+h|T} = \Psi_0 \varepsilon_{T+h} + \Psi_1 \varepsilon_{T+h-1} + \cdots + \Psi_{h-1} \varepsilon_{T+1},$$

where $\Psi_j = \Phi_j A^{-1} B$. If we denote the ijth element of Ψ_n by $\psi_{ij,n}$, the kth element of the forecast error vector becomes

$$y_{k,T+h} - y_{k,T+h|T} = \sum_{n=0}^{h-1} (\psi_{k1,n} \varepsilon_{1,T+h-n} + \cdots + \psi_{kK,n} \varepsilon_{K,T+h-n}).$$

Given that the ε_{kt}s are contemporaneously and serially uncorrelated and have unit variances by construction, it follows that the corresponding forecast error variance is

$$\sigma_k^2(h) = \sum_{n=0}^{h-1} (\psi_{k1,n}^2 + \cdots + \psi_{kK,n}^2) = \sum_{j=1}^{K} (\psi_{kj,0}^2 + \cdots + \psi_{kj,h-1}^2).$$

The term $(\psi_{kj,0}^2 + \cdots + \psi_{kj,h-1}^2)$ is interpreted as the contribution of variable j to the h-step forecast error variance of variable k. This interpretation makes sense if the ε_{it}s can be viewed as shocks in variable i. Dividing the preceding terms by $\sigma_k^2(h)$ gives the percentage contribution of variable j to the h-step forecast error variance of variable k,

$$\omega_{kj}(h) = (\psi_{kj,0}^2 + \cdots + \psi_{kj,h-1}^2)/\sigma_k^2(h).$$

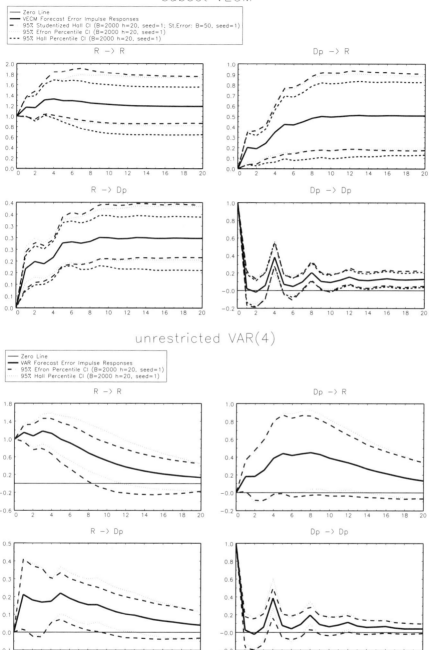

Figure 4.1. Forecast error impulse responses of German interest rate–inflation system based on subset VECM (3.41) (upper panel) and an unrestricted VAR(4) model (lower panel).

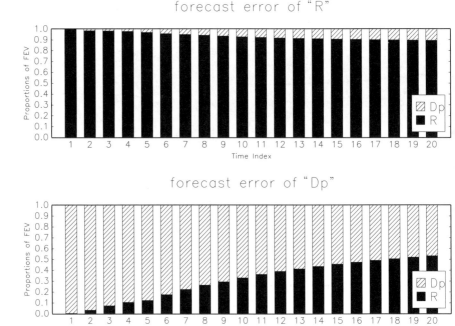

Figure 4.2. Forecast error variance decomposition of German interest rate–inflation system based on subset VECM (3.41).

These quantities, computed from estimated parameters, are often reported for various forecast horizons. Clearly, their interpretation as forecast error variance components may be criticized on the same grounds as structural impulse responses because they are based on the latter quantities.

In Figure 4.2, a forecast error variance decomposition of the German interest rate–inflation system based on the subset VECM (3.41) from Chapter 3 is shown. It is based on a Choleski decomposition of the covariance matrix. In Figure 4.2 it appears that the interest rate dominates the system to some extent. Its forecast errors are largely attributable to own innovations whereas the forecast errors of the inflation rate are partly determined by interest rate changes – at least for longer term forecasts. This interpretation has to be viewed with caution, however, because the forecast error variance components are computed from estimated quantities and are therefore uncertain. Also, in the present case, one may wonder whether the picture changes if the order of the variables is interchanged. Recall that the forecast error variance decomposition is based on the orthogonalized impulse responses for which the order of the variables matters. Although the instantaneous residual correlation is small in our subset VECM, it will have some impact on the outcome of a forecast error variance decomposition. For the present example the impact is small, however. Therefore, we do not show the result but encourage the reader to perform his or her own analysis.

4.7 Examples

In this section we illustrate the use of SVAR models by applying the methods discussed in previous sections. We start with the simple IS–LM model considered in Section 4.2 to illustrate the AB-model. Then we discuss the Blanchard–Quah model as an example for using long-run restrictions for the effects of shocks in the SVAR framework. The main emphasis in these two examples is on illustrating specific SVAR issues. In the final example we consider a Canadian labor market model and go through the different steps of an analysis in more detail.

4.7.1 A Simple AB-Model

In the first example we follow Breitung (2000) and estimate the stylized IS–LM model considered in Section 4.2 using U.S. macroeconomic time series. The empirical model is a simple trivariate VAR that includes the log of real GDP (q_t), a three-month interbank interest rate (i_t), and the log of the real monetary base (m_t). Therefore the vector of time series variables is $y_t = (q_t, i_t, m_t)'$. We use quarterly, seasonally adjusted data for the period from $1970Q1$ to $1997Q4$ from the Federal Reserve Economic Data (FRED) database maintained at the Federal Reserve Bank of St. Louis. Investigating the trending properties reveals evidence for a unit root in each of the three time series. As mentioned earlier, the estimation procedure from Section 4.4.1 may be applied to a VAR model fitted to the levels even if variables have unit roots; hence, possible cointegration restrictions are ignored. This is frequently done in SVAR modeling to avoid imposing too many restrictions, and we follow that road here. The specification of the reduced form in our analysis is the model used in Breitung (2000). More precisely, the starting point of the analysis is a reduced-form VAR(4) including a trend and a constant as deterministic terms. Using the first four observations as presample values, we have $T = 108$ observations for estimation. Alternative reduced-form model specifications may be used for the subsequent structural analysis. For instance, lag length criteria point to a smaller lag length ($p = 2$ or $p = 3$), whereas results from residual autocorrelation tests indicate a lag length of $p = 6$. We encourage the reader to explore these possibilities as well. As mentioned before, the main purpose of our analysis is an illustration of the AB-model. Therefore, we do not consider alternative specifications here.

Using the reduced form VAR(4), we impose the just-identifying restrictions discussed in Section 4.2 and estimate the structural parameters by means of the ML estimator considered in Section 4.4. The resulting structural parameter estimates of the matrices A and B are given by

$$
\tilde{A} = \begin{bmatrix} 1 & \underset{(-0.25)}{-0.04} & 0 \\ \underset{(-0.51)}{-0.14} & 1 & \underset{(4.92)}{0.73} \\ 0 & 0 & 1 \end{bmatrix} \text{ and } \tilde{B} = \begin{bmatrix} \underset{(13.9)}{0.0068} & 0 & 0 \\ 0 & \underset{(14.5)}{0.0087} & 0 \\ 0 & 0 & \underset{(14.7)}{0.0056} \end{bmatrix},
$$

where we list asymptotic t-ratios in parentheses below the coefficient estimates. It turns out that the estimated coefficient a_{12} is negative – and thus has the wrong sign ($\hat{a}_{12} = -0.04$) – but is statistically insignificant. The parameters of the inverted money demand relation have the expected sign; however, the coefficient for the output innovation (-0.14) is not significant at conventional levels.

Once the structural model has been identified and estimated, the effects of the structural shocks ε_t can be investigated through an impulse response analysis. The results of the impulse response analysis are often more informative than the structural parameter estimates themselves. For this purpose, the estimated contemporaneous impact matrix can be obtained from the ML estimates of the structural parameters:

$$
\tilde{A}^{-1}\tilde{B} = \begin{bmatrix} 0.69 & 0.03 & -0.02 \\ 0.10 & 0.88 & -0.42 \\ 0.00 & 0.00 & 0.56 \end{bmatrix} \times 10^{-2}.
$$

Figure 4.3 gives the responses (multiplied by 100) of the three system variables to the identified structural shocks together with 95% Hall bootstrap confidence intervals based on 2,000 bootstrap replications. According to our estimated SVAR model, an IS or spending shock (ε^{IS}) increases output immediately, increases interest rates for about twelve quarters with a maximal response after two years, and gradually drives down real money holdings. These effects are predicted by the IS–LM model. Moreover, an LM shock (ε^{LM}) leads to an increase in the interest rate and a decrease in real money holdings as well as a decrease of output for about three years. A positive money supply shock (ε^m) drives output down after roughly a year, which is at odds with economic theory. Although this effect is only marginally significant, it might suggest that money supply shocks are not appropriately captured by our stylized model. However, this money supply shock leads to an immediate drop in the interest rate and to a gradual increase of real money balances. This reaction is known as the "liquidity effect" and has also been observed in more complex SVAR models. This example demonstrates that even a very simple model produces results that are largely in line with predictions of a basic IS–LM model.

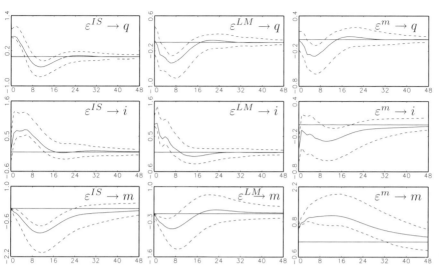

Figure 4.3. Responses of output (q), interest rate (i), and real money (m) in an IS–LM model with 95% confidence intervals based on 2,000 replications of the Hall bootstrap.

4.7.2 The Blanchard–Quah Model

Our second example provides estimates for the Blanchard–Quah model introduced in Section 4.3. Their model is a simple bivariate VAR model for the growth rates of output and the unemployment rate U_t. The growth rate is measured as the first differences of log output denoted as ΔQ_t. Consequently, $y_t = (\Delta Q_t, U_t)'$. We use quarterly U.S. time series data for the period between $1948Q2$ and $1987Q4$, as in the original study by Blanchard & Quah (1989). The data are available from the data archive of the *Journal of Applied Econometrics* [see data for Weber (1995)]. In the data set, the growth rate of output is adjusted for a constant mean with a structural break at $1974Q1$, whereas the unemployment rate is adjusted for a linear time trend. ADF unit root tests for both variables clearly reject the hypothesis of a unit root, indicating that both series are stationary.

Blanchard & Quah (1989) have identified aggregate demand shocks by assuming that they have merely transitory effects on the level of output. In contrast, aggregate supply shocks may have permanent effects on Q_t (see also Section 4.3). In other words, the vector of structural shocks $\varepsilon_t = (\varepsilon_t^s, \varepsilon_t^d)'$ is identified by restricting the long-run effect of the demand shock ε_t^d on output [i.e., the (1,2)-element of the matrix Ψ] to zero. This restriction implies a lower triangular structure for Ψ such that $\hat{\Psi}$ can be obtained by a Choleski decomposition of the long-run covariance matrix (see Section 4.4). Results from lag-length information criteria suggest a VAR order of $p = 2$ and, apart from some nonnormality in the residuals of the unemployment equation, a VAR(2) is a well-specified

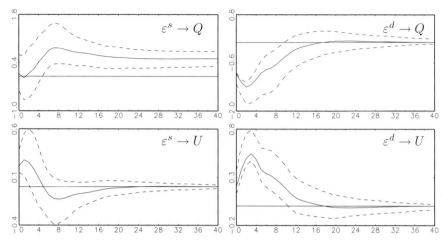

Figure 4.4. Responses of output and unemployment to supply and (negative) demand shock based on an unrestricted VAR(8) with 95% Hall bootstrap confidence intervals using 2,000 bootstrap replications.

model. Whereas the reader is invited to perform the following analysis based on a VAR(2) specification, we follow Blanchard & Quah (1989) and use a VAR(8) with a constant term to estimate the reduced-form model in order to replicate the original results as closely as possible. Checking the t-values of the VAR(8) reveals many insignificant coefficient estimates. Therefore a subset model may be another alternative reduced-form model. Based on the unrestricted VAR(8), we estimate the structural decomposition by computing the contemporaneous impact matrix B as well as the identified total long-run impact matrix Ψ:

$$\hat{\mathsf{B}} = \begin{bmatrix} \underset{(0.270)}{0.075} & \underset{(-7.02)}{-0.930} \\ \underset{(3.18)}{0.220} & \underset{(2.98)}{0.208} \end{bmatrix} \text{ and } \widehat{\Psi} = \begin{bmatrix} \underset{(4.29)}{0.519} & 0 \\ \underset{(0.005)}{0.008} & \underset{(3.01)}{4.044} \end{bmatrix}, \quad (4.30)$$

where we give t-statistics based on 2,000 bootstrap draws in parentheses. The t-statistics have been obtained using the standard bootstrap method from Section 4.5.2. These estimates suggest that supply shocks have a significant, positive long-run effect on output, whereas the long-run effect of a (negative) demand shock is restricted to zero.

Figure 4.4 shows the implied impulse response functions for the Blanchard–Quah example together with approximate 95% confidence intervals obtained from Hall's bootstrap method using 2,000 replications. Because we are interested in the effects of the structural shocks on the level of output, the first row in Figure 4.4 shows the accumulated impulse responses for ΔQ_t which are the responses of Q_t. As already suggested by the estimate of $\widehat{\Psi}$, positive supply

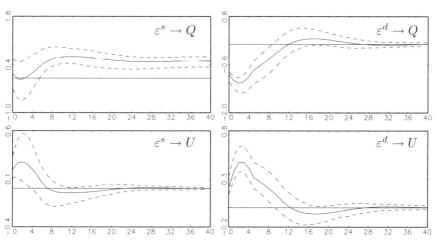

Figure 4.5. Responses of output and unemployment to supply and (negative) demand shock based on a subset VAR model with 95% Hall bootstrap confidence intervals using 2,000 bootstrap replications.

shocks increase output in the long-run. The interval estimate indicates, however, that output does not react significantly to supply shocks for about one year after the shock has occurred. Interestingly, a positive supply shock increases unemployment for about one year before it returns to its initial level. The response of output to a negative demand shock given in the upper-right panel of Figure 4.4 represents the identifying long-run restriction imposed. After first decreasing, output returns to its initial level after about two years. Similarly, unemployment goes up, reaching its peak one year after the shock has occurred, and then returns to its equilibrium level. Overall, the results seem compatible with the usual interpretation of demand and supply effects.

Just to illustrate the impact of imposing subset restrictions on the present model, we have also determined estimates of B and Ψ based on a subset model obtained using the sequential selection procedure in conjunction with the AIC described in Section 3.4.5. The resulting estimates are

$$
\hat{B} = \begin{bmatrix} 0.129 & -0.896 \\ {\scriptstyle (0.55)} & {\scriptstyle (-10.0)} \\ 0.199 & 0.214 \\ {\scriptstyle (3.23)} & {\scriptstyle (4.31)} \end{bmatrix} \quad \text{and} \quad \widehat{\Psi} = \begin{bmatrix} 0.507 & 0 \\ {\scriptstyle (6.63)} & \\ 0.990 & 2.842 \\ {\scriptstyle (1.09)} & {\scriptstyle (4.69)} \end{bmatrix}.
$$

Although these estimates are somewhat different from those in (4.30), the corresponding impulse responses shown in Figure 4.5 do not look very different from those in Figure 4.4. In the latter figure the confidence intervals are a bit wider in general, however. Thus, imposing subset restrictions may result in

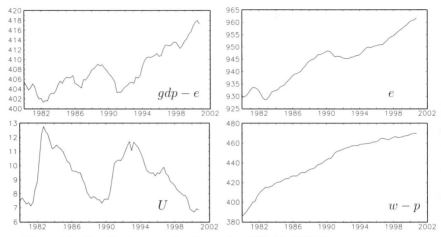

Figure 4.6.   Canadian labor market time series, $1980Q1–2000Q4$.

more precise estimates of the impulse responses provided, of course, that the subset restrictions are valid.

4.7.3 An SVECM for Canadian Labor Market Data

In this section, we use the theoretical framework considered in Section 4.3.2 to identify macroeconomic shocks to the labor market within a VECM for Canadian data. In particular, the empirical VAR model is specified for labor productivity, employment, unemployment rate, and real wages. In our analysis we use quarterly, seasonally adjusted data for Canada constructed from data obtained from the OECD database for the period from $1980Q1$ to $2000Q4$. Productivity ($gdp - e$) is constructed by subtracting the log of employment (e) from the log real GDP (gdp), U denotes the unemployment rate, and $w - p$ is the log of a real wage index. The time series vector used in our analysis is thus given by

$$y_t = [(gdp_t - e_t), e_t, U_t, (w_t - p_t)]',$$

and we show the time series plots in Figure 4.6.

   The time series for productivity, employment, and real wages clearly show upward trending behavior. Although this upward trend cannot be observed in the unemployment series, none of the four time series look stationary. There-fore, we conduct ADF unit root tests in a first step before proceeding with the reduced-form model specification. The unit root test results are summarized in Table 4.1. Given the shape of the time series in Figure 4.6, we include a constant and a deterministic time trend in the test regressions for $gdp - e$, e, and $w - p$. Accordingly, we only use a constant when testing for a unit root in

Table 4.1. *Augmented Dickey–Fuller unit root tests for Canadian data*

Variable	Deterministic terms	Lags	Test value	Critical values 1%	5%	10%
$gdp - e$	constant,trend	2	-1.99	-3.96	-3.41	-3.13
$\Delta(gdp - e)$	constant	1	-5.16^{***}	-3.43	-2.86	-2.57
e	constant,trend	2	-1.91	-3.96	-3.41	-3.13
Δe	constant	1	-4.51^{***}	-3.43	-2.86	-2.57
U	constant	1	-2.22	-3.43	-2.86	-2.57
ΔU	—	0	-4.75^{***}	-2.56	-1.94	-1.62
$(w - p)$	constant,trend	4	-2.05	-3.96	-3.41	-3.13
$\Delta(w - p)$	constant	3	-2.62^{*}	-3.43	-2.86	-2.57
$\Delta(w - p)$	constant	0	-5.60^{***}	-3.43	-2.86	-2.57

Note: Critical values from Davidson & MacKinnon (1993, Table 20.1).

unemployment. As the number of lagged differences included in the Dickey–Fuller test, we use values suggested by the AIC criterion when employing a maximum lag order of $p_{max} = 8$. Given the test results in Table 4.1, unit roots cannot be rejected in the levels of all four variables. To test for unit roots in the first differences of our variables, we include a constant in the test regression of $\Delta(gdp - e)$, Δe and $\Delta(w - p)$ and no deterministic terms in the equation for ΔU. Moreover, compared with the level test regressions, the number of lagged differences is decreased by one. These specifications are obtained by taking first differences of the levels model. The unit root hypothesis is rejected at the 1% level for the first differences of productivity, employment, and unemployment, whereas for $\Delta(w - p)$ it can only be rejected on the 10% level. The conclusions of the ADF test for productivity, employment, and the unemployment rate are quite clear and are not sensitive to the choice of the lag length. The test statistic for the real wages, however, is only slightly larger than the 10% critical value, but varying the number of lagged differences (e.g., to 0, 1, or 2) in the test regressions leads to the rejection of a unit root at the 1% level. As an example, we included the test result for the specification with no lagged differences as suggested by the SC. Overall, the results in Table 4.1 suggest that $gdp - e$, e, U, and $w - p$ can be treated as I(1) variables.

Given the integration and trending properties of the time series, cointegration between the four variables is possible. Therefore, the next step in our analysis is the specification of an initial, unrestricted VAR model that forms the basis for systems cointegration tests as discussed in Chapter 3. For this purpose we employ information criteria to select the lag length of a VAR specification, including a constant and a deterministic trend. If we choose a maximum lag order of $p_{max} = 8$, AIC and FPE suggest $p = 3$, HQ proposes $p = 2$, and SC chooses $p = 1$. For all the suggested lag lengths, we conduct a series of diagnostic tests.

Table 4.2. *Diagnostic tests for VAR(p) specifications for Canadian data*

	Q_{16}	Q_{16}^*	FLM_5	LJB_4	LJB_4^L	$MARCH_{LM}(5)$
$p = 3$	174.0 [0.96]	198.0 [0.68]	0.99 [0.51]	8.63[0.37]	9.67 [0.29]	512.0 [0.35]
$p = 2$	209.7 [0.74]	236.1 [0.28]	1.20 [0.16]	3.23[0.92]	2.28 [0.97]	528.1 [0.19]
$p = 1$	233.5 [0.61]	256.9 [0.22]	1.74 [0.00]	9.71[0.24]	9.92 [0.27]	570.1 [0.02]

Note: p-values in brackets.

In particular, we test against autocorrelation, nonnormality, and ARCH effects in the VAR residuals (see Chapter 3 for details on the diagnostic tests). We list the results for $p = 1, 2$, and 3 in Table 4.2. For $p = 3$ and $p = 2$, none of the diagnostic tests indicate signs of misspecification. The VAR(1) suggested by the SC criterion, however, shows some signs of residual autocorrelation and residual ARCH effects. Moreover, univariate Lomnicki–Jarque–Bera tests (results not shown) indicate some signs of nonnormality for the employment and unemployment equation if $p = 1$ is used. Therefore, the lag length $p = 1$ seems too restrictive as an initial choice. Using the tools of stability analysis for $p = 2$ and $p = 3$ reveals some signs of parameter non-constancy. In particular, some significant Chow tests, the visual inspection of recursive coefficients, and some large recursive residuals point to instability of some VAR model parameters. Although, in principle, it would be desirable to model these effects, we continue the analysis using a time-invariant VAR model.

To test for cointegration we use, the VAR(2) and VAR(3) specifications. As deterministic terms, we include a constant and a linear trend. With $p = 3$, the Johansen cointegration test (see Section 3.4.2) rejects the null hypothesis of no cointegration at the 1% level. In contrast, the null of $r = 1$ cannot be rejected at conventional significance levels. Note, however, that the value of the test statistic is not too far away from the critical values. Nevertheless, formally, the Johansen test indicates a cointegrating rank of $r = 1$, and for illustration we proceed by assuming a cointegrating rank of $r = 1$. Against the background

Table 4.3. *Johansen cointegration tests for Canadian system*

	Test statistics		Critical values		
H_0	$p = 3$	$p = 2$	90%	95%	99%
$r = 0$	84.92	86.12	58.96	62.61	70.22
$r = 1$	36.42	37.33	39.08	42.20	48.59
$r = 2$	18.72	15.65	22.95	25.47	30.65
$r = 3$	3.85	4.10	10.56	12.39	16.39

Notes: Deterministic terms: constant and linear trend (restricted to long-run part). Critical values from Johansen (1995a, Table 15.4).

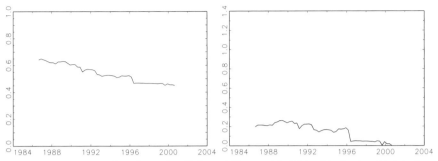

Figure 4.7. Recursive eigenvalue (left) and $\mathcal{T}$-test with 10% critical value (right) of VECM with two lagged differences and $r = 1$.

of the theoretical model discussed in Section 4.3.2, which suggests up to two cointegration relations, the reader is invited to perform a sensitivity analysis using $r = 2$ as an alternative specification.

We estimate a VECM based on the VAR(3) specification suggested by AIC and FPE under the rank restriction $r = 1$, that is, we include two lags of the differences of the variables. The diagnostic tests for this VECM do not indicate signs of misspecification. Moreover, we show the recursive eigenvalues and the corresponding $\mathcal{T}$-tests in Figure 4.7. They do not give rise to concern about instability of the model. Hence, we regard the VECM as an adequate description of the data. Table 4.4 shows the Johansen ML estimate of the cointegration relation β, where we have normalized the coefficient of real wages to one. This cointegration vector may be interpreted as a stationary wage-setting relation in which real wages are related to productivity and unemployment, as in equation (4.17). Rewriting the vector in the form of a wage-setting relation gives

$$(w - p)_t = -0.545(gdp - e)_t + 0.013e_t - 1.727U_t + 0.709t + ec_t.$$

$$(4.31)$$

Productivity enters the wage relation with the wrong sign, but this may be just a consequence of including a linear trend in (4.31). This trend may be interpreted

Table 4.4. *Cointegration vector and loading parameters for VECM with two lagged differences and cointerating rank $r = 1$*

	$gdp - e$	e	U	$w - p$	t
$\hat{\beta}'$	0.545	−0.013	1.727	1	−0.709
	(0.90)	(−0.02)	(1.19)		(−2.57)
$\hat{\alpha}'$	−0.012	−0.016	−0.009	−0.085	
	(−0.92)	(−2.16)	(−1.49)	(−5.71)	

Note: t-statistics in parentheses.

as a proxy for productivity that picks up the effects of productivity increases. The coefficient for employment is relatively small and insignificant. In line with theoretical arguments, real wages are negatively related to unemployment, although the coefficient is not significant at conventional levels. Hence, outsiders may influence the wage-setting in Canada. The estimates of the adjustment coefficients α support the interpretation of the cointegration vector as a wage setting schedule. According to the significant loading estimates from Table 4.4, excess real wages drive real wage growth down and also decrease employment growth.

Having specified the reduced form model, we now turn to the structural analysis. The reader is encouraged to specify a satisfactory subset model for the present data set. We continue our analysis based on a full VECM with two lagged differences and cointegrating rank 1. For this purpose, we next discuss the identification of shocks to the Canadian labor market.

Identification of labor market shocks. Recall from Section 4.3.2 that the vector of structural shocks is given by $\varepsilon_t = (\varepsilon_t^{gdp}, \varepsilon_t^d, \varepsilon_t^s, \varepsilon_t^w)'$. To derive the set of identifying assumptions, we make use of the theoretical labor market model discussed in Section 4.3.2. If we let $A = I_K$, we need $\frac{1}{2}K(K-1) = 6$ linearly independent restrictions to just-identify the parameters in B. We have $k^* = K - r = 3$ shocks with permanent effects in our VECM, whereas $r = 1$ shock merely has transitory effects. The cointegration analysis suggests that the wage-setting relation is stationary. Accordingly, wage shocks ε^w have no long-run impact on the variables included in y_t, which corresponds to four zero restrictions in the last column of the identified long-run impact matrix ΞB. Owing to the reduced rank of ΞB, this only imposes $k^* r = 3$ linearly independent restrictions. To identify the $k^* = 3$ permanent shocks, $k^*(k^* - 1)/2 = 3$ additional restrictions are necessary. If constant returns to scale are assumed, productivity is only driven by technology shocks ε^{gdp} in the long-run. These restrictions are imposed by setting the elements $(\Xi B)_{1j}$, $j = 2, 3, 4$ equal to zero. Because $(\Xi B)_{14} = 0$ is already imposed by the first set of restrictions, only two additional linearly independent restrictions are provided by assuming constant returns to scale. Consequently, one additional restriction is needed for just-identification of the SVECM. Because the theoretical model does not suggest an additional long-run restriction, we choose one contemporaneous restriction, that is, a zero restriction for B. As in Section 4.3.2, we assume that labor demand shocks do not affect real wages on impact, that is, $B_{42} = 0$. In Section 4.3.2 this restriction was needed to identify the two transitory shocks. In the present empirical analysis, only one shock is transitory and consequently no contemporaneous restrictions are needed to identify it. Here, the restriction is used to identify the permanent shocks. Taken together, these identifying assumptions are exactly identifying and correspond to the following structure on the contemporaneous impact matrix B and the identified long-run impact matrix ΞB:

$$
B = \begin{pmatrix} * & * & * & * \\ * & * & * & * \\ * & * & * & * \\ * & 0 & * & * \end{pmatrix} \quad \text{and} \quad \Xi B = \begin{pmatrix} * & 0 & 0 & 0 \\ * & * & * & 0 \\ * & * & * & 0 \\ * & * & * & 0 \end{pmatrix}. \tag{4.32}
$$

Using the estimation procedure described in Section 4.4.2, we obtain the following estimates for the contemporaneous and long-run impact matrix:

$$
\tilde{B} = \begin{pmatrix}
\underset{(5.94)}{0.58} & \underset{(0.61)}{0.07} & \underset{(-0.66)}{-0.15} & \underset{(0.92)}{0.07} \\
\underset{(-1.72)}{-0.12} & \underset{(4.15)}{0.26} & \underset{(-0.88)}{-0.16} & \underset{(2.12)}{0.09} \\
\underset{(0.44)}{0.03} & \underset{(-5.22)}{-0.27} & \underset{(0.09)}{0.01} & \underset{(1.53)}{0.05} \\
\underset{(0.73)}{0.11} & 0 & \underset{(0.74)}{0.48} & \underset{(5.99)}{0.49}
\end{pmatrix} \tag{4.33}
$$

and

$$
\widetilde{\Xi B} = \begin{pmatrix}
\underset{(5.21)}{0.79} & 0 & 0 & 0 \\
\underset{(0.86)}{0.20} & \underset{(3.10)}{0.58} & \underset{(-0.85)}{-0.49} & 0 \\
\underset{(-1.38)}{-0.16} & \underset{(-3.59)}{-0.34} & \underset{(0.91)}{0.14} & 0 \\
\underset{(-0.84)}{-0.15} & \underset{(3.59)}{0.60} & \underset{(-0.91)}{-0.25} & 0
\end{pmatrix}. \tag{4.34}
$$

In parentheses we provide bootstrapped t-values obtained using 2,000 bootstrap replications. The estimated long-run effects of labor market shocks on unemployment are given in the third row of (4.34). Note that, according to our estimate, only labor demand shocks significantly decrease the unemployment rate in Canada in the long-run. Conditional on the set of just-identifying restrictions, it is also possible to test further restrictions on the effects of structural shocks. For instance, checking whether labor supply shocks have no long-run effects on unemployment corresponds to testing the hypothesis $H_0 : (\Xi B)_{33} = 0$. In our example, the corresponding LR test statistic has a $\chi^2(1)$-distribution and is given by $LR = 6.07$ with a p-value $= 0.014$. Hence, the null hypothesis is rejected on the 5% significance level. Using the estimates $\tilde{B}$ in (4.33), we may also compute the responses to the structural shocks ε_t, which provide a more informative picture of the dynamic effects of macroeconomic shocks to the Canadian labor market.

Figure 4.8 shows the responses of unemployment to a technology, a labor demand, a labor supply, and a wage-setting shock together with 95% Hall bootstrap confidence intervals based on 2,000 bootstrap replications. The point estimates suggest that a technology shock (ε^{gdp}) drives unemployment down. However,

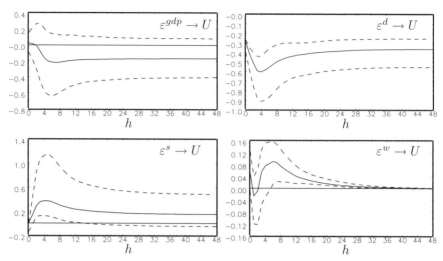

Figure 4.8. Responses of unemployment to economic shocks with 95% Hall bootstrap confidence intervals based on 2,000 bootstrap replications.

this effect is not significant either in the short-run or in the long-run. A labor demand shock (ε^d) leads to a significant drop in unemployment reaching the maximum effect after about one year. A positive labor supply (ε^s) shock has a significant positive impact on unemployment for about two years. In the long-run there is no significant effect of the labor supply shock, which is in line with the bootstrap t-values of the estimated long-run impact matrix. Finally, unemployment increases after a shock to wage-setting (ε^w). This effect becomes significant only about six quarters after the shock. In the long-run the response to wage shocks is zero as imposed by our identifying assumption. Note, however, that compared with responses to other shocks in the system, the reaction of wages is relatively small. Overall, the impulse responses are in line with what one would have expected from economic theory. Moreover, the adjustment to a new labor market equilibrium takes about three to five years.

To assess the relative importance of the identified labor market shocks, we list for different horizons h the forecast error variance decomposition of unemployment in Table 4.5. Clearly, according to our estimates, labor demand shocks are the dominant source for Canadian unemployment. Even in the long-run about 70% of the variation in the unemployment variable can be attributed to the labor demand shocks. Although technology shocks are not important at short horizons, they become more and more important as h increases. After $h = 48$ periods, technology shocks explain a fraction of 12% of the variance in unemployment. In contrast, wage-setting shocks are not an important source for the determination of unemployment in the long-run. Note that this result

Table 4.5. *Forecast error variance decomposition of Canadian unemployment*

h	ε^{gdp}	ε^d	ε^s	ε^w
1	0.01	0.96	0.00	0.03
4	0.01	0.78	0.21	0.01
8	0.05	0.69	0.24	0.01
12	0.08	0.68	0.23	0.01
24	0.10	0.69	0.21	0.01
48	0.12	0.70	0.18	0.00

for the wage-setting shocks is implied by the identifying restrictions of the shocks.

As in every structural VAR analysis, the results may depend to some extent on the specification of the reduced-form model and the choice of identifying assumptions. Here, the main purpose was to illustrate the use of structural VECMs. Therefore, we used only one specification. The reader is invited to check the robustness of the results with respect to different reduced-form model specifications and alternative identifying assumptions.

4.8 Conclusions

In this chapter tools for analyzing dynamic time series models have been discussed. If the dynamic interactions between the variables of a given system are of interest, impulse response analysis can give useful insights. A major problem, however, is the identification of those innovations that actually reflect the ongoings in the system. We have discussed how information from subject matter theory can be used to identify unique impulses that can be traced through the system and may convey useful information on the relations of the variables. Imposing such restrictions means considering structural VARs or VECMs. Forecast error variance decompositions are alternative tools for a dynamic analysis. They can also be based on structural VARs or VECMs.

Although imposing structural restrictions resolves the nonuniqueness problem of the innovations, it may be worth remembering that Sims (1980) advocated VAR models as alternatives to econometric simultaneous equations models because he regarded the identifying restrictions used for them as "incredible." Thus, structural VAR modeling may be criticized on the same grounds. Even if the restrictions imposed are firmly based on some economic theory, they may not truly reflect what goes on in the actual underlying system. Thus, all we can hope for in an impulse response analysis is getting information on the question of whether some theory or theoretical concept is compatible with the data or rather whether the data can be interpreted in such a way as to reflect a specific theory. It is much harder to reject a specific theory on the basis of a VAR or VECM analysis because, if the implications of the theory are not reflected in the impulse responses, for instance, this can have various reasons. Not choosing the identifying restrictions properly is only one source of possible error. Other sources may be a wrong choice of variables, inappropriate data, or poor modeling and estimation. Therefore, conclusions from analyzing a dynamic model are conditional on several assumptions and choices of the analyst. These reservations should be kept in mind and they should be a challenge for improving one's analysis.

5 Conditional Heteroskedasticity

Helmut Herwartz

5.1 Stylized Facts of Empirical Price Processes

Price processes observed at speculative markets such as foreign exchanges or stock, bond, or commodity markets have been attracting a huge interest in the academic world for decades. A particular time series model that has been proven to approximate empirical (log) price processes quite accurately is the random walk model [Fama (1965)]. According to this model the best forecast of a future price is today's price and, thus, the latter summarizes efficiently the (publicly) available information for prediction. Although the concept of weak market efficiency may also cover some degree of predictability of future price changes [Campbell, Lo & MacKinlay (1997)], there is a wide consensus that (log) speculative prices are nonstationary and, more precisely, show dynamic properties in line with processes that are integrated of order one.

Given nonstationarity of actual price processes, the statistical analysis mostly concentrates on speculative returns. Changes of log speculative prices (compounded returns) are typically not, or at most weakly, autocorrelated [Campbell et al. (1997)]. Measured at some higher frequency, daily price variations, for example, exhibit positive autocorrelation. Periods of higher and smaller price variations alternate; empirical volatilities tend to cluster. The latter property is easily found in the empirical autocorrelation function of squared returns. Thus, although price processes are hardly predictable, the variance of the forecast error is time dependent and can be estimated by means of observed past variations. As a consequence of volatility clustering, it turns out that the unconditional distribution of empirical returns is at odds with the hypothesis of normally distributed price changes that had been put forth by Bachelier (1900) and was powerfully rejected by Fama (1965). Yet, the phenomenon of time-varying volatility is well known and has generated a vast body of econometric literature following the seminal contributions by Engle (1982), Bollerslev (1986), and Taylor (1986) introducing the (generalized) autoregressive conditionally heteroskedastic ((G)ARCH) process and the stochastic volatility model, respectively. The former class of time series processes has been introduced briefly in Chapter 2 and will be discussed in more detail in the next section.

Different price processes measured on financial markets are often contemporaneously related. For instance, stock prices of firms acting on the same market may show similar patterns in the sequel of news important for the entire market. Similarly, one observes relatedness of the worlds leading exchanges [Engle, Ito & Lin (1990), King, Sentana & Wadhwani (1994)]. In addition to these stylized facts one may also expect relatedness of speculative prices in the light of economic theory. For instance, interest rate parities formalize a close link between interest rates and foreign exchange rates. Long- and short-term interest rates are also dependent. Therefore, one may regard the analysis of financial market data within a system of related variables as a fruitful means of improving the understanding of volatility dynamics. Moreover, a multivariate framework allows modeling of time-depending patterns of covariances. In the Capital Asset Pricing Model (CAPM) [Sharpe (1964), Lintner (1965)], the ratio of the covariance between returns on a particular asset and the so-called market portfolio and the variance of the latter measures the undiversifiable risk of the asset. This ratio has become popular as the asset's "beta," and, if one regards the market portfolio's variance as depending on time, it is quite natural to make allowance for time-varying covariances. Multivariate versions of the GARCH model are considered in Section 5.3.

This chapter will concentrate throughout on the class of GARCH models. As another important approach to modeling time varying second order moments the class of stochastic volatility models is not considered here. For detailed reviews of the latter field the reader may consult Taylor (1986) or Shephard (1996). More detailed surveys of GARCH models are offered, for instance, by Bera & Higgins (1993), Bollerslev, Engle & Nelson (1994), Bollerslev, Chou & Kroner (1992), Pagan (1996) and Palm (1996).

5.2 Univariate GARCH Models

Since its introduction, the univariate GARCH model has been applied in countless empirical studies. The GARCH(1,1) model has turned out to be particularly useful for describing a wide variety of financial market data [Bollerslev et al. (1994)]. Therefore, this chapter focuses mainly on this parsimonious specification of conditional heteroskedasticity. This section will first briefly discuss theoretical properties of GARCH models and thereby address most of the preceding issues, volatility clustering and forecasting, unconditional leptokurtosis, and stationarity. The second part addresses estimation of GARCH specifications and gives properties of the maximum likelihood estimator. Then, two directions to extend the basic GARCH model motivated from empirical experiences, conditional leptokurtosis, and asymmetry of volatility, will be considered. A few remarks on diagnostic testing are also made.

5.2.1 Basic Features of GARCH Processes

Representation. A representation of the GARCH(q, p) model [Bollerslev (1986)] has been given already in Chapter 2. Equivalently, a GARCH process u_t can be written as

$$u_t = \xi_t \sigma_t, \quad \xi_t \sim \text{iid } N(0, 1), \tag{5.1}$$

$$\sigma_t^2 = \gamma_0 + \gamma_1 u_{t-1}^2 + \gamma_2 u_{t-2}^2 + \ldots + \gamma_q u_{t-q}^2 + \beta_1 \sigma_{t-1}^2$$

$$+ \ldots + \beta_p \sigma_{t-p}^2 \tag{5.2}$$

$$= z_t' \theta. \tag{5.3}$$

Note that the case $p = 0$ in (5.2) covers the ARCH(q) process [Engle (1982)]. In the compact notation (5.3), $z_t = (1, u_{t-1}^2, \ldots, u_{t-q}^2, \sigma_{t-1}^2, \ldots, \sigma_{t-p}^2)'$ and the $p + q + 1$ vector $\theta = (\gamma_0, \gamma_1, \ldots, \gamma_q, \beta_1, \ldots, \beta_p)'$ collects the parameters of interest. The following are sufficient conditions for the conditional variances σ_t^2 to be positive:

$$\gamma_0 > 0, \quad \gamma_i, \beta_j \geq 0, \quad i = 1, \ldots, q, \, j = 1, \ldots, p.$$

Necessary as well as less restrictive sufficient conditions for $\sigma_t^2 > 0$ can be found in Nelson & Cao (1992). Using lag-polynomials, one may specify σ_t^2 in (5.2) as

$$(1 - \beta_1 L - \ldots - \beta_p L^p)\sigma_t^2 = \gamma_0 + (\gamma_1 L + \ldots + \gamma_q L^q)u_t^2$$

$$\Leftrightarrow (1 - \beta(L))\sigma_t^2 = \gamma_0 + \gamma(L)u_t^2. \tag{5.4}$$

If the roots of the polynomial $(1 - \beta(z))$ are larger than 1 in absolute value, the GARCH(q, p) process has an ARCH representation of infinite order:

$$\sigma_t^2 = (1 - \beta(L))^{-1}\gamma_0 + (1 - \beta(L))^{-1}\gamma(L)u_t^2 \tag{5.5}$$

$$= \gamma_0^* + \sum_{i=1}^{\infty} \gamma_i^* u_{t-i}^2. \tag{5.6}$$

Volatility forecasting. Defining a zero-mean process as

$$v_t = u_t^2 - \sigma_t^2, \tag{5.7}$$

the GARCH(q, p) model yields a representation of squared observations u_t^2, which is similar to the ARMA process introduced in Chapter 2, that is,

$$u_t^2 = \gamma_0 + \sum_{i=1}^{\max(p,q)} (\gamma_i + \beta_i)u_{t-i}^2 + v_t - \sum_{i=1}^{p} \beta_i v_{t-i}. \tag{5.8}$$

In (5.8) $\gamma_i = 0$, $i > q$, or $\beta_i = 0$, $i > p$ are set implicitly if $q < p$ or $p < q$, respectively. Although the error process v_t can be shown to be uncorrelated, it is still dependent with respect to higher order moments, thereby weakening the analogy of the GARCH(q, p) and ARMA(p, q) model to some extent.

Since the squared GARCH(q, p) process u_t^2 has an autoregressive representation, the corresponding conditional expectation σ_t^2 is also autoregressive. The latter argument is of particular importance for ex-ante forecasting of conditional variances. For this issue, the following representation of σ_t^2 is useful:

$$\sigma_t^2 = \gamma_0^* + \sum_{i=1}^{\infty} \gamma_i^* \sigma_{t-i}^2 + \sum_{i=1}^{\infty} \gamma_i^* v_{t-i}. \tag{5.9}$$

Since $E[v_{T+h}|\Omega_T] = 0$, $h > 0$, the usual recursive forecasting formulas apply to predict the mean of σ_{T+h}^2 conditional on Ω_T, the set of information available in time T.

Unconditional moments. Although the distribution of the basic model given in (5.1) is conditionally normal, it turns out that the unconditional distribution of a GARCH process is leptokurtic. In comparison with the normal distribution, the unconditional distribution of u_t shows higher mass around the zero mean and in its tails. The latter result becomes evident from investigating the unconditional moments of the GARCH process. To facilitate the presentation, consider the GARCH(1,1) model. Then, applying the law of iterated expectations, we find that the unconditional variance is

$$E[u_t^2] = E[E[u_t^2|\Omega_{t-1}]]$$
$$= \gamma_0 + \gamma_1 E[u_{t-1}^2] + \beta_1 E[E[u_{t-1}^2|\Omega_{t-2}]]$$
$$= (1 - \gamma_1 - \beta_1)^{-1}\gamma_0. \tag{5.10}$$

Accordingly, one obtains $E[u_t^2] = (1 - \gamma(1) - \beta(1))^{-1}\gamma_0$ for the general GARCH(q, p) case. Along similar lines it can be shown that all odd order moments of the GARCH(q, p) process are zero. Moreover, under conditional normality the fourth-order moment of the GARCH(1,1) process is

$$E[u_t^4] = \frac{3\gamma_0^2(1 + \gamma_1 + \beta_1)}{(1 - \gamma_1 - \beta_1)(1 - \beta_1^2 - 2\gamma_1\beta_1 - 3\gamma_1^2)}. \tag{5.11}$$

Note that $E[u_t^4]$ only exists if

$$(\beta_1^2 + 2\gamma_1\beta_1 + 3\gamma_1^2) < 1.$$

From the results in (5.10) and (5.11), the kurtosis of the GARCH(1,1) under conditional normality is derived as

$$\kappa = \frac{E[u_t^4]}{(E[u_t^2])^2} = \frac{3(1 - \gamma_1 - \beta_1)(1 + \gamma_1 + \beta_1)}{(1 - \beta_1^2 - 2\gamma_1\beta_1 - 3\gamma_1^2)}. \tag{5.12}$$

Under the parameter restrictions made for positivity of conditional variances and existence of the fourth-order moment, it holds that $\kappa > 3$, indicating leptokurtosis of u_t. Note that it is essentially the ARCH-parameter γ_1 that governs volatility clustering and leptokurtosis. In case $\gamma_1 = 0$, the GARCH(1,1) model is not identified ($\kappa = 3$), and for $\beta_1 = 0$ excess kurtosis increases with γ_1.

Stationarity. Nelson (1990) has provided a detailed discussion of stationarity and ergodicity of the GARCH(1,1) process. In particular, σ_t^2 and u_t are strictly stationary and ergodic if $E[\log(\beta_1 + \gamma_1 \xi_t^2)] < 0$. Furthermore $E[u_t] = 0$ if $E[(\beta_1 + \gamma_1 \xi_t^2)^{1/2}] < 1$. Imposing the stronger restriction $E[\beta_1 + \gamma_1 \xi_t^2] < 1$, we can show that $E[u_t^2] = \sigma^2 < \infty$ and u_t is weakly (covariance) stationary. Note that these moment conditions depend on the distribution of the innovations ξ_t. Since the condition under which the GARCH(1,1) is strictly stationary is weaker as the requirement for covariance or weak stationarity, it can happen that a particular GARCH process is strictly stationary but fails to be weakly stationary. A prominent example for this case is the so-called integrated GARCH(1,1) process [Engle & Bollerslev (1986)]:

$$u_t = \sigma_t \xi_t, \ \xi_t \sim \text{ iid } N(0, 1),$$

$$\sigma_t^2 = \gamma_0 + \gamma_1 u_{t-1}^2 + \beta_1 \sigma_{t-1}^2, \ \gamma_1 + \beta_1 = 1. \tag{5.13}$$

In the light of the apparent similarity between the IGARCH(1,1) model in (5.13) and the familiar random walk model with deterministic drift, it is worthwhile to stress that the dynamic properties of both specifications differ sharply. Whereas the random walk is nonstationary, the variance process in (5.13) remains strictly stationary and ergodic.

5.2.2 Estimation of GARCH Processes

To discuss maximum likelihood (ML) estimation of GARCH models, we assume for the moment that a finite stretch of observations u_t, $t = 1, \ldots, T$ is available. In a more general context, GARCH-type disturbances could also appear on the right-hand side of (auto)regression models. In this case the GARCH process will not be directly observable. For a wide variety of common empirical models, however, the variance parameters can be estimated given some (consistent) estimate of the conditional mean such that the methods outlined below apply if estimation residuals $\hat{u}_t$ replace the u_t, $t = 1, \ldots, T$. A few additional remarks on this issue are given in Section 5.2.4.

Specifying the joint density of $u_1, u_2, \ldots, u_T$ makes use of its representation as the product of some conditional and the corresponding marginal density. Let $\mathcal{U}_{T-1}$ denote the sequence of random variables $u_0, u_1, \ldots, u_{T-1}$. On the assumption that u_0 is constant or is drawn from a known distribution, the joint distribution of a finite stretch of observations from a GARCH process is

$$f(u_1, \ldots, u_T) = f(u_T | \mathcal{U}_{T-1}) \cdot f(\mathcal{U}_{T-1})$$
$$= f(u_T | \mathcal{U}_{T-1}) f(u_{T-1} | \mathcal{U}_{T-2}) \cdots f(u_1 | \mathcal{U}_0) f(\mathcal{U}_0).$$

(5.14)

The conditional distributions in (5.14) are available from the definition of the GARCH(q, p) process in (5.2). Then, the log-likelihood function is, conditional on some initialization σ_0, given as

$$l(\theta | u_1, \ldots, u_T) = \sum_{t=1}^{T} l_t$$

(5.15)

$$= \sum_{t=1}^{T} \left(-\frac{1}{2} \log(2\pi) - \frac{1}{2} \log \sigma_t^2 - \frac{1}{2} \frac{u_t^2}{\sigma_t^2} \right).$$

(5.16)

Compared with the common case with independent random variables, the ML estimator $\hat{\theta}$ cannot be obtained analytically but requires iterative optimization routines. A particular optimization routine that is often used to estimate the model in (5.2) is the BHHH algorithm named after Berndt, Hall, Hall & Hausman (1974). According to this algorithm the ith step estimate is obtained as

$$\hat{\theta}_i = \hat{\theta}_{i-1} + \phi \left(\sum_{t=1}^{T} \frac{\partial l_t}{\partial \theta} \frac{\partial l_t}{\partial \theta'} \Big|_{\theta = \hat{\theta}_{i-1}} \right)^{-1} \sum_{t=1}^{T} \frac{\partial l_t}{\partial \theta} \Big|_{\theta = \hat{\theta}_{i-1}},$$

(5.17)

where $\phi > 0$ is used to modify the step length.

Under regularity conditions [Davidson (2000)] the ML estimator $\hat{\theta}$ converges at rate $\sqrt{T}$ and is asymptotically normally distributed, that is,

$$\sqrt{T}(\hat{\theta} - \theta) \overset{d}{\to} N(0, S^{-1}),$$

(5.18)

where S is the expectation of the outer product of the scores of $l_t(\theta)$,

$$S = \sum_{t=1}^{T} \mathsf{E} \left[\frac{\partial l_t}{\partial \theta} \frac{\partial l_t}{\partial \theta'} \right].$$

The log-likelihood function in (5.16) is determined under the assumption of conditional normality stated in (5.1), which in turn was more ad hoc than based on statistical or economic reasoning. In the empirical literature on GARCH processes, it turned out that conditional normality of speculative returns is more an exception than the rule. Therefore, issues arising for estimation and inference under conditional nonnormality have also attracted a large interest in the theoretical literature on GARCH processes. Maximum likelihood estimation in presence of leptokurtic innovations ξ_t will be sketched in Section 5.2.3. If nonnormality of innovations ξ_t is ignored the log-likelihood function will be misspecified. Maximizing the misspecified Gaussian log-likelihood function is, however, justified by quasi-maximum likelihood theory. Asymptotic theory on properties of the QML estimator in univariate GARCH models is well developed. Consistency and asymptotic normality of the QML estimator have been shown for a wide variety of strictly stationary GARCH processes, including the IGARCH(1,1) process or even the mildly explosive specification with $\gamma_1 + \beta_1$ (slightly) exceeding unity [Bollerslev & Wooldridge (1992), Lumsdaine (1996), Lee & Hansen (1994)]. If the normality assumption is violated, the covariance matrix of the QML estimator is

$$\sqrt{T}(\hat{\theta} - \theta) \overset{d}{\to} N(0, D^{-1}SD^{-1}), \tag{5.19}$$

where D is the negative expectation of the matrix of second-order derivatives

$$D = -\mathsf{E}\left[\frac{\partial^2 l}{\partial\theta\partial\theta'}\right]. \tag{5.20}$$

Analytical expressions for the derivatives necessary to implement the BHHH algorithm and a practical guide through (Q)ML estimation and inference are given in Bollerslev (1986) and Fiorentini, Calzolari & Panattoni (1996).

5.2.3 Extensions

Asymmetry and leverage effects. As provided in (5.2), the GARCH model is characterized by a symmetric response of current volatility to positive and negative lagged errors u_{t-1}. Positive and negative innovations that are equal in absolute value imply the same impact on the conditional variance σ_t^2. Since u_t is uncorrelated with its history, it could be interpreted conveniently as a measure of news entering a financial market in time t. From the empirical literature on returns of risky assets, it is known that future volatility of stock returns is much more affected by negative compared with positive news [Black (1976)]. In the light of economic theory, such an effect might be explained via a firm's debt-to-equity ratio. Negative news will increase this measure and, thus, the corresponding asset will be more risky. The described asymmetry in response to market news has become popular as the so-called leverage effect, which is obviously not captured by the basic GARCH process discussed so far.

To allow for different impacts of lagged positive and negative innovations, threshold GARCH (TGARCH) models have been introduced by Glosten, Jagannathan & Runkle (1993) for the variance and by Zakoian (1994) for the standard deviation. According to the former, the TGARCH(1,1) model takes the following form:

$$\sigma_t^2 = \gamma_0 + \gamma_1 u_{t-1}^2 + \gamma_1^- u_{t-1}^2 I(u_{t-1} < 0) + \beta_1 \sigma_{t-1}^2. \tag{5.21}$$

In (5.21), $I(\cdot)$ denotes an indicator function. The leverage effect is covered by the TGARCH model if $\gamma_1^- > 0$.

In addition to threshold specifications, many other parametric as well as non-parametric volatility models have been designed to capture asymmetries in the conditional variance. Engle & Ng (1993) and Hentschel (1995) have provided comparative reviews on this issue. Nelson (1991) has proposed the exponential GARCH model (EGARCH). Under conditional normality the EGARCH(1,1) model reads as follows:

$$\log(\sigma_t^2) = \tilde{\gamma}_0 + \tilde{\gamma}_1 (|\xi_{t-1}| - \mathsf{E}[|\xi_{t-1}|]) + \tilde{\gamma}_1^- \xi_{t-1} + \tilde{\beta}_1 \log(\sigma_{t-1}^2).$$

(5.22)

Note that under normality $\mathsf{E}[|\xi_t|] = \sqrt{2/\pi}$. If $\tilde{\gamma}_1 > 0$, the process in (5.22) is convenient to generate volatility clustering. In addition, $\tilde{\gamma}_1^- < 0$ will deliver a leverage effect. Owing to its specification in terms of $\log(\sigma_t^2)$ the EGARCH model has the advantage that, irrespective of the parameter values, conditional variances will be positive throughout. As a particular drawback of the EGARCH model, Engle & Ng (1993) have pointed out that, owing to the exponential structure, the model may tend to overestimate the impact of outliers on volatility.

Conditional leptokurtosis. As it is often argued in empirical contributions, the normal distribution specified in (5.1) is rarely supported by real data. The normality assumption is often rejected for the estimated GARCH innovations ($\hat{\xi}_t$). As outlined in Section 5.2.2, QML estimation is consistent and provides asymptotically valid distributional results for the rescaled and centered vector of parameter estimates $\sqrt{T}(\hat{\theta} - \theta)$ under suitable conditions. If an alternative parametric distribution can reasonably be assumed, exact ML methods may outperform QML estimation in terms of efficiency. ML estimation under misspecification of the (non-Gaussian) conditional distribution, however, may yield inconsistent parameter estimates [Newey & Steigerwald (1997)].

Moreover, if the normality assumption is violated it is no longer possible to provide valid forecasting intervals for u_{T+h} given Ω_T by means of quantiles of the Gaussian distribution. To improve interval forecasting it pays to consider a leptokurtic distribution of ξ_t. In addition to statistical aspects like interval forecasting or efficiency excess, it is worthwhile to mention that conditional leptokurtosis is an important feature that has to be taken into account for practical economic issues like derivative pricing [Duan (1995, 1999), Hafner & Herwartz (2001a)] or Value-at-Risk evaluation [Jorion (2001)].

Given the often apparent violation of conditional normality on the one hand and uncertainty concerning the true underlying distribution of innovations ξ_t on the other hand, Engle & Gonzalez-Rivera (1991) have proposed a semi-parametric GARCH model in which the conditional distribution is left unspecified. Parametric models covering conditional leptokurtosis require an appropriate distribution to be assumed explicitly. For instance, Bollerslev (1987) and Nelson (1991) have advocated evaluating the sample log-likelihood under the assumptions that innovations ξ_t follow a standardized t-distribution and a standardized general error distribution (GED), respectively. For given variance dynamics, leptokurtic innovations will, in comparison with normally distributed innovations, strengthen the leptokurtosis of the unconditional distribution of a GARCH process. Moreover, outlying observations are more likely to occur. The implementation of GARCH models under the conditional t-distribution and the GED is now briefly considered in turn.

GARCH WITH t-DISTRIBUTED INNOVATIONS. A random variable u_t is t-distributed with v degrees of freedom, mean zero, and variance σ_t^2 if it has the following density:

$$f(u_t|\theta, v) = \frac{v^{v/2}\Gamma\left(\frac{v+1}{2}\right)}{\sqrt{\pi}\,\Gamma(\frac{v}{2})\sqrt{\frac{(v-2)\sigma_t^2}{v}}}\left(v + \frac{v \cdot u_t^2}{(v-2)\sigma_t^2}\right)^{-\left(\frac{v+1}{2}\right)}. \qquad (5.23)$$

In (5.23), $\Gamma(.)$ denotes the Gamma function, $\Gamma(h) = \int_0^\infty x^{h-1}\exp(-x)dx$, $h > 0$. Recall that for $v \to \infty$, the density in (5.23) coincides with the Gaussian density. The contribution of a single observation to the log-likelihood function is

$$l_t(\theta, v) = \log(f(u_t|\Omega_{t-1})) \qquad (5.24)$$

$$= \log\left(v^{v/2}\Gamma\left(\frac{v+1}{2}\right)\right) - \log\left(\sqrt{\pi}\,\Gamma\left(\frac{v}{2}\right)\sqrt{\frac{(v-2)\sigma_t^2}{v}}\right)$$

$$-\frac{v+1}{2}\log\left(v + \frac{v \cdot u_t^2}{(v-2)\sigma_t^2}\right). \qquad (5.25)$$

Noting that $\sigma_t^2 = z_t'\theta$, we find that analytical scores of the log-likelihood function are

$$\frac{\partial l_t}{\partial \theta} = -\frac{1}{2}\frac{1}{\sigma_t^2} \cdot z_t + \frac{v+1}{2}\left(v + \frac{v \cdot u_t^2}{(v-2)\sigma_t^2}\right)^{-1}$$

$$\times \frac{v \cdot u_t^2}{(v-2)\sigma_t^4} \cdot z_t, \qquad (5.26)$$

$$\frac{\partial l_t}{\partial v} = \frac{1}{2}\Bigg\{\log(v) + 1 + \Gamma^{-1}\left(\frac{v+1}{2}\right)\Gamma'\left(\frac{v+1}{2}\right)$$

$$-\Gamma^{-1}\left(\frac{v}{2}\right)\Gamma'\left(\frac{v}{2}\right) - \frac{1}{v-2} + \frac{1}{v} - \log\left(v + \frac{v \cdot u_t^2}{(v-2)\sigma_t^2}\right)$$

$$-(v+1)\left(v + \frac{v \cdot u_t^2}{(v-2)\sigma_t^2}\right)^{-1}\left(1 - \frac{2 \cdot u_t^2}{(v-2)^2 \sigma_t^2}\right)\Bigg\}. \qquad (5.27)$$

GENERALIZED ERROR DISTRIBUTION (*GED*). The discussion of the GARCH process under generally distributed error terms is almost analogous to the latter case. According to this distribution, with shape parameter v, a zero-mean random variable u_t with variance σ_t^2 has the following density:

$$f(u_t|\theta, v) = v \exp\left(-\frac{1}{2}\left|\frac{u_t}{\lambda \cdot \sigma_t}\right|^v\right)\left[2^{\frac{v+1}{v}}\Gamma\left(\frac{1}{v}\right)\lambda \cdot \sigma_t\right]^{-1}, \quad (5.28)$$

where λ is defined as

$$\lambda = \left[\frac{\Gamma(\frac{1}{v})}{2^{\frac{2}{v}}\Gamma(\frac{3}{v})}\right]^{0.5}. \quad (5.29)$$

In case $v = 2$, the density in (5.28) is equal to the $N(0, \sigma_t^2)$ density and the distribution becomes leptokurtic if $v < 2$. For $v = 1$ ($v \to \infty$) the GED coincides with the (approximates the) double exponential (rectangular) distribution [Harvey (1990)]. Under GARCH, the contribution of a single observation to the sample log-likelihood and its analytical scores are given as

$$l_t = \log(v) - \frac{1}{2}\left|\frac{u_t}{\lambda \cdot \sigma_t}\right|^v - \log\left\{2^{\frac{v+1}{v}}\Gamma\left(\frac{1}{v}\right)\lambda\right\} - \frac{1}{2}\log(\sigma_t^2),$$

$$(5.30)$$

$$\frac{\partial l_t}{\partial \theta} = 0.25v\left|\frac{u_t}{\lambda \cdot \sigma_t}\right|^v\frac{1}{\sigma_t^2} \cdot z_t - \frac{1}{2\sigma_t^2} \cdot z_t, \quad (5.31)$$

$$\frac{\partial l_t}{\partial v} = \frac{1}{v} - \frac{1}{2}\left|\frac{u_t}{\lambda \cdot \sigma_t}\right|^v\left\{\log\left(\left|\frac{u_t}{\lambda \cdot \sigma_t}\right|\right) - v\frac{\lambda'}{\lambda}\right\}$$

$$+ \frac{1}{v^2}\left\{\log(2) + \Gamma^{-1}\left(\frac{1}{v}\right)\Gamma'\left(\frac{1}{v}\right)\right\} - \frac{\lambda'}{\lambda}, \quad (5.32)$$

where

$$\lambda' = \lambda^{-1}2^{\frac{v-2}{2}}v^{-2}\Gamma^{-1}\left(\frac{3}{v}\right)\left\{2\log(2)\Gamma\left(\frac{1}{v}\right)\right.$$

$$\left. - \Gamma'\left(\frac{1}{v}\right) + 3\Gamma^{-1}\left(\frac{3}{v}\right)\Gamma'\left(\frac{3}{v}\right)\Gamma\left(\frac{1}{v}\right)\right\}.$$

5.2.4 Blockdiagonality of the Information Matrix

So far ML estimation of variance dynamics has been discussed for an observed GARCH process or estimates obtained from consistent first-step estimates for the conditional mean equation. Separating the estimation of the conditional mean on the one hand and volatility dynamics on the other is justified whenever the information matrix of the underlying model is blockdiagonal with respect to the parameters governing first- and second-order dynamics, respectively [Engle (1982)]. Two prominent cases in which blockdiagonality of the information matrix does not hold are the (auto)regression with EGARCH error terms and the so-called (G)ARCH-in-mean model [Engle, Lilien & Robins (1987)] in which the conditional mean of some variable depends on the current state of volatility. For the class of (auto)regression models with (T)GARCH disturbances, block-diagonality of the information matrix holds if the distribution of the underlying innovations ξ_t is not skewed, that is, $E[\xi_t^3] = 0$ [Linton (1993), Lundbergh & Teräsvirta (2002)].

5.2.5 Specification Testing

Apart from a visual inspection of the autocorrelation function of a squared (estimated) GARCH process, u_t^2, $t = 1, \ldots, T$, $(\hat{u}_t^2)$ formal tests of homoskedasticity against the presence of ARCH-type variances are in widespread use. To test the null hypothesis of a homoskedastic error variance, McLeod & Li (1983) derived a portmanteau-type test building on the autocorrelation function of the squared GARCH process. Based on the Lagrange multiplier (LM) principle, an asymptotically equivalent test, the familiar ARCH–LM test, is given in Engle (1982). The latter principle often allows the test statistic to be derived from the degree of explanation offered by simple auxiliary regressions. Engle & Ng (1993) proposed LM tests of the symmetric GARCH model against volatility models allowing asymmetry, so-called size effects, or both. Once a particular GARCH model has been estimated, issues of diagnostic testing are naturally focused on the implied GARCH innovations $\hat{\xi}_t = u_t/\hat{\sigma}_t$. For instance, the analyst should be led to respecify the model if $\hat{\xi}_t$, $t = 1, \ldots, T$, show remaining conditional heteroskedasticity. Although applying standard diagnostic tests for $\hat{\xi}_t$ such as the ARCH–LM test may give some indication of remaining misspecification, the asymptotic distributions of such tests are unknown in general. Li & Mak (1994) and Lundbergh & Teräsvirta (2002) have formulated portmanteau and LM tests for testing the null hypothesis of "no remaining ARCH," respectively. Moreover, Lundbergh & Teräsvirta (2002) have exploited the LM principle to cover the issue of testing the symmetric, structurally invariant GARCH process against asymmetric and nonlinear smooth-transition GARCH processes [Hagerud (1997)] on the one hand and against smoothly changing parameters on the other. Specifying a smooth transition GARCH process under the alternative hypothesis, the TGARCH process and a model with a single shift point are nested when diagnosing the symmetric GARCH. More specific tests of the structural stability of GARCH-type volatility dynamics, as introduced by Chu (1995) or Lin & Yang (1999), only allow a single structural shift in the variance parameters.

5.2.6 An Empirical Illustration with Exchange Rates

To illustrate practical issues involved when analyzing empirical price processes, this section investigates the dynamic properties of a bivariate exchange rate series composed of the prices of the U.S. dollar (USD) in terms of the British pound sterling (GBP) and the deutsche mark (DEM) using JMuTi. The investigated sample consists of 4,367 daily observations covering the period

Figure 5.1. Log exchange rate series (-- GBP/USD, — DEM/USD); 2 January 1986 to 27 September 2002; $T = 4,367$.

2 January 1986 to 27 September 2002. Note that, with the advent of the euro in 1999, the DEM/USD rate is actually an implicit price of the USD. As shown in Figure 5.1, both log price series are nonstationary and, more precisely, have an evolution similar to a random walk process without a drift term. Since the difference between the two log exchange rates yields the implicit log price of the GBP in terms of the DEM, that is,

$$\log\left(\frac{DEM}{GBP}\right) = \log\left(\frac{DEM}{USD}\right) - \log\left(\frac{GBP}{USD}\right),$$

the two investigated series are presumably not cointegrated.

Log exchange rate changes are depicted in Figure 5.2. Both series of log price variations show marked patterns of volatility clustering. It appears that the process of log GBP/USD changes is more concentrated around zero and shows more outlying observations than is the case for the DEM/USD rate.

Autocorrelation and partial autocorrelation patterns, as shown in Figure 5.3 for changes of the log GBP/USD rate, do not indicate any predictability of the conditional mean. Similar results are obtained for the DEM/USD rate and are thus not shown to economize on space. In sharp contrast, the corresponding diagnostics for squared-log exchange rate changes confirm the diagnosed

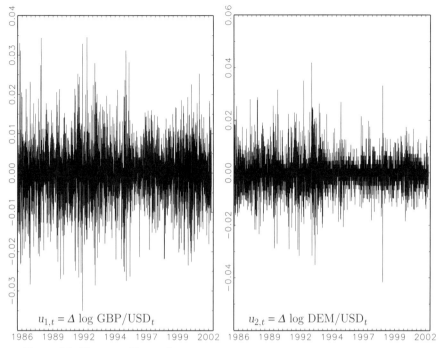

Figure 5.2. Changes of log exchange rates.

volatility clustering. From Figure 5.4 it is evident that second-order moments of exchange rate changes have significant positive autocorrelation. Comparing the magnitude of the estimated autocorrelations of second-order moments indicates that volatility clustering is more pronounced in the GBP/USD series as against the DEM/USD rate. A similar conclusion is offered from kernel density estimates for the unconditional distribution of standardized log price changes, which are depicted in Figures 5.5 and 5.6. For convenience of presentation, the graphs provide a corresponding density estimate for a sample drawn from the $N(0, 1)$ distribution. Excess kurtosis is stronger in the case of the GBP/USD rate.

Given the descriptive results obtained so far it is appropriate to estimate a parametric model covering time-varying variances such as GARCH(1,1). Estimation results for this specification are shown in Table 5.1. ML estimation has been implemented on the assumption of three alternative conditional distributions, the basic normal model, the t-distribution, and the GED. For both processes and all distributional assumptions, the obtained parameters are in line with other empirical applications of the GARCH process. The $\hat{\gamma}_1$ estimate is small but significant, and $\hat{\beta}_1$ is about 0.95 and also significant. Interestingly, estimates of the parameters governing volatility clustering ($\hat{\gamma}_1$) or excess conditional kurtosis ($\hat{v}$) indicate that both properties are more pronounced for the

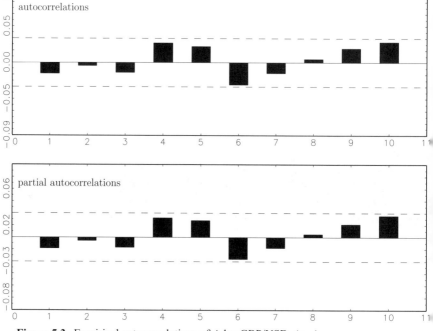

Figure 5.3. Empirical autocorrelations of $\Delta \log \text{GBP/USD}_t$ ($u_{1,t}$).

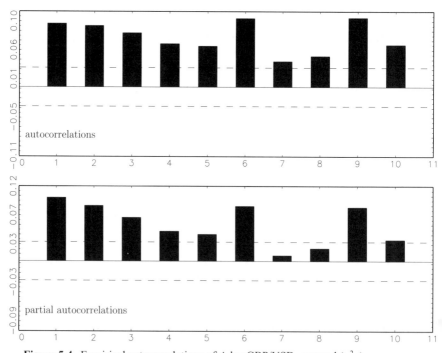

Figure 5.4. Empirical autocorrelations of $\Delta \log \text{GBP/USD}_t$ squared ($u_{1,t}^2$).

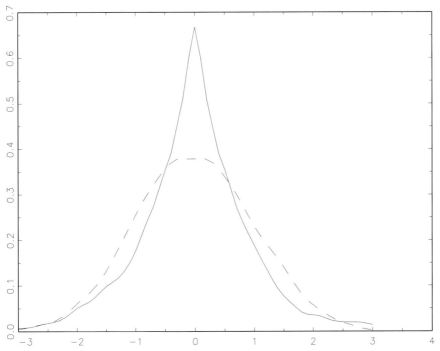

Figure 5.5. Density estimation for $\Delta \log \text{GBP/USD}_t$ $(u_{1,t})$ (solid line, Gaussian kernel with $h = 0.127$) and standard normal observations (broken line, Gaussian kernel with $h = 0.185$).

GBP/USD rate. In comparison with the DEM/USD rate, $\hat{\gamma}_1$ is slightly higher throughout when modeling the former rate. Moreover, for the GBP/USD rate, estimated degrees of freedom for the t-distribution ($\hat{v} = 4.18$) or the estimated shape parameter of the GED ($\hat{v} = 0.78$) are larger and smaller, respectively, in comparison with the DEM/USD rate. Thus, the latter rate shows less conditional leptokurtosis than log price changes of the GBP/USD rate. Comparing the obtained maximum values of the alternative log-likelihood functions discloses that the GED provides the closest fit to the empirical processes. In comparison with the conditional t-distribution involving the same number of unknown parameters, this specification improves the maximum of the log-likelihood by 91.4 and 39.2 points, respectively. The Gaussian approximation is clearly outperformed by both alternatives. Given that the underlying innovations are not normally distributed, the ML t-ratios given for the basic GARCH specification should be treated with care.

Diagnostic statistics computed for $\hat{\xi}_t$, the implied GARCH(1,1) residuals, are also given in Table 5.1. It turns out that the GARCH(1,1) model is convenient for capturing the time-varying variances of both processes entirely. LM statistics testing the hypothesis of homoskedasticity against remaining

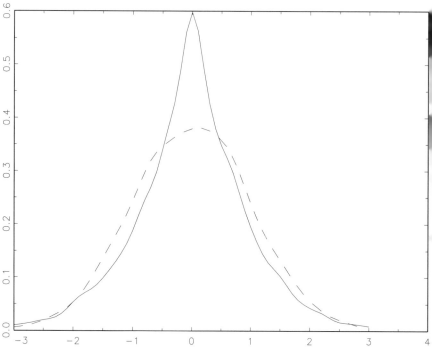

Figure 5.6. Density estimation for $\Delta \log \text{DEM/USD}_t$ $(u_{2,t})$ (solid line, Gaussian kernel with $h = 0.135$) and standard normal observations (broken line, Gaussian kernel with $h = 0.178$).

conditional heteroskedasticity are insignificant throughout. Moreover, employing more general models, that is, extending the basic GARCH(1,1) to higher order processes or towards a TGARCH(1,1), does not indicate misspecification of the volatility model discussed. Detailed estimation results for more general univariate volatility specifications are not given here because of space considerations. Not surprisingly, the Lomnicki–Jarque–Bera test on normality delivers strong evidence against the Gaussian model. Again, excess kurtosis is larger when considering the GBP/USD rate ($\kappa \approx 5.3$) in comparison with the DEM/USD ($\kappa \approx 4.5$).

5.3 Multivariate GARCH Models

Having introduced the univariate GARCH approach to time-varying volatility, this section will discuss aspects of multivariate conditionally heteroskedastic processes. Being conceptually straightforward, however, the generalization of univariate towards multivariate GARCH models involves very large parameter spaces and thus will prove to be analytically and computationally quite demanding. Specification issues for multivariate GARCH processes are discussed

Table 5.1. *Univariate GARCH(1,1) estimates and diagnostics for* $\hat{\xi}_t$

	GBP/USD			DEM/USD		
Statistics	$N(0, \sigma_t^2)$	$t(v, 0, \sigma_t^2)$	$\text{GED}(v, 0, \sigma_t^2)$	$N(0, \sigma_t^2)$	$t(v, 0, \sigma_t^2)$	$\text{GED}(v, 0, \sigma_t^2)$
$\hat{\gamma}_0$	3.03e-07 (5.93)	2.28e-07 (2.70)	2.42e-07 (1.85)	6.86e-07 (5.28)	5.61e-07 (2.93)	5.77e-07 (2.75)
$\hat{\gamma}_1$	3.61e-02 (15.1)	3.61e-02 (6.70)	4.47e-02 (5.24)	3.49e-02 (9.46)	3.54e-02 (6.03)	3.48e-02 (5.52)
$\hat{\beta}_1$	9.57e-01 (322.8)	9.61e-01 (174.5)	9.59e-01 (123.9)	9.51e-01 (168.7)	9.55e-01 (122.8)	9.53e-01 (107.6)
$\hat{v}$	4.18e+00 (12.5)	7.83e-01 (37.5)		5.05e+00 (10.4)	1.14e+00 (33.6)	
log lik.	1.615e+04	1.633e+04	1.642e+04	1.567e+04	1.579e+04	1.583e+04
No remaining ARCH (LM, 1 lag)						
F test	0.326	0.276	0.372	0.123	0.093	0.088
p-value	0.568	0.600	0.567	0.726	0.911	0.766
Lomnicki–Jarque–Bera test						
LJB	959.9	981.3	975.4	405.5	411.6	410.1
p-value	.000	.000	.000	.000	.000	.000
skewness	0.153	0.153	0.150	−0.061	−0.066	−0.065
kurtosis	5.277	5.303	5.296	4.488	4.499	4.496

first. QML estimation of these processes is also addressed. Some extensions of the symmetric, conditionally normally distributed multivariate GARCH model close this section.

5.3.1 Alternative Model Specifications

The half-vec Model. In principle, the generalization of the univariate GARCH process towards a dynamic model describing second-order moments of a serially uncorrelated but conditionally heteroskedastic K-dimensional vector of error terms, $u_t = (u_{1,t}, u_{2,t}, \ldots, u_{K,t})'$, is straightforward. Doing so requires relating the covariance matrix Σ_t and the information generated by the history of the process (Ω_{t-1}) parametrically. The vector u_t follows a multivariate GARCH(q, p) process (MGARCH) if

$$u_t | \Omega_{t-1} \sim N(0, \Sigma_t),$$

$$\text{vech}(\Sigma_t) = \tilde{\gamma}_0 + \sum_{j=1}^{q} \tilde{\Gamma}_j \text{vech}(u_{t-j} u'_{t-j}) + \sum_{j=1}^{p} \tilde{B}_j \text{vech}(\Sigma_{t-j}),$$

$$(5.33)$$

where vech(.) is the half-vectorization operator that stacks the elements of a quadratic ($K \times K$) matrix from the main diagonal downwards in a $\frac{1}{2}K(K+1)$-dimensional vector; $\tilde{\Gamma}_j$, $j = 1, \ldots, q$, and $\tilde{B}_j$, $j = 1, \ldots, p$, are fixed ($\frac{1}{2}K(K+1) \times \frac{1}{2}K(K+1)$) coefficient matrices; and $\tilde{\gamma}_0$ is a $\frac{1}{2}K(K+1)$ dimensional column vector collecting time invariant (co) variance components. The special case where $p = 0$ formalizes the multivariate ARCH(q) process. Introduced by Bollerslev, Engle & Wooldridge (1988), the representation in (5.33) has become popular as the so-called half-vec (vech) MGARCH model.

Within such a multivariate model, dynamics of second-order moments easily become intractable owing to the large parameter space involved. Recall that the estimation of GARCH processes requires iterative numerical procedures. Apart from computational infeasibility one may imagine that it is cumbersome in applied work to restrict the admissible parameter space of the half-vec model such that the implied matrices $\Sigma_t, t = 1, \ldots, T$ are positive definite. For these reasons, there are only rare (if any) empirical applications of the half-vec model. Since most of the more restrictive specifications have an implied half-vec representation, however, the model in (5.33) has become a useful tool to investigate theoretical properties of multivariate GARCH processes such as covariance stationarity or to implement recursive forecasting schemes.

Volatility forecasting and covariance stationarity. Consider for convenience the MGARCH(1,1) case and define a vector of serially uncorrelated, mean-zero error terms

$$v_t = \text{vech}(u_t u'_t) - \text{vech}(\Sigma_t). \tag{5.34}$$

Then, substituting $\text{vech}(u_t u_t')$ in (5.33), we obtain a vector autoregressive scheme for $\text{vech}(\Sigma_t)$ that can be used for covariance forecasting:

$$\text{vech}(\Sigma_t) = \tilde{\gamma}_0 + (\tilde{\Gamma}_1 + \tilde{B}_1)\text{vech}(\Sigma_{t-1}) + \tilde{\Gamma}_1 v_{t-1}. \tag{5.35}$$

The unconditional mean of $\text{vech}(u_t u_t')$, $\mathsf{E}[\text{vech}(u_t u_t')] = \mathsf{E}[\text{vech}(\Sigma_t)]$ is available from (5.35) by successive substitutions as

$$\mathsf{E}[\text{vech}(\Sigma_t)] = (I + (\tilde{\Gamma}_1 + \tilde{B}_1) + (\tilde{\Gamma}_1 + \tilde{B}_1)^2 + (\tilde{\Gamma}_1 + \tilde{B}_1)^3 + \cdots)\tilde{\gamma}_0. \tag{5.36}$$

The relation in (5.36) provides a finite solution for $\mathsf{E}[\text{vech}(\Sigma_t)]$ if the series of matrix powers $(\tilde{\Gamma}_1 + \tilde{B}_1)^h$ converges to a zero matrix with increasing horizon h. This condition holds if the eigenvalues of $(\tilde{\Gamma}_1 + \tilde{B}_1)$ have modulus less than unity. In this case the MGARCH process is covariance stationary.

Constant correlation and diagonal MGARCH. Various strategies have been followed to reduce the complexity of the dynamic structure in (5.33) and to improve the scope of multivariate GARCH modeling in practice. Let $\sigma_{ij,t}$ denote a typical element of Σ_t. To economize on the number of parameters, one may regard the systems' variances to be generated by univariate GARCH processes of order $p = q = 1$ for instance, as follows:

$$\sigma_{ii,t} = \gamma_{ii,0} + \gamma_{ii,1}u_{i,t-1}^2 + \beta_{ii,1}\sigma_{ii,t-1}, \ i = 1, \ldots, K. \tag{5.37}$$

To specify covariance dynamics, Bollerslev (1990) introduced the constant correlation model, where

$$\sigma_{ij,t} = \rho_{ij}\sqrt{\sigma_{ii,t}\sigma_{jj,t}}, \ i, j = 1, \ldots, K. \tag{5.38}$$

This MGARCH version implies strong restrictions compared with the general model in (5.33). For instance, in the bivariate MGARCH(1,1) case the model in (5.38) and (5.37) contains only seven parameters as against twenty one parameters encountered in (5.33). A particular advantage of constant correlation models is that, given suitable initial conditions, the assumptions $|\gamma_{ii} + \beta_{ii}| < 1$, $|\rho_{ij}| < 1, i, j = 1, \ldots, K$ are sufficient to guarantee positive definiteness of the time path of implied covariances Σ_t. The price paid for parsimony and feasibility is, however, a very specific dynamic structure that might not be met by empirical processes [Tsui & Yu (1999)]. Applying this model in practice will therefore require some pretest for constant correlation [Tse (2000), Engle (2002)].

To estimate a dynamic generalization of the CAPM, Bollerslev et al. (1988) made use of the restriction that all off-diagonal elements in $\tilde{\Gamma}_j$ and $\tilde{B}_j$ are zero, thereby introducing the diagonal model. In this framework, variance processes, as in (5.37) are combined with ARMA-type dynamics governing the covariances, that is,

$$\sigma_{ij,t} = \gamma_{ij,0} + \gamma_{ij,1}u_{i,t-1}u_{j,t-1} + \beta_{ij,1}\sigma_{ij,t-1}, \ i, j = 1, \ldots, K. \tag{5.39}$$

For the bivariate case, the diagonal model has nine parameters and thus is less parsimonious than the constant correlation model. A specific difficulty for practical work is to control the parameters in off-diagonal equations such that covariance matrices $\Sigma_t, t = 1, 2, \ldots, T$ are positive definite. Ding & Engle (1994) demonstrated that, in spite of its parsimony, the diagonal model is not computationally feasible for systems exceeding dimension $K = 5$. For such systems the interaction of parameters is too complex for existing optimization algorithms to converge.

The BEKK form. A particular drawback of the constant correlation and diagonal models is the possibility that important cross-sectional dynamics, as allowed by the half-vec model, will be ruled out by construction. Assume, for instance, that a bivariate system is composed of returns for a particular asset and a market portfolio. In this case, one may immediately take current volatility of the asset to depend partially on information processed in the aggregated stock market. Tests on causality in variance [Cheung & Ng (1996), Hafner & Herwartz (2004)] may be employed to indicate if an empirical vector return process exhibits cross-sectional relationships. The so-called BEKK model [Baba, Engle, Kraft & Kroner (1990)] formalizes a multivariate volatility specification that incorporates cross-equation dynamics. Engle & Kroner (1995) have discussed this model in detail. The BEKK form of the GARCH(q, p) process is

$$\Sigma_t = \Gamma_0'\Gamma_0 + \sum_{n=1}^{N}\sum_{i=1}^{q} \Gamma_{ni}' u_{t-i} u_{t-i}' \Gamma_{ni} + \sum_{n=1}^{N}\sum_{i=1}^{p} B_{ni}' \Sigma_{t-i} B_{ni}. \quad (5.40)$$

In (5.40), Γ_0 is a ($K \times K$) upper triangular matrix and Γ_{ni}, $i = 1, \ldots, q$, and B_{ni}, $i = 1, \ldots, p$, are ($K \times K$) parameter matrices. When the order parameter N is increased, the BEKK–specification allows more general forms of the dynamic dependence of Σ_t on Ω_{t-1}. For an appropriate choice of N the BEKK model can be shown to span the entire space of positive definite symmetric matrices. In practice, however, mostly $N = 1$ is chosen such that, for the bivariate GARCH(1,1) model, eleven parameters control the time path of second-order moments. In the following discussion we implicitly assume $N = 1$ throughout the presentation. Then parameter matrices Γ_{1i} and $-\Gamma_{1i}$ (or B_{1i} and $-B_{1i}$) imply identical volatility processes. Thus, for the purpose of identification, $\gamma_{11} > 0$ ($\beta_{11} > 0$) is assumed. A particular advantage of the BEKK-representation is that only squared terms enter the right-hand side of (5.40). Therefore, given positive definite initial covariances $\Sigma_0, \ldots, \Sigma_{1-p}$, time paths of second-order moments $\Sigma_t, t = 1, \ldots, T$ are positive definite under the weak (sufficient) condition that at least one of the matrices Γ_0 or B_{1i} has full rank [Engle & Kroner (1995)].

Compared with the diagonal model, the BEKK specification economizes on the number of parameters by restricting the half-vec model within and across equations. To illustrate this issue it is interesting to regard the dynamic structure implied by the BEKK model separately for each element in Σ_t, that is,

$$\sigma_{11,t} = [\Gamma_0'\Gamma_0]_{11} + \gamma_{11}^2 u_{1,t-1}^2 + 2\gamma_{11}\gamma_{21}u_{1,t-1}u_{2,t-1}$$
$$+\gamma_{21}^2 u_{2,t-1}^2, \tag{5.41}$$

$$\sigma_{21,t} = [\Gamma_0'\Gamma_0]_{21} + \gamma_{11}\gamma_{12}u_{1,t-1}^2$$
$$+(\gamma_{21}\gamma_{12} + \gamma_{11}\gamma_{22})u_{1,t-1}u_{2,t-1} + \gamma_{21}\gamma_{22}u_{2,t-1}^2, \tag{5.42}$$

$$\sigma_{22,t} = [\Gamma_0'\Gamma_0]_{22} + \gamma_{12}^2 u_{1,t-1}^2 + 2\gamma_{12}\gamma_{22}u_{1,t-1}u_{2,t-1}$$
$$+\gamma_{22}^2 u_{2,t-1}^2. \tag{5.43}$$

For convenience of presentation, autoregressive dynamics are excluded in (5.41) to (5.43). Since the coefficients in Γ_{11} (and B_{11}) enter the second moments non-linearly, a decided drawback of the model is that the role of particular parameters for the evolution of conditional (co)variances over time is not obvious. Therefore, numerous approaches to impulse response analysis have been advocated to uncover the dynamic structure of multivariate nonlinear models in general [Gallant, Rossi & Tauchen (1993), Koop, Pesaran & Potter (1996)] and MGARCH models in particular [Lin (1997), Herwartz & Lütkepohl (2000), Hafner & Herwartz (2001b)].

5.3.2 Estimation of Multivariate GARCH Models

Conceptually, estimation of multivariate GARCH models is a straightforward extension of the univariate benchmark. The contribution of an observed vector u_t to the (quasi) log-likelihood function is given as

$$\log(f(u_t|\Omega_{t-1})) = -\frac{K}{2}\log(2\pi) - \frac{1}{2}\log|\Sigma_t| - \frac{1}{2}u_t'\Sigma_t^{-1}u_t.$$

With respect to asymptotic properties of the (Q)ML estimator on the one hand and to computational issues involved when maximizing the log-likelihood function on the other hand, the multivariate estimation problem is substantially more involved than its univariate counterpart. These two issues are now considered in turn.

Asymptotic properties of the QML estimator. In the multivariate framework, results for the asymptotic properties of the (Q)ML estimator have been derived recently. Jeantheau (1998) proved the QML estimator to be consistent under the main assumption that the multivariate process is strictly stationary and ergodic. For a vector ARMA model with MGARCH disturbances exhibiting constant conditional correlation, Ling & McAleer (2003) proved consistency and asymptotic normality of the QML estimator assuming finiteness of unconditional second- and sixth-order moments of u_t, respectively. With finite unconditional moments up to order eight, Comte & Lieberman (2003) derived asymptotic normality of the QML estimator within the BEKK model. The asymptotic distribution of the rescaled QML estimator of $\theta' = (\text{vech}(\Gamma_0')', \text{vec}(\Gamma_{11})', \text{vec}(B_{11})')$ is analogous to the univariate case given in (5.19). If, however, a particular GARCH process fails to have finite eighth-order moments, the common approach to evaluate the covariance matrix of $\hat{\theta}$ given in (5.19) provides, strictly speaking, little more than a rule of thumb.

Numerical issues. Implementing the BHHH algorithm (5.17) and evaluating the covariance matrix of the QML estimator require first- and second-order derivatives of the Gaussian log-likelihood function. Although software packages such as GAUSS provide algorithms to evaluate these derivatives numerically, analytical derivatives may be preferable for their precision and shorter computing time [McCullough & Vinod (1999)]. Explicit formulas for analytical scores for the multivariate regression model with BEKK-type conditionally heteroskedastic error terms are given in Lucchetti (2002). Comte & Lieberman (2003) have provided the following general expressions for first- and second-order derivatives:

$$\frac{\partial l_t}{\partial \theta_i} = -\frac{1}{2}\text{tr}[\dot{\Sigma}_{t,i}\Sigma_t^{-1} - u_t u_t' \Sigma_t^{-1} \dot{\Sigma}_{t,i}\Sigma_t^{-1}], \tag{5.44}$$

$$\frac{\partial^2 l_t}{\partial \theta_i \partial \theta_j} = -\frac{1}{2}\text{tr}[\ddot{\Sigma}_{t,j,i}\Sigma_t^{-1} - \dot{\Sigma}_{t,j}\Sigma_t^{-1}\dot{\Sigma}_{t,i}\Sigma_t^{-1}$$
$$+ u_t u_t' \Sigma_t^{-1}\dot{\Sigma}_{t,i}\Sigma_t^{-1}\dot{\Sigma}_{t,j}\Sigma_t^{-1} + u_t u_t' \Sigma_t^{-1}\dot{\Sigma}_{t,j}\dot{\Sigma}_{t,j}\Sigma_t^{-1}$$
$$\times \dot{\Sigma}_{t,i}\Sigma_t^{-1} - u_t u_t' \Sigma_t^{-1}\ddot{\Sigma}_{t,i,j}\Sigma_t^{-1}]. \tag{5.45}$$

In (5.44) and (5.45), $\dot{\Sigma}_{t,j}$ ($\ddot{\Sigma}_{t,i,j}$) is a $(K \times K)$ matrix containing the first- (second-) order derivatives of each element of Σ_t with respect to θ_i (θ_i and θ_j). Building on (5.44) and (5.45), Hafner & Herwartz (2003) have given explicit first- and second-order derivatives for the simplest version of the BEKK model ($N = p = q = 1$). Moreover, they have demonstrated, by means of a Monte Carlo experiment, that the empirical size properties of QML inference are considerably closer to their nominal counterparts when using analytical instead of numerical second-order derivatives.

5.3.3 Extensions

The basic multivariate volatility models discussed so far may be generalized along similar lines, as discussed in Section 5.2.3 for the univariate case. Multivariate processes incorporating an asymmetric response of (co)variances to negative versus positive news have been introduced, for example, by Braun, Nelson & Sunier (1995) to generalize the univariate EGARCH [Nelson (1991)]. Hafner & Herwartz (1998) and Herwartz & Lütkepohl (2000) have formalized

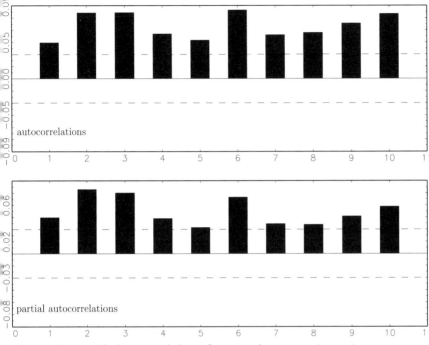

Figure 5.7. Empirical autocorrelations of cross-product process $(u_{1,t}u_{2,t})$.

asymmetry of (co)variances in the spirit of the TGARCH [Glosten et al. (1993)]. The assumption of conditional multivariate normality made in (5.33) could be replaced by a multivariate t-distribution as in Hafner & Herwartz (2001b) and Fiorentini, Sentana & Calzolari (2002). Adopting a semiparametric approach, Hafner & Rombouts (2002) have left the conditional distribution unspecified.

As outlined, the huge parameter spaces typically involved when employing multivariate GARCH processes make it practically impossible to analyze large-scale systems of empirical price variations. Recently, a few contributions have been aimed at modeling high-dimensional systems via the GARCH approach, namely the Dynamic Conditional Correlation MGARCH [Engle (2002)] and the Flexible MGARCH [Ledoit, Santa-Clara & Wolf (2002)]. Both approaches involve the estimation of univariate variance processes. Then, by means of the former procedure, transformed first-step residuals are used to yield dynamic correlation estimates. According to the Flexible MGARCH approach, unrestricted "univariate" covariance estimates are obtained from an equation like (5.39). In a second step, unrestricted estimates of $\gamma_{ij,0}, \gamma_{ij,1}, \beta_{ij,1}$ are transformed such that the resulting matrices of parameter estimates deliver positive definite covariances $\hat{\Sigma}_t$.

Table 5.2. *MGARCH estimates for bivariate exchange rate series*

	Estimates		ML t-ratios		QML t-ratios	
$\hat{\Gamma}_0$	9.41e-04	5.98e-04	14.9	6.14	5.47	3.68
	−	7.92e-04		11.9		11.2
$\hat{\Gamma}_1$	0.240	−0.053	25.8	−3.95	6.81	−1.93
	−0.027	0.220	−2.85	16.9	−0.743	8.99
$\hat{B}_1$	0.957	0.012	279.	2.70	99.6	1.45
	0.006	0.964	1.66	211.1	0.677	145.0

5.3.4 Continuing the Empirical Illustration

Having investigated the univariate case of time-varying volatility for the log price changes of the GBP/USD and DEM/USD rates in Section 5.2.6, we now turn our attention to joint second-order dynamics exhibited by these series. As a first indication of contemporaneous correlation, Figure 5.7 shows the autocorrelation and partial autocorrelation functions for the process of the product of

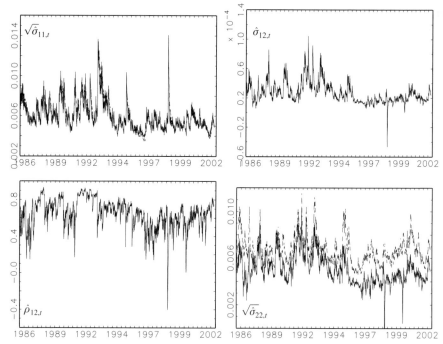

Figure 5.8. Estimated second-order moments (conditional standard deviations of u_{it}, covariance, and correlation between u_{1t} and u_{2t}). Univariate GARCH (--) versus MGARCH (—).

the two log price changes. Evidently, this moment process shows persistent positive autocorrelation, thereby motivating a multivariate approach to modeling volatility of the two exchange rates under study.

Estimates of the BEKK representation of the bivariate GARCH(1,1) model are shown in Table 5.2. In addition to the parameter estimates ML and QML, t-ratios are provided. Given the apparent violation of the Gaussian assumption obtained from the univariate exercises, the latter should be preferred when interpreting the estimation results. QML t-ratios are smaller than the ML counterparts throughout, indicating that ignoring conditional leptokurtosis will overestimate the significance of estimated dynamics. The parameter estimates obtained imply that the eigenvalues of the variance dynamics are smaller than 1 and, thus, the estimated process is covariance stationary. Estimated diagonal coefficients are plausible in the light of the univariate results. In the parameter matrix $\hat{\Gamma}_1$ ($\hat{B}_1$), the diagonal elements are 0.024 and 0.022 (0.957 and 0.964) and, thus, are close to the square root of their univariate counterparts given in Table 5.1. Cross-sectional dynamics are indicated if off-diagonal elements of these matrices are significant. Evaluating QML t-ratios, we find that only $\hat{\gamma}_{12,1} = -0.053$ is significant at the 10% level but fails slightly to be significant at the 5% level. Using (5.43) reveals that, in the present case, this coefficient governs the impact of log GBP/USD changes on the conditional variance of the log DEM/USD rate. From the latter results, one may expect that the bivariate and the univariate approaches to volatility estimation will deliver different time paths for the DEM/USD volatility but will give similar results with respect to the GBP/USD rate.

Time paths of standard deviations implied by the univariate and the bivariate volatility models are depicted on the diagonal of Figure 5.8. The upper-right and lower-left panels show the conditional covariance process and the implied correlations, respectively. Recall that the evaluation of the latter quantities requires a multivariate approach to volatility estimation. Apparently, the estimated standard deviations correspond to the volatility clusters and outlying observations documented in Figure 5.2. Whereas both approaches, the univariate and multivariate models, deliver almost identical estimates of GBP/USD volatility, it turns out that, relative to the BEKK model, the univariate GARCH(1,1) tends to overestimate the volatility of the DEM/USD rate. This effect is particularly evident in the second half of the sample period. Time-varying correlation estimates are almost uniformly positive and vary mostly between 0.2 and 0.9. Though not being a formal test one may conclude from a graphical inspection of the correlation pattern that the assumption of constant correlation would hardly be appropriate for this bivariate exchange rate process.

6 Smooth Transition Regression Modeling

Timo Teräsvirta

6.1 Introduction

Nonlinear models have gained a foothold in both macroeconomic and financial modeling. Linear approximations to nonlinear economic phenomena have served macroeconomic modelers well, but in many cases nonlinear specifications have turned out to be useful. Nonlinear econometric models can be divided in two broad categories. The first one contains the models that do not nest a linear model as a special case. Disequilibrium models [e.g., Fair & Jaffee (1972)] are a case in point. The second category embraces several popular models that do nest a linear model. The switching regression model, various Markov-switching models, and the smooth transition regression model are examples of models that belong to this class. Researchers interested in applying them can then choose a linear model as their starting-point and consider nonlinear extensions should they turn out to be necessary. In this chapter, the discussion is centered on modeling of economic time series using the family of smooth transition regression models as a tool.

This chapter is organized as follows. The smooth transition regression model is presented in Section 6.2. The modeling cycle, consisting of specification, estimation and evaluation stages, is the topic of Section 6.3. In Section 6.4, the modeling strategy and its application using JMulTi is illustrated by two empirical examples. Section 6.5 presents some final remarks.

6.2 The Model

The smooth transition regression (STR) model is a nonlinear regression model that may be viewed as a further development of the switching regression model that Quandt (1958) introduced. The univariate version of the switching regression model has long been known as the threshold autoregressive model; for a thorough review, see Tong (1990). The two-regime switching regression model with an observable switching variable is a special case of the standard

STR model, but switching regression models with more than two regimes are generally not nested in it. Accordingly, the univariate smooth transition autoregressive (STAR) model contains the two-regime threshold autoregressive model as a special case. The STR model originated as a generalization of a particular switching regression model in the work of Bacon & Watts (1971). These authors considered two regression lines and devised a model in which the transition from one line to the other is smooth. One of the two data sets Bacon & Watts (1971) used as examples will be reconsidered in Section 6.4. In the time series literature, Chan & Tong (1986) suggested the univariate STAR model. The earliest references in the econometrics literature are Goldfeld & Quandt (1972, pp. 263–264) and Maddala (1977, p. 396). Recent accounts include Granger & Teräsvirta (1993), Teräsvirta (1994, 1998), Franses & van Dijk (2000), and van Dijk, Teräsvirta & Franses (2002).

The standard STR model is defined as follows:

$$\begin{aligned}
y_t &= \phi' \mathbf{z}_t + \theta' \mathbf{z}_t G(\gamma, c, s_t) + u_t \\
&= \{\phi + \theta G(\gamma, c, s_t)\}' \mathbf{z}_t + u_t, \quad t = 1, \ldots, T,
\end{aligned} \tag{6.1}$$

where $\mathbf{z}_t = (\mathbf{w}_t', \mathbf{x}_t')'$ is a vector of explanatory variables, $\mathbf{w}_t = (1, y_{t-1}, \ldots, y_{t-p})'$, and $\mathbf{x}_t = (x_{1t}, \ldots, x_{kt})'$, which is a vector of exogenous variables. Furthermore, $\phi = (\phi_0, \phi_1, \ldots, \phi_m)'$ and $\theta = (\theta_0, \theta_1, \ldots, \theta_m)'$ are $((m + 1) \times 1)$ parameter vectors and $u_t \sim \text{iid}(0, \sigma^2)$. Transition function $G(\gamma, c, s_t)$ is a bounded function of the continuous transition variable s_t, continuous everywhere in the parameter space for any value of s_t, γ is the slope parameter, and $c = (c_1, \ldots, c_K)'$, which is a vector of location parameters, $c_1 \leq \ldots \leq c_K$. The last expression in (6.1) indicates that the model can be interpreted as a linear model with stochastic time-varying coefficients $\phi + \theta G(\gamma, c, s_t)$. In this chapter it is assumed that the transition function is a general logistic function

$$G(\gamma, c, s_t) = \left(1 + \exp\{-\gamma \prod_{k=1}^{K}(s_t - c_k)\}\right)^{-1}, \gamma > 0 \tag{6.2}$$

where $\gamma > 0$ is an identifying restriction. Equations (6.1) and (6.2) jointly define the logistic STR (LSTR) model. The most common choices for K are $K = 1$ and $K = 2$. For $K = 1$, the parameters $\phi + \theta G(\gamma, c, s_t)$ change monotonically as a function of s_t from ϕ to $\phi + \theta$. For $K = 2$, they change symmetrically around the midpoint $(c_1 + c_2)/2$, where this logistic function attains its minimum value. The minimum lies between zero and $1/2$. It reaches zero when $\gamma \to \infty$ and equals $1/2$ when $c_1 = c_2$ and $\gamma < \infty$. Slope parameter γ controls the slope and c_1 and c_2 the location of the transition function. Transition function (6.2) with $K = 1$ is also the one that Maddala (1977) proposed, whereas Goldfeld & Quandt (1972) and Chan & Tong (1986) favored the cumulative distribution function of a normal random variable. In fact, these two functions are close substitutes.

The LSTR model with $K = 1$ (LSTR1 model) is capable of characterizing asymmetric behavior. As an example, suppose that s_t measures the phase of the business cycle. Then the LSTR1 model can describe processes whose dynamic properties are different in expansions from what they are in recessions, and the transition from one extreme regime to the other is smooth. On the other hand, the LSTR2 model ($K = 2$) is appropriate in situations in which the local dynamic behavior of the process is similar at both large and small values of s_t and different in the middle. For further work on parameterizing the transition in the STR framework, see Öcal & Osborn (2000) and van Dijk & Franses (1999).

When $\gamma = 0$, the transition function $G(\gamma, c, s_t) \equiv 1/2$, and thus the STR model (6.1) nests the linear model. At the other end, when $\gamma \to \infty$, the LSTR1 model approaches the switching regression model with two regimes that have equal variances. When $\gamma \to \infty$ in the LSTR2 model, the result is another switching regression model with three regimes such that the outer regimes are identical and the midregime is different from the other two. Note that an alternative to the LSTR2 model exists, the so-called exponential STR (ESTR) model. It is (6.1) with the transition function

$$G_E(\gamma, c, s_t) = 1 - \exp\{-\gamma(s_t - c_1^*)^2\}, \gamma > 0. \tag{6.3}$$

This function is symmetric around $s_t = c_1^*$ and has, at low and moderate values of slope parameter γ, approximately the same shape, albeit a different minimum value (zero), as (6.2). Because this function contains one parameter less than the LSTR2 model, it can be regarded as a useful alternative to the corresponding logistic transition function. It has a drawback, however. When $\gamma \to \infty$, (6.1) with (6.3) becomes practically linear, for the transition function equals zero at $s_t = c_1^*$ and unity elsewhere. The ESTR model is therefore not a good approximation to the LSTR2 model when γ in the latter is large and $c_2 - c_1$ is at the same time not close to zero.

In practice, the transition variable s_t is a stochastic variable and very often an element of $\mathbf{z}_t$. It can also be a linear combination of several variables. In some cases, it can be a difference of an element of $\mathbf{z}_t$; see Skalin & Teräsvirta (2002) for a univariate example. A special case, $s_t = t$, yields a linear model with deterministically changing parameters.

When $\mathbf{x}_t$ is absent from (6.1) and $s_t = y_{t-d}$ or $s_t = \Delta y_{t-d}$, $d > 0$, the STR model becomes a univariate smooth transition autoregressive model; see Teräsvirta (1994) for more discussion. The exponential STAR (ESTAR) model is a slight generalization of the Exponential Autoregressive model that Haggan & Ozaki (1981) have already introduced.

6.3 The Modeling Cycle

In this section we consider modeling nonlinear relationships using STR model (6.1) with transition function (6.2). We present a modeling cycle consisting of three stages: specification, estimation, and evaluation. Previous presentations of the modeling strategy can be found in Teräsvirta (1994), completed by Eitrheim & Teräsvirta (1996) (the STAR model) and Teräsvirta (1998) (the STR model). We will now discuss the three stages of the cycle separately, beginning with specification, continuing with estimation, and ending with evaluation.

6.3.1 Specification

The specification stage entails two phases. First, the linear model forming the starting point is subjected to linearity tests, and then the type of STR model (LSTR1 or LSTR2) is selected. Economic theory may give an idea of which variables should be included in the linear model but may not be particularly helpful in specifying the dynamic structure of the model. The linear specification including the dynamics may in that case be obtained by various model selection techniques described in Chapters 2 and 3. If the model is a purely autoregressive one, however, it may be advisable not to create gaps in the lag structure by omitting lags shorter than the maximum lag selected for the model. The reason is that such omissions may reduce the power of the linearity tests. Models for strongly seasonal time series constitute an obvious exception to this rule. For example, when the seasonal series is a monthly one and model selection criteria suggest omitting several consecutive lags shorter than 12, it may be sensible to do that.

Linearity is tested against an STR model with a predetermined transition variable. If economic theory is not explicit about this variable, the test is repeated for each variable in the predetermined set of potential transition variables, which is usually a subset of the elements in $\mathbf{z}_t$. The purpose of these tests is twofold. First, they are used to test linearity against different directions in the parameter space. If no rejections of the null hypothesis occur, the model builder accepts the linear model and does not proceed with STR models. Second, the test results are used for model selection. If the null hypothesis is rejected for at least one of the models, the model against which the rejection, measured in the p-value, is strongest is chosen to be the STR model to be estimated. Details of this follow next.

Testing linearity. Testing linearity against STAR or STR has been discussed, for example, in Luukkonen, Saikkonen & Teräsvirta (1988a) and Teräsvirta (1994, 1998). The STR model shares with many other nonlinear models the property that the model is only identified under the alternative, not the null, hypothesis of linearity; see Hansen (1996) for a general discussion. The ensuing identification problem in testing linearity can, in the STR context, be circumvented by approximating the transition function (6.2) in (6.1) by a Taylor expansion around the null hypothesis $\gamma = 0$. It is customary to assume $K = 1$ in (6.2) and use the third-order Taylor approximation: see, for example, Teräsvirta (1998). The resulting test has power against both the LSTR1 ($K = 1$) and LSTR2 ($K = 2$) models.

Assume now that the transition variable s_t is an element in $\mathbf{z}_t$ and let $\mathbf{z}_t = (1, \widetilde{\mathbf{z}}_t)'$, where $\widetilde{\mathbf{z}}_t$ is an ($m \times 1$) vector. The approximation yields, after merging terms and reparameterizing, the following auxiliary regression:

$$y_t = \beta_0' \mathbf{z}_t + \sum_{j=1}^{3} \beta_j' \widetilde{\mathbf{z}}_t s_t^j + u_t^*, \quad t = 1, \ldots, T, \tag{6.4}$$

where $u_t^* = u_t + R_3(\gamma, c, s_t)\theta' \mathbf{z}_t$ with the remainder $R_3(\gamma, c, s_t)$. The null hypothesis is $H_0 : \beta_1 = \beta_2 = \beta_3 = 0$ because each β_j, $j = 1, 2, 3$, is of the form $\gamma \widetilde{\beta}_j$, where, $\widetilde{\beta}_j \neq 0$ is a function of θ and c. This is a linear hypothesis in a linear (in parameters) model. Because $u_t^* = u_t$ under the null hypothesis, the asymptotic distribution theory is not affected if an LM-type test is used. The asymptotic distribution theory of the resulting χ^2-test requires the existence of $\mathrm{E}s_t^6 \widetilde{\mathbf{z}}_t \widetilde{\mathbf{z}}_t'$. If the model is a univariate STAR model, this is equivalent to requiring $\mathrm{E}y_t^8 < \infty$. This assumption naturally implies restrictions on β_0.

The test statistic has an asymptotic χ^2-distribution with $3m$ degrees of freedom when the null hypothesis is valid. But then, the χ^2-statistic can be severely size-distorted in small and even moderate samples. The corresponding F-statistic is recommended instead. It has an approximate F-distribution with $3m$ and $T - 4m - 1$ degrees of freedom under the null hypothesis. JMulTi always uses the F-version of the test.

In building STR models, the test is applied as follows. First, select a set of potential transition variables $S = \{s_{1t}, \ldots, s_{kt}\}$. It may contain the same elements as $\widetilde{\mathbf{z}}_t$, but economic theory or other considerations may restrict the set or suggest adding other variables. After defining S, perform the test using each element in S in turn as the transition variable. If the null hypothesis is rejected for several transition variables, select the one for which the p-value of the test is minimized. The logic behind this suggestion is that the rejection of the null hypothesis is stronger against the correct alternative than other alternative models. However, if several small p-values are close to each other, it may be useful to proceed by estimating the corresponding STR models and leaving the choice between them to the evaluation stage. For more discussion about this procedure, see Teräsvirta (1998).

Choosing the type of the model. When linearity has been rejected and a transition variable subsequently selected, the next step will be to choose the model type. The available choices are $K = 1$ and $K = 2$ in (6.2). As mentioned in Section 6.2, the former choice leads to the LSTR1 model, whose parameters change monotonically as a function of the transition variable. Note, however, that they do not need to change in the same direction. When $K = 2$, the parameters change symmetrically around $(c_1 + c_2)/2$ (LSTR2 model). Alternatively, instead of $K = 2$, one may in some situations use the exponential transition function (6.3), which is symmetric around c (ESTR model). This can be the case when, for example, the sequences of estimates of c_1 and c_2 in the iterative estimation converge toward the same value. As already discussed, the LSTR1 and the LSTR2 models describe different types of behavior. The former ($K = 1$) has two extreme regimes that are different. For example, if the transition variable is a business cycle indicator, one regime will be related to business cycle expansions and the other to contractions. The latter has two identical extremes (for both very large and small values of the transition variable), whereas the midregime is different. As an example, a nonlinear equilibrium correction in which the strength of attraction varies nonlinearly as a function of the size of the deviation from the equilibrium can be characterized by an LSTR2 model.

The choice between these two types of models can be based on the auxiliary regression (6.4). The coefficient vectors β_j, $j = 1, 2, 3$, in (6.4) are functions of the parameters in (6.1). In the special case $c = 0$, it can be shown that $\beta_2 = 0$ when the model is an LSTR1 model, whereas $\beta_1 = \beta_3 = 0$ when the model is an LSTR2 or ESTR model; see Teräsvirta (1994) for details. Even when $c \neq 0$, β_2 is closer to the null vector than β_1 or β_3 when the model is an LSTR1 model, and vice versa for the LSTR2 model. This suggests the following short test sequence:

1. Test the null hypothesis $H_{04} : \beta_3 = 0$ in (6.4).
2. Test $H_{03} : \beta_2 = 0 | \beta_3 = 0$.
3. Test $H_{02} : \beta_1 = 0 | \beta_2 = \beta_3 = 0$.

If the test of H_{03} yields the strongest rejection measured in the p-value, choose the LSTR2 or ESTR model. Otherwise, select the LSTR1 model. All three hypotheses can simultaneously be rejected at a conventional significance level such as 0.05 or 0.01; that is why the strongest rejection counts. This procedure was simulated in Teräsvirta (1994) and appeared to work satisfactorily. It is implemented in JMulTi. Escribano & Jordá (1999) suggested an alternative procedure that requires adding the component $\beta_4' \tilde{z}_t s_t^4$ to (6.4) and leads to the general linearity hypothesis $\beta_1 = \beta_2 = \beta_3 = \beta_4 = 0$.

In choosing the STR model type, either one of the two test sequences has proved useful in practice. It is also possible to fit both an LSTR1 and an LSTR2 (or ESTR) model to the data and make the choice between them at the evaluation stage. In practice, this is a sensible way of proceeding if the test sequence does not provide a clear-cut choice between the two alternatives in the sense that p-values of the test of H_{03}, on the one hand, and of H_{02} or H_{04} on the other, are close to each other.

Reducing the size of the model. As in linear models, the model builder often wants to reduce the size of the model by eliminating redundant variables. In (6.1), eliminating an element in $\mathbf{z}_t$ such as z_{jt} requires the restriction $\phi_j = \theta_j = 0$. Unlike the situation for linear models, two other types of exclusion restrictions are of interest. One is $\phi_j = 0$. This restriction limits the combined coefficient of z_{jt} to zero for $G(\gamma, c, s_t) = 0$ so that z_{jt} does not contribute in that regime. A mirror image of this restriction is $\phi_j = -\theta_j$, which limits the combined coefficient to zero when $G(\gamma, c, s_t) = 1$. Thus, in reducing the number of parameters, restrictions $\phi_j = 0$ and $\phi_j = -\theta_j$ should both be considered. Naturally, restricting z_{jt} to only appear linearly ($\theta_j = 0$) in (6.1) has to be considered as well.

All of the preceding procedures require estimating several ST(A)R models. In some cases, estimating the unrestricted STR model may be difficult owing to a small sample size because the estimation algorithm may not converge. In such situations, it may be useful to begin with a complete linear component $\phi' z_t$ and introduce zeroes in the nonlinear component. Success is not guaranteed, however, if the true model contains restrictions of type $\phi_j = -\theta_j$. Imposing such restrictions has to be considered as well.

6.3.2 Estimation of Parameters

Initial values. The parameters of the STR model are estimated using conditional maximum likelihood. The log-likelihood is maximized numerically, and JMulTi uses the iterative BFGS algorithm [see, for example, Hendry (1995, Appendix A5)] with numerical derivatives for the purpose. Finding good starting-values for the algorithm is important. One way of obtaining them is the following. When γ and c in transition function (6.2) are fixed, the STR model is linear in parameters. This suggests constructing a grid. Estimate the remaining parameters ϕ and θ conditionally on (γ, c_1), or (γ, c_1, c_2) for $K = 2$, and compute the sum of squared residuals. Repeat this process for N combinations of these parameters. Select the parameter values that minimize the sum of squared residuals. Because the grid is only two- or three-dimensional (in the three-dimensional case, the restriction $c_1 \leq c_2$ constrains the size of the grid further), this procedure is computationally manageable.

When constructing the grid, note that γ is not a scale-free parameter. The exponent of the transition function is therefore standardized by dividing it by the Kth power of the sample standard deviation of the transition variable s_t, which we will call $\widehat{\sigma}_s$. The transition function becomes

$$G(\gamma, c, s_t) = \left(1 + \exp\{-(\gamma/\widehat{\sigma}_s^K)\prod_{k=1}^{K}(s_t - c_k)\}\right)^{-1}, \gamma > 0. \quad (6.5)$$

This makes the slope parameter γ in (6.5) scale-free, which in turn facilitates the construction of an effective grid.

A numerical problem. A specific numerical problem exists in the estimation of STR models. It is present when γ in (6.5) is large and the model is consequently close to a switching regression model. This makes the estimation of γ difficult in small samples because determining the curvature of (6.2) then requires many observations in the neighborhood of c ($K = 1$) and c_1 and c_2 ($K = 2$). It is unlikely that such clusters can be found in small samples. For discussion, see Bates & Watts (1988, p. 87), Seber & Wild (1989, pp. 480–481), or Teräsvirta (1994, 1998). This lack of information manifests itself in the standard deviation estimate of $\widehat{\gamma}$, which becomes large. Contrary to first intuition, the ensuing small value of the t-ratio does not, in that case, suggest redundancy of the nonlinear component ("insignificant $\widehat{\gamma}$"). Besides, quite apart from the numerical problem, the identification problem mentioned in Section 6.3.1 invalidates the standard interpretation of the t-ratio as a test of the hypothesis $\gamma = 0$.

6.3.3 Evaluation

Testing the STR model. Like any linear model, the estimated STR model needs to be evaluated before it can be used for forecasting or other purposes. Misspecification tests are an important tool in checking the quality of an estimated nonlinear model as they are in the case of linear models. Eitrheim & Teräsvirta (1996) and Teräsvirta (1998) have considered misspecification testing in ST(A)R models. The tests to be discussed here are generalizations of correponding tests for evaluation of linear models. They are an LM test of no error autocorrelation, an LM-type test of no additive nonlinearity, and another LM-type test of parameter constancy. Consistency and asymptotic normality of the maximum likelihood estimators are required for the asymptotic statistical theory behind the tests to be valid.

Test of no error autocorrelation. The test of no error autocorrelation applicable to STR models is a special case of a general test discussed in Godfrey (1988) (see also the corresponding test for linear models described in Chapter 2). Assume that $M(z_t; \psi)$ is at least twice continuously differentiable with respect to the parameters everywhere in the sample space and that

$$y_t = M(z_t; \psi) + u_t, \quad t = 1, \ldots, T, \quad (6.6)$$

where $u_t = \alpha' v_t + \varepsilon_t$ with $\alpha = (\alpha_1, \ldots, \alpha_q)'$, $v_t = (u_{t-1}, \ldots, u_{t-q})'$, and $\varepsilon_t \sim$ iid $N(0, \sigma^2)$. The null hypothesis of no error autocorrelation against the alternative of autocorrelation of at most order q in u_t in (6.6) is $\alpha = 0$.

The STR model satisfies the differentiability condition for $\gamma < \infty$. The details of applying Godfrey's LM test to the STR model are discussed in Teräsvirta (1998). Briefly, the test consists of regressing the residuals $\tilde{u}_t$ of the estimated STR model on the lagged residuals $\tilde{u}_{t-1}, \ldots, \tilde{u}_{t-q}$ and the partial derivatives of the log-likelihood function with respect to the parameters of the model evaluated at the maximizing value $\psi = \hat{\psi}$. Let n be the number of parameters in the model. Then the test statistic

$$F_{LM} = \{(SSR_0 - SSR_1)/q\}/\{SSR_1/(T - n - q)\},$$

where SSR_0 is the sum of squared residuals of the STR model and SSR_1 the corresponding sum from the auxiliary regression just described, has an approximate F-distribution with q and $T - n - q$ degrees of freedom under the null hypothesis. The F-version of the test is preferable to the corresponding χ^2-statistic based on the asymptotic distribution theory. The reason is that the latter statistic can be severely size distorted in small and moderate samples. When the model is linear, the test collapses into the well-known test of no serial correlation of Breusch (1978) and Godfrey (1978), already discussed in Chapter 3.

Test of no additive nonlinearity. After an STR model has been fitted to the data, it is important to ask whether the model adequately characterizes the nonlinearity originally found in the data by applying linearity tests or to ask whether some nonlinearity remains unmodeled. In the STR framework, a natural alternative to consider in this context is an additive STR model. It can be defined as follows:

$$y_t = \phi' z_t + \theta' z_t G(\gamma_1, c_1, s_{1t}) + \psi' z_t H(\gamma_2, c_2, s_{2t}) + u_t, \qquad (6.7)$$

where $H(\gamma_2, c_2, s_{2t})$ is another transition function of type (6.2) and $u_t \sim$ iid $N(0, \sigma^2)$. For notational simplicity, assume $H(0, c_2, s_{2t}) = 0$. Then the null hypothesis of no additive nonlinearity can be defined as $\gamma_2 = 0$ in (6.7). The model is only identified under the alternative: both ψ and c_2 are nuisance parameters under the null hypothesis. The identification problem can be solved as in Section 6.3.1 by approximating the transition function H by its Taylor expansion around $\gamma_2 = 0$, merging terms, and reparameterizing. If a third-order expansion is assumed, this yields the following auxiliary model:

$$y_t = \beta_0' \mathbf{z}_t + \theta' \mathbf{z}_t G(\gamma_1, c_1, s_{1t}) + \sum_{j=1}^{3} \beta_j'(\tilde{\mathbf{z}}_t s_{2t}^j) + u_t^*, \qquad (6.8)$$

where $u_t^* = u_t + \psi' \mathbf{z}_t R_3(\gamma_2, c_2, s_{2t})$, R_3 being the remainder from the polynomial approximation. The null hypothesis is $\beta_1 = \beta_2 = \beta_3 = 0$ in (6.8). If we set $\theta = 0$, (6.8) collapses into equation (6.4).

Deriving the LM-type test for testing this hypothesis is straightforward. The only difference compared with the case of testing linearity in Section 6.3.1 is that z_t in (6.4) is replaced by the gradient vector $v_t = (\mathbf{z}_t', \mathbf{z}_t' G(\widetilde{\gamma}_1, \widetilde{c}_1, s_{1t}), g_t(\widetilde{\gamma}), g_t(\widetilde{c}_1)')'$, where

$$g_t(\gamma) = \partial G(\gamma_1, c_1, s_{1t})/\partial \gamma_1 |_{(\gamma_1, c_1)=(\widetilde{\gamma}_1, \widetilde{c}_1)}$$

and

$$g_t(\widetilde{c}_1) = \partial G(\gamma_1, c_1, s_{1t})/\partial c_1 |_{(\gamma_1, c_1)=(\widetilde{\gamma}_1, \widetilde{c}_1)}.$$

The moment requirement is $\mathsf{E} s_t^6 \mathbf{z}_t \mathbf{z}_t' < \infty$. The test can be restricted to concern only a subvector of ψ by assuming that some elements of ψ equal zero a priori.

This test can in practice be applied in the same way as the linearity test by defining the set S of potential transition variables and carrying out the test against every variable in the set. In practice, S may often be the same set as the one used at the specification stage.

As a special case, one may test restrictions imposed on the STR model. Assume that the estimated equation contains the exclusion restriction $\phi^{(0)} = 0$ or, alternatively, $\phi^{(0)} = -\theta^{(0)}$, where $\phi^{(0)}$ and $\theta^{(0)}$ are subsets of elements of ϕ and θ. For notational simplicity, consider the former case. The validity of the restriction may be tested after estimating the restricted model by testing the hypothesis $\phi^{(0)} = 0$ in the linearly augmented STR equation

$$y_t = \phi^{(1)'}\mathbf{z}_t^{(1)} + \theta'\mathbf{z}_t G(\gamma_1, c_1, s_{1t}) + \phi^{(0)'}\mathbf{z}_t^{(0)} + u_t,$$

where $\mathbf{z}_t = (\mathbf{z}_t^{(0)'}, \mathbf{z}_t^{(1)'})'$ and the elements in $\mathbf{z}_t^{(i)}$ correspond to the coefficients in $\phi^{(i)}$, $i = 0, 1$. The test is a straightforward LM test as no identification problem is present in this situation. A corresponding test is available for testing the validity of $\phi^{(0)} = -\theta^{(0)}$.

An alternative parsimonious misspecification test would be the RESET of Ramsey (1969) that is also mentioned in Chapter 2. In this context, RESET is carried out by testing the hypothesis $\beta_2 = \cdots = \beta_h$ in another linearly augmented STR equation

$$y_t = \phi'\mathbf{z}_t + \theta'\mathbf{z}_t G(\gamma_1, c_1, s_{1t}) + \sum_{j=2}^{h} \beta_j \widetilde{y}_t^j + u_t,$$

where $\widetilde{y}_t$ is the fitted value of y_t from the estimated STR model. It should be pointed out, however, that, in practice, RESET has turned out not to be a very powerful test in detecting misspecification of the STR model. It may be best viewed as a complement to the other tests available for evaluating the STR model.

Testing parameter constancy. Parameter nonconstancy may indicate misspecification of the model or genuine change over time in the economic relationship described by the model. Either way, parameter constancy is one of the hypotheses that has to be tested before the estimated model can be used for forecasting or policy simulations. The alternative to parameter constancy allows smooth continuous change in parameters. This is different from the considerations in Chapter 3, where the alternative is a single structural break. The present alternative does, however, contain a structural break as a special case. To consider the test, rewrite (6.1) as follows:

$$y_t = \phi(t)'\mathbf{z}_t + \theta(t)'\mathbf{z}_t G(\gamma, c, s_t) + u_t, \quad \gamma > 0, \tag{6.9}$$

where

$$\phi(t) = \phi + \lambda_\phi H_\phi(\gamma_\phi, c_\phi, t^*) \tag{6.10}$$

and

$$\theta(t) = \theta + \lambda_\theta H_\theta(\gamma_\theta, c_\theta, t^*), \tag{6.11}$$

where $t^* = t/T$ and $u_t \sim$ iid $N(0, \sigma^2)$. Functions $H_\phi(\gamma_\phi, c_\phi, t^*)$ and $H_\theta(\gamma_\theta, c_\theta, t^*)$ are defined as in (6.2) with $s_t = t^*$. They represent two time-varying parameter vectors whose values vary smoothly between ϕ and $\phi + \lambda_\phi$ and θ and $\theta + \lambda_\theta$, respectively. Equations (6.9), (6.10), and (6.11) define a time-varying, smooth transition regression (TV–STR) model. Its univariate counterpart, the TV–STAR model, is discussed in detail in Lundbergh, Teräsvirta & van Dijk (2003). The null hypothesis of parameter constancy equals $\gamma_\phi = \gamma_\theta = 0$, whereas the alternative H$_1$: "either $\gamma_\phi > 0$ or $\gamma_\theta > 0$ or both." Testing subhypotheses is possible by setting elements of λ_ϕ and λ_θ to zero a priori.

In principle, it would also be possible to construct similar alternative hypotheses for the parameters γ and c in the transition function G. Time variation implied by such alternatives would, however, be more difficult to detect in practice than time variation in ϕ and θ. For this reason, testing constancy of γ and c is not considered here.

The TV–STR model is only identified when $\gamma_\phi, \gamma_\theta > 0$. To circumvent the problem, we proceed as in Section 6.3.1 and expand (6.10) and (6.11) into Taylor series around the null hypothesis. A first-order Taylor expansion around $\gamma_\psi = 0$, if the order of the logistic function $K = 3$, has the following form after reparameterization:

$$T(\gamma_\psi, c_\psi, t^*) = (1/2) + (\gamma_\psi/2)\{\delta_0^{(\psi)} + \delta_1^{(\psi)}t^* + \delta_2^{(\psi)}(t^*)^2 + \delta_3^{(\psi)}(t^*)^3\}$$
$$+ R_1(\gamma_\psi, c_\psi, \gamma_\psi, c_\psi, t^*) \tag{6.12}$$

for $\psi = \phi, \theta$, where R_1 is the remainder. If one approximates (6.9) using (6.10) and (6.11) using (6.12) and reparameterizes the following nonlinear auxiliary regression results:

$$y_t = \beta_0' \mathbf{z}_t + \sum_{j=1}^{3} \beta_j' \{\mathbf{z}_t(t^*)^j\} + \sum_{j=1}^{3} \beta_{j+3}' \{\mathbf{z}_t(t^*)^j\} G(\gamma, c, s_t) + u_t^*,$$

(6.13)

where $\beta_j = 0, j = 1, \ldots, 6$, if and only if the null hypothesis $\gamma_\phi = \gamma_\theta = 0$ holds. Note that $u_t^* = u_t$ under the null hypothesis. The new null hypothesis thus equals $\beta_j = 0, j = 1, \ldots, 6$. As already mentioned, testing subhypotheses by assuming that the parameters not under test are constant, is possible and results in obvious modifications in (6.13); see Teräsvirta (1998) for discussion.

The LM-type test for testing the current null hypothesis is analogous to the ones in the preceding sections. The auxiliary regression now consists of regressing residual $\tilde{u}_t$ (or y_t) on

$$v_t = [\mathbf{z}_t', \mathbf{z}_t' t^*, \mathbf{z}_t'(t^*)^2, \ldots, \mathbf{z}_t'(t^*)^3 G(\gamma, c, s_t)]'.$$

The F-version of the test is recommended because v_t is a $(7(m+1) \times 1)$ vector and the number of degrees of freedom in the χ^2-test would equal $6(m+1)$. Modifying the test for other values of K is straightforward. When $\theta = 0$ in (6.1), the test collapses into the corresponding parameter constancy test in a linear model discussed in Eitrheim & Teräsvirta (1996) and Teräsvirta (1998). In what follows, we call the test statistic LMK, where K indicates the order of the polynomial in the exponent of $H_\phi(\gamma_\phi, c_\phi, t^*)$ and $H_\theta(\gamma_\theta, c_\theta, t^*)$. Carrying out the test for a small number of parameters at a time is advisable, for the results may yield important information about causes of possible misspecification of the model.

Note that in Eitrheim & Teräsvirta (1996) and Teräsvirta (1998) it is assumed that $\gamma_\phi = \gamma_\theta$. This restriction, however, affects neither the form nor the asymptotic null distribution of the test statistic and has implications only if the alternative model is actually estimated. This need not automatically be the case because a rejection of parameter constancy may often be interpreted as an indication of missing variables or other misspecification of the functional form.

Other tests. Although the tests just discussed may be the most obvious ones to use when an estimated STR model is evaluated, other tests may be useful. One may, for example, test the null hypothesis of no ARCH using tests discussed in Chapter 2. Applied to macroeconomic equations, these tests may most conveniently be regarded as general misspecification tests because it is unlikely that ARCH would be present, for example, in quarterly macroeconometric equations. Notice, however, that such tests cannot be expected to be very powerful against misspecification in the conditional mean. In fact, as

Luukkonen, Saikkonen & Teräsvirta (1988b) pointed out, the LM test of no ARCH only has trivial local power against misspecification of that kind. The Lomnicki–Jarque–Bera normality test (see Chapter 2) is also available here. It is sensitive to outliers, and the result should be considered jointly with a visual examination of the residuals.

What to do when at least one test rejects. Although carrying out the misspecification tests just discussed is straightforward, it may not always be easy to decide what to do when some of them reject the null hypothesis. Error autocorrelation indicates misspecification but is not specific about its nature. The test may not only have power against misspecified dynamics but also against omitted variables. Rejecting the null of no additive nonlinearity may suggest adding another STR component to the model. But then, because a rejection as such does not say anything definite about the cause, the idea of extending the model further has to be weighted against other considerations such as the risk of overfitting. Some protection against overfitting may be obtained by applying low significance levels. This is important because the number of tests typically carried out at the evaluation stage can be large.

Parameter constancy tests are also indicative of general misspecification, and there is no unique way of responding to a rejection. Note, however, that carrying out the test for subsets of parameters can provide important information about the shortcomings of the model and may suggest what to do next. In certain cases, it may be reasonable to respond to a rejection by extending an estimated ST(A)R model into a TV-ST(A)R model. Recent work by van Dijk, Strikholm & Teräsvirta (2003) and Teräsvirta, Strikholm & van Dijk (2003) on time-varying seasonal patterns in quarterly industrial production series constitutes an example in which the TV–STAR model is an essential tool of the analysis.

6.4 Two Empirical Examples

In this section we consider two empirical examples of nonlinear modeling using STR models. Our purpose is to illustrate the phases of the modeling cycle presented in Section 6.3 and give examples of decisions the modeler has to make during modeling. The first example is based on data from a chemical experiment considered in Bacon & Watts (1971), who introduced the STR model. The second example is from Lütkepohl, Teräsvirta & Wolters (1999). The topic of the authors is modeling the demand for narrow money (M1) in Germany.

6.4.1 Chemical Data

The observations in this modeling experiment come from Example 1 of Bacon & Watts (1971). The purpose of the experiment they considered was to investigate

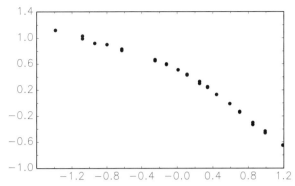

Figure 6.1. Observations of the logarithmic flow (cm), x-axis, and the logarithm of the height of the stagnant layer (g/cm. s), y-axis. Source: Bacon & Watts (1971).

the effect of water flow down an inclined channel on the height of a stagnant surface layer containing a certain surfactant. The thickness of the layer was assumed to be a nonlinear function of the flow. The sample consisted of 29 independent observations ($T = 29$) of the thickness of the stagnant layer Y_t measured in centimeters and of flow X_t measured in grams per centimeter and second. The experimenter controlled X and observed the corresponding value Y. The authors fitted an STR model to the logarithmic data using Bayesian techniques. They defined the transition function as a hyperbolic tangent function closely resembling the logistic function that has been a common choice in later work. Figure 6.1 demonstrates a clearly nonlinear relationship between the logarithmic flow (x-axis) and the logarithmic thickness of stagnant layer (y-axis). When the flow is sufficiently strong, the thinning rate of the the stagnant layer moves to a higher level.

We repeat the example of Bacon and Watts by using our STR model. Fitting a linear model to the data yields

$$y_t = \underset{(0.023)}{0.38} - \underset{(0.032)}{0.67}\, x_t + \tilde{\varepsilon}_t \tag{6.14}$$

$$T = 29,\ \tilde{\sigma}_L = 0.124,\ R^2 = 0.943,\quad p^{RESET}(2, 25) = 0.28,$$

where $\tilde{\sigma}_L$ equals the residual standard deviation and p^{RESET} is the p-value of the RESET. The test does not indicate any misspecification of (6.14). On the other hand, the residuals arranged according to x_t in ascending order and graphed in Figure 6.2 show that the linear model is not adequate. The results of the linearity tests in Section 6.3.1 appearing in Table 6.1 support this conclusion. The p-values are remarkably small.

Hypothesis H_0 is the general null hypothesis based on the third-order Taylor expansion of the transition function; see (6.4). Hypotheses H_{04}, H_{03}, and H_{02} are the ones discussed in Section 6.3.1. Because the p-value of the test of H_{03}

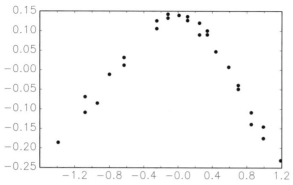

Figure 6.2. Residuals of (6.14) arranged in ascending order of x_t (x-axis: the value of x_t; y-axis: residual $\widetilde{\varepsilon}_t$).

is much larger than the ones corresponding to testing H_{04} and H_{02}, the choice of $K = 1$ in (6.2) (the LSTR1 model) is quite clear. This is also obvious from Figure 6.1, for there appears to be a single transition from one regression line to the other.

The next step is to estimate the LSTR1 model, which yields

$$y_t = \underset{(0.043)}{0.57} - \underset{(0.034)}{0.39}\,x_t$$

$$-(\underset{(0.28)}{0.21} + \underset{(0.14)}{0.49}\,x_t)(1 + \exp\{-(\underset{(0.30)}{2.5}\,/\widehat{\sigma}_x^1)(x_t - \underset{(0.24)}{0.30})\})^{-1} + \widehat{u}_t$$

$$(6.15)$$

$$T = 29,\ \widehat{\sigma} = 0.014\ R^2 = 0.9994,\ \widetilde{\sigma}_L/\widehat{\sigma} = 0.115,$$

where $\widehat{\sigma}_x^1$ is the sample standard deviation of x_t, and $\widehat{\sigma}$ is the residual standard deviation. Note that there are two large standard deviations, which suggests that the full model may be somewhat overparameterized. This is often the case when the STR model is based on the linear model without any restrictions. Model (6.15) is a "mini-example" of such a situation. It may appear strange that the need to reduce the size of the model is obvious in this model already because

Table 6.1. *p-Values of the linearity tests of model (6.14)*

Hypothesis	Transition variable x_t
H_0	7×10^{-22}
H_{04}	9×10^{-7}
H_{03}	0.011
H_{02}	8×10^{-18}

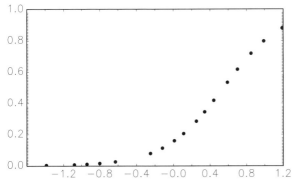

Figure 6.3. Transition function of model (6.16) as a function of the transition variable. Each dot corresponds to at least one observation.

it only has a single explanatory variable. On the other hand, the number of observations is as small as 29, which probably explains this outcome.

The first reaction of the modeler would perhaps be to tighten the specification by removing the nonlinear intercept. Another possibility would be to restrict the intercepts by imposing the other exclusion restriction $\phi_0 = -\theta_0$. In fact, the latter alternative yields a model with a slightly better fit than the former one. The model estimated with this restriction is

$$y_t = \underset{(0.21)}{0.61} - \underset{(0.017)}{0.37} \, x_t$$

$$-(\underset{(0.21)}{0.61} + \underset{(0.040)}{0.27} \, x_t)(1 + \exp\{-(\underset{(0.21)}{2.3} \, /\widehat{\sigma}_x^1)(x_t - \underset{(0.025)}{0.55})\})^{-1} + \widehat{u}_t$$

$$(6.16)$$

$$T = 29, \ \widehat{\sigma} = 0.014, \ R^2 = 0.9994, \ \widetilde{\sigma}_L/\widehat{\sigma} = 0.114.$$

The estimated standard deviations of all estimates in (6.16) are now appreciably small, and thus further reduction of the model size is not necessary. The fit of both (6.15) and (6.16) is vastly superior to that of (6.14), whereas there is little difference between the two LSTR1 models. The residual standard deviation of these models is only about one-tenth of the corresponding figure for (6.14). Such an improvement is unthinkable when economic time series are being modeled. The graph of the transition function as a function of the observations in Figure 6.3 shows that the transition is indeed smooth. The graph does not convey the fact that eight observations (slightly less than one-third of the total) lie to the right of 0.55, the estimate of the location parameter c.

The test of no additive nonlinearity [$H_0 : \beta_1 = \beta_2 = \beta_3 = 0$ in (6.8)] has the p-value 0.71. In testing $H_{02} : \beta_1 = 0|\beta_2 = \beta_3 = 0$, a test based on a first-order Taylor expansion of $H(\gamma_2, c_2, s_{2t})$ and thus one against another LSTR1 component, we find that the p-value of the test equals 0.30. These results show that nonlinearity in this data set has been adequately characterized by the LSTR1 model. The tests of no error autocorrelation and parameter constancy are not meaningful here in the same way as they are in connection with time series models, and they have therefore not been applied to model (6.16).

6.4.2 Demand for Money (M1) in Germany

The second example concerns modeling the demand for money in Germany and follows Lütkepohl et al. (1999), which we will abbreviate, as LTW. The authors considered the stability of a German demand-for-money function and were also interested in possible nonlinearity. In particular, the effects of the German unification on the demand for money (M1) were of interest. The observation period covered the quarters from $1960Q1$ to $1995Q4$. The main variables were the logarithm of money stock (M1) m_t, the logarithm of gross national product y_t, the logarithm of the GNP deflator p_t, and a long interest rate R_t. The exact definitions of variables can be found in LTW.

A cointegration analysis (see Chapter 3 for discussion) gives the result that there is a single cointegrating relationship among the nonstationary variables of interest. As in LTW, this cointegrating combination of m_t, y_t, and R_t is denoted by z_t^*. STR modeling, to be reviewed here, has been preceded by an analysis showing that the seasonal pattern in the demand of money has changed as a result of German Monetary Unification on 1 July 1990. This has resulted in the introduction of a set of seasonal dummies complementing the ones already in the model. The new dummies obtain nonzero values only from $1990Q3$ onwards.

Our description of the modeling process begins at the stage where the new seasonals have been incorporated in the linear model of m_t. The estimated equation has the form

$$\Delta m_t = \underset{(0.057)}{0.16} \Delta y_t - \underset{(0.044)}{0.12} \Delta y_{t-1} - \underset{(0.055)}{0.17} \Delta y_{t-2} - \underset{(0.23)}{0.52} \Delta R_t$$
$$- \underset{(0.080)}{0.54} \Delta p_t - \underset{(0.25)}{0.81} \Delta R_{t-1} - \underset{(0.021)}{0.16} z_{t-1}^* - \underset{(0.028)}{0.13} + \widetilde{\alpha}_t' d_t + \widetilde{\varepsilon}_t$$

$$(6.17)$$

$$T = 140[1961(1) - 1995(4)], \ \widetilde{\sigma}_L = 0.013, \ \overline{R}^2 = 0.94,$$

$$pLJB = 0.14,$$

$$pLM_{ARCH}(1) = 0.32, \ pLM_{ARCH}(4) = 0.31,$$

$$pLM_{AR}(1) = 0.60, \ pLM_{AR}(4) = 0.97, \ p^{RESET}(2, 124) = 0.23,$$

where $\widetilde{\alpha}_t' d_t$ is the estimated linear combination of the seasonal dummies, $\widetilde{\sigma}_L$ is the residual standard deviation, $pLJB$ is the p-value of the Lomnicki–Jarque–Bera normality test, $pLM_{ARCH}(q)$ is the p-value of the LM test of no ARCH

Table 6.2. *p-values of parameter constancy tests of model (6.18)*

Hypothesis	Test statistic		
	LM1	LM2	LM3
Constant (only) under H_0 :			
All parameters except new seasonals	0.45	0.18	0.21
Intercept and regular seasonal dummies	0.66	0.83	0.87
Coefficient of z_{t-1}^*	0.64	0.89	0.74
Coefficient of ΔR_t	0.083	0.044	0.077

against ARCH at most of order q, and $pLM_{AR}(q)$ is the p-value of the LM test of no error autocorrelation against autocorrelation at most of order q. All these tests have been discussed in Chapter 2. Not one of these tests, including RESET, indicates misspecification of the model. Results of tests of parameter constancy can be found in Table 6.2.

They show, by and large, that model (6.18) has constant parameters. In particular, the introduction of the postunification seasonal dummies has stabilized the seasonal parameters. The effect of the error correction term on Δm_t is stable. Note that z_{t-1}^* is treated in the same way as the other variables, although it contains estimated parameters. As explained in Chapter 3, the estimators of these parameters are superconsistent, and the estimates can therefore be taken as constants in this context. The last row of Table 6.2 contains the smallest p-values found in the tests (not all results are reported). They concern the coefficient of the unlagged long-term interest rate variable ΔR_t. Given the large number of tests, they are not deemed worthy of further consideration.

A stable linear equation offers a good starting point for testing linearity. The results of the linearity tests can be found in Table 6.3. The p-values of tests of H_{04} and H_{03} are not reported in cases where H_0 is not rejected at the 5% level of significance. The results show that there is only weak evidence of nonlinearity and that it centers around the error correction z_{t-1}^* and the quarterly rate of

Table 6.3. *p-values of linearity tests of model (6.18)*

Hypothesis	Transition variable					
	Δy_{t-1}	Δy_{t-2}	ΔR_t	ΔR_{t-1}	Δp_t	z_{t-1}^*
H_0	0.81	0.15	0.083	0.91	0.047	*
H_{04}					0.11	*
H_{03}					0.27	*
H_{02}	0.32	0.62	0.14	0.98	0.087	0.063

Note: An asterisk means that the value of the test statistic has not been computed owing to near singularity of the moment matrix.

inflation Δp_t. It has not been possible to test the null hypothesis when z^*_{t-1} is the transition variable in the alternative because the moment matrix to be inverted has been nearly singular. If Δp_t is chosen to be the transition variable of the STR model, the test sequence discussed in Section 6.3.1 clearly points to an LSTR1 model.

A sensible decision in this situation is to consider STR models with both Δp_t and z^*_{t-1} as transition variables. The ultimate choice of LTW is a model with Δp_t as a transition variable. The final model estimated following a reduction in size has the following form:

$$
\Delta m_t = \underset{(0.069)}{0.37}\,\Delta y_t - \underset{(0.052)}{0.19}\,\Delta y_{t-2} - \underset{(0.21)}{0.59}\,\Delta R_t - \underset{(0.22)}{0.95}\,\Delta R_{t-1}
$$

$$
-\underset{(0.12)}{0.48}\,\Delta p_t - \underset{(0.043)}{0.28}\,z^*_{t-1} - \underset{(0.056)}{0.28} + \widehat{\alpha}'\boldsymbol{d}_t + (\,\underset{(0.061)}{0.19} - \underset{(0.051)}{0.17}\,\Delta y_t
$$

$$
- \underset{(0.045)}{0.18}\,\Delta y_{t-1} + \underset{(0.046)}{0.15}\,z^*_{t-1})(1+\exp\{-(\,\underset{(54)}{47}/\widehat{\sigma}^1_{\Delta p})\Delta p_t\})^{-1} + \widehat{\varepsilon}_t
$$

$$\tag{6.18}$$

$$
T = 140[1961(1)\text{-}1995(4)],\ \widehat{\sigma} = 0.012,\ \widetilde{\sigma}_L/\widehat{\sigma} = 0.965,\ R^2 = 0.96
$$

$$
pLJB = 7 \times 10^{-4},\ pLM_{ARCH}(1) = 0.86,\ pLM_{ARCH}(4) = 0.52
$$

$$
pLM_{AR}(1) = 0.94,\ pLM_{AR}(4) = 0.83,
$$

where $\widehat{\sigma}^1_{\Delta p}$ is the sample standard deviation of Δp_t and $\widehat{\sigma}$ is the residual standard deviation.

LTW discuss the economic interpretation of the STR-equation (6.18) – its nonlinear features in particular. In this exposition, details related to modeling will be in the foreground. First, note that the reduction in the residual standard deviation, compared with (6.18), is only 3.5%. This accords with the fact that linearity was not rejected very strongly. Second, it may seem surprising that normality of errors is rejected: that was not the case in equation (6.18). A comparison of residuals from both models shows that the STR model has practically eliminated a few large positive residuals present in (6.18) but has not done anything to the largest negative residuals in that model. This has led to negative skewness in the residuals of (6.18) and caused a rejection of normality. Third, the estimate of the slope parameter γ in the transition function has a large standard deviation. This is an example of the situation discussed in Section 6.3.2. As seen from Figure 6.4, the transition function has a steep slope, quite different from the one in the previous example, and the large standard deviation estimate is a numerical consequence of this fact.

The other statistics below the estimated STR equation do not indicate misspecification. An interesting issue is whether the model is a satisfactory

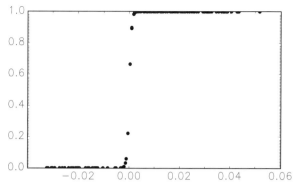

Figure 6.4. Transition function of (6.18) as a function of observations. Each dot corresponds to an observation. The transition variable is Δp_t.

characterization of the nonlinearity detected at the specification stage. This is considered using the tests of no additive nonlinearity. The results can be found in Table 6.4.

The results for the two hypotheses H_{04} and H_{03} have been omitted because H_0 is not strongly rejected. Two details deserve attention. First, the nonlinearity indicated by the results in columns Δp_t and z_{t-1}^* of Table 6.3 has been adequately modeled. The corresponding p-values in Table 6.4 are large. On the other hand, the trace of nonlinearity signaled by the linearity test against STR with the interest rate variable ΔR_t as the transition variable has remained and become slightly more visible. But then, the p-values in the corresponding column of Table 6.4 are not sufficiently small to cause any action.

Model (6.18) already had constant parameters. The STR model (6.18) passes all parameter constancy tests, and results of the tests are therefore not reported here. It should be mentioned, however, that the three tests for the coefficients of ΔR_t now have p-values between 0.13 and 0.26. As a whole, the model appears adequate. This does not exclude the possibility that some other nonlinear model would not fit the data better than (6.18), but within the STR family and the given information set, (6.18) appears to be a reasonable specification.

Table 6.4. *p-values of the test of no additive nonlinearity in model (6.18)*

Hypothesis	Δy_t	Δy_{t-1}	Δy_{t-2}	ΔR_t	ΔR_{t-1}	Δp_t	z_{t-1}^*
			Transition variable				
H_0	0.28	0.80	0.077	0.062	0.91	0.44	*
H_{02}	0.055	0.41	0.46	0.071	0.94	0.999	0.622

Note: An asterisk indicates that the value of the statistic has not been computed owing to near-singularity of the moment matrix.

6.5 Final Remarks

This chapter has emphasized the modeling cycle for building STR models. Nevertheless, the linearity tests discussed in Section 6.3.1 can also be used as general tests against nonlinearity. Even the builders of switching regression or threshold autoregressive models may use them because the tests also have power against these nonlinear models. In that case they may be seen as a computationally simple alternative offered by JMuiTi to the simulation or bootstrap-based linearity tests against threshold autoregressive models that Hansen (1999) has advocated. Likewise, as Eitrheim & Teräsvirta (1996) have pointed out, the test of no additive nonlinearity can be applied to checking the adequacy of a switching regression or a threshold autoregressive model.

7 Nonparametric Time Series Modeling

Rolf Tschernig

7.1 Introduction

As the previous chapters have shown, parametric time series modeling offers a great wealth of modeling tools. Linear time series models are generally the starting point for modeling both univariate and multivariate time series data. Such data may also exhibit nonstationary behavior caused by the presence of unit roots, structural breaks, seasonal influences, and the like. If one is interested in nonlinear dynamics, it is no longer sufficient to consider linear models. This situation arises if, for example, the strength of economic relationships depends on the state of the business cycle or if the adjustment speed toward long-run equilibrium relationships is not proportional to the deviation from the long-run equilibrium. Chapter 6 discusses how to build nonlinear parametric models for various kinds of nonlinear dynamics, including those of business cycles. There it is also explained how the parameter estimates can be used to understand the underlying nonlinear dynamic behavior.

However, nonlinear parametric modeling also has its drawbacks. Most importantly, it requires an a priori choice of parametric function classes for the function of interest. The framework of smooth transition regression models discussed in Chapter 6, for example, is widely used. Although it is an appropriate modeling framework for many empirical problems, it may not always capture features that are relevant to the investigator. In the latter case, one has to choose alternative nonlinear parametric models like neural networks or Markov-switching models to name a few. Thus, nonlinear parametric modeling implies the difficult choice of a model class.

In contrast, when using the nonparametric modeling approach, one can avoid this choice. For example, when using local linear estimation it is sufficient to assume that the function of interest is continuously differentiable up to second order.

This generality has its price. Nonparametric estimators are known to suffer from the "curse of dimensionality." This means that the rate of convergence of

243

the estimates decreases with the number of explanatory variables in the model (see Section 7.2.2). The "curse of dimensionality" becomes even more of a problem if one wants to estimate multivariate time series models with many dimensions and a large number of lagged variables nonparametrically. For that reason nonparametric multivariate modeling is generally not very useful for small samples. One promising alternative is the use of semiparametric multivariate time series models. They are, however, beyond the scope of this chapter.

Therefore, we focus in this chapter on the nonparametric estimation of univariate nonlinear time series models. These models may contain conditionally heteroskedastic errors and seasonal features. Deferring seasonal models to Section 7.6, we assume that a univariate stochastic process $\{y_t\}_{t \geq 1}$ is generated by the *conditionally heteroskedastic nonlinear autoregressive* (NAR) *model*

$$y_t = \mu(x_t) + \sigma(x_t)\xi_t, \qquad (7.1)$$

where $x_t = (y_{t-i_1}, y_{t-i_2}, \ldots, y_{t-i_m})'$ is the $(m \times 1)$ vector of all m correct lagged values, $i_1 < i_2 < \cdots < i_m$, the ξ_t's, $t = i_m + 1, i_m + 2, \ldots$, denote a sequence of iid random variables with zero mean and unit variance, and $\mu(\cdot)$ and $\sigma(\cdot)$ denote the conditional mean and volatility function, respectively. To facilitate notation, (7.1) is written such that the conditional mean $\mu(\cdot)$ and the conditional volatility function $\sigma(\cdot)$ are based on the same lags. However, the estimators and their asymptotic theory presented in this chapter also hold as long as the lags needed for modeling $\sigma(\cdot)$ are also required for modeling $\mu(\cdot)$ but not vice versa. Thus, a nonlinear time series with homoskedastic errors is included in the present setup. Note that the vector x_t does not necessarily include consecutive lags. This would unnecessarily increase the "curse of dimensionality" if not all lags are relevant. Therefore, lag selection must be more advanced than simply determining the order of the model, i_m, as it is usually done in the case of linear autoregressive models. It should also be mentioned that it is possible to extend the vector x_t by exogenous variables, but this option is not further discussed in this chapter.

In practice, the functions $\mu(\cdot)$ and $\sigma(\cdot)$, the number of lags m, and the lag indices $i_1, i_2, \ldots, i_m$ are unknown and have to be estimated or selected. In this chapter we provide a brief introduction to nonparametric modeling of the NAR model (7.1) and some extensions.

The chapter is organized as follows. In Section 7.2 we derive the local linear and the Nadaraya–Watson estimator for the conditional mean function $\mu(\cdot)$ on the assumption that the correct lags $i_1, \ldots, i_m$ and thus x_t are known. In Section 7.3 we present nonparametric methods for estimating the asymptotically optimal bandwidth and for selecting the relevant lags. Section 7.4 briefly discusses some diagnostic tests for checking the residuals. All these steps are illustrated with a running example. The nonparametric estimation of the conditional volatility function $\sigma(\cdot)$ is presented in Section 7.5. In Section 7.6 the nonparametric theory for fitting NAR models is extended to various seasonal nonlinear autoregressive models. The last two sections illustrate the presented nonparametric tools. Section 7.7 shows how to model the conditional mean function of the monthly changes of U.S. average weekly working hours. Section 7.8 discusses the modeling of a conditional volatility function for the daily returns of the XETRA Dax index.

7.2 Local Linear Estimation

First we will explain the principles of local polynomial estimation applied to the estimation of the conditional mean function and derive the local constant and local linear estimator. We then present their asymptotic properties including a heuristic discussion of the required assumptions. The construction of confidence intervals is also explained. At the end of this section we show how one can partially visualize the function estimates in the case of higher dimensional regressors and how to obtain forecasts.

7.2.1 The Estimators

Local estimation of $\mu(x)$ means estimating $\mu(\cdot)$ separately for each $(m \times 1)$ vector $x = (x_1, x_2, \ldots, x_m)'$ of interest. Note that x is scalar if $m = 1$ and x_t is scalar. The starting point for deriving the *local linear estimator* is the fact that, although $\mu(x)$ is not observable, it appears in a first-order Taylor expansion of $\mu(x_t)$ taken at x,

$$\mu(x_t) = \mu(x) + \frac{\partial \mu(x)}{\partial x'}(x_t - x) + R(x_t, x), \tag{7.2}$$

where $R(x_t, x)$ denotes the remainder term. Inserting this expansion into the model equation (7.1) yields

$$y_t = \mu(x)1 + \frac{\partial \mu(x)}{\partial x'}(x_t - x) + R(x_t, x) + \varepsilon_t,$$

where we now use the symbol ε_t for the stochastic error term. Observe that the right-hand side contains two known terms, the constant one multiplied by the unknown $\mu(x)$ and the known term $(x_t - x)$ multiplied by the vector of unknown first partial derivatives $\frac{\partial \mu(x)}{\partial x'}$. Thus, were there no remainder term $R(x_t, x)$, one would have a simple OLS regression problem in which the estimated parameters correspond to the estimated function value $\hat{\mu}(x)$ at x and the estimated vector $\frac{\partial \mu(x)}{\partial x'}$ of first partial derivatives also evaluated at x.

However, whenever the conditional mean function is nonlinear, the remainder term $R(x_t, x)$ may be nonzero at x. Using standard OLS estimation would then result in biased estimates for which the size of the bias depends on all remainder terms $R(x_t, x)$, $t = 1, \ldots, T$. One possibility to reduce the bias is to use only those observations x_t that are in some sense close to x. More generally, one downweighs those observations that are not in a local neighborhood of x. If more data become available, it is possible to decrease the size of the local neighborhood, where the estimation variance and the bias can decrease. In this sense, the approximation error of the model can decline with sample size. This is the main idea underlying nonparametric estimation.

Technically, the weighing is controlled by a so-called *kernel function* $K(u)$, where in the following it is assumed that this function is a symmetric, compactly supported, nonnegative, univariate probability density so that $\int K(u)du = 1$. Typical examples are the uniform density $K(u) = I(|u| \leq 1/2)$ or the quartic kernel $K(u) = \frac{15}{16}(1 - u^2)I(|u| \leq 1)$ (see also Chapter 2). Here $I(\cdot)$ denotes the indicator function. In practice, one can also use the Gaussian density. To adjust the size of the neighborhood one introduces a *bandwidth* h such that for a scalar x the kernel function becomes

$$\frac{1}{h} K\left(\frac{x_t - x}{h}\right).$$

Thus, the larger h is chosen, the larger is the neighborhood around x, where sample observations receive a large weight and the larger may be the estimation bias. Because a larger h implies function estimates will look smoother, the bandwidth h is sometimes also called a *smoothing parameter*. Since the observations in the local neighborhood of x are the most important, this estimation approach is called *local estimation*.

If $m > 1$ and $x = (x_1, \ldots, x_m)'$ is a vector, one uses a *product kernel*

$$K_h(x_t - x) = \prod_{i=1}^{m} \frac{1}{h^m} K\left(\frac{x_{ti} - x_i}{h}\right).$$

Here x_{ti} denotes the ith component of x_t. Instead of using a scalar bandwidth that imposes the same degree of smoothing in all directions, it is also possible to use a vector bandwidth that determines the amount of smoothing in each direction separately. The latter option is further discussed, for example, in Yang & Tschernig (1999). In Section 7.2.2, we will see that quantities such as the kernel variance $\sigma_K^2 = \int u^2 K(u)du$ and the kernel constant $||K||_2^2 := \int K(u)^2 du$ influence the asymptotic behavior of the local linear estimator.

Owing to the introduction of a kernel function, one now has to solve a weighted least-squares problem

$$\{\hat{c}, \hat{c}_1, \ldots, \hat{c}_m\} =$$

$$\arg\min_{\{c, c_1, \ldots, c_m\}} \sum_{t=i_m+1}^{T} \left\{y_t - c - \sum_{i=1}^{m} c_i(x_{ti} - x_i)\right\}^2 K_h(x_t - x),$$

which delivers the local linear function estimate $\hat{\mu}(x, h) = \hat{c}$ at the point x. The bandwidth h is also included as an argument to indicate the dependence of the estimation result on the bandwidth. This estimator is described as being *local linear* because it is based on the first-order Taylor approximation (7.2). Since no parameters in the sense of parametric models are estimated, this estimation approach is called *nonparametric*. Note that estimating the function $\mu(\cdot)$ on the complete support of x would require infinitely many estimations. In practice, however, it is sufficient to estimate $\mu(\cdot)$ on a grid or just at specific values.

With the matrices

$$e = (1, 0_{1\times m})', \quad \mathbf{Z}(x) = \begin{pmatrix} 1 & \cdots & 1 \\ x_{i_m+1} - x & \cdots & x_T - x \end{pmatrix}',$$

$$W(x, h) = \text{diag}\,\{K_h(x_t - x)/T\}_{t=i_m+1}^T, \quad \mathbf{y} = \left(y_{i_m+1}, \ldots, y_T\right)',$$

the local linear function estimator can also be written as a generalized least-squares estimator

$$\widehat{\mu}(x, h) = e' \left\{\mathbf{Z}'(x)W(x, h)\mathbf{Z}(x)\right\}^{-1} \mathbf{Z}'(x)W(x, h)\mathbf{y}. \tag{7.3}$$

An even simpler local estimator is the *local constant function estimator*, better known as the *Nadaraya–Watson estimator*, which is derived from a zero-order Taylor approximation

$$\widehat{\mu}_{NW}(x, h) = \hat{c} = \arg\min_{\{c\}} \sum_{t=i_m+1}^T \{y_t - c\}^2 K_h(x_t - x).$$

The latter can also be written as

$$\widehat{\mu}_{NW}(x, h) = \left\{\mathbf{Z}'_{NW}W(x, h)\mathbf{Z}_{NW}\right\}^{-1}\mathbf{Z}'_{NW}W(x, h)\mathbf{y}$$

$$= \frac{\sum_{t=i_m+1}^T K_h(x_t - x)y_t}{\sum_{t=i_m+1}^T K_h(x_t - x)}, \tag{7.4}$$

where $\mathbf{Z}_{NW} = (1, \ldots, 1)'_{1\times(T-i_m)}$. The local linear estimator has preferable asymptotic properties, however (see Section 7.2.2).

The local constant and local linear estimators are the simplest cases of *local polynomial estimators*. Other local polynomial estimators are obtained by using higher-order Taylor expansions. In Section 7.3.1, a local quadratic estimator is used to estimate second-order partial derivatives of $\mu(\cdot)$.

To apply the local linear estimator (7.3), one has to decide on a value for the *bandwidth* h. If x_t is one- or two-dimensional, one may plot the estimated function on a grid for various values of h. Knowing that increasing the bandwidth potentially increases the estimation bias, whereas decreasing the bandwidth lowers the estimation variance, one then may choose a bandwidth that produces a smooth enough plot. Such a choice, however, is very subjective. A better method for bandwidth choice, which is based on statistical procedures, is presented in Section 7.3.1. A well-grounded bandwidth choice is also necessary for valid asymptotic properties of these estimators.

7.2.2 Asymptotic Properties

We first state the asymptotic distribution for the local linear estimator (7.3) and then discuss the required assumptions. Let $f(x)$ denote the density of the lag vector at the point x and tr(A) the trace of a matrix A. Then the *asymptotic normal distribution* of the local linear estimator (7.3) is given by

$$\sqrt{Th^m} \left\{ \widehat{\mu}(x, h) - \mu(x) - b(x)h^2 \right\} \overset{d}{\to} N\left(0, v(x)\right),\tag{7.5}$$

where the *asymptotic bias* $b(x)$ and *asymptotic variance* $v(x)$ are

$$b(x) = \frac{\sigma_K^2}{2} \operatorname{tr}\left(\frac{\partial^2 \mu(x)}{\partial x \, \partial x'} \right),\tag{7.6}$$

$$v(x) = \frac{\sigma^2(x) \|K\|_2^{2m}}{f(x)}.\tag{7.7}$$

From (7.5) it becomes clear that, for the asymptotic normal distribution to exist, one has to require $Th^m \to \infty$ and $h \to 0$ as $T \to \infty$. Otherwise, the asymptotic distribution would "collapse to a point" or the bias would grow infinitely large. Further assumptions are required.

Inspecting the asymptotic bias term (7.6) more closely reveals that the second-order partial derivatives of $\mu(x)$ have to exist. In fact, for (7.5) to hold this has to be the case in a neighborhood of x. For this reason one has to assume that $\mu(\cdot)$ is twice continuously differentiable on the support of $f(x)$. Because both the density $f(x)$ and the conditional variance $\sigma^2(x)$ enter the asymptotic variance (7.7), one also has to assume that both are continuous and the latter is positive on the support of $f(x)$.

Initially, the asymptotic distribution (7.5) was derived under the assumption that $\{y_t, x_t\}$ is a sample of iid observations. Then x_t does not contain lags of y_t and there is no stochastic dependence between observations at different times. In the current situation, where x_t is a vector of lagged y_ts, a stochastic dependence clearly exists. Note that autocorrelation measures the linear stochastic dependence within the y_ts. As in the case of linear autoregressive models, where one has to assume that the autocorrelations decrease fast enough if the distance between observations increases, for (7.5) to hold one has to guarantee that the stochastic dependence in general dies out quickly enough. In the present context it is not sufficient to consider only dependence measured by the first moments since the NAR process (7.1) is a nonlinear stochastic process, and thus higher moments of the process y_t matter as well. In the literature several measures exist for quantifying stochastic dependence. Härdle & Yang (1998) showed that the

asymptotic behavior of the local linear estimator (7.3) is the same as that encountered in the case of iid variables if the stochastic dependence is sufficiently
weak. At this point it is sufficient to state that a stationary linear ARMA(p, q)
process satisfies the required conditions if its driving error process is not completely ill-behaved [see Doukhan (1994, Theorem 6) and Yang & Tschernig
(2002, Theorem 2) for a precise statement]. For empirical work, it is most important to transform a given time series to be stationary. Thus, prior to local
linear estimation one has to remove unit roots (see Section 2.7 in Chapter 2 for
unit root testing).

Let us now discuss some implications of the asymptotic normal distribution
(7.5). Rewriting it in a somewhat sloppy way gives

$$\widehat{\mu}(x, h) \approx N\left(\mu(x) + b(x)h^2, \frac{1}{Th^m}v(x)\right), \tag{7.8}$$

which nicely shows the asymptotic bias-variance trade-off. If h gets larger, the
bias increases but the variance diminishes and vice versa. In Section 7.3.1,
this asymptotic trade-off will be used to obtain an asymptotically optimal bandwidth. Inspecting its formula given by (7.19) below shows that its rate of decline
is $T^{-1/(m+4)}$. Thus, if we denote a positive constant by β, any bandwidth for
which $h = \beta T^{-1/(m+4)}$ holds has the optimal rate to guarantee a balanced decline of bias and variance. Inserting $h = \beta T^{-1/(m+4)}$ into (7.5) delivers the
rate of convergence of the local linear estimator with respect to the number of
observations T, that is,

$$T^{2/(4+m)}\{\widehat{\mu}(x, h) - \mu(x)\} \xrightarrow{d} N\left(b(x)\beta^2, \frac{1}{\beta^m}v(x)\right). \tag{7.9}$$

It becomes apparent that the rate of convergence of the local linear estimator
depends on the number m of lags and becomes quite slow if there are many
lags. This is frequently called the "*curse of dimensionality*" of nonparametric
estimators. Note that the rate of convergence is slower than for parametric
estimators even if $m = 1$. This is the price one pays in non-parametric estimation
for allowing the model complexity to increase with the number of observations
and thus to let the bias reduce with sample size. Such an increase in model
complexity is in general not possible if one wants to obtain the parametric
$\sqrt{T}$-rate.

By inspecting (7.6), one can see that the estimation bias also depends on the
second partial derivatives of the conditional mean function as well as on the
kernel variance σ_K^2. The asymptotic variance (7.7) increases with the conditional
variance $\sigma^2(x)$ and decreases with the density $f(x)$. The intuition for the latter
is that the larger the density, the more observations are on average close to the
point x and are thus available for local estimation, which in turn reduces the
estimation variance. The bias term $b(x)$ can be estimated using (7.23) in Section
7.3.1. The estimation of $v(x)$ requires estimating the density $f(x)$, for example,

by (7.44) in the appendix to this chapter and the conditional variance $\sigma^2(x)$ by one of the nonparametric estimators presented in Section 7.5.1.

The asymptotic distribution of the Nadaraya–Watson estimator (7.4) has been derived under various conditions [see, e.g., the survey of Härdle, Lütkepohl & Chen (1997)]. One also obtains asymptotic normality, but the asymptotic bias term $b(x)$ in (7.5) has to be replaced by

$$b_{NW}(x) = b(x) + \sigma_K^2 \frac{\partial f(x)}{\partial x'} \frac{\partial \mu(x)}{\partial x} \Big/ f(x). \tag{7.10}$$

Thus, the asymptotic bias of the Nadaraya–Watson estimator includes a further term that contains the first partial derivatives of the density $f(x)$ and of the conditional mean function $\mu(x)$. Its bias is therefore not design-adaptive since the bias depends on the density at x.

7.2.3 Confidence Intervals

From the asymptotic distribution (7.8), one can also derive an asymptotic $(1 - \alpha)$-percent *confidence interval* for $\mu(x)$,

$$\left[\widehat{\mu}(x, h) - b(x)h^2 - z_{\alpha/2}\sqrt{\frac{v(x)}{Th^m}}, \ \widehat{\mu}(x, h) - b(x)h^2 + z_{\alpha/2}\sqrt{\frac{v(x)}{Th^m}} \right],$$

where $z_{\alpha/2}$ denotes the $(1 - \alpha/2)$ quantile of the normal distribution. Note first that the length as well as the location of the confidence interval depends on the chosen bandwidth h. Second, the asymptotic bias $b(x)$ and the asymptotic variance $v(x)$ have to be consistently estimated, for example, by the methods discussed in Section 7.3.1. As will be seen there, a consistent bias estimate requires the estimation of second-order partial derivatives. Such estimates can be prone to a large variance, particularly if m is large and the sample size is small. Thus, it may make sense to compute confidence intervals without the bias correction $b(x)h^2$ as follows:

$$\left[\widehat{\mu}(x, h) - z_{\alpha/2}\sqrt{\frac{v(x)}{Th^m}}, \ \widehat{\mu}(x, h) + z_{\alpha/2}\sqrt{\frac{v(x)}{Th^m}} \right]. \tag{7.11}$$

It should be noted that if the stochastic process (7.1) is homoskedastic, one has $\sigma(x) = \sigma$ and $v(x)$ given by (7.7) facilitates to $\sigma^2 \|K\|_2^{2m}/f(x)$. In Section 7.5 we will discuss how to estimate $\sigma(x)$ and σ. The density $f(x)$ can be estimated by (7.44) in the appendix to this chapter.

Often one is not only interested in the confidence interval for the function value at a single x but for the function itself. If it is sufficient, to consider confidence intervals jointly for a finite number J of grid points $\{x^{(1)}, x^{(2)}, \ldots, x^{(J)}\}$, then one can use *Bonferroni* confidence intervals (see the appendix for their derivation). In this case, the length of the confidence intervals depends on the number of grid points J. If a confidence set not only for a finite number of points of the function but for the function itself is needed, one has to estimate confidence bands [see Neumann & Polzehl (1998) for their derivation and estimation in case of nonlinear autoregressive processes (7.1)].

7.2.4 Plotting the Estimated Function

In general, one is not only interested in the function value $\mu(x)$ at one particular regression point x but in the behavior of the function on important parts of its domain. In this case, one may compute and plot the function on a grid of points $\{x^{(1)}, \ldots, x^{(J)}\}$. If x is scalar, the J grid points are equidistantly chosen on the interval $[\min_t x_t, \max_t x_t]$.

For a two-dimensional regressor vector x, J^2 grid points are used with J equidistant points in direction i covering the interval $[\min_t x_{ti}, \max_t x_{ti}]$. Because this grid is rectangular, the function $\mu(\cdot)$ may also be computed at points outside the data range. Such estimates exhibit a large estimation variance since the density $f(\cdot)$ at such points is very small and thus, by (7.7), the asymptotic estimation variance $v(x)$ is likely to be much larger than within the data range. Therefore, all function estimates at points outside the data range should be suppressed from a function plot.

For an illustration, consider the time series of seasonally adjusted, quarterly German consumption for the period $1960Q1$–$1982Q4$. In later sections this example will be picked up again to illustrate other aspects of the nonparametric modeling procedure. This data set was already analyzed in Section 2.9 of Chapter 2 using linear models. There it was found that a linear autoregressive model with lags 2 and 3 describes the first differences of the logged data well. Using the same lags and using the plug-in bandwidth (7.24) derived in Section 7.3.1, Figure 7.1(a) shows the local linear estimates of $\mu(\cdot)$ on the described grid with $J = 30$.

Inspecting the plot suggests that there are a few observations that are somewhat outside the main data range. If this is the case, then such data points can be expected to have a small density just like points that are completely outside the data range. One therefore may wish to exclude such points from the plot as well. Therefore, it may be useful to remove all function estimates from the plot at points for which the estimated density $\widehat{f}(x, h)$ is in the β-percent quantile of lowest density values. If the plot is redrawn using $\beta = 0.1$, one obtains the plot in Figure 7.1(b). Note that for the latter plot the data were standardized with standard deviation 0.0110, and thus the labeling of the axes is useful. Now the function plot has become easier to evaluate. Overall, the function looks quite linear although, some curvature is still visible.

One quick way to explore the statistical relevance of the nonlinearity is to plot Bonferroni confidence intervals given by (7.11) and (7.43) in the appendix of this chapter. Since plotting three surfaces into one graph is not very instructive,

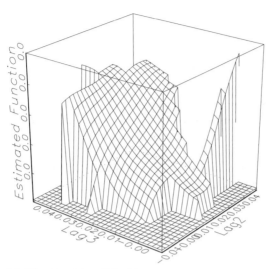

(a) All grid points within data range

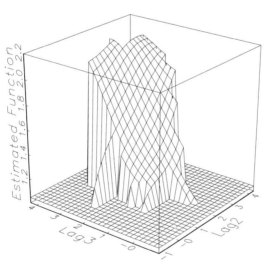

(b) All grid points for which the estimated density is within the 10%-quantile are removed and the data are standardized with standard deviation 0.0110

Figure 7.1. Plot of the estimated conditional mean function of the growth rate of the seasonally adjusted, quarterly German consumption.

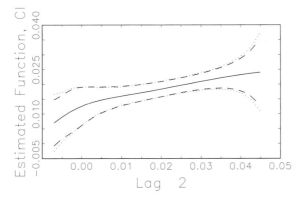

Figure 7.2. Plot of Bonferroni confidence intervals (CI) with 95% confidence level around the estimated conditional mean function of the growth rate of the seasonally adjusted, quarterly German consumption with the third lag set to the estimated mean. (Dashed lines are based on conditionally heteroskedastic errors, and dotted lines are based on homoskedastic errors; 10% of the observations with the lowest density are removed.)

one may plot confidence intervals by letting the grid vary only in direction i and keeping the other directions fixed. With x_3 set to the estimated mean, the estimated Bonferroni confidence intervals for $\mu(x_2^{(1)}, x_3), \ldots, \mu(x_2^{(J)}, x_3)$ of the German consumption are shown in Figure 7.2. The figure contains two confidence intervals with 95% confidence level. The dashed lines are based on the estimated conditional volatility $\sigma(x)$, whereas the dotted lines are obtained under the assumption of a homoskedastic process. All estimates for which the density estimate is within the 10%-quantile are removed. Both confidence intervals do not indicate any significant nonlinearity because one can imagine replacing the nonlinear function estimates by a straight line without touching the boundaries of the confidence intervals. Repeating this exercise for other values of x_3 does not lead to different results nor does switching the role of lag 2 and lag 3.

Keep in mind that this procedure cannot replace a nonlinearity test. It can, however, help to determine regions where nonlinearities are important. Nonparametric nonlinearity tests have been developed, for example, by Hjellvik, Yao & Tjøstheim (1998) or Lee & Ullah (2001). As an alternative one can use the parametric nonlinearity tests developed by Eitrheim & Teräsvirta (1996) (see Chapter 6). Another possibility for checking the importance of estimated nonlinearities is to conduct rolling-over, out-of-sample forecasts. They are described in Section 7.4.

Of course, the function graph cannot be plotted if there are more than two lags. However, it is then still possible to graph the function if the grid is taken in two user-specified directions with the value of x in the remaining directions kept fixed. When interpreting such plots, one has to bear in mind that changing the conditioning values also changes the plot. Thus, the absence of nonlinearity for several conditioning values does not rule out nonlinearity in other data regions. For an example with more than two lags, see Section 7.7.

7.2.5 Forecasting

It is easy to obtain a *nonparametric, one-period-ahead forecast* for a time series. One need only estimate $\mu(x_{T+1})$ local linearly. By following a procedure similar to that used to compute a confidence interval for the function estimate, one can compute a *prediction interval*. In the confidence intervals (7.11), one simply replaces the standard deviation of estimation $\sqrt{v(x)/(Th^m)}$ by the standard deviation of prediction $\sqrt{\sigma^2(x) + v(x)/(Th^m)}$.

In practice, one is often interested in h-step ahead forecasts. Such forecasts can be obtained by setting the first lag i_1 to h. Then it is possible to construct $x_{T+h} = (y_{T+h-i_1}, \ldots, y_{T+h-i_m})$, where the first component is just y_T. For a detailed discussion of such h-step-ahead forecasts, see Tschernig & Yang (2000a).

We now turn to nonparametric methods for the estimation of the bandwidth h and the relevant lags $i_1, \ldots, i_m$.

7.3 Bandwidth and Lag Selection

The methods for nonparametric bandwidth and lag selection described in the following are mainly based on Tschernig & Yang (2000b). For lag selection it is necessary to specify a set of possible lag vectors a priori by choosing the maximal lag M. Denote the full lag vector containing all lags up to M by $x_{t,M} = (y_{t-1}, y_{t-2}, \ldots, y_{t-M})'$. The lag selection task is now to eliminate from the full lag vector $x_{t,M}$ all lags that are redundant.

For both bandwidth estimation and lag selection, it is first necessary to choose an optimality criterion. A widely used criterion is the mean-integrated squared error of prediction, which is commonly known as the *final prediction error* (FPE) (see also Chapter 2). Here we state it by using a weight function $w(\cdot)$ needed for obtaining consistency of the lag selection procedure. One has to choose a weight function $w(\cdot)$ that is continuous and nonnegative and for which $f(x_M) > 0$ for x_M in the support of $w(\cdot)$. The weight function must further have a compact support with nonempty interior. The simplest example is the indicator function being 1 on a specified set. To state the FPE for an arbitrary set of lags, lag indices and other quantities that may differ from the correct ones are indexed with a "+". For a given bandwidth h and lag vector $i_1^+, \ldots, i_{m+}^+$, the FPE is given by

$$FPE(h, i_1^+, \ldots, i_{m^+}^+) = \mathsf{E}\left(\left(\breve{y}_t - \widehat{\mu}(\breve{x}_t^+, h)\right)^2 w(\breve{x}_{t,M})\right)$$

$$= \int \left[\int \left(\breve{y} - \widehat{\mu}(\breve{x}^+, h)\right)^2 w(\breve{x}_M) f(\breve{y}, \breve{x}_M) d\breve{y} d\breve{x}_M\right]$$

$$\times f(y_1, \ldots, y_T) dy_1 \cdots dy_T. \tag{7.12}$$

Here, the stochastic process $\{\breve{y}_t\}$ is assumed to be independent of the process $\{y_t\}$ but to have the same stochastic properties. Note that the outer integral averages over all possible realizations of the estimator $\widehat{\mu}(\breve{x}^+, h)$, which vary for a given $\breve{x}^+$, and bandwidth h with the sample realizations $y_1, \ldots, y_T$.

Were the $FPE(h, i_1^+, \ldots, i_{m^+}^+)$ observable for all lag vectors under consideration, $i_1^+, \ldots, i_{m^+}^+$, $m^+ = 0, 1, \ldots, M$, then one would clearly select the lag vector and bandwidth minimizing the FPE across all lag combinations considered.

Because the $FPE(h, i_1^+, \ldots, i_{m^+}^+)$ is not observable, it has to be estimated. In the literature, mainly two approaches have been suggested for estimating the unknown $FPE(\cdot)$ or variants thereof, namely, cross validation [Vieu (1994), Yao & Tong (1994)] or the estimation of an asymptotic expression of the $FPE(\cdot)$ [Auestad & Tjøstheim (1990), Tjøstheim & Auestad (1994), Tschernig & Yong (2000)].

In addition to the previously stated assumptions, one has to assume that the errors ξ_t, $t \geq i_m + 1$ have a finite fourth moment m_4. This assumption is needed to guarantee that the variance of estimators of the $FPE(\cdot)$ is bounded. This assumption also must be made for standard lag selection in linear models.

Under the stated assumptions, Tschernig & Yang (2000b, Theorem 2.1) have shown that, for the local linear estimator (7.3) and the correct lag vector $i_1, \ldots, i_m$, one obtains

$$FPE(h, i_1, \ldots, i_m) =$$
$$AFPE(h, i_1, \ldots, i_m) + o\left(h^4 + (T - i_m)^{-1}h^{-m}\right), \tag{7.13}$$

where the three terms of the *asymptotic final prediction error* (AFPE)

$$AFPE(h, i_1, \ldots, i_m) = A + b(h)B + c(h)C \tag{7.14}$$

are the integrated variance, the integrated variance of estimation, and the integrated squared bias of estimation with the (unknown) constants

$$A = \int \sigma^2(x) w(x_M) f(x_M) dx_M = \mathsf{E}\left(\sigma^2(x_t) w(x_{t,M})\right), \tag{7.15}$$

$$B = \int \sigma^2(x) w(x_M) f(x_M) / f(x) dx_M = \mathsf{E}\left(\sigma^2(x_t) \frac{w(x_{t,M})}{f(x_t)}\right), \tag{7.16}$$

$$C = \int \left(\text{tr} \left\{ \frac{\partial^2 \mu(x)}{\partial x \partial x'} \right\} \right)^2 w(x_M) f(x_M) dx_M$$

$$= \mathsf{E} \left(\left(\text{tr} \left\{ \frac{\partial^2 \mu(x_t)}{\partial x_t \partial x_t'} \right\} \right)^2 w(x_{t,M}) \right) \tag{7.17}$$

and

$$b(h) = ||K||_2^{2m} (T - i_m)^{-1} h^{-m}, \quad c(h) = \sigma_K^4 h^4 / 4, \tag{7.18}$$

where the last two terms depend on the bandwidth and kernel constants. Note that one can interpret A also as the FPE of the true function $\mu(\cdot)$. Further note that the integrated variance of estimation and the integrated squared bias of estimation go to 0 for increasing sample size if $h \to 0$ and $Th^m \to \infty$ as $T \to \infty$ holds.

Inspecting B more closely reveals why the definition of the FPE (7.12) includes a weight function. Without a weight function with compact support, one would have in the case of a homoskedastic process, $\sigma(x) = \sigma$, an integral $\sigma^2 \int dx$ that is unbounded and thus an infinite B.

The first-order asymptotic expansion of the FPE given by (7.13) to (7.18) has to be slightly modified if a lag vector different from the correct one is chosen. Consider first the case in which all correct lags are included plus some additional ones and index all corresponding variables with a $+$ as before. The modified FPE expansion is then obtained by replacing m by m^+, i_m by $i_{m^+}^+$, x by x^+, and h by h^+ in equations (7.13) to (7.18) [Tschernig & Yang (2000b, Theorem 3.3)].

Now consider the case in which not all correct lags are included in the chosen lag vector and all correct variables are relevant in the range of the weight function that specifies the range of interest. The latter condition rules out a situation where, for example, lag 1 enters the function $\mu(\cdot)$ only outside the range of interest. If a relevant lag in the chosen lag vector is left out and underfitting occurs, then the $AFPE(\cdot)$ of the underfitting and the correct model differ by a constant independent of the bandwidth and sample size [Tschernig & Yang (2000b, Theorem 3.4)].

Next we show how to use (7.14) for bandwidth estimation.

7.3.1 Bandwidth Estimation

From minimizing the AFPE (7.14) with respect to h, that is, by solving the variance-bias trade-off between $b(h)B$ and $c(h)C$, one obtains the *asymptotically optimal bandwidth*

$$h_{\text{opt}} = \left\{ \frac{m ||K||_2^{2m} B}{(T - i_m) \sigma_K^4 C} \right\}^{1/(m+4)}. \tag{7.19}$$

Note that, in order for the asymptotically optimal bandwidth to be finite, one has to assume that C defined in (7.17) is positive and finite. This requirement implies that, in case of local linear estimation, an asymptotically optimal bandwidth h_{opt} for linear processes that is finite does not exist. This is because a first-order approximation bias does not exist, and thus a larger bandwidth has no cost. Clearly, in this case one should take a bandwidth as large as possible.

It should be noted that h_{opt} is asymptotically optimal on the range where the weight function $w(\cdot)$ is positive. For this reason it is also called the *global* asymptotically optimal bandwidth. Starting from the mean-squared error of prediction,

$$\int \left[\int (\check{y} - \widehat{\mu}(x, h))^2 \, f(\check{y}|x) d\check{y} \right] f(y_1, \dots, y_T) dy_1 \cdots dy_T,$$

which is computed at a given x, one would obtain a *local* asymptotically optimal bandwidth, which, by construction, may vary with x.

If h_{opt} is estimated by using consistent estimators for the unknown constants B and C defined by (7.16) and (7.17), the resulting bandwidth estimate is known as a plug-in bandwidth $\widehat{h}_{\text{opt}}$. One way to estimate the expected value B consistently is given by averaging the weighted squared errors from the local linear estimates

$$\widehat{B}(h_B) = \frac{1}{T - i_m} \sum_{t=i_m+1}^{T} \{y_t - \widehat{\mu}(x_t, h_B)\}^2 \, w(x_{t,M})/\widehat{f}(x_t, h_B), \quad (7.20)$$

where $\widehat{f}(\cdot)$ is the Gaussian kernel estimator (7.44) of the density $f(x)$. For estimating h_B, one may use Silverman's rule-of-thumb bandwidth [Silverman (1986)]

$$\widehat{h}_B = \widehat{\sigma} \left(\frac{4}{m+2} \right)^{1/(m+4)} T^{-1/(m+4)} \tag{7.21}$$

with $\widehat{\sigma} = \left(\prod_{i=1}^{m} \sqrt{\text{Var}(x_{ti})} \right)^{1/m}$ denoting the geometric mean of the standard deviation of the regressors.

An estimator of C is given by

$$\widehat{C}(h_C) = \frac{1}{T - i_m} \sum_{t=i_m+1}^{T} \left[\sum_{j=1}^{m} \widehat{\mu}^{(jj)}(x_t, h_C) \right]^2 w(x_{t,M}), \tag{7.22}$$

where $\mu^{(jj)}(\cdot)$ denotes the second-order direct derivative of the function $\mu(\cdot)$ with respect to x_{tj}. For estimating higher-order derivatives, one can use local polynomial estimation of appropriate order. For the current problem of estimating second-order direct derivatives it is sufficient to use the *direct local quadratic estimator*

$$\{\widehat{c}_0, \widehat{c}_{11}, \dots, \widehat{c}_{1m}, \widehat{c}_{21}, \dots, \widehat{c}_{2m}\} = \arg\min_{\{c_0, c_{11}, \dots, c_{1m}, c_{21}, \dots, c_{2m}\}}$$

$$\sum_{t=i_m+1}^{T} \{y_t - c_0 - c_{11}(x_{t1} - x_1) - \dots - c_{1m}(x_{tm} - x_m) \quad (7.23)$$

$$-c_{21}(x_{t1} - x_1)^2 - \dots - c_{2m}(x_{tm} - x_m)^2\}^2 K_h(x_t - x).$$

The estimates of the direct second derivatives are then given by $\widehat{\mu}^{(jj)}(x, h) = 2\widehat{c}_{2j}$, $j = 1, \dots, m$. Excluding all cross terms does not affect the convergence rate while keeping the increase in the "parameters" $c_0, c_{1j}, c_{2j}, j = 1, \dots, m$ linear in the number of lags m. This approach is a simplification of the partial cubic estimator proposed by Yang & Tschernig (1999), who also showed that the rule-of-thumb bandwidth

$$\widehat{h}_C = 2\widehat{\sigma} \left(\frac{4}{m+4} \right)^{1/(m+6)} T^{-1/(m+6)}$$

has the optimal rate.

The *plug-in bandwidth* $\widehat{h}_{\text{opt}}$ is then given by

$$\widehat{h}_{\text{opt}} = \left\{ \frac{m\|K\|_2^{2m} \widehat{B}(\widehat{h}_B)}{(T - i_m)\widehat{C}(\widehat{h}_C)\sigma_K^4} \right\}^{1/(m+4)}. \quad (7.24)$$

Inserting (7.24) into (7.14) shows that the minimal AFPE for the correct lag vector is given by

$$AFPE_{\text{opt}} = A + k(m, \|K\|_2^2, B, C, \sigma_K)(T - i_m)^{4/(4+m)}, \quad (7.25)$$

where the interested reader can find the specification of $k(m, \|K\|_2^2, B, C, \sigma_K)$ in Tschernig & Yang (2000b, Corollary 2.1). This shows how the convergence rate of the minimal AFPE towards A depends on the number of lags m. The larger m, the slower the convergence.

7.3.2 Lag Selection

Since the $FPE(\cdot)$s are not available for lag selection, the $AFPE(\cdot)$s are used instead. In addition to the estimation of B and C discussed in Section 7.3.1, this requires estimating the integrated variance A given by (7.15) by taking the sample average

$$\widehat{A}(h) = (T - i_m)^{-1} \sum_{t=i_m+1}^{T} \{y_t - \widehat{\mu}(x_t, h)\}^2 w(x_{t,M}) \quad (7.26)$$

of the squared estimated residuals of the local linear estimates $\widehat{\mu}(x_t, h)$. From Section 7.2.2 it is known that local linear estimates are biased. This carries over to the estimator $\widehat{A}(h)$. For estimating the AFPE (7.14), the term A is the most important one because it does not vanish with increasing sample size. It is therefore useful to take its estimation bias into account when replacing A by $\widehat{A}(h)$ in (7.14). In fact, under the stated assumptions the asymptotic behavior of $\widehat{A}(h)$ is given by [Tschernig & Yang (2000b, Theorem 3.1)]

$$\widehat{A}(h) = AFPE(h) - 2K(0)^m (T - i_m)^{-1} h^{-m} B \tag{7.27}$$
$$+ o\left(h^4 + (T - i_m)^{-1} h^{-m}\right) + O_p\left((T - i_m)^{-1/2}\right).$$

Rearranging (7.27) and computing at h_{opt} immediately delivers an estimator for the AFPE

$$AFPE = \widehat{A}(h_{\text{opt}}) + 2K(0)^m (T - i_m)^{-1} h_{\text{opt}}^{-m} \widehat{B}(h_B). \tag{7.28}$$

In practice, the asymptotically optimal bandwidth h_{opt} is replaced by the plug-in bandwidth (7.24), and h_B is estimated by (7.21). Note that one can interpret the second term in (7.28) as a penalty term to punish overfitting or choosing superfluous lags. This penalty term decreases with sample size because h_{opt} is of order $T^{-1/(m+4)}$. Under some additional smoothness assumptions that allow the estimation of the plug-in bandwidth, the minimal AFPE (7.25) remains valid for (7.28).

Note that inserting (7.14) into (7.27) reveals that the estimate of the integrated variance A has a bias of order $h^4 + (T - i_m)^{-1} h^{-m}$. This bias can be eliminated by estimating the relevant bias terms. If the plug-in bandwidth has been calculated, this is easily possible since then estimates for B and C are available. The asymptotically unbiased estimated $\widehat{A}_{\text{ub}}(\widehat{h}_{\text{opt}})$ of the integrated variance A is given by

$$\widehat{A}_{\text{ub}}(\widehat{h}_{\text{opt}}) = \widehat{A}(\widehat{h}_{\text{opt}}) - \left\{ b(\widehat{h}_{\text{opt}}) - 2K(0)^m (T - i_m)^{-1} \widehat{h}_{\text{opt}}^{-m} \right\} \widehat{B}(\widehat{h}_B)$$
$$- c(\widehat{h}_{\text{opt}}) \widehat{C}(\widehat{h}_C). \tag{7.29}$$

It is worth pointing out that, in case of a homoskedastic process, one has $A = \sigma^2 E(u(x_{t,M}))$ from (7.15). If $w(\cdot)$ is chosen to be the indicator function and its support is such that integrating the density over that support delivers almost 1, $A \approx \sigma^2$ results. In practice, this allows (7.29) to be used to estimate σ^2 if the process is homoskedastic and the support of the weight function is taken to be larger than the data sample.

To select the adequate lag vector, one replaces m by m^+ in (7.28) and computes it for all possible lag combinations with $m^+ \leq M$ and then chooses the lag vector with the smallest AFPE. Under the stated assumptions and a further technical condition, Tschernig & Yang (2000b, Theorem 3.2) showed that this procedure is *weakly consistent*, that is, the probability of choosing the correct lag vector, if it is included in the set of lags considered, approaches 1 with increasing sample size.

This consistency result may look surprising since the linear FPE is known to be inconsistent. However, in case of lag vectors that include in addition to the m correct lags l superfluous lags, the convergence rate of the optimal bandwidth becomes $(T - i_{m+l}^{+})^{-1/(m+l+4)}$, and thus the rate of the penalty term in (7.28) turns to $(T - i_{m+l}^{+})^{-4/(m+l+4)}$, which is slower than that for the correct lag vector. This implies that models that are too large are ruled out asymptotically. Note that this feature is intrinsic to the local estimation approach since the number of lags influences the rate of convergence (see (7.9)).

We remark that the consistency result breaks down if $C = 0$, that is, if $\mu(\cdot)$ is a linear function. In this case, overfitting (including superfluous lags in addition to the correct ones) is more likely. The breakdown of consistency can be avoided by using the Nadaraya–Watson instead of the local linear estimator because the former will also be biased in case of linear processes. In this instance the bias term (7.10) also includes the first partial derivatives of the design density, which makes the estimation of the plug-in bandwidth more difficult.

Note that the asymptotic properties of the lag selection method also rely on the argument that the weight function $w(\cdot)$ is the full lag vector $x_{t,M}$. In practice, however, one can choose $w(\cdot)$ to be the indicator function on the range of the observed data.

In Tschernig & Yang (2000b) it is also shown that it is asymptotically more likely to overfit than to underfit (miss some correct lags). To reduce overfitting and therefore increase correct fitting, they suggest correcting the AFPE and estimating the *corrected asymptotic final prediction error* (CAFPE):

$$CAFPE = AFPE \left\{ 1 + m(T - i_m)^{-4/(m+4)} \right\}. \tag{7.30}$$

The correction does not affect consistency under the stated assumptions, whereas additional lags are punished more heavily in finite samples. One chooses the lag vector with the smallest CAFPE. Both lag selection criteria, AFPE and CAFPE are available in JMulTi. However, Monte Carlo simulations conducted in the cited paper clearly suggest using CAFPE in practice since AFPE is found to be strongly overfitting.

We note that, for weak consistency it is not necessary to use the same number of start values and number of observations $T - M$ for all lag vectors. Instead, one can also use as many observations as possible and use only i_{m+}^{+} start values for lag vector $\{i^{+}, \dots, i_{m+}^{+}\}$. To keep comparability with the linear lag selection procedures we recommend, however, always using M start values.

If the number of total lags M and the sample size T are large, then a full search through all lag combinations may take too long. In this case, one can do a directed search, as suggested by Tjøstheim & Auestad (1994). Lags are added as long as they reduce the selection criterion, and one adds the lag from the remaining ones that delivers the largest reduction. In the light of the terminology of Section 3.4.5, this procedure may also be called sequential adding of regressors.

To exploit available sample information as well as possible and to exclude boundary effects from the estimations, some robustification measures may be used, which are reported in the appendix to this chapter.

7.3.3 Illustration

Section 7.2.4 explained the use of local linear estimation techniques to estimate the autoregression function of the growth rate of the seasonally adjusted, quarterly German consumption for the period $1960Q2$–$1982Q4$. There we used the lags obtained in Section 2.9 of Chapter 2 with a linear lag selection procedure. Now we conduct a nonparametric lag selection using the CAFPE criterion (7.30), doing a full search up to lag $M = 8$ and always using M start values. Table 7.1 shows the lag vectors that exhibit a minimal CAFPE for each number $m^+ = 0, 1, \ldots, M$ of lags. The overall minimal CAFPE is obtained for two lags containing lags 2 and 3. This result corresponds to the selected lags based on linear models. The table also shows that the largest reduction in the lag selection criterion is obtained by selecting lag 2.

If instead of a full search a directed (or sequential) search is carried out, the selected lags corresponding up to a total of three lags remain unchanged and thus also the optimal lags. The single lag 8 is selected if for each lag vector $i_{m^+}^+$ start values are used. If the total number of lags and the start values are set to $M = 5$, lags 1 and 3 are selected. Thus, the number of start values available for estimating each lag vector can matter – particularly in small samples.

When conducting nonparametric lag selection, keep in mind that, as shown in Section 7.3.2, lag selection based on the (C)AFPE criterion and local linear estimation is not consistent if the underlying data generating process is linear, that is, if $C = 0$. In this case, there is a positive probability of choosing additional lags in addition to the correct ones. To check whether some lags are possibly

Table 7.1. *Lag selection for the growth rate of the seasonally adjusted, quarterly German consumption*

No. of selected lags	Selected lag vector	CAFPE (10^{-3})	Plug-in bandwidth
0	—	0.120	—
1	2	0.108	0.0074
2	2, 3	0.106	0.011
3	2, 3, 5	0.114	0.011
4	1, 2, 3, 8	0.135	0.0093
5	1, 2, 4, 7, 8	0.332	0.0098
6	1, 2, 3, 5, 7, 8	0.782	0.012
7	1, 2, 3, 5, 6, 7, 8	2.26	0.014
8	1, 2, 3, 4, 5, 6, 7, 8	6.09	0.016

due to overfitting, compare the result of nonparametric lag selection with the results for linear lag selection criteria such as the FPE, AIC, HQ, or SC (see Chapter 2).

For the current example, the SC criterion also selects lags 2 and 3 if M start values are used and M is either 5 or 8. However, in case of different start values, the optimal lag vector contains in addition lag 6. This illustrates that the issue of start values matters independently of the method chosen.

7.4 Diagnostics

As in parametric time series modeling, one has to check whether the model is correctly specified in the sense that there is no relevant structure left in the residuals. For testing residuals resulting from local polynomial estimation, there are no simple tests with known asymptotic distributions as there are for the residuals of many parametric models. However, one can still use some of these tests as an explorative device. For example, the Portmanteau test for residual autocorrelation, the LM test for residual autocorrelation in linear AR models also known as the Godfrey (1988) test, the ARCH–LM test, and the Lomnicki–Jarque–Bera test for nonnormality may be used. Conducting the Godfrey (1988) test that explicitly allows for nonlinear autoregression functions (see Section 6.3.3 for its implementation for parametric nonlinear models) is more difficult within the nonparametric framework because it additionally requires nonparametric estimation of the first-order partial derivatives. It is also possible to estimate the spectrum and the density of the residuals (see Section 2.6 of Chapter 2 for details on these tests and estimators). One just has to keep in mind that the asymptotic properties stated there may not hold if the residuals are obtained from local estimation. These diagnostics may nevertheless indicate possible misspecification owing to neglected autocorrelation or heteroskedasticity. It can also be useful to plot the autocorrelation function of the residuals.

If there is some indication of autocorrelation at certain lags, the largest lag M in the lag search may be increased beyond the lag for which the residual autocorrelation appears significant and the lag selection redone. If M was already chosen large enough, one may simply sequentially add the indicated lags and reestimate the model. Alternatively, lags suggested by linear lag selection criteria may be added. Such an extended model may not, however, provide better overall results because higher-order dependence with respect to the initially selected lags is more important than weak autocorrelation at larger lags (see Section 7.7 for an empirical example of this situation).

A further possibility for checking the adequacy of a chosen lag vector is to conduct *rolling-over, one-step-ahead forecasts*. This is done by splitting the data set in a sample for estimation that contains the first T' values and taking the remaining $T - T'$ values for out-of-sample forecasting. The first forecast is computed for $y_{T'+1}$ based on all observations available up to time T'. In the next step, one forecasts $y_{T'+2}$ based on the sample $\{y_1, \ldots, y_{T'+1}\}$. This procedure is iterated until $T - 1$ observations are used and y_T is forecasted. The rolling-over, one-step-ahead prediction error is then computed as follows:

$$PE = \frac{1}{T - T'} \sum_{j=T'+1}^{T} (\widehat{y}_j - y_j)^2. \qquad (7.31)$$

Three modes are supported in JMulTi for forecasting the $\widehat{y}_j$'s in (7.31). In the first mode, all forecasts are computed by using a user-specified lag vector. In the second mode, a CAFPE-based lag selection is conducted on the basis of the initial estimation sample up to time T', and then this selected lag vector is maintained for all remaining periods. In the third mode, a lag selection is carried out for each forecast. The latter mode can be computationally very demanding if the sample size is large, a full search is conducted for each lag selection, or both.

Conducting all diagnostics for the residuals of the local linear model fitted in Section 7.2.4 to the growth rates of German consumption did not reveal any misspecification. The rolling-over, one-step-ahead forecasts of the last 19 observations delivered a prediction error of $1.780 \cdot 10^{-4}$, where lags 2, 3, and 8 were selected before the first forecast. In comparison, the AIC selected lags 2, 3, and 6, and the selected linear autoregressive model produced a prediction error of $1.412 \cdot 10^{-4}$. Thus, the linear model predicts better than the nonparametric model. This underlines the conjecture of Section 7.2.4 about the linearity of the data-generating process. It is interesting to note that the prediction error of the linear autoregressive model is still larger than the variance of the true values, which is $1.266 \cdot 10^{-4}$. This remains true if the SC or HQ lag selection criteria are used. The p-values of the ARCH–LM test of the null hypothesis of homoskedasticity are above 0.65 for four and eight lags. Thus, there is no evidence for ARCH-type heteroskedasticity.

7.5 Modeling the Conditional Volatility

Since we allow the nonlinear autoregressive process (7.1) to be conditionally heteroskedastic, computing confidence intervals (7.11) requires estimating the conditional volatility function $\sigma(x)$ because the latter enters the asymptotic variance (7.7) of the local linear estimator of $\mu(x)$.

Estimating the conditional volatility $\sigma(x)$ is also one of the basic tasks in modeling financial time series. We therefore discuss how the tools presented in the previous sections can be modified appropriately for the estimation of $\sigma(x)$. Then, we discuss how to select an appropriate bandwidth. Because, in the present setting it is permissible for the lag vector of $\sigma(\cdot)$ to be a subvector of $\mu(\cdot)$, we discuss lag selection as well. Finally, we investigate under which conditions a NAR process is a generalization of an ARCH(q) process.

7.5.1 Estimation

In case of conditionally homoskecastic errors, $\sigma^2(x_t) = \sigma^2$. As mentioned in Section 7.3.2, σ^2 can be estimated by (7.29) and may then be used to compute confidence intervals under the assumption of homoskedastic errors.

To derive local estimators of the conditional volatility, assume for the moment that the conditional mean function $\mu(\cdot)$ is known. Defining $\varepsilon_t = y_t - \mu(x_t)$, one can rewrite the NAR process (7.1) as $\varepsilon_t = \sigma(x_t)\xi_t$. Squaring both sides and adding and subtracting $\sigma^2(x_t)$ yield

$$\varepsilon_t^2 = \sigma^2(x_t) + \sigma^2(x_t)\left(\xi_t^2 - 1\right)$$
$$= \sigma^2(x_t) + u_t, \quad t = i_m + 1, \ldots, \tag{7.32}$$

where we define $u_t = \sigma^2(x_t)\left(\xi_t^2 - 1\right)$. It can be shown that

$$\mathsf{E}(u_t u_s) = \begin{cases} \sigma_u^2 & \text{if } t = s, \\ 0 & \text{otherwise.} \end{cases}$$

Thus, the process $\{u_t\}$ is a white noise process. Note, however, that the variance of u_t only exists if $\mathsf{E}(\sigma^4(x_t)) < \infty$ and that the fourth moment m_4 of ξ_t is finite such that $(\xi_t^2 - 1)$ has bounded variance.

Because u_t in (7.32) is white noise, the only difference between the stochastic processes (7.32) and (7.1) is that the input variables of the present "conditional mean function" $\sigma^2(x)$ do not include lags of the dependent variable ε_t^2. One can nevertheless use the local estimators derived in Section 7.2 if the dependent variable y_t is replaced by the squared residuals ε_t^2.

In general, the conditional mean function $\mu(\cdot)$ is unknown, and thus the errors $\varepsilon_t, t = i_m + 1, \ldots, T$ have to be estimated by $\widehat{\varepsilon}_t = y_t - \widehat{\mu}(x_t, h)$. If $\widehat{\mu}(x_t, h)$ is the local linear estimator (7.3), then a *local linear estimator* of the conditional variance $\sigma^2(x_t)$ is obtained by replacing in (7.3) y_t by $\widehat{\varepsilon}_t^2$. This delivers

$$\widehat{\sigma}^2(x, h) = e'\left\{\mathbf{Z}'(x)W(x, h)\mathbf{Z}(x)\right\}^{-1}\mathbf{Z}'(x)W(x, h)\widehat{\varepsilon}^2, \tag{7.33}$$

where $\widehat{\varepsilon}^2 = \left(\widehat{\varepsilon}_{i_m+1}^2, \ldots, \widehat{\varepsilon}_T^2\right)'$. The Nadaraya–Watson estimator (7.4) has to be modified to

$$\widehat{\sigma}_{NW}^2(x, h) = \frac{\sum_{t=i_m+1}^T K_h(x_t - x)\widehat{\varepsilon}_t^2}{\sum_{t=i_m+1}^T K_h(x_t - x)}. \tag{7.34}$$

Under the assumptions mentioned before plus some further regularity conditions on the NAR process (7.1) and continuous differentiability of $\sigma^2(\cdot)$,

Tschernig & Yang (2000a, Theorem 3) derived the asymptotic bias and variance and the asymptotic normality of the local linear volatility estimator (7.33).

Note that in finite samples the local linear estimator (7.33) may lead to negative estimates $\widehat{\sigma}^2(x)$ even for a very large bandwidth h. This is especially likely if x is close to the boundary of the sample data. To see this, imagine that x is scalar and just at the boundary of the sample. Then almost all deviations $x_t - x, t = i_m + 1, \ldots, T$ entering $\mathbf{Z}(x)$ and $W(x, h)$ are either nonpositive or nonnegative, and thus almost all sample points are either to the left or to the right of the vertical axis in a scatter plot of $(x_t - x)$ and $\widetilde{\varepsilon}_t^2$. Then the estimated constant and thus $\widehat{\sigma}^2(x)$ may be negative. Such an outcome is extremely unlikely if x is around the mean of the sample because the $(x_t - x)$'s are scattered evenly around the vertical axis. Therefore, one should check the sign of $\widehat{\sigma}^2(x)$. If it is negative, use the Nadaraya–Watson estimator (7.34), which is not subject to this problem.

7.5.2 Bandwidth Choice

We just saw how the local estimators of the conditional mean function need to be modified for the estimation of the conditional volatility. Similarly, one can adjust the FPE criterion (7.12) to the stochastic process (7.32) by replacing y_t by ε_t^2 and the estimated conditional mean function $\widehat{\mu}(\cdot)$ by the estimated conditional variance $\widehat{\sigma}^2(\cdot)$. As in Section 7.3.1, an asymptotically optimal bandwidth for $\widehat{\sigma}^2(x, h)$ can then be derived that can be used to obtain a plug-in bandwidth. The plug-in bandwidth is obtained by replacing in (7.20), (7.22), and (7.24) y_t by ε_t^2 and $\widehat{\mu}(\cdot)$ by $\widehat{\sigma}^2(\cdot)$ and the total number of observations T by the number of residuals T_σ as well as the start values i_m by the start values i_{σ, m_σ}. The resulting equations are presented in the appendix of this chapter.

Note that the local linear estimator (7.33) and the Nadaraya–Watson estimator (7.34) only have the same asymptotically optimal bandwidth if the design is uniform ($\mu(\cdot)$ is constant on its support). In case of homoskedastic errors, all first- and second-order partial derivatives of $\sigma^2(\cdot)$ are zero; thus, the asymptotic first-order bias of the Nadaraya–Watson and the local linear estimators is zero and no asymptotically optimal bandwidths exist because the bias-variance trade-off then fails. This implies that a plug-in bandwidth was chosen too small, and the resulting conditional volatility estimates consequently exhibit a variance that is too large. For the local linear estimator, that effect also occurs if $\sigma(\cdot)$ is linear on the support of the weight function.

Thus, in case of homoskedastic errors, confidence intervals (7.11) based on $\widehat{\sigma}^2(x_t)$ can be misleading. As mentioned before, one should in this case use (7.29) to estimate σ^2. Because without testing one does not know in practice which situation is given, JMuITi computes two confidence intervals. For one of them, conditional heteroskedasticity is allowed for and (7.33) is used with the same lag vector as for $\mu(x)$; for the other confidence interval homoskedasticity is assumed and (7.29) is used.

7.5.3 Lag Selection

For obtaining the modified (C)AFPE criteria one applies the same replacements as before to the (C)AFPE estimators (7.28) and (7.30) as well as to (7.26). The resulting equations are also shown in the appendix. As before, the lag vector that exhibits the smallest estimated modified (C)AFPE criterion given by (7.45) and (7.46) in the appendix is chosen.

Currently, the asymptotic properties of this lag selection procedure can only be derived for the special case in which the conditional mean function $\mu(\cdot)$ is known to be a constant. If, in addition, the assumptions required for selecting the lags of the conditional mean function are adequately modified, then, according to Tschernig & Yang (2000b), the lag selection for the conditional volatility function $\sigma(x)$ using the modified (C)AFPE estimators given by (7.45) and (7.46) in the appendix is weakly consistent. One important requirement for such a result is that the variance of u_t exist.

If the lags entering $\mu(\cdot)$ are known but not the function itself, we expect that it will be possible to show that the lag selection is weakly consistent if the set of lags to be chosen from is completely contained in the set of lags of $\mu(\cdot)$.

The case in which the lags of $\mu(\cdot)$ also have to be estimated remains to be analyzed. Since this case is predominant in practice, we have to conclude that the properties of local linear lag selection methods for the conditional volatility function are not yet fully investigated. The difficulty is that the behavior of the lag selection procedure for $\sigma(\cdot)$ always depends on the lag selection and estimation result for $\mu(\cdot)$. It is worth noting that this problem also occurs in the case of parametric methods.

Two remarks are necessary. First, for bandwidth choice and lag selection the problem of possibly obtaining negative variance estimates from (7.33) is ignored because, as was argued in Section 7.5.1, it is a boundary problem and therefore does not affect too many observations as long as the number of lags m is not too large.

Second, if the NAR process (7.1) is homoskedastic, lag selection using the modified (C)AFPE cannot be consistent because the local linear estimator (7.33) has no first-order bias and we face the same situation as in the case of a linear conditional mean function $\mu(\cdot)$ (see Section 7.3.2 for details). In such a situation, one may frequently observe overfitting: some lags are selected although selecting no lags is correct.

In practice one can deal with this possibility basically in two ways. The first solution is to investigate potential heteroskedasticity by the tools just presented with all the potential problems and use the results as a basis for further parametric modeling and testing. The second one is to model the conditional volatility only if the ARCH–LM test rejects homoskedastic errors (see Section 7.4). However, as is discussed next, the ARCH–LM test may have only little power against some types of conditional heteroskedasticity that are allowed for in an NAR process (7.1).

7.5.4 ARCH Errors

We will first show that the stochastic process (7.32) of the squared residuals can be seen as a generalization of an ARCH(q) process if $\mu(\cdot) = 0$. For the latter, the conditional variance is given by

$$\sigma_t^2 = \gamma_0 + \gamma_1 \varepsilon_{t-1}^2 + \cdots + \gamma_q \varepsilon_{t-q}^2, \tag{7.35}$$

where one has to assume $\gamma_i > 0, i = 0, \ldots, q$. For details on ARCH processes, see Chapter 5. In the special case of $\mu(\cdot) = 0$ one has $\varepsilon_t = y_t$, and thus (7.35) can be written as

$$\sigma^2(x_t) = \gamma_0 + \gamma_1 y_{t-1}^2 + \cdots + \gamma_q y_{t-q}^2,$$

where $x_t = (y_{t-1}, y_{t-2}, \ldots, y_{t-q})'$. In that case, the conditional variance $\sigma^2(x_t)$ is a sum of weighted, squared, lagged observations. This implies, for example, for an ARCH(2) process that $\sigma^2(x_t)$ is in terms of y_{t-1} and y_{t-2} a two-dimensional parabola.

If $\mu(y_{t-1}, y_{t-2}, \ldots, y_{t-m}) \neq 0$ and (7.35) holds, the conditional variance $\sigma^2(\cdot)$ no longer has a simple form since

$$\sigma^2(y_{t-1}, \ldots, y_{t-q-m}) = \gamma_0 + \gamma_1 \left(y_{t-1} - \mu(y_{t-2}, \ldots, y_{t-1-m}) \right)^2$$
$$+ \cdots + \gamma_q \left(y_{t-q} - \mu(y_{t-q-1}, \ldots, y_{t-q-m}) \right)^2,$$

which is no longer a straightforward function in terms of the $y_{t-i'}$'s. Note further that $\sigma^2(\cdot)$ includes more lags than $\mu(\cdot)$ because it consists of all lags from 1 to m plus those from $m + 1$ to $m + q$. This violates the assumption that $\sigma(\cdot)$ may contain all lags of $\mu(\cdot)$ but no more (see Section 7.1). Thus, the NAR model (7.1) does not in general include ARCH errors (except if $\mu(\cdot) = 0$).

It may be, however, that a conditional volatility function $\sigma(x_t)$ can be approximated to some extent by an ARCH(∞) model. If a reasonably good approximation for the underlying conditional volatility function does not exist, the ARCH–LM test can be expected to have only little power. To see the latter case, consider the conditionally heteroskedastic AR(1) model

$$y_t = \alpha y_{t-1} + \sqrt{y_{t-1}} \xi_t, \quad 0 < \alpha < 1,$$

which plays an important role in modeling the term structure of interest rates. By inverting the AR(1) model, one obtains an MA(∞) model $y_t = \sum_{i=0}^{\infty} \alpha^i \varepsilon_{t-i}$, where, as before, $\varepsilon_t = \sigma(x_t)\xi_t$. Replacing y_{t-1} in the conditional variance function by its MA(∞) representation delivers

$$\sigma^2(x_t) = \sigma^2(y_{t-1}) = y_{t-1} = \sum_{i=0}^{\infty} \alpha^i \varepsilon_{t-i-1},$$

which cannot be captured by an ARCH(∞) model.

An example of a partial approximation of $\sigma(x_t)$ by an ARCH(∞) model is the following. Let the conditionally heteroskedastic AR(1) model

$$y_t = \alpha y_{t-1} + \sigma(y_{t-1})\xi_t \quad |\alpha| < 1$$

have conditional volatility function $\sigma^2(y) = 1 + \frac{y^2}{1+y^2}$. Taking the first-order Taylor approximation of $\sigma^2(y)$ with respect to y^2 at $y_0 = 0$ yields

$$\sigma^2(y) \approx 1 + \frac{y_0^2}{1+y_0^2} + \frac{1}{(1+y_0^2)^2}(y^2 - y_0^2) = 1 + y^2.$$

By inserting the MA(∞) representation into the Taylor approximation, one obtains

$$\sigma^2(y_{t-1}) \approx 1 + \left(\sum_{i=0}^{\infty} \alpha^i \varepsilon_{t-1-i} \right)^2$$

$$= 1 + \sum_{i=0}^{\infty} \alpha^{2i} \varepsilon_{t-1-i}^2 + \sum_{i \neq j} \alpha^i \alpha^j \varepsilon_{t-1-i} \varepsilon_{t-1-j}.$$

This approximation contains an ARCH(∞) part with $\gamma_i = \alpha^{2(i-1)}, i = 1, 2, \ldots$. Therefore, an ARCH–LM test can be expected to have some power in this case.

In Section 7.4 it was seen that, for the example of the growth rates of the seasonally adjusted, quarterly German consumption, the ARCH–LM test did not indicate any conditional heteroskedasticity. In light of the previous discussion, this finding does not rule out the presence of conditional heteroskedasticity. Nevertheless, we will not investigate this issue further. Instead, we refer to the reader to Section 7.8, which illustrates how to use the presented tools for modeling the conditional volatility function of the returns of the XETRA Dax index.

7.6 Local Linear Seasonal Modeling

Economic time series frequently exhibit a seasonal pattern. Although economic data are often available in a seasonally adjusted format, using seasonally adjusted data should be avoided if possible. The main reason is that seasonal adjustment procedures, which are used in public agencies, commonly contain nonlinear transformations. Thus, finding evidence of nonlinearity in a seasonally adjusted series may be the result of the seasonal adjustment procedure. In this section we therefore discuss several seasonal extensions of the NAR model (7.1). The presented models and nonparametric modeling procedures were derived in Yang & Tschernig (2002), and the interested reader is referred to this reference for details.

7.6.1 The Seasonal Nonlinear Autoregressive Model

To represent seasonal processes it is convenient to replace the time index t by $t = s + S\tau$, where $s = 1, 2, \ldots, S$ denotes the season and $\tau = 0, 1, \ldots$ represents a new time index.

The *seasonal nonlinear autoregressive* (SNAR) *model* is given by

$$y_{s+\tau S} = \mu_s(x_{s+\tau S}) + \sigma(x_{s+\tau S})\xi_{s+\tau S}, \tag{7.36}$$

where $x_{s+\tau S}$ denotes, as before, the vector of all correct lagged variables. In this seasonal extension of the standard nonlinear autoregression model (7.1), the regression functions $\mu_s(\cdot)$, $s = 1, \ldots, S$ may vary with the S seasons. This is also a nonlinear generalization of the periodic AR (PAR) model

$$y_{s+\tau S} = b_s + \sum_{i=1}^{p} \alpha_{is} y_{s+\tau S-i} + \epsilon_{s+\tau S} \tag{7.37}$$

[see, for example, Lütkepohl (1991, Chapter 12)]. For this reason, one can also view the SNAR model as a periodic nonlinear autoregression.

The local estimators for estimating $\mu_s(\cdot)$, $s = 1, \ldots, S$, are readily obtained by estimating each seasonal function separately using only data of season s. The local linear and Nadaraya–Watson estimators described in Section 7.2.1 have to be modified accordingly. The quantities for computing the plug-in bandwidth and the (C)AFPE estimator described in Sections 7.3.1 and 7.3.2 are now obtained by taking the mean of the quantities computed for each season. These modifications are more or less straightforward, and we refer the interested reader to the paper of Yang & Tschernig (2002).

We note that the computation of the (C)AFPE is facilitated if there is an equal number of observations for each season. This is done in the following way. To guarantee that one has at least $M \geq i_m$ starting values for each season, estimation has to start in $\tau = i_{M,S}$, where $i_{M,S}$ is the smallest integer equal to or greater than M/S. The largest value of the nonseasonal index τ is given by $T_S = \left[\frac{T}{S}\right]$, where $[a]$ truncates the fractional portion of a. Finally, $T_{M,S} = T_S - i_{M,S} + 1$ denotes the number of observations per season available for estimation if the largest lag is M.

Yang & Tschernig (2002) have shown that, under an appropriate extension of the stated assumptions, nonparametric lag selection based on (C)AFPE is weakly consistent. Of course, consistency breaks down if $\mu(\cdot)$ is a linear function and the SNAR model (7.36) reduces to a PAR model (7.37). In order to be able to check lag selection under the assumption of linearity, in JMulTi one can conduct lag selection for the PAR model using either the linear FPE, AIC, HQ, or SC.

Note that for both the SDNAR and the PAR models the number of observations available for estimating each function is about $T_S \approx T/S$. The effective sample size is therefore too small for some macroeconomic applications such as the German consumption data discussed in Sections 7.2.4, 7.3.3, and 7.4. In other words, the SNAR model (7.36) provides too much flexibility for 30 years of quarterly data. This clearly limits the applicability of the SNAR model. We next present two seasonal models with effective sample size T.

7.6.2 The Seasonal Dummy Nonlinear Autoregressive Model

To increase the effective sample size to T, one has to restrict the seasonal flexibility in the conditional mean functions. One possible restriction is given by $\mu_s(\cdot) = \mu(\cdot) + b_s$, $s = 1, 2, \ldots, S$, where $b_1 = 0$ is defined for identification. Then the seasonal variation of the functions between the sth and the first season is restricted to the constant shifts b_s. The resulting process,

$$y_{s+\tau S} = \mu(x_{s+\tau S}) + b_s + \sigma(x_{s+\tau S})\xi_{s+\tau S}, \tag{7.38}$$

is a restricted seasonal nonlinear autoregression. In Yang & Tschernig (2002) this is called a *seasonal dummy nonlinear autoregressive model* (SDNAR model) since it is a generalization of the seasonal dummy linear autoregressive model (SDAR model)

$$y_{s+\tau S} = b_s + \sum_{i=1}^{p} \alpha_i y_{s+\tau S-i} + \epsilon_{s+\tau S}. \tag{7.39}$$

If the seasonal parameters b_s, $s = 2, \ldots, S$ are known, one can subtract them from the dependent variable and obtain a model in which the conditional mean and volatility function are independent of any season,

$$\widetilde{y}_{s+\tau S} = \mu(x_{s+\tau S}) + \sigma(x_{s+\tau S})\xi_{s+\tau S}, \tag{7.40}$$

and where

$$\widetilde{y}_{s+\tau S} = y_{s+\tau S} - b_s, \quad \tau = i_{M,S}, \ldots, T_S, \quad s = 2, \ldots, S.$$

As in Section 7.5, we have the situation that the dependent variable is different from the lags in $x_{s+\tau S}$. It is therefore easy to modify the standard local estimators, the standard plug-in bandwidth, and the lag selection criteria presented in Sections 7.2 and 7.3. In this situation the rate of convergence clearly depends on the sample size T.

In practice, the seasonal parameters b_s, $s = 2, \ldots, S$ have to be estimated. Yang & Tschernig (2002) have suggested a semiparametric estimator that exhibits a convergence rate faster than that of the local linear estimator for $\mu(\cdot)$. It is thus possible to replace the b_ss in (7.40) by their estimates $\bar{b}_s(h)$ (7.41) and then continue as if the b_ss were known. In the cited paper it is shown that, under some regularity conditions, this does not affect the asymptotic behavior of the local linear estimators and lag selectors for $\mu(\cdot)$.

We now briefly show the basic steps underlying the semiparametric estimates $\bar{b}_s(h)$, $s = 2, \ldots, S$. In the first step one ignores the assumption that b_s is constant and allows it to vary with x. A local linear estimator is used to estimate b_s at all observations, which delivers $\widehat{b}_s(x_{s+i_{M,s}S}, h), \ldots, \widehat{b}_s(x_{s+T_SS}, h)$. In the second step, one uses the fact that b_s is assumed to be a constant, which makes it possible to average the preceding estimates as follows:

$$\bar{b}_s(h) = \frac{\sum_{\tau=i_{M,S}}^{T_S} w(x_{s+\tau S,M})\widehat{b}_s(x_{s+\tau S}, h)}{\sum_{\tau=i_{M,S}}^{T_S} w(x_{s+\tau S,M})}, \quad s = 2, \ldots, S. \quad (7.41)$$

The averaging implies that the variances of the single estimates are to some extent smoothed out. This is why the convergence rate of the semiparametric estimator (7.41) is faster than that of the function estimates [Yang & Tschernig (2002, Theorem 5)]. In (7.40) the unknown seasonal parameters b_s, $s = 2, \ldots, S$, can therefore be replaced by their estimates $\bar{b}_s(h)$, and one may then continue as if the b_s's were known.

7.6.3 Seasonal Shift Nonlinear Autoregressive Model

Another way of restricting the seasonal nonlinear autoregression model (7.36) is to assume that the seasonal process is additively separable into a seasonal mean shift δ_s, $s = 1, 2, \ldots, S$ and a nonseasonal, nonlinear autoregression z_t, that is, $y_{s+\tau S} = \delta_s + z_{s+\tau S}$. One may call

$$y_{s+\tau S} - \delta_s = \mu \left(y_{s+\tau S-i_1} - \delta_{\{s-i_1\}}, \ldots, y_{s+\tau S-i_m} - \delta_{\{s-i_m\}} \right) \quad (7.42)$$

$$+ \sigma \left(y_{s+\tau S-i_1} - \delta_{\{s-i_1\}}, \ldots, y_{s+\tau S-i_m} - \delta_{\{s-i_m\}} \right) \xi_{s+\tau S}$$

a *seasonal shift nonlinear autoregressive model* (SHNAR model), where $\{a\}$ is defined as

$$\{a\} = \begin{cases} S & \text{if } a \text{ modulo } S = 0, \\ a \text{ modulo } S & \text{otherwise.} \end{cases}$$

For identifiability, it is assumed that $\delta_1 = 0$. This seasonal shift nonlinear autoregressive model is another way of generalizing the SDAR model (7.39), where the constants $\delta_1, \ldots, \delta_S$ of the linear model are obtained up to an additive constant via the system of linear equations $b_s = \delta_s - \sum_{j=1}^{p} \alpha_j \delta_{\{s-j\}}$, $s = 1, 2, \ldots, S$.

If the seasonal mean shifts $\delta_1, \ldots, \delta_S$ were known, one could obtain the nonseasonal process $z_{s+\tau S} = y_{s+\tau S} - \delta_s$, which is a NAR process (7.1) for z_t. It therefore could be analyzed by the standard nonparametric methods presented in Sections 7.2 and 7.3.

If the seasonal mean shifts $\delta_1, \ldots, \delta_S$ are unknown, they can easily be estimated by taking the seasonal averages $\widehat{\delta}_s = T_{M,S}^{-1} \sum_{\tau=i_{M,S}}^{T_S} (y_{s+\tau S} - y_{1+\tau S})$, $s = 2, \ldots, S$. Since this parametric estimator has $\sqrt{T_S}$ convergence that is faster than the convergence rate of the local linear estimator, one can also use the standard nonparametric methods even if the seasonal mean shifts have to be estimated.

We are now ready to apply the various presented nonparametric estimators to two different economic time series.

7.7 Example I: Average Weekly Working Hours in the United States

In this section we will illustrate the complete nonparametric modeling procedure for the average weekly hours worked in the United States. The 478 monthly observations cover the period from 1960M1 to 1999M11 and were seasonally adjusted and provided by The Conference Board, www.tcb.org. Figure 7.3 displays the time series of the data. The two largest drops in the average weekly hours occur in January 1982 and January 1996. Visual inspection and standard ADF unit root tests suggest taking first differences in order to obtain a stationary series. The time series of the first differences is also shown in Figure 7.3. A large drop in the level series turns into a sequence of one large negative spike followed by a large positive one. Capturing these large changes will be one of the modeling challenges. On the basis of the (partial) autocorrelations of the first differences, which are also shown in Figure 7.3, one may consider lags 1 and 2. Note the significance of lag 12 which may result from the seasonal adjustment procedure.

Because higher-order dependence cannot be seen from the estimated autocorrelations, lag selection should be conducted by means of the nonparametric methods described in Section 7.3. Doing a full search with the CAFPE criterion (7.30) for a maximum number of eight lags up to lag 8, $M = 8$, identifies lags 1 and 2 as the relevant ones, as can be seen from Table 7.2. The table shows the optimal selection of lags for each number of lags as well as the plug-in bandwidth underlying the function estimates and the resulting CAFPE. For example, $\mu(y_{t-1}, y_{t-2})$ was estimated with plug-in bandwidth 0.158 and the resulting CAFPE value is 0.0524. The same lags, 1 and 2, are suggested when a full lag search is conducted within linear AR models using the FPE, AIC, HQ, or SC lag selection criteria. These lag selection results are in line with the autocorrelations estimated for the changes in the average weekly working hours shown in Figure 7.3.

In Figure 7.4 the estimated conditional mean function with lags 1 and 2 is plotted from two different angles. All function estimates outside the data region and those for which the estimated density of the grid points is within the lower 10% quantile are removed. The graph of the function looks somewhat like a

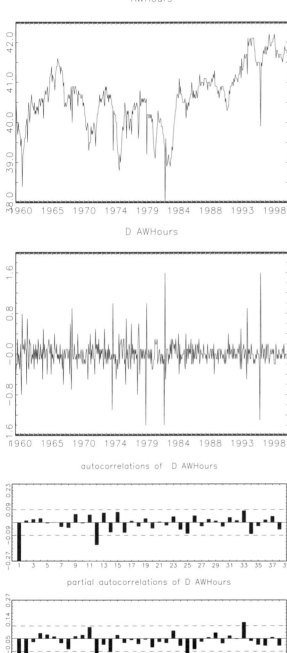

Figure 7.3. Monthly observations of the average weekly working hours in the United States, January 1960–November 1999, with first differences (D AWHours), autocorrelations, and partial autocorrelations of first differences.

Table 7.2. *Lag selection for the conditional mean function of the monthly changes of U.S. average weekly working hours up to lag 8*

No. of selected lags	Selected lag vector	CAFPE	Plug-in bandwidth
0	—	0.0731	—
1	1	0.0540	0.142
2	1, 2	0.0524	0.158
3	1, 2, 8	0.0554	0.174
4	1, 3, 6, 8	0.0772	0.204
5	1, 2, 4, 7, 8	0.1224	0.207
6	1, 2, 3, 4, 5, 7	0.2214	0.227
7	1, 2, 3, 4, 5, 7, 8	0.3937	0.236
8	1, 2, 3, 4, 5, 6, 7, 8	1.2787	0.274

large armchair, indicating strong nonlinearities in the direction of the first lag. To confirm this impression, one may investigate a cut through the function surface in the direction of lag 1. Such a one-dimensional graph can be seen in Figure 7.5, where lag 2 is fixed at its mean. The dashed lines are Bonferroni 95% confidence intervals ((7.11) combined with (7.43)) of the function estimates evaluated at the grid points where conditionally heteroskedastic errors are assumed. The dotted lines are obtained by assuming homoskedastic errors. Since the confidence intervals turned out to be very large at several grid points that are close to the boundary, it is useful to exclude such points from the plot. Thus, only those estimates for which the density of the grid points is within the larger 70% quantile are shown. One can clearly see that the monthly changes of the average weekly working hours are quite small as long as the change in the previous month is smaller than 0.4 in absolute value. In contrast, a strong downswing in the previous month (being larger than 0.4 in absolute value) will be followed by an even stronger upswing. This evidence of nonlinear dynamics is statistically supported by the fact that it is not possible to fit a straight line in between the confidence intervals. Note that testing linearity by one of the tests proposed in the previous chapter leads to a clear rejection of linearity.

We now turn to diagnostic tests of the estimated residuals. Recall from Section 7.4 that the asymptotic distribution results of the standard diagnostic tests are not yet proven to be valid for nonparametrically estimated residuals. To begin with, there is no evidence for conditional heteroskedasticity. First of all, the *p*-value of the ARCH–LM test with four lags is 0.81. Second, a lag search for the conditional volatility function suggests no lags. However, the residuals are far from being normally distributed since the *p*-value of the Lomnicki–Jarque–Bera test is 0.00. This is due to the very large kurtosis of about 13.5. This value reflects the large negative outliers in the residuals, which are plotted in Figure 7.6. Note that the large positive spikes that are visible in the original data in

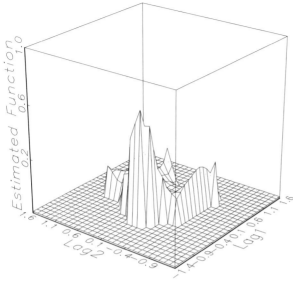

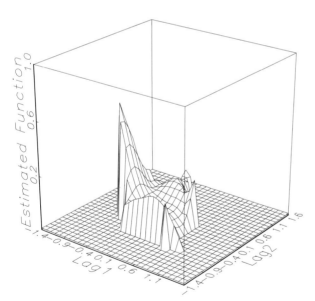

Figure 7.4. Two different views of the estimated conditional mean function of monthly changes of U.S. average weekly working hours: Lags 1 and 2; estimates for which the estimated density of the grid points is within the lower 10% quantile are removed.

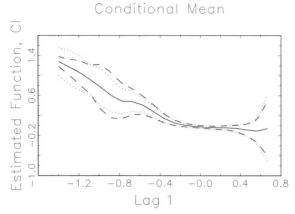

Figure 7.5. Estimated conditional mean function of monthly changes of U.S. average weekly working hours: Bonferroni confidence intervals (CI) with 95% confidence level with the second lag set to the estimated mean; dashed lines are based on conditionally heteroskedastic errors, and dotted lines are based on homoskedastic errors; 30% of the observations with the lowest density are removed.

Figure 7.3 are captured by the nonlinear, conditional mean function. There is a simple reason for this finding. The large downswing occurs first and cannot be well predicted from past observations whereas the large upswing always follows in the month after and is thus much easier to predict if one allows for nonlinear models. This is exactly reflected in the function plots in Figures 7.4 and 7.5.

The estimated (partial) autocorrelations of the residuals are also plotted in Figure 7.6. One can see that the autocorrelation for lag 12 is outside the 95% confidence interval that is given by the dashed lines. This was already the case for the original data (see Figure 7.3) and seems to cause a rather low p-value of 0.118 for the Ljung–Box statistic with sixteen lags. The p-value for the F-statistic of the Godfrey test is even as low as 0.076.

The relevance of lag 12 may be due to overadjusting in the seasonal adjustment procedure. Thus, one may either add lags or try to remove remaining seasonality with one of the seasonal nonlinear autoregressive models described in Section 7.6. The latter will be done first using the seasonal shift nonlinear autoregressive model (7.42). It also seems useful to extend the lag search over all lags up to lag 15. We will do this but only allow for a maximum of four lags. Setting the seasonal shift parameter of January to zero, we estimate all other seasonal shift parameters between 0.02 and 0.19. Note that these estimates are independent of the lags selected. Thus, average weekly working hours in January are lower than in any other month. However, taking that into account does not lead to another lag selection. The autocorrelation in the residuals at lag 12 remains large, and the p-values of the autocorrelation tests even fall below the significance level of 5%.

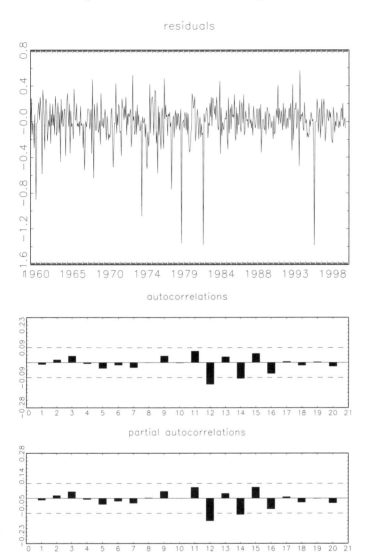

Figure 7.6. Diagnostics for the conditional mean function of the monthly changes of U.S. average weekly working hours.

The seasonal dummy nonlinear autoregressive model (7.38) is an alternative restricted seasonal model but is not available in JMulTi for monthly data. Finally, there is the seasonal nonlinear autoregressive model (7.36), which is the most flexible one. Because for each season there are only forty observations, a nonparametric estimation is not very promising and is therefore not performed here.

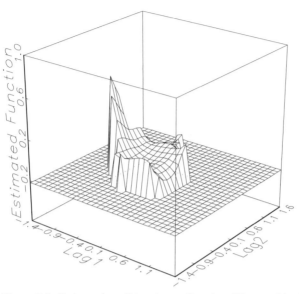

Figure 7.7. Estimated conditional mean function of the monthly changes of U.S. average weekly working hours with lags 1, 2, and 12; lag 12 is set to the estimated mean; estimates for which the estimated density of the grid points is within the lower 10% quantile are removed.

Alternatively, one may include further lags in the conditional mean function $\mu(\cdot)$ of the nonseasonal model (7.1). Accordingly, we rerun a lag search in the same setup as for the seasonal models with all lags up to lag 15 and a maximum of four lags. Doing a full search with CAFPE, which requires some computation time, delivers lags 1 and 9. A faster directed sequential search leads to the same lags. The function plot looks similar to the one obtained with lags 1 and 2 shown in Figure 7.4 and is thus not shown here. Moreover, the diagnostics are similar as well except that now the p-values of the autocorrelation tests are smaller. This result clearly shows that nonlinear lag selection also considers stochastic dependence in higher moments. In fact, nonlinear lag selection may trade off some linear autocorrelation for some more substantial dependence in higher moments, as in the present case. The latter may turn out much more important for forecasting, as will be seen below in this section.

If it is important to eliminate the remaining autocorrelation, one may add those lags that are suggested by linear lag selection procedures. Doing a full search, the FPE and AIC criteria suggest lags 1, 2, 12, and 15, whereas the HQ and the SC criteria select lags 1, 2, and 12 only. Thus, one may add lag 12 to the original set of lags 1 and 2. Figure 7.7 displays the function plot in which lags 1

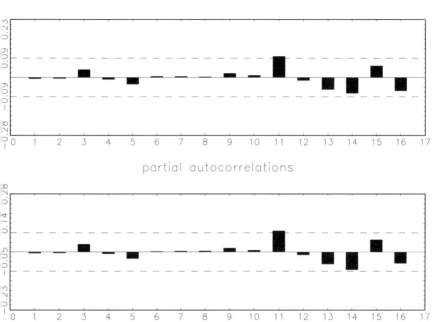

Figure 7.8. Autocorrelations and partial autocorrelations of residuals of the monthly changes of U.S. average weekly working hours. The estimation is based on lags 1, 2, and 12.

and 2 vary on the grid and lag 12 is kept fixed at its mean. Comparing this graph with the plot of the two-dimensional function with lags 1 and 2 in Figure 7.4 does not reveal much difference. However, the autocorrelations of the residuals look somewhat better, as can be seen from Figure 7.8. Also, the p-values of the diagnostics for remaining autocorrelation are all above 50%. Summarizing the results up to now, one may say that, with respect to capturing first-order correlation, the nonparametric, nonseasonal model with lags 1, 2, and 12 has a slight advantage over the more parsimonious model with lags 1 and 2.

Another check of the validity of the nonparametric modeling procedure is to conduct rolling-over, out-of-sample, one-step-ahead forecasts. A nonparametric lag selection and prediction is conducted for the change in the average weekly working hours occurring in $1991M12$ using data up to $1991M11$. In the next step all data up $1991M12$ are used for predicting $1992M1$ without reselecting the lags, however. This is repeated until the prediction of $1999M11$, which covers a period of seven years. Then, the prediction error (7.31) is computed. The lags are selected with a directed search for four lags out of fifteen. Table 7.3 displays the results for the nonparametric CAFPE procedure and parametric

Table 7.3. *Prediction errors for rolling-over, out-of-sample,*
one-step-ahead forecasts of the monthly changes of U.S. average
weekly working hours

Criterion	CAFPE	FPE, AIC, HQ	SC
Lags selected at $1991M11$	1, 9	1, 2, 12, 15	1, 12
Prediction error	0.0550	0.0615	0.0615

Note: The prediction period is $1991M12$ to $1999M11$; four out of fifteen lags can be selected.

procedures based on linear autoregressive models using the FPE, AIC, HQ, and SC criteria.

It can be seen that the linear criteria all include lags 1 and 12 and exhibit the same prediction error. The nonparametric CAFPE selects lags 1 and 9 for the smaller sample and exhibits a prediction error that is 10% lower than those of the linear models. It is worth noting that the smallest prediction error for the nonparametric procedure is obtained if one restricts the largest lag to be considered to be 8. In that case, lags 1 and 2 are chosen like for the complete sample and the prediction error is 0.0495, leading to an almost 20% improvement over linear models. Allowing only lags up to 8 worsens the prediction error of the linear models compared with those before. Finally, computing the nonparametric prediction error for lags 1, 2, and 12 produces a prediction error of 0.0557. In sum, the results from rolling-over forecasts favor the parsimonious nonlinear specification with lags 1 and 2 that was obtained at the very beginning. They also clearly show the superiority of the more general nonparametric modeling procedure owing to the importance of the underlying nonlinear dynamics.

7.8 Example II: XETRA Dax Index

To illustrate nonparametric volatility estimation, consider 1,029 daily observations of the closing values of the XETRA Dax index ranging from 1 January 1999 to 31 January 2003. The data were downloaded from Yahoo. Because the index is nonstationary, we consider the returns by taking first differences after taking logarithms. To obtain nice scales on the plots, the returns are multiplied by 100 and shown in Figure 7.9.

Before we can estimate the conditional volatility function, we have to identify the conditional mean function. Figure 7.9 also displays the autocorrelation and partial autocorrelation function of the returns. Up to lag 20, only lag 19 is significant and lags 5 and 6 are the smallest lags with almost significant values. Thus, it is not surprising that a full lag search based on linear autoregressive

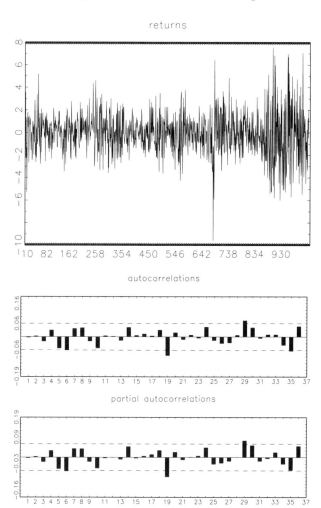

Figure 7.9. Daily returns (multiplied by 100) of the XETRA Dax index, 1 January 1999 to 31 January 2003 with autocorrelations and partial autocorrelations.

models, the SC criterion, and all lags up to lag 8 suggests using no lags. The AIC leads to lags 5 and 6 with a value of 1.245. For comparison, the AIC of the white noise model is 1.254 and is thus only marginally larger. The estimated parameter values are -0.052 and -0.063, where only the latter is significant at the 5% level. One can conclude that the autoregressive model has almost no explanatory power. For later reference we conduct rolling-over, one-step-ahead forecasts for the last 206 observations. To avoid any use of out-of-sample information, the lags are reselected using the first 822 observations and the AIC criterion. Now lag 4 is chosen. It turns out that the prediction variance (7.31)

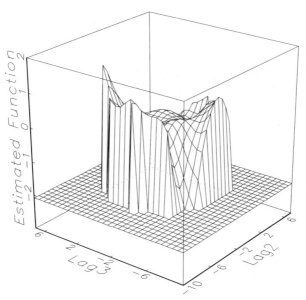

(a) Lags 2 and 3; estimates for which the estimated density of the grid points is within the lower 10% quantile are removed

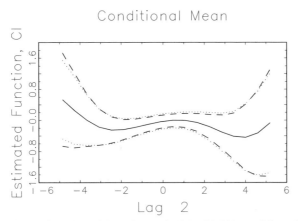

(b) Bonferroni confidence intervals (CI) with 99% confidence level and the third lag set to the estimated mean: dashed lines are based on conditional heteroskedastic errors, and dotted lines are based on homoskedastic errors; 40% of the observations with the lowest density are removed

Figure 7.10. Estimated conditional mean function of daily returns of the XETRA Dax index.

of the one-step-ahead forecasts is 7.89, whereas the variance of the returns to be predicted is 7.79. Thus, the linear model is not of much use for forecasting purposes.

To select the relevant lags of a nonlinear autoregressive model, the CAFPE criterion (7.30) is applied with a directed search up to lag 8 and a total number of eight lags. The selected lags are 2 and 3 with a CAFPE value of 3.28, which is about 7% smaller than the corresponding value of 3.50 for the white noise model. Figure 7.10(a) displays the conditional mean function where those estimates were removed for which the estimated density of the grid points is within the lower 10% quantile. Inspecting the plot shows that the estimated function is about 0 except in the front corner. Thus, the nonparametric model seems to allow better capture of extreme events. Figure 7.10(b) displays 99%-Bonferroni confidence intervals for lag 2 with lag 3 kept fixed at its mean. In the plot all grid points for which their density is within the 40% lower quantile are suppressed because confidence intervals become very large in that region. The plot shows that the zero line is contained within the confidence intervals. Estimating this function with lag 3 kept fixed at -2 or 2 does not change this conclusion. Thus, there is no substantial nonlinearity in the main regions of the data.

To check the forecasting power of the estimated conditional mean function, we conduct rolling-over, one-step-ahead predictions using the CAFPE criterion. On the basis of the first 822 observations, lag 5 is selected in addition to lags 2 and 3. This specification delivers a prediction error of 15.95, which is about twice as large as the one of the linear autoregressive model analyzed earlier. This result underlines the previous conclusion that the nonlinearities occur only in rare events but do not help to improve forecasts on average.

Performing the diagnostic tests of Section 7.4 shows no remaining autocorrelation. However, the ARCH–LM test with 4 lags rejects the null of conditional homoskedasticity at a significance level of 0.5%, and the Lomnicki–Jarque–Bera test rejects normality of the residuals at the same significance level. Therefore, there is a strong need for modeling conditional heteroskeasticity, and we now turn to this approach.

In the light of the very weak evidence of a nonzero conditional mean function, we assume for the following analysis of the conditional volatility that the conditional mean function is 0. For selecting the lags of the conditional volatility function, we use the CAFPE criterion as described in Section 7.5. A directed search is conducted up to lag 8. Lags 4, 5, and 6 are selected according to the results in Table 7.4. Next we estimate this specification and analyze the residuals. The latter are plotted in Figure 7.11 and indicate neither remaining heteroskecasticity nor autocorrelation. The p-value of the ARCH–LM test of homoskedasticity is now 0.27 with four lags and 0.13 with ten lags. Furthermore, the normality of the residuals cannot be rejected since the Lomnicki–Jarque–Bera test has a p-value of 0.90. The relevance of modeling the conditional

Table 7.4. *Lag selection for the conditional volatility function of daily returns of the XETRA Dax index*

No. of selected lags	Selected lag vector	CAFPE	Plug-in bandwidth
0	—	46.58	—
1	5	41.27	0.71
2	5, 6	35.61	0.95
3	4, 5, 6	32.16	1.19
4	4, 5, 6, 8	42.25	1.46
5	4, 5, 6, 7, 8	159.25	2.08
6	1, 4, 5, 6, 7, 8	454.10	2.57
7	1, 3, 4, 5, 6, 7, 8	2492.02	3.67
8	1, 2, 3, 4, 5, 6, 7, 8	4713.01	4.00

volatility can also be seen by comparing the residuals in Figure 7.11 with the original returns in Figure 7.9.

In Figure 7.12(a) the estimated conditional volatility function is visualized on a grid with lag 4 kept fixed at its mean. As before, those grid points for which the density is within the lower 10% quantile are removed. Recall from Section 7.5.4 that, in the case of $\mu(\cdot) = 0$, the estimated conditional mean function generalizes ARCH models. In the case of an ARCH(2) process, the graph of $\sigma^2(x_t)$ is given by a two-dimensional parabola. From the plot in Figure 7.12(a) it is difficult to

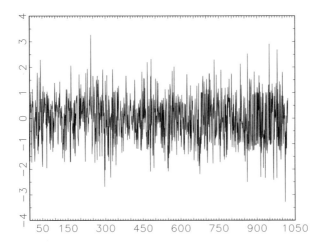

Figure 7.11. Estimated residuals of nonparametric estimates of the conditional volatility function for the daily returns of the XETRA Dax index.

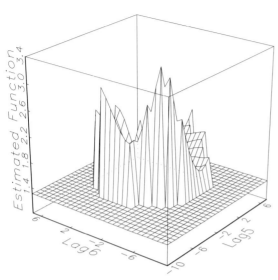

(a) Lags 4, 5 and 6; lag 4 set to estimated mean; 10% of the observations with the lowest density are removed

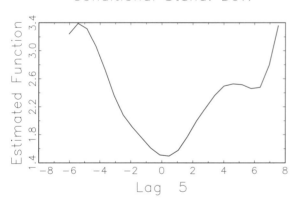

(b) Lag 5; 20% of the observations with the lowest density are removed

Figure 7.12. Estimated conditional volatility function of the daily returns of the XETRA Dax index.

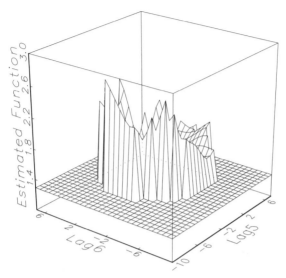

Figure 7.13. Estimated conditional volatility function of the daily returns of the XETRA Dax index; lags 4, 5, and 6; lag 4 set to estimated mean; based on residuals resulting from estimating the conditional mean function with lags 2 and 3; 10% of the observations with the lowest density are removed.

see if the graph of the estimated function deviates substantially from a parabola. As an explorative device one may estimate the volatility function for lag 5 only. The function estimates are displayed in Figure 7.12(b) and reveal asymmetric behavior. The increase of volatility is steeper for increasing negative returns than for increasing positive returns. This is what one may expect, although it should be kept in mind that these estimates are biased owing to omitted lags. If parametric modeling is intended, a TGARCH model should be superior to the symmetric ARCH model (see Chapter 5 for a discussion of ARCH-type models).

   To check the robustness of these results, this analysis may be repeated with the estimated conditional mean function. One then finds that all CAFPE values are much smaller and that the lags selected for the conditional volatility are again lags 4, 5, and 6 and, hence, remain unchanged. Figure 7.13 displays the estimated function. Comparing it with the plot in Figure 7.12(a) when $\mu(\cdot) = 0$ was assumed does not indicate large differences. To conclude, we find that the returns of the XETRA Dax index exhibit strong conditional volatility, where the amount of the volatility differs nonlinearly with respect to the magnitude and the sign of the past returns.

Appendix

Bonferroni confidence intervals. Denote for grid point $x^{(j)}$ the event $\left|\left(\widehat{\mu}(x^{(j)}, h) - \mu(x^{(j)})\right) / \sqrt{\frac{v(x^{(j)})}{Th^m}}\right| < z_{\alpha_j/2}$ by A_j. Then the joint confidence intervals for all grid points with confidence level $1 - \alpha_j$ are defined by $P(\bigcap_{j=1}^{J} A_j) = 1 - \alpha$. Using the Bonferroni inequality, we find that this probability can be approximated by

$$P\left(\bigcap_{j=1}^{J} A_j\right) \geq \sum_{j=1}^{J} P(A_j) - (J - 1),$$

which is equivalent to $1 - \alpha \geq J(1 - \alpha_j) - (J - 1)$. Solving for $1 - \alpha_j$ delivers $1 - \alpha_j \leq 1 - \frac{\alpha}{J}$. Thus, replacing α in (7.11) by

$$\alpha_j = \frac{\alpha}{J} \tag{7.43}$$

for each grid point guarantees that the overall confidence level is at least the desired confidence level $(1 - \alpha)$.

Robustification and implementation. The computation of $\widehat{B}(h_b)$ given by (7.20) requires division by the density estimate $\widehat{f}(\cdot)$. This estimate may become unreliable if data are scarce in the neighborhood of x_t. To exploit all available data for estimating $f(x)$, in JMuITi the kernel estimator

$$\widehat{f}(x, h) = (T - i_m + i_1)^{-1} \sum_{i=i_m+1}^{T+i_1} K_h(x_i - x) \tag{7.44}$$

is used, where the vectors x_i, $i = T + 1, \ldots, T + i_1$, are all available from the observations y_t, $t = 1, \ldots, T$. For example, x_{T+i_1} is given by $(y_T, \ldots, y_{T+i_1-i_m})^T$. This robustification, which was suggested by Tjøstheim & Auestad (1994), is switched off if the sum stops at T.

In addition, for computing $\widehat{B}(h_B)$, 5% of those observations whose density values $\widehat{f}(\cdot)$ are the lowest are screened off.

In practice it may also happen that the rule-of-thumb bandwidths $\widehat{h}_B$ and $\widehat{h}_C$ are chosen too small such that for some x, for example, the inversion in (7.3) is numerically unreliable. In such cases, these rule-of-thumb bandwidths are increased until numerical stability is obtained. It was also found that the Gaussian kernel is numerically more stable than the quartic kernel. For this reason one should use the Gaussian kernel.

Estimators for bandwidth and lag selection for conditional volatility. The plug-in bandwidth for (7.33) is computed by

$$\widehat{h}_{\sigma,\text{opt}} = \left\{ m \|K\|_2^{2m} \widehat{B}_\sigma(\widehat{h}_B)(T_\sigma - i_{\sigma,m})^{-1} \widehat{C}_\sigma(\widehat{h}_C)^{-1} \sigma_K^{-4} \right\}^{1/(m+4)},$$

where T_σ denotes the number of residuals, $i_{\sigma,m}$ the number of start values, and

$$\widehat{B}_\sigma(h_B) = \sum_{t=i_{\sigma,m}+1}^{T} \left\{\varepsilon_t^2 - \widehat{\sigma}^2(x_t, h_B)\right\}^2 w(x_{t,M})/\widehat{f}(x_t, h_B),$$

$$\widehat{C}_\sigma(h_C) = \frac{1}{T_\sigma - i_{\sigma,m}} \sum_{t=i_{\sigma,m}+1}^{T} \left[\sum_{j=1}^{m} (\widehat{\sigma}^2)^{(jj)}(x_t, h_C)\right]^2 w(x_{t,M}).$$

The AFPE criterion is computed as

$$AFPE_\sigma = \widehat{A}_\sigma(h_{\sigma,opt}) + 2K(0)^m(T_\sigma - i_{\sigma,m})^{-1}h_{\sigma,opt}^{-m}\widehat{B}_\sigma(h_B), \qquad (7.45)$$

where

$$\widehat{A}_\sigma(h) = (T_\sigma - i_{\sigma,m})^{-1} \sum_{t=i_{\sigma,m}+1}^{T} \left\{\varepsilon_t^2 - \widehat{\sigma}^2(x_t, h)\right\}^2 w(x_{t,M}).$$

The modified CAFPE criterion is given by

$$CAFPE_\sigma = AFPE_\sigma \left\{1 + m_\sigma(T - i_{\sigma,m_\sigma})^{-4/(m_\sigma+4)}\right\}. \qquad (7.46)$$

If ε_t^2 is not available, it is replaced by $\widehat{\varepsilon}_t^2$.

8   The Software JMulTi

Markus Krätzig

8.1 Introduction to JMulTi

8.1.1 Software Concept

This chapter gives a general overview of the software by which the examples in this book can be reproduced; it is freely available via the Internet.[1] The information given here covers general issues and concepts of JMulTi. Detailed descriptions on how to use certain methods in the program are left to the help system installed with the software.

JMulTi is an interactive JAVA application designed for the specific needs of time series analysis. It does not compute the results of the statistical calculations itself but delegates this part to a computational engine via a communications layer. The range of its own computing functions is limited and is only meant to support data transformations to provide input for the various statistical routines.

Like other software packages, JMulTi contains graphical user interface (GUI) components that simplify tasks common to empirical analysis – especially reading in data, transforming variables, creating new variables, editing data, and saving data sets. Most of its functions are accessible by simple mouse interaction.

Originally the software was designed as an easy-to-use GUI for complex and difficult-to-use econometric procedures written in GAUSS that were not available in other packages. Because this concept has proved to be quite fruitful, JMulTi has now evolved into a comprehensive modeling environment for multiple time series analysis. The underlying general functionality has been bundled in the software framework JStatCom, which is designed as a ready-made platform for the creation of various statistical applications by developers.

---

[1]   The homepage is http://www.jmulti.de

8.1.2 Operating JMulTi

Much effort has been invested in making the use of JMulTi as intuitive as possible. Therefore it is not necessary to read this chapter before using the program. Some options are explained in detail, however. Thus it may be a good strategy to read this chapter after a first acquaintance with the software.

JMulTi is a JAVA program and consequently relies on the availability of an appropriate JAVA Runtime Environment (JRE)[2] that needs to be installed as well. Users new to JAVA programs should be aware that the user interface looks slightly different from the one of native programs and is sometimes a bit less responsive. This does not mean that the speed of the statistical calculations is slower than with other software packages. The difference results from the way the JAVA GUI components are painted on the screen. The speed of the calculations is only lowered by the overhead imposed by the communications interface between JMulTi and the computational engine. This is a tolerable fixed cost that does not affect the performance of the algorithms.

In the following sections some conventions for numbers, dates and variable names, data input, and data handling will be discussed. Section 8.4 describes how various time series operations can be carried out, and Section 8.6 gives a very general overview of the underlying software framework. This is especially meant for developers who consider writing graphical user interfaces for their algorithms.

8.2 Numbers, Dates, and Variables in JMulTi

8.2.1 Numbers

JMulTi stores numbers as 64-bit, double-precision, floating point values as defined in IEEE (754–1985). Special values are NaN, Infinity and -Infinity. NaN stands for Not-a-Number and is used to code missing values in data files. Infinities are not allowed for data points but occur in the definition of intervals or for coding special values.

To input numbers that are used by a procedure, JMulTi provides special text fields with input-validating capabilities. Usually these text fields display a reasonable default value. The decimal delimiter is a point. The number displayed is rounded to the precision required for the respective purpose. Very often the number of fraction digits is zero, which allows only for integer input. If the given value cannot be parsed to a number or if it is not in the allowed range, a descriptive message will pop up and any other action is canceled. It is always possible to input values coded in exponential notation (e.g., 1.234e-10). The respective text field formats the input value in a way that makes sense for the given context.

---

[2] The Sun JRE can be downloaded from http://www.java.sun.com.

Range of numbers. Sometimes it is necessary to input a range defined by two numbers. JMulTi also provides special text fields for this purpose that make sure that the given range is valid and within the enclosing interval. Text fields with this behavior are marked with angular brackets. The two numbers defining the range must be separated by a comma.

8.2.2 Numbers in Tables

JMulTi often uses tables to display an array of numbers. The tables frequently have a right mouse pop-up menu for useful tasks on that table. The default menu for number tables allows the precision and the notation of the numbers displayed to be changed. If a table is editable, the same rules hold as for number text fields.

  In certain contexts, such as for the specification of subset restrictions, the number table renders certain values with special symbols (e.g., '*' or '---'). Usually these tables can be edited by just clicking on a cell such that the value switches to the next valid one and the symbol changes accordingly.

8.2.3 Dates

In JMulTi dates are objects defined by a main period, a frequency, and a sub-period. They can be specified in various ways with the respective text fields for date input. All three pieces of information must be retrieved from the input. The following formats are recognized, where D stands for the main period, S for the subperiod, and F for the frequency or periodicity:

- D S/F, for example 1960 1/6. This format is always possible and is used as default format if no special identifier for the frequency is defined.
- D 'Q' S, for example 1960 Q 1. This format is used for quarterly data.
- D 'M' S, for example 1960 M 11. This format is used for monthly data.
- D, for example 1960. This format is used for annual data.
- D ['I','II'], for example 1960 II. This format is used for half-yearly data.
- D.S, for example 1960.1. This format is just for input convenience and can be used when the program already knows the frequency from the context, which is often the case.

Date input must conform to the given rules and is validated against a range defined by two dates. If the input is wrong in any way, the previous value is restored and a descriptive message is shown.

Range of dates. Sometimes it is necessary to define a time range by specifying its first and the last date. JMulTi provides special text fields for that purpose as well. Like the ones for number ranges, they are marked with angular brackets and validated against an enclosing date range. The two dates must be separated by a comma.

8.2.4 Variable Names

As a general convention throughout the program, variable names can contain letters, numbers, and '_' but must start with a nonnumber. For example, _invest, invest and i2 would be valid names, whereas 2i, gov exp or cons+inv would be invalid. This is enforced wherever variable names can be set within the program but must also be followed when specifying variable names in a data file. Variable names are case insensitive, meaning that two variable names differing only in the case of one or more letters are considered equal.

8.3 Handling Data Sets

8.3.1 Importing Data

JMulTi is meant to be used for empirical data analysis. Therefore the first step is always to read in a data set that is stored in a file. In case the available data is in a format that is not directly readable by JMulTi, it should always be possible to transform the data easily into one of the accessible formats.

When the data are read in, JMulTi automatically identifies dummy and trend variables as deterministic. In general, reading in variables that are either an intercept, a deterministic trend, or seasonal dummy variables is not recommended because JMulTi offers automatic generation of these variables wherever it is necessary for a certain procedure.

8.3.2 Excel Format

JMulTi can read in Microsoft® Excel 97 files. Earlier versions are not supported, whereas the file format did not change with later versions of Excel. There is an appropriate file filter for *.xls files. When the file is opened, a dialog asks for some additional information. Only one Excel table can be read in at a time.

The Excel file should have the variable names in the first row and the numeric values starting in one of the next rows. The parser also recognizes cells that contain formulas and evaluates them. If JMulTi finds no variable names, it creates defaults from the filename and an index. Other cells with nonnumbers will be treated as missing values and coded as NaN. Whether the decimal delimiter is a comma or a point depends on the local settings. A number is recognized if Excel has stored the content of the cell as a number.

8.3.3 ASCII Format

An ASCII data file example with an optional description looks like this:

```
/*seasonally adjusted, West Germany:
fixed investment, disposable income, consumption expen-
ditures */
180 451 415
179 465 421
...
```

The file should contain the data of each variable in a column. Missing values may be coded with NaN. It makes no difference whether the numbers are coded with a decimal comma or a decimal point. The exponential notation (e.g., 1.23e-4) is recognized as well. When the file is opened, a dialog asks for additional information. It is possible to add a description enclosed by /* ... */ to the data set somewhere in the file.

8.3.4 JMulTi .dat Format

JMulTi has a file format that is a slight extension of the ASCII format and allows for easy data recognition without further user interaction. The following is an example of a .dat file with an optional description:

```
/*seasonally adjusted, West Germany:
fixed investment, disposable income, consumption expen-
ditures */
3 1960.1 4
invest income cons
180 451 415
179 465 421
...
```

where the first number defines the number of variables, the second number the start date, and the last number the periodicity of the data set. The start date must be a valid date for the given periodicity. In the example, 1960.1 stands for the first quarter of 1960 because 4 defines quarterly data. Yearly data has periodicity 1. The periodicity can be chosen to be any positive integer. It should be noticed that, for monthly data, January is coded with 1960.01, whereas 1960.1 or 1960.10 stands for October 1960.

8.4 Selecting, Transforming, and Creating Time Series

8.4.1 Time Series Selector

Once a data set has been read in, the single variables can be accessed via the time series selector. All time series appear in a list and can easily be combined even if they stem from different files. It is not possible, however, to select time series together for some operation that have a different periodicity. Time series of the same periodicity must have at least two overlapping observations in a common time range to be eligible for common operations. Various tasks on the selected variables can be accessed by a menu that pops up when the user right clicks over selected variables in the time series selector. The tasks in the pop-up menu do not take the selected range into account but always operate on the whole range of the selected time series.

The time series selector is used to select the set of variables, the order of the variables, and the time range for the various econometric methods and models. The respective selection is only valid within its context (e.g., for unit root tests). The selection made there has no influence on the model selection – for instance for a VAR model. The selection mechanism is also adjusted to its context, which means that only one variable can be selected for unit root tests, whereas for VAR modeling the number of variables is not restricted.

Sometimes the ordering of the variables is important for a model or for analysis. The selector uses the order in which the variables have been clicked on. For multiple selection, it is necessary to keep either the Shift or the Ctrl button depressed while the mouse is clicked over a series. The selected variables are displayed in the correct order in the control area of the selector after the selection has been confirmed.

The time range of the selection can be adjusted by editing the respective text field. The valid range is the largest common range of all selected time series, where NaN missing values have been automatically truncated from the beginning and the end of each series. The smallest legal range must contain two observations. Once a range selection is made, this selection is kept as long as it is valid. The maximum possible range can easily be set via a button. This mechanism enables the user to keep an edited time range as long as possible but allows a quick switch back to the maximum range as well.

In general, all variable names in JMulTi are case insensitive, which means that there is no distinction between, say, GNP and gnp. However, the variables in the selector are displayed as they have been read in or named with the case of the characters unchanged.

The time series selector displays variables with their names and with a symbol tagging their property. Within the context of time series analysis the three possible properties are endogenous, exogenous, and deterministic. Through these properties variables can be grouped and treated differently by a certain procedure or model. It is possible to change the property of a variable via the right mouse menu. The following tasks are available through this pop-up menu as well:

Delete. All selected time series can be deleted. This operation is also accessible by pressing the Del key.

Rename. The first selected time series can be renamed. The new name must be unique among all time series in the list. The rules for variable names described earlier apply.

Creating dummies. For dummy creation, first a variable needs to be selected as a reference for the time range and the periodicity. A dialog allows specification of the date of the impulse or the range of a shift. As already mentioned, seasonal dummies should usually not be added to the data set explicitly because they can be created for each specific analysis where they are needed.

Transforming time series. Some common transformations are also accessible via the transform dialog. New variables are generated with a descriptive suffix. If logarithm is selected, it is always applied first. The selected original variables do not change.

Editing time series. The selected time series can be edited as well. Changes are only stored if the dialog is confirmed with OK. If series with different ranges are selected, the missing values at the beginning or the end are displayed with NaN.

Exporting data. It is possible to combine the selected time series with a new data set that will be saved in the .dat format described earlier. The data set can then be read in again without further interaction.

8.4.2 Time Series Calculator

The time series calculator is a very flexible tool to create new variables by combining existing time series with arithmetic operations and functions. It provides the minilanguage TSCalc that operates with one-dimensional arrays and scalars. The operation is as follows:

1. First one has to select the variables to be combined in the time series selector.
2. The names appear in the list Available Variables and are put into the variable space of the calculator.
3. One can write one or more commands to the command area and execute them with Execute or Ctrl+E. Newly created variables appear in the list of available variables.
4. Finally, the selected variables in Available Variables can be added to the workspace with Add Selected.

The syntax of TSCalc is very easy, and only a few simple rules apply:

* New variables can be defined with
  newvariable = some expression;.

- Several commands can be executed at once by separating them with ' ; '.
- The content of a variable can be printed out by just writing the variable name to the command line.
- The conventions for variable names hold as described in Section 8.2.4.
- All array operations are applied elementwise.
- TSCalc understands exponential notation; for example, 1.234e-3.

By double clicking on a variable in the list, the name appears in the command window and can be combined with commands from the calculator. Apart from basic arithmetic operations, TSCalc provides a range of other functions like sin, cos, tan, min, max, lagn, log, stdc, meanc, rndn, ones, trend. For a complete list of possible operators and functions, consult the help system. In case there are syntax errors, a descriptive message is printed to the output window. If the selection in the time series selector is changed, the workspace of the calculator is overwritten. Variables that have not been added to the workspace are lost.

8.5 Managing Variables in JMulTi

JMulTi uses a sophisticated system to share variables between different components. This makes the internal design of the program much clearer, but it also has the benefit for the user that there is a great deal of transparency over almost all variables that are used by the system. It is possible to check input parameters as well as results being read back after a procedure has finished.

The tool to access the variable space is the Variable Control Frame. A tree structure allows browsing through the variables by their names. Each variable can be displayed in a table, and a description is usually available on what is stored in it and what type and dimension it has. The variables in the tree always belong to a certain scope that is defined by the location of the variable in the component hierarchy. For example, a variable stored for the VEC model is not accessible from the VAR model. This structure is reflected in the tree.

As a special feature it is possible to save every selected variable to an ASCII text file to reuse it in another program. This feature can also be used for exporting output and using it in another program for creating graphics for a publication. The main idea of this facility is to provide as much flexibility as possible and to offer a way of overcoming the limitations of JMulTi by using its export functions.

8.6 Notes for Econometric Software Developers

8.6.1 General Remark

The following short overview should serve as a motivation for interested researchers to use the software described in this chapter not only as a ready-made tool but also as a platform to quickly create new applications for various purposes in econometrics. For example, with the proper tools it would be possible to create a user interface for a new test or estimation routine in a few hours without a deep knowledge in object-oriented programming techniques. On the other hand, the system is flexible enough to serve as a platform for more demanding applications as well. The technical details of how to implement this capability are not described here, but the general idea of the underlying framework is presented. For more information the interested reader is referred to the homepage[3] of the project.

8.6.2 The JStatCom Framework

As mentioned in the introduction, JMuLTi is based on a software framework called JStatCom. A software framework is a set of reusable classes that make up a reusable design for a class of software [see Johnson & Foote (1988), Deutsch (1989)]. This means that it already provides a structure as well as key functionality for applications in a certain problem domain. The designer of an application can reuse not only classes but the whole design of the framework and concentrate on specific aspects of his or her implementation [Gamma, Helm, Johnson & Vlissides (1995)]. The problem domain for JStatCom is time series analysis, but it could well be extended to statistical modeling in general or simulation, such as for macroeconomic models.

JStatCom is a set of JAVA classes together with additional native libraries necessary to communicate to certain computational engines. It is organized into several packages as shown in Figure 8.1. The dashed lines indicate dependencies between packages, and it can easily be seen that the model package contains the core classes on which all other packages depend. For time series analysis the ts package defines all relevant functionality. The other packages are largely independent of each other. All classes and components within that framework can be accessed by a well-documented application programming interface (API). A special feature of JStatCom is that it makes heavy use of the JavaBeans component architecture as defined by Sun Microsystems (1.01-1997). Components can be configured and plugged together in a standardized way, which can speed up development significantly.

8.6.3 Component Structure

To understand the underlying general design better, Figure 8.2 summarizes the relationships between JStatCom, JMuLTi, the computational engine, and statistical procedures written for a certain engine. All components together make a runnable application. The main building blocks of the software are clearly separated from each other and can be developed independently.

---

[3] The homepage is http://www.jstatcom.com.

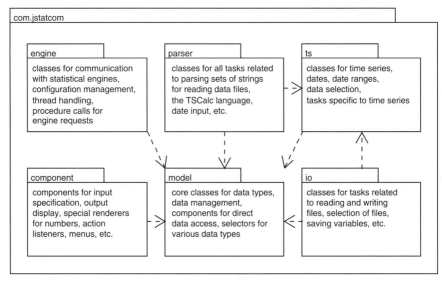

Figure 8.1. JStatCom JAVA Package Structure.

The application developer needs to implement the statistical procedures for a specific engine, and he or she must create the user interface for the application. The first task should be familiar to researchers because it means just using a programming language to implement the desired algorithm.

The task of creating the JAVA application on the other hand is greatly simplified by the framework design of JStatCom. Many sophisticated classes and components are available and can easily be reused. The general functionality described earlier in this chapter is immediately available if the respective

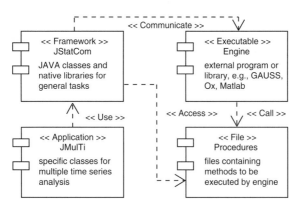

Figure 8.2. Collaboration of components.

components are used. As a developer, one only needs to think about the special needs of a certain procedure, which basically means input and output specification. Although some programming in JAVA is always needed, most steps can be done in a standardized way.

The design splits the complex task of creating an application for time series analysis into smaller units, which can be solved separately. The problems that occur in literally every analysis have been solved in the JAVA framework already. The task of creating the GUI and the task of programming a complex statistical procedure are almost completely separated and can even be done by different people. That way it is possible to reuse already written code efficiently and to enhance its value by integrating it with a graphical user interface.

8.7 Conclusion

JMuTi uses the functionality of JStatCom to implement interesting, new, and otherwise difficult-to-use methods in time series econometrics. It is freely available, using free code provided by many authors.

On the other hand, the development of JStatCom would not at all have been possible without the experiences gained from creating, using, and extending JMuTi. The framework is an extract of all general solutions that have been found to be useful and are not related to a specific model but occur frequently when implementing new methods. Both pieces of software will, it is hoped, continue to be improved, maintained, and extended with new features in the future. It is likely that the software will change much faster than this book; therefore, users are advised to check the respective websites for the latest developments.

References

Ahn, S. K. (1988). Distribution of residual autocovariances in multivariate autoregressive models with structured parameterization, *Biometrika* **75**: 590–593.

Ahn, S. K. & Reinsel, G. C. (1990). Estimation of partially nonstationary multivariate autoregressive models, *Journal of the American Statistical Association* **85**: 813–823.

Akaike, H. (1973). Information theory and an extension of the maximum likelihood principle, *in* B. Petrov & F. Csáki (eds.), *2nd International Symposium on Information Theory*, Académiai Kiadó, Budapest, pp. 267–281.

Akaike, H. (1974). A new look at the statistical model identification, *IEEE Transactions on Automatic Control* **AC-19**: 716–723.

Amisano, G. & Giannini, C. (1997). *Topics in Structural VAR Econometrics*, 2nd ed., Springer-Verlag, Berlin.

Anderson, T. W. (1984). *An Introduction to Multivariate Statistical Analysis*, John Wiley, New York.

Andrews, D. W. K. (1993). Tests for parameter instability and structural change with unknown change point, *Econometrica* **61**: 821–856.

Andrews, D. W. K. & Ploberger, W. (1994). Optimal tests when a nuisance parameter is present only under the alternative, *Econometrica* **62**: 1383–1414.

Ansley, C. F. & Kohn, R. (1983). Exact likelihood of vector autoregressive-moving average process with missing or aggregated data, *Biometrika* **70**: 275–278.

Arellano, C. & Pantula, S. G. (1995). Testing for trend stationarity versus difference stationarity, *Journal of Time Series Analysis* **16**: 147–164.

Auestad, B. & Tjøstheim, D. (1990). Identification of nonlinear time series: First order characterization and order determination, *Biometrika* **77**: 669–687.

Baba, Y., Engle, R. F., Kraft, D. F. & Kroner, K. F. (1990). Multivariate simultaneous generalized ARCH, *mimeo*, Department of Economics, University of California, San Diego.

Bachelier, L. (1900). Theory of speculation, *in* P. Cootner (ed.), *The Random Character of Stock Market Prices*, MIT Press, Cambridge, Massachusetts, pp. 17–78.

Bacon, D. W. & Watts, D. G. (1971). Estimating the transition between two intersecting straight lines, *Biometrika* **58**: 525–534.

Banerjee, A., Dolado, J. J., Galbraith, J. W. & Hendry, D. F. (1993). *Co-integration,*

Error-Correction, and the Econometric Analysis of Non-stationary Data, Oxford University Press, Oxford.

Bartel, H. & Lütkepohl, H. (1998). Estimating the Kronecker indices of cointegrated echelon form VARMA models, *Econometrics Journal* **1**: C76–C99.

Bartlett, M. S. (1950). Periodogram analysis and continuous spectra, *Biometrika* **37**: 1–16.

Basu, A. K. & Sen Roy, S. (1987). On asymptotic prediction problems for multivariate autoregressive models in the unstable nonexplosive case, *Calcutta Statistical Association Bulletin* **36**: 29–37.

Bates, D. M. & Watts, D. G. (1988). *Nonlinear Regression Analysis and its Applications*, Wiley, New York.

Beaulieu, J. J. & Miron, J. A. (1993). Seasonal unit roots in aggregate U.S. data, *Journal of Econometrics* **55**: 305–328.

Benkwitz, A., Lütkepohl, H. & Neumann, M. (2000). Problems related to bootstrapping impulse responses of autoregressive processes, *Econometric Reviews* **19**: 69–103.

Benkwitz, A., Lütkepohl, H. & Wolters, J. (2001). Comparison of bootstrap confidence intervals for impulse responses of German monetary systems, *Macroeconomic Dynamics* **5**: 81–100.

Bera, A. K. & Higgins, M. L. (1993). ARCH models: Properties, estimation and testing, *Journal of Economic Surveys* **7**: 305–366.

Bernanke, B. (1986). Alternative explanations of the money–income correlation, *Carnegie–Rochester Conference Series on Public Policy*, North-Holland, Amsterdam.

Berndt, E. K., Hall, B. H., Hall, R. E. & Hausman, J. A. (1974). Estimation and inference in nonlinear structural models, *Annals of Economic and Social Measurement* **3/4**: 653–665.

Black, F. (1976). Studies in stock price volatility changes, *Proceedings of the 1976 Meeting of the Business and Economics Statistics Section*, American Statistical Association, pp. 177–181.

Blanchard, O. & Quah, D. (1989). The dynamic effects of aggregate demand and supply disturbances, *American Economic Review* **79**: 655–673.

Bollerslev, T. (1986). Generalized autoregressive conditional heteroskedasticity, *Journal of Econometrics* **31**: 307–327.

Bollerslev, T. (1987). A conditionally heteroskedastic time series model for speculative prices and rates of return, *Review of Economics and Statistics* **69**: 542–547.

Bollerslev, T. (1990). Modelling the coherence in short-run nominal exchange rates: A multivariate generalized ARCH model, *Review of Economics and Statistics* **72**: 498–505.

Bollerslev, T., Chou, R. Y. & Kroner, K. F. (1992). ARCH modelling in finance: A review of the theory and empirical evidence, *Journal of Econometrics* **52**: 5–59.

Bollerslev, T., Engle, R. F. & Nelson, D. B. (1994). ARCH models, *in* R. Engle & D. McFadden (eds.), *Handbook of Econometrics, Vol. 4*, Elsevier Science Publishers, Amsterdam.

Bollerslev, T., Engle, R. F. & Wooldridge, J. M. (1988). A capital asset pricing model with time-varying covariances, *Journal of Political Economy* **96**: 116–131.

Bollerslev, T. & Wooldridge, J. (1992). Quasi maximum likelihood estimation and inference in dynamic models with time varying covariances, *Econometric Reviews* **11**: 143–172.

Boswijk, H. P. (1995). Efficient inference on cointegration parameters in structural error correction models, *Journal of Econometrics* **69**: 133–158.

Box, G. E. P. & Jenkins, G. M. (1976). *Time Series Analysis: Forecasting and Control*, Holden-Day, San Francisco.

Braun, P. A., Nelson, D. B. & Sunier, A. M. (1995). Good news, bad news, volatility and betas, *Journal of Finance* **50**: 1575–1603.

Breitung, J. (2000). *Structural Inference in Cointegrated Vector Autoregressive Models*, Habilitationsschrift, Humboldt-Universität zu Berlin.

Breitung, J. (2001). A convenient representation for structural vector autoregressions, *Empirical Economics* **26**: 447–459.

Breusch, T. (1978). Testing for autocorrelation in dynamic linear models, *Australian Economic Papers* **17**: 334–355.

Brockwell, P. J. & Davis, R. A. (1987). *Time Series: Theory and Methods*, Springer-Verlag, New York.

Brown, R. L., Durbin, J. & Evans, J. M. (1975). Techniques for testing the constancy of regression relationships over time, *Journal of the Royal Statistical Society B* **37**: 149–192.

Brüggemann, R. & Lütkepohl, H. (2001). Lag selection in subset VAR models with an application to a U.S. monetary system, *in* R. Friedmann, L. Knüppel & H. Lütkepohl (eds.), *Econometric Studies: A Festschrift in Honour of Joachim Frohn*, LIT Verlag, Münster, pp. 107–128.

Burridge, P. & Taylor, A. M. R. (2001). On the properties of regression-based tests for seasonal unit roots in the presence of higher-order serial correlation, *Journal of Business & Economic Statistics* **19**: 374–379.

Campbell, J., Lo, A. & MacKinlay, A. (1997). *The Econometrics of Financial Markets*, Princeton University Press, Princeton, New Jersey.

Candelon, B. & Lütkepohl, H. (2001). On the reliability of Chow-type tests for parameter constancy in multivariate dynamic models, *Economics Letters* **73**: 155–160.

Canova, F. & Hansen, B. E. (1995). Are seasonal patterns constant over time? A test for seasonal stability, *Journal of Business & Economic Statistics* **13**: 237–252.

Chan, K. S. & Tong, H. (1986). On estimating thresholds in autoregressive models, *Journal of Time Series Analysis* **7**: 178–190.

Cheung, Y. W. & Ng, L. K. (1996). A causality in variance test and its application to financial market prices, *Journal of Econometrics* **72**: 33–48.

Christiano, L. J., Eichenbaum, M. & Evans, C. (1999). Monetary shocks: What have we learned and to what end? *in* J. Taylor & M. Woodford (eds.), *The Handbook of Macroeconomics*, Amsterdam: Elsevier Science Publishers.

Chu, C.-S. (1995). Detecting parameter shifts in GARCH models, *Econometric Reviews* **14**: 241–266.

Comte, F. & Lieberman, O. (2003). Asymptotic theory for multivariate GARCH processes, *Journal of Multivariate Analysis* **84**: 61–84.

Cooley, T. F. & LeRoy, S. F. (1985). Atheoretical macroeconometrics: A critique, *Journal of Monetary Economics* **16**: 283–308.

Davidson, J. (2000). *Econometric Theory*, Blackwell, Oxford.

Davidson, R. & MacKinnon, J. (1993). *Estimation and Inference in Econometrics*, Oxford University Press, London.

Deutsch, L. P. (1989). Design reuse and frameworks in the smalltalk-80 system, *in* T. J. Biggerstaff & A. J. Perlis (eds.), *Software Reusability, Volume II: Applications and Experience*, Addison-Wesley, Reading, MA, pp. 57–71.

Dickey, D. A. & Fuller, W. A. (1979). Estimators for autoregressive time series with a unit root, *Journal of the American Statistical Association* **74**: 427–431.

Dickey, D. A., Hasza, H. P. & Fuller, W. A. (1984). Testing for unit roots in seasonal time series, *Journal of the American Statistical Association* **79**: 355–367.

Ding, Z. & Engle, R. F. (1994). Large scale conditional covariance matrix modeling, estimation and testing, *mimeo*, UCSD.

Dolado, J. J. & Lütkepohl, H. (1996). Making Wald tests work for cointegrated VAR systems, *Econometric Reviews* **15**: 369–386.

Doornik, J. A. & Hansen, H. (1994). A practical test of multivariate normality, unpublished paper, Nuffield College.

Doornik, J. A. & Hendry, D. F. (1994). *PcFiml 8.0, Interactive Econometric Modelling of Dynamic Systems*, Thomson Publishing.

Doornik, J. A. & Hendry, D. F. (1997). *Modelling Dynamic Systems Using PcFiml 9.0 for Windows*, International Thomson Business Press, London.

Doornik, J. A., Hendry, D. F. & Nielsen, B. (1998). Inference in cointegrating models: UK M1 revisited, *Journal of Economic Surveys* **12**: 533–572.

Doukhan, P. (1994). *Mixing. Properties and Examples*, Lecture Notes in Statistics, Springer-Verlag, New York.

Duan, J.-C. (1995). The GARCH option pricing model, *Mathematical Finance* **5**: 13–32.

Duan, J.-C. (1999). Conditionally fat-tailed distributions and the volatility smile in options, Working paper, Hong Kong University of Science and Technology, Department of Finance.

Dufour, J.-M. & Renault, E. (1998). Short run and long run causality in time series: Theory, *Econometrica* **66**: 1099–1125.

Edgerton, D. & Shukur, G. (1999). Testing autocorrelation in a system perspective, *Econometric Reviews* **18**: 343–386.

Efron, B. & Tibshirani, R. J. (1993). *An Introduction to the Bootstrap*, Chapman & Hall, New York.

Eitrheim, Ø. & Teräsvirta, T. (1996). Testing the adequacy of smooth transition autoregressive models, *Journal of Econometrics* **74**: 59–75.

Engle, R. F. (1982). Autoregressive conditional heteroscedasticity with estimates of the variance of United Kingdom inflation, *Econometrica* **50**: 987–1007.

Engle, R. F. (2002). Dynamic conditional correlation: A simple class of multivariate generalized autoregressive conditional heteroskedasticity models, *Journal of Business & Economic Statistics* **20**: 339–350.

Engle, R. F. & Bollerslev, T. (1986). Modelling the persistence of conditional variances, *Econometric Reviews* **5**: 81–87.

Engle, R. F. & Gonzalez-Rivera, G. (1991). Semiparametric ARCH models, *Journal of Business & Economic Statistics* **9**: 345–360.

Engle, R. F. & Granger, C. W. J. (1987). Cointegration and error correction: Representation, estimation and testing, *Econometrica* **55**: 251–276.

Engle, R. F., Hendry, D. F. & Richard, J.-F. (1983). Exogeneity, *Econometrica* **51**: 277–304.

Engle, R. F., Ito, T. & Lin, W. L. (1990). Meteor showers or heat waves? Heteroskedastic intra-daily volatility in the foreign exchange market, *Econometrica* **58**: 525–542.

Engle, R. F. & Kroner, K. F. (1995). Multivariate simultaneous generalized GARCH, *Econometric Theory* **11**: 122–150.

Engle, R. F., Lilien, D. M. & Robins, R. P. (1987). Estimating the varying risk premia in the term structure: The GARCH-M model, *Econometrica* **55**: 391–407.

Engle, R. F. & Ng, V. K. (1993). Measuring and testing the impact of news on volatility, *Journal of Finance* **48**: 1749–1778.

Engle, R. F. & Yoo, B. S. (1987). Forecasting and testing in cointegrated systems, *Journal of Econometrics* **35**: 143–159.

Ericsson, N. R., Hendry, D. F. & Mizon, G. E. (1998). Exogeneity, cointegration, and economic policy analysis, *Journal of Business & Economic Statistics* **16**: 370–387.

Escribano, A. & Jordá, O. (1999). Improved testing and specification of smooth transition regression models, *in* P. Rothman (ed.), *Nonlinear Time Series Analysis of Economic and Financial Data*, Kluwer Academic Publishers, Dordrecht, pp. 289–319.

Fair, R. C. & Jaffee, D. M. (1972). Methods of estimation for markets in disequilibrium, *Econometrica* **40**: 497–514.

Fama, E. F. (1965). The behaviour of stock market prices, *Journal of Business* **38**: 34–105.

Fiorentini, G., Calzolari, G. & Panattoni, L. (1996). Analytic derivatives and the computation of GARCH estimates, *Journal of Applied Econometrics* **11**: 399–417.

Fiorentini, G., Sentana, E. & Calzolari, G. (2002). Maximum likelihood estimation and inference in multivariate conditionally heteroskedastic dynamic regression models with student-t innovations, mimeo.

Franses, P. H. (1990). Testing for seasonal unit roots in monthly data, *Econometric Institute Report 9032A*, Erasmus University, Rotterdam.

Franses, P. H. & Hobijn, B. (1997). Critical values for unit root tests in seasonal time series, *Journal of Applied Statistics* **24**: 25–46.

Franses, P. H. & van Dijk, D. (2000). *Non-Linear Time Series Models in Empirical Finance*, Cambridge University Press, Cambridge.

Fuller, W. A. (1976). *Introduction to Statistical Time Series*, John Wiley & Sons, New York.

Galí, J. (1992). How well does the IS-LM model fit postwar U.S. data? *Quarterly Journal of Economics* **107**: 709–738.

Galí, J. (1999). Technology, employment, and the business cycle: Do technology shocks explain aggregate fluctuations? *American Economic Review* **89**: 249–271.

Gallant, A. R., Rossi, P. E. & Tauchen, G. (1993). Nonlinear dynamic structures, *Econometrica* **61**: 871–907.

Gamma, E., Helm, R., Johnson, R. & Vlissides, J. (1995). *Design Patterns: Elements of Reusable Object-Oriented Software*, Addison-Wesley, Reading, MA.

Glosten, L., Jagannathan, R. & Runkle, D. (1993). Relationship between the expected value and the volatility of the nominal excess return on stocks, *Journal of Finance* **48**: 1779–1801.

Godfrey, L. G. (1978). Testing against general autoregressive and moving average error models when the regressors include lagged dependent variables, *Econometrica* **46**: 1293–1302.

Godfrey, L. G. (1988). *Misspecification Tests in Econometrics*, Cambridge University Press, Cambridge.

Goldfeld, S. M. & Quandt, R. (1972). *Nonlinear Methods in Econometrics*, North-Holland, Amsterdam.

Gonzalo, J. & Pitarakis, J.-Y. (1998). Specification via model selection in vector error correction models, *Economics Letters* **60**: 321–328.

Granger, C. W. J. (1966). The typical spectral shape of an economic variable, *Econometrica* **34**: 150–161.

Granger, C. W. J. (1969). Investigating causal relations by econometric models and cross-spectral methods, *Econometrica* **37**: 424–438.

Granger, C. W. J. (1981). Some properties of time series data and their use in econometric model specification, *Journal of Econometrics* **16**: 121–130.

Granger, C. W. J. & Teräsvirta, T. (1993). *Modelling Nonlinear Economic Relationships*, Oxford University Press, Oxford.

Haase, K., Lütkepohl, H., Claessen, H., Moryson, M. & Schneider, W. (1992). *MulTi: A Menu-Driven GAUSS Program for Multiple Time Series Analysis*, Universität Kiel, Kiel, Germany.

Hafner, C. M. & Herwartz, H. (1998). Structural analysis of portfolio risk using beta impulse response functions, *Statistica Neerlandica* **52**: 336–355.

Hafner, C. M. & Herwartz, H. (2001a). Option pricing under linear autoregressive dynamics, heteroskedasticity, and conditional leptokurtosis, *Journal of Empirical Finance* **8**: 1–34.

Hafner, C. M. & Herwartz, H. (2001b). Volatility impulse response functions for multivariate GARCH models, *Discussion paper 2001/39*, CORE.

Hafner, C. M. & Herwartz, H. (2003). Analytical quasi maximum likelihood inference in BEKK-GARCH models, *mimeo EI 2003-21*, Econometric Institute, Erasmus University, Rotterdam.

Hafner, C. M. & Herwartz, H. (2004). Causality tests for multivariate GARCH models, Working paper, Institute for Statistics and Econometrics, University of Kiel, 156/2004.

Hafner, C. M. & Rombouts, J. V. K. (2002). Semiparametric multivariate GARCH models, *Discussion Paper 2002/XX*, CORE.

Hagerud, G. E. (1997). A new nonlinear GARCH model, EFI, Stockholm School of Economics.

Haggan, V. & Ozaki, T. (1981). Modelling non-linear random vibrations using an amplitude-dependent autoregressive time series model, *Biometrika* **68**: 189–196.

Haldrup, N. (1998). An econometric analysis of I(2) variables, *Journal of Economic Surveys* **12**: 595–650.

Hall, P. (1992). *The Bootstrap and Edgeworth Expansion*, Springer-Verlag, New York.

Hamilton, J. D. (1994). *Time Series Analysis*, Princeton University Press, Princeton, New Jersey.

Hannan, E. J. & Deistler, M. (1988). *The Statistical Theory of Linear Systems*, Wiley, New York.

Hannan, E. J. & Quinn, B. G. (1979). The determination of the order of an autoregression, *Journal of the Royal Statistical Society* **B41**: 190–195.

Hannan, E. J. & Rissanen, J. (1982). Recursive estimation of mixed autoregressive-moving average order, *Biometrika* **69**: 81–94.

Hansen, B. E. (1996). Inference when a nuisance parameter is not identified under the null hypothesis, *Econometrica* **64**: 413–430.

Hansen, B. E. (1997). Approximate asymptotic *p* values for structural-change tests, *Journal of Business & Economic Statistics* **15**: 60–67.

Hansen, B. E. (1999). Testing for linearity, *Journal of Economic Surveys* **13**: 551–576.

Hansen, H. & Johansen, S. (1999). Some tests for parameter constancy in cointegrated VAR-models, *Econometrics Journal* **2**: 306–333.

Hansen, P. R. (2003). Structural changes in the cointegrated vector autoregressive model, *Journal of Econometrics* **114**: 261–295.

Härdle, W., Lütkepohl, H. & Chen, R. (1997). A review of nonparametric time series analysis, *International Statistical Review* **65**: 49–72.

Härdle, W., Tsybakov, A. & Yang, L. (1998). Nonparametric vector autoregression, *Journal of Statistical Planning and Inference* **68**: 221–245.

Harvey, A. C. (1990). *The Econometric Analysis of Time Series*, 2nd ed., Philip Allan, Hemel, Hempstead.

Hatanaka, M. (1996). *Time-Series-Based Econometrics: Unit Roots and Co-Integration*, Oxford University Press, Oxford.

Hendry, D. F. (1995). *Dynamic Econometrics*, Oxford University Press, Oxford.

Hentschel, L. (1995). All in the family: Nesting symmetric and asymmetric GARCH models, *Journal of Financial Economics* **39**: 71–104.

Herwartz, H. & Lütkepohl, H. (2000). Multivariate volatility analysis of VW stock prices, *International Journal of Intelligent Systems in Accounting, Finance and Management* **9**: 35–54.

Hjellvik, V., Yao, Q. & Tjøstheim, D. (1998). Linearity testing using local polynomial approximation, *Journal of Statistical Planning and Inference* **68**: 295–321.

Hodrick, R. J. & Prescott, E. C. (1997). Postwar U.S. business cycles: An empirical investigation, *Journal of Money Credit and Banking* **29**: 1–16.

Hubrich, K., Lütkepohl, H. & Saikkonen, P. (2001). A review of systems cointegration tests, *Econometric Reviews* **20**: 247–318.

Hylleberg, S., Engle, R. F., Granger, C. W. J. & Yoo, B. S. (1990). Seasonal integration and cointegration, *Journal of Econometrics* **44**: 215–238.

IEEE (754-1985). IEEE standard for binary floating-point arithmetic, *ANSI/IEEE Standard*.

Jacobson, T., Vredin, A. & Warne, A. (1997). Common trends and hysteresis in Scandinavian unemployment, *European Economic Review* **41**: 1781–1816.

Jarque, C. M. & Bera, A. K. (1987). A test for normality of observations and regression residuals, *International Statistical Review* **55**: 163–172.

Jeantheau, T. (1998). Strong consistency of estimators for multivariate ARCH models, *Econometric Theory* **14**: 70–86.

Johansen, S. (1988). Statistical analysis of cointegration vectors, *Journal of Economic Dynamics and Control* **12**: 231–254.

Johansen, S. (1991). Estimation and hypothesis testing of cointegration vectors in Gaussian vector autoregressive models, *Econometrica* **59**: 1551–1581.

Johansen, S. (1992). Determination of cointegration rank in the presence of a linear trend, *Oxford Bulletin of Economics and Statistics* **54**: 383–397.

Johansen, S. (1994). The role of the constant and linear terms in cointegration analysis of nonstationary time series, *Econometric Reviews* **13**: 205–231.

Johansen, S. (1995a). *Likelihood-based Inference in Cointegrated Vector Autoregressive Models*, Oxford University Press, Oxford.

Johansen, S. (1995b). A statistical analysis of cointegration for I(2) variables, *Econometric Theory* **11**: 25–59.

Johansen, S., Mosconi, R. & Nielsen, B. (2000). Cointegration analysis in the presence of structural breaks in the deterministic trend, *Econometrics Journal* **3**: 216–249.

Johnson, R. E. & Foote, B. (1988). Designing reusable classes, *Journal of Object-Oriented Programming* **1**: 22–35.

Johnston, J. (1984). *Econometric Methods*, 3rd edn., McGraw-Hill, New York.

Jones, R. (1980). Maximum likelihood fitting of ARMA models to time series with missing observations, *Technometrics* **22**: 389–395.

Jorion, P. (2001). *Value at Risk*, McGraw-Hill, New York.

Judge, G. G., Griffiths, W. E., Hill, R. C., Lütkepohl, H. & Lee, T.-C. (1985). *The Theory and Practice of Econometrics*, 2nd ed., John Wiley and Sons, New York.

Kilian, L. (1998). Small-sample confidence intervals for impulse response functions, *Review of Economics and Statistics* **80**: 218–230.

King, M., Sentana, E. & Wadhwani, S. (1994). Volatility and links between international stock markets, *Econometrica* **62**: 901–923.

King, R. G., Plosser, C. I., Stock, J. H. & Watson, M. W. (1991). Stochastic trends and economic fluctuations, *American Economic Review* **81**: 819–840.

Kiviet, J. F. (1986). On the rigor of some mis-specification tests for modelling dynamic relationships, *Review of Economic Studies* **53**: 241–261.

Koop, G., Pesaran, M. H. & Potter, S. M. (1996). Impulse response analysis in nonlinear multivariate models, *Journal of Econometrics* **74**: 119–147.

Krämer, W., Ploberger, W. & Alt, R. (1988). Testing for structural change in dynamic models, *Econometrica* **56**: 1355–1369.

Krämer, W. & Sonnberger, H. (1986). *The Linear Regression Model under Test*, Physica-Verlag, Heidelberg.

Kwiatkowski, D., Phillips, P. C. B., Schmidt, P. & Shin, Y. (1992). Testing the null of stationarity against the alternative of a unit root: How sure are we that the economic time series have a unit root? *Journal of Econometrics* **54**: 159–178.

Lanne, M., Lütkepohl, H. & Saikkonen, P. (2002). Comparison of unit root tests for time series with level shifts, *Journal of Time Series Analysis* **23**: 667–685.

Lanne, M., Lütkepohl, H. & Saikkonen, P. (2003). Test procedures for unit roots in time series with level shifts at unknown time, *Oxford Bulletin of Economics and Statistics* **65**: 91–115.

Ledoit, O., Santa-Clara, P. & Wolf, M. (2003). Flexible multivariate GARCH modeling with an application to international stock markets, *Review of Economics and Statistics*, **85**: 735–747.

Lee, S. W. & Hansen, B. E. (1994). Asymptotic theory for the GARCH(1,1) quasi-maximum likelihood estimator, *Econometric Theory* **10**: 29–52.

Lee, T. & Ullah, A. (2001). Nonparametric bootstrap tests for neglected nonlinearity in time series regression models, *Journal of Nonparametric Statistics* **13**: 425–451.

Lewis, R. & Reinsel, G. C. (1985). Prediction of multivarate time series by autoregressive model fitting, *Journal of Multivariate Analysis* **16**: 393–411.

Leybourne, S. J. & McCabe, D. P. M. (1994). A consistent test for a unit root, *Journal of Business & Economic Statistics* **12**: 157–166.

Li, W. K. & Mak, T. K. (1994). On the squared residual autocorrelations in nonlinear time series with conditional heteroskedasticity, *Journal of Time Series Analysis* **15**: 627–636.

Lin, C.-F. & Yang, J. (1999). Testing shifts in financial models with conditional heteroskedasticity: An empirical distribution function approach, *mimeo*, University of Technology, Quantitative Finance Research Group, Sydney.

Lin, W. L. (1997). Impulse response functions for conditional volatility in GARCH models, *Journal of Business & Economic Statistics* **15**: 15–25.

Ling, S. & McAleer, M. (2003). Asymptotic theory for a new vector ARMA GARCH model, *Econometric Theory* **19**: 280–310.

Lintner, J. (1965). Security prices, risk and maximal gains from diversification, *Journal of Finance* **20**: 587–615.

Linton, O. (1993). Adaptive estimation in ARCH models, *Econometric Theory* **9**: 539–569.

Ljung, G. M. & Box, G. E. P. (1978). On a measure of lack of fit in time-series models, *Biometrika* **65**: 297–303.

Lomnicki, Z. A. (1961). Tests for departure from normality in the case of linear stochastic processes, *Metrika* **4**: 37–62.

Lucchetti, R. (2002). Analytical scores for multivariate GARCH models, *Computational Economics* **19**: 133–143.

Lumsdaine, R. (1996). Consistency and asymptotic normality of the quasi-maximum likelihood estimator in IGARCH(1,1) and covariance stationary GARCH(1,1) models, *Econometrica* **64**: 575–596.

Lundbergh, S. & Teräsvirta, T. (2002). Evaluating GARCH models, *Journal of Econometrics* **110**: 417–435.

Lundbergh, S., Teräsvirta, T. & van Dijk, D. (2003). Time-varying smooth transition autoregressive models, *Journal of Business & Economic Statistics* **21**: 104–121.

Lütkepohl, H. (1988). Asymptotic distribution of the moving average coefficients of an estimated vector autoregressive process, *Econometric Theory* **4**: 77–85.

Lütkepohl, H. (1991). *Introduction to Multiple Time Series Analysis*, Springer-Verlag, Berlin.

Lütkepohl, H. (1993). Testing for causation between two variables in higher dimensional VAR models, *in* H. Schneeweiss & K. F. Zimmermann (eds.), *Studies in Applied Econometrics*, Physica-Verlag, Heidelberg, pp. 75–91.

Lütkepohl, H. (1996). Testing for nonzero impulse responses in vector autoregressive processes, *Journal of Statistical Planning and Inference* **50**: 1–20.

Lütkepohl, H. (2001). Vector autoregressions, *in* B. H. Baltagi (ed.), *A Companion to Theoretical Econometrics*, Blackwell, Oxford, pp. 678–699.

Lütkepohl, H. & Breitung, J. (1997). Impulse response analysis of vector autoregressive processes, *in* C. Heij, H. Schumacher, B. Hanzon & C. Praagman (eds.), *System Dynamics in Economic and Financial Models*, Wiley, Chichester.

Lütkepohl, H. & Claessen, H. (1997). Analysis of cointegrated VARMA processes, *Journal of Econometrics* **80**: 223–239.

Lütkepohl, H. & Poskitt, D. S. (1991). Estimating orthogonal impulse responses via vector autoregressive models, *Econometric Theory* **7**: 487–496.

Lütkepohl, H. & Poskitt, D. S. (1996a). Specification of echelon form VARMA models, *Journal of Business & Economic Statistics* **14**: 69–79.

Lütkepohl, H. & Poskitt, D. S. (1996b). Testing for causation using infinite order vector autoregressive processes, *Econometric Theory* **12**: 61–87.

Lütkepohl, H. & Poskitt, D. S. (1998). Consistent estimation of the number of cointegration relations in a vector autoregressive model, *in* R. Galata & H. Küchenhoff (eds.), *Econometrics in Theory and Practice. Festschrift for Hans Schneeweiß*, Physica-Verlag, Heidelberg, pp. 87–100.

Lütkepohl, H. & Reimers, H.-E. (1992). Impulse response analysis of cointegrated systems, *Journal of Economic Dynamics and Control* **16**: 53–78.

Lütkepohl, H. & Saikkonen, P. (1997). Impulse response analysis in infinite order cointegrated vector autoregressive processes, *Journal of Econometrics* **81**: 127–157.

Lütkepohl, H. & Saikkonen, P. (1999). Order selection in testing for the cointegrating rank of a VAR process, *in* R. F. Engle & H. White (eds.), *Cointegration, Causality, and Forecasting. A Festschrift in Honour of Clive W. J. Granger*, Oxford University Press, Oxford, pp. 168–199.

Lütkepohl, H. & Saikkonen, P. (2000). Testing for the cointegrating rank of a VAR process with a time trend, *Journal of Econometrics* **95**: 177–198.

Lütkepohl, H., Saikkonen, P. & Trenkler, C. (2001a). Maximum eigenvalue versus trace tests for the cointegrating rank of a VAR process, *Econometrics Journal* **4**: 287–310.

Lütkepohl, H., Saikkonen, P. & Trenkler, C. (2001b). Testing for the cointegrating rank of a VAR process with level shift at unknown time, *Discussion Paper 63*, SFB 373, Humboldt Universität.

Lütkepohl, H., Teräsvirta, T. & Wolters, J. (1999). Investigating stability and linearity of a German M1 money demand function, *Journal of Applied Econometrics* **14**: 511–525.

Lütkepohl, H. & Wolters, J. (2003). The transmission of German monetary policy in the pre-euro period, *Macroeconomic Dynamics* **7**: 711–733.

Luukkonen, R., Saikkonen, P. & Teräsvirta, T. (1988a). Testing linearity against smooth transition autoregressive models, *Biometrika* **75**: 491–499.

Luukkonen, R., Saikkonen, P. & Teräsvirta, T. (1988b). Testing linearity in univariate time series models, *Scandinavian Journal of Statistics* **15**: 161–175.

Maddala, D. S. (1977). *Econometrics*, McGraw-Hill, New York.

Maddala, G. S. & Kim, I.-M. (1998). *Unit Roots, Cointegration, and Structural Change*, Cambridge University Press, Cambridge.

McCullough, B. D. & Vinod, H. D. (1999). The numerical reliability of econometric software, *Journal of Economic Literature* **37**: 633–655.

McLeod, A. I. & Li, W. K. (1983). Diagnostic checking of ARMA time series models using squared residual autocorrelations, *Journal of Time Series Analysis* **4**: 269–273.

Moryson, M. (1998). *Testing for Random Walk Coefficients in Regression and State Space Models*, Physica-Verlag, Heidelberg.

Mosconi, R. & Giannini, C. (1992). Non-causality in cointegrated systems: Representation, estimation and testing, *Oxford Bulletin of Economics and Statistics* **54**: 399–417.

Nelson, D. B. (1990). Stationarity and persistence in the GARCH(1,1) model, *Econometric Theory* **6**: 318–334.

Nelson, D. B. (1991). Conditional heteroskedasticity in asset returns: A new approach, *Econometrica* **59**: 347–370.

Nelson, D. & Cao, C. Q. (1992). Inequality constraints in univariate GARCH models, *Journal of Business & Economics Statistics* **10**: 229–235.

Neumann, M. & Polzehl, J. (1998). Simultaneous bootstrap confidence bands in nonparametric regression, *Journal of Nonparametric Statistics* **9**: 307–333.

Newey, W. K. & Steigerwald, D. G. (1997). Asymptotic bias for quasi-maximum-likelihood estimators in conditional heteroskedasticity models, *Econometrica* **65**: 587–599.

Ng, S. & Perron, P. (1995). Unit root tests in ARMA models with data-dependent methods for the selection of the truncation lag, *Journal of the American Statistical Association* **90**: 268–281.

Öcal, N. & Osborn, D. R. (2000). Business cycle nonlinearities in UK consumption and production, *Journal of Applied Econometrics* **15**: 27–43.

Pagan, A. (1995). Three econometric methodologies: An update, *in* L. Oxley, D. A. R. George, C. J. Roberts & S. Sayer (eds.), *Surveys in Econometrics*, Basil Blackwell, Oxford.

Pagan, A. (1996). The econometrics of financial markets, *Journal of Empirical Finance* **3**: 15–102.

Palm, F. (1996). GARCH models of volatility, *in* G. Maddala & C. Rao (eds.), *Handbook of Statistics, Vol. 14*, Elsevier, Amsterdam, pp. 209–240.

Pantula, S. G. (1989). Testing for unit roots in time series data, *Econometric Theory* **5**: 256–271.

Park, J. Y. & Phillips, P. C. B. (1988). Statistical inference in regressions with integrated processes: Part 1, *Econometric Theory* **4**: 468–497.

Park, J. Y. & Phillips, P. C. B. (1989). Statistical inference in regressions with integrated processes: Part 2, *Econometric Theory* **5**: 95–131.

Parzen, E. (1961). Mathematical considerations in the estimation of spectra, *Technometrics* **3**: 167–190.

Paulsen, J. (1984). Order determination of multivariate autoregressive time series with unit roots, *Journal of Time Series Analysis* **5**: 115–127.

Perron, P. (1989). The great crash, the oil price shock, and the unit root hypothesis, *Econometrica* **57**: 1361–1401.

Phillips, P. C. B. (1987). Time series regression with a unit root, *Econometrica* **55**: 277–301.

Phillips, P. C. B. (1991). Optimal inference in cointegrated systems, *Econometrica* **59**: 283–306.

Phillips, P. C. B. & Durlauf, S. N. (1986). Multiple time series regression with integrated processes, *Review of Economic Studies* **53**: 473–495.

Phillips, P. C. B. & Hansen, B. E. (1990). Statistical inference in instrumental variables regression with I(1) processes, *Review of Economic Studies* **57**: 99–125.

Phillips, P. C. B. & Loretan, M. (1991). Estimating long-run economic equilibria, *Review of Economic Studies* **58**: 407–436.

Phillips, P. C. B. & Perron, P. (1988). Testing for a unit root in time series regression, *Biometrika* **75**: 335–346.

Ploberger, W. & Krämer, W. (1992). The CUSUM test with OLS residuals, *Econometrica* **60**: 271–285.

Ploberger, W., Krämer, W. & Kontrus, K. (1989). A new test for structural stability in the linear regression model, *Journal of Econometrics* **40**: 307–318.

Priestley, M. B. (1981). *Spectral Analysis and Time Series*, Academic Press, London.

Quandt, R. E. (1958). The estimation of parameters of a linear regression system obeying two separate regimes, *Journal of the American Statistical Association* **53**: 873–880.

Ramsey, J. B. (1969). Tests for specification errors in classical linear least-squares regression analysis, *Journal of the Royal Statistical Society B* **31**: 350–371.

Rao, C. R. (1973). *Linear Statistical Inference and Its Applications*, 2nd ed., John Wiley and Sons, New York.

Ravn, M. O. & Uhlig, H. (2001). On adjusting the HP-filter for the frequency of observations, *Working Paper 479*, CESifo.

Reimers, H.-E. (1991). *Analyse kointegrierter Variablen mittels vektorautoregressiver Modelle*, Physica-Verlag, Heidelberg.

Reinsel, G. C. (1993). *Elements of Multivariate Time Series Analysis*, Springer-Verlag, New York.

Rissanen, J. (1978). Modeling by shortest data description, *Automatica* **14**: 465–471.

Said, S. E. & Dickey, D. A. (1984). Testing for unit roots in autoregressive-moving average models of unknown order, *Biometrika* **71**: 599–607.

Saikkonen, P. (1992). Estimation and testing of cointegrated systems by an autoregressive approximation, *Econometric Theory* **8**: 1–27.

Saikkonen, P. & Lütkepohl, H. (1996). Infinite order cointegrated vector autoregressive processes: Estimation and inference, *Econometric Theory* **12**: 814–844.

Saikkonen, P. & Lütkepohl, H. (1999). Local power of likelihood ratio tests for the cointegrating rank of a VAR process, *Econometric Theory* **15**: 50–78.

Saikkonen, P. & Lütkepohl, H. (2000a). Asymptotic inference on nonlinear functions of the coefficients of infinite order cointegrated VAR processes, *in* W. A. Barnett, D. F. Hendry, S. Hylleberg, T. Teräsvirta, D. Tjøstheim & A. Würtz (eds.), *Nonlinear Econometric Modeling in Time Series Analysis*, Cambridge University Press, Cambridge, pp. 165–201.

Saikkonen, P. & Lütkepohl, H. (2000b). Testing for the cointegrating rank of a VAR process with an intercept, *Econometric Theory* **16**: 373–406.

Saikkonen, P. & Lütkepohl, H. (2000c). Testing for the cointegrating rank of a VAR process with structural shifts, *Journal of Business & Economic Statistics* **18**: 451–464.

Saikkonen, P. & Lütkepohl, H. (2000d). Trend adjustment prior to testing for the cointegrating rank of a vector autoregressive process, *Journal of Time Series Analysis* **21**: 435–456.

Saikkonen, P. & Lütkepohl, H. (2002). Testing for a unit root in a time series with a level shift at unknown time, *Econometric Theory* **18**: 313–348.

Saikkonen, P. & Luukkonen, R. (1993a). Point optimal tests for testing the order of differencing in ARIMA models, *Econometric Theory* **9**: 343–362.

Saikkonen, P. & Luukkonen, R. (1993b). Testing for a moving average unit root in autoregressive integrated moving average models, *Journal of the American Statistical Association* **88**: 596–601.

Saikkonen, P. & Luukkonen, R. (1997). Testing cointegration in infinite order vector autoregressive processes, *Journal of Econometrics* **81**: 93–129.

Sargent, T. J. (1978). Estimation of dynamic labor demand schedules under rational expectations, *Journal of Political Economy* **86**: 1009–1044.

Schmidt, P. & Phillips, P. C. B. (1992). LM tests for a unit root in the presence of deterministic trends, *Oxford Bulletin of Economics and Statistics* **54**: 257–287.

Schwarz, G. (1978). Estimating the dimension of a model, *Annals of Statistics* **6**: 461–464.

Schwert, G. W. (1989). Tests for unit roots: A Monte Carlo investigation, *Journal of Business & Economic Statistics* **7**: 147–159.

Seber, G. A. F. & Wild, C. J. (1989). *Nonlinear Regression*, Wiley, New York.

Shapiro, M. & Watson, M. W. (1988). Sources of business cycle fluctuations, *NBER Macroeconomics Annual* **3**: 111–156.

Sharpe, W. F. (1964). Capital asset prices: A theory of market equilibrium under conditions of risk, *Journal of Finance* **19**: 425–442.

Shephard, N. (1996). Statistical aspects of ARCH and stochastic volatility, *in* D. R. Cox, D. V. Hinkley & O. Barndorff-Nielsen (eds.), *Time Series Models in Econometrics, Finance and Other Fields.Monographs on Statistics and Applied Probability 65*, Chapman & Hall, pp. 1–67.

Silverman, B. W. (1986). *Density Estimation for Statistics and Data Analysis*, Chapman & Hall, London.

Sims, C. A. (1980). Macroeconomics and reality, *Econometrica* **48**: 1–48.

Sims, C. A. (1981). An autoregressive index model for the U.S. 1948-1975, *in* J. Kmenta & J. B. Ramsey (eds.), *Large-Scale Macro-Econometric Models*, North-Holland, Amsterdam, pp. 283–327.

Sims, C. A. (1986). Are forecasting models usable for policy analysis? *Quarterly Review, Federal Reserve Bank of Minneapolis* **10**: 2–16.

Sims, C. A., Stock, J. H. & Watson, M. W. (1990). Inference in linear time series models with some unit roots, *Econometrica* **58**: 113–144.

Skalin, J. & Teräsvirta, T. (2002). Modeling asymmetries and moving equilibria in unemployment rates, *Macroeconomic Dynamics* **6**: 202–241.

Stock, J. H. (1994). Unit roots, structural breaks and trends, *in* R. F. Engle & D. L. McFadden (eds.), *Handbook of Econometrics, Volume IV*, Elsevier, Amsterdam, pp. 2739–2841.

Sun Microsystems (1.01-1997). Java beans api specification.

Tanaka, K. (1990). Testing for a moving average unit root, *Econometric Theory* **6**: 433–444.

Taylor, S. J. (1986). *Modelling Financial Time Series*, John Wiley & Sons, Chichester.

Teräsvirta, T. (1994). Specification, estimation, and evaluation of smooth transition autoregressive models, *Journal of the American Statistical Association* **89**: 208–218.

Teräsvirta, T. (1998). Modeling economic relationships with smooth transition regressions, *in* A. Ullah & D. E. Giles (eds.), *Handbook of Applied Economic Statistics*, Dekker, New York, pp. 507–552.

Teräsvirta, T., Strikholm, B. & van Dijk, D. (2003). Changing seasonal patterns in quarterly industrial production in Finland and Sweden, *in* R. Höglund, M. Jäntti & G. Rosenqvist (eds.), *Statistics, Econometrics and Society. Essays in Honour of Leif Nordberg*, Statistics Finland, Helsinki, pp. 229–246.

Tjøstheim, D. & Auestad, B. (1994). Nonparametric identification of nonlinear time-series: Projections, *Journal of the American Statistical Association* **89**: 1398–1409.

Toda, H. Y. & Phillips, P. C. B. (1993). Vector autoregressions and causality, *Econometrica* **61**: 1367–1393.

Toda, H. Y. & Yamamoto, T. (1995). Statistical inference in vector autoregressions with possibly integrated processes, *Journal of Econometrics* **66**: 225–250.

Tong, H. (1990). *Non-Linear Time Series. A Dynamical System Approach*, Oxford University Press, Oxford.

Tsay, R. S. (1993). Testing for noninvertible models with applications, *Journal of Business & Economic Statistics* **11**: 225–233.

Tschernig, R. & Yang, L. (2000a). Nonparametric estimation of generalized impulse response functions, *SFB 373 Discussion Paper 89, 2000*, Humboldt-Universität Berlin.

Tschernig, R. & Yang, L. (2000b). Nonparametric lag selection for time series, *Journal of Time Series Analysis* **21**: 457–487.

Tse, Y. K. (2000). A test for constant correlations in a multivariate GARCH model, *Journal of Econometrics* **98**: 107–127.

Tsui, A. K. & Yu, Q. (1999). Constant conditional correlation in a bivariate GARCH model: Evidence from the stock market in China, *Mathematics and Computers in Simulation* **48**: 503–509.

van Dijk, D. & Franses, P. H. (1999). Modeling multiple regimes in the business cycle, *Macroeconomic Dynamics* **3**: 311–340.

van Dijk, D., Strikholm, B. & Teräsvirta, T. (2003). The effects of institutional and technological change and business cycle fluctuations on seasonal patterns in quarterly industrial production series, *Econometrics Journal* **6**: 79–98.

van Dijk, D., Teräsvirta, T. & Franses, P. H. (2002). Smooth transition autoregressive models – A survey of recent developments, *Econometric Reviews* **21**: 1–47.

Vieu, P. (1994). Choice of regressors in nonparametric estimation, *Computational Statistics & Data Analysis* **17**: 575–594.

Vlaar, P. (1998). On the asymptotic distribution of impulse response functions with long run restrictions, *DNB Staff reports 22*, De Nederlandsche Bank.

Watson, M. W. (1994). Vector autoregressions and cointegration, *in* R. F. Engle & D. L. McFadden (eds.), *Handbook of Econometrics, Vol. IV*, Elsevier, New York.

Weber, C. E. (1995). Cyclical output, cyclical unemployment, and Okun's coefficient: A new approach, *Journal of Applied Econometrics* **10**: 433–445.

Wold, H. (1960). A generalization of causal chain models, *Econometrica* **28**: 443–463.

Yang, L. & Tschernig, R. (1999). Multivariate bandwidth selection for local linear regression, *Journal of the Royal Statistical Society, Series B* **61**: 793–815.

Yang, L. & Tschernig, R. (2002). Non- and semiparametric identification of seasonal nonlinear autoregression models, *Econometric Theory* **18**: 1408–1448.

Yao, Q. & Tong, H. (1994). On subset selection in non-parametric stochastic regression, *Statistica Sinica* **4**: 51–70.

Zakoian, J. M. (1994). Threshold heteroskedastic functions, *Journal of Economic Dynamics and Control* **18**: 931–955.

Zellner, A. (1962). An efficient method of estimating seemingly unrelated regressions and tests of aggregation bias, *Journal of the American Statistical Association* **57**: 348–368.

Index